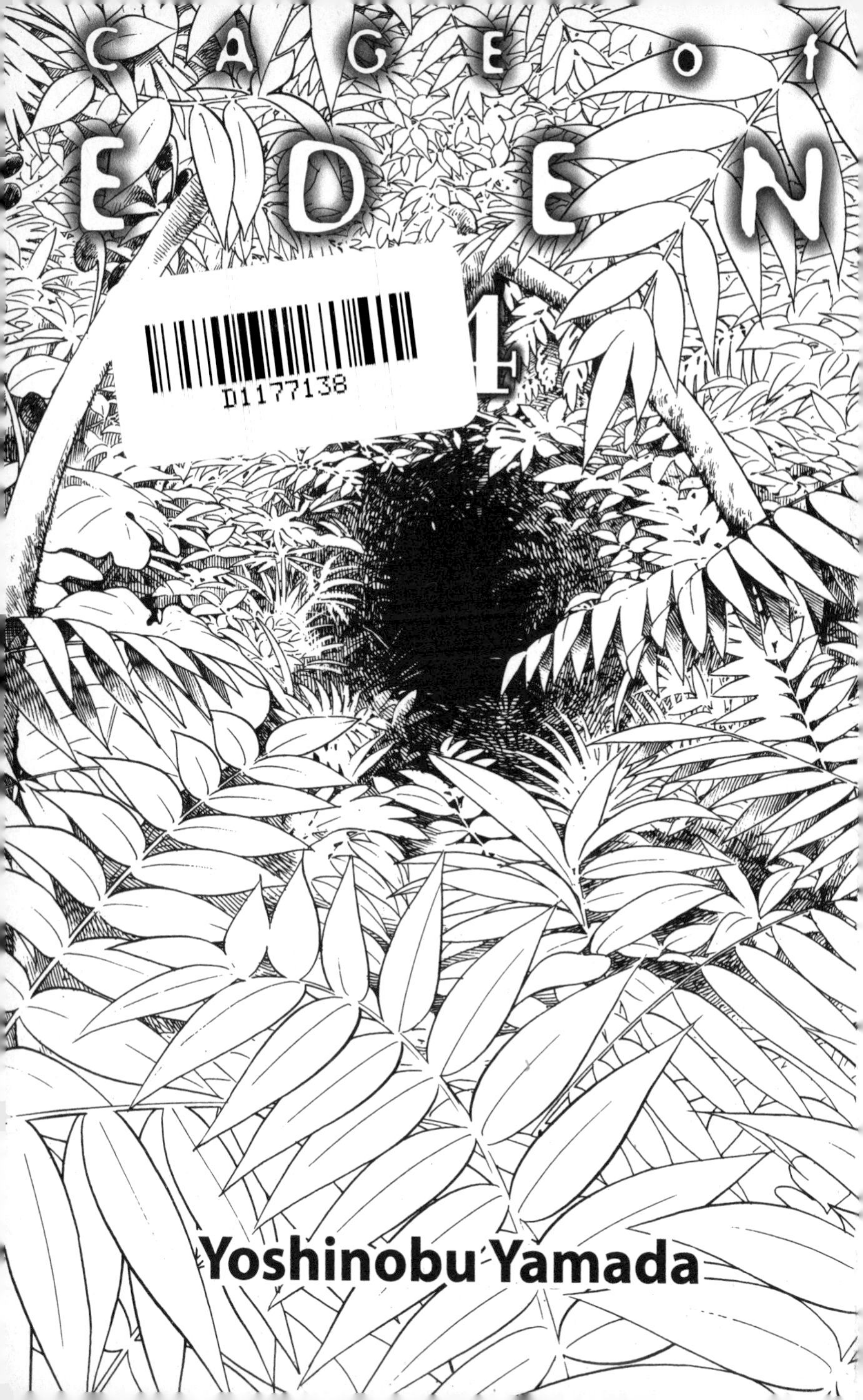
CAGE of
EDEN
4
Yoshinobu Yamada

CAGE of EDEN

CONTENTS

Chapter 113: THE TOWER OF TERROR 3
Chapter 114: DARKNESS AND DEATH.................... 23
Chapter 115: THE WAY TO GO...................... 45
Chapter 116: UNDERGROUND................................ 65
Chapter 117: PROFOUND DARKNESS 85
Chapter 118: B3 103
Chapter 119: TOO LARGE............................. 123
Chapter 120: DEEPER AND DEEPER..................... 143
Chapter 121: STRANGE PLANTS 163

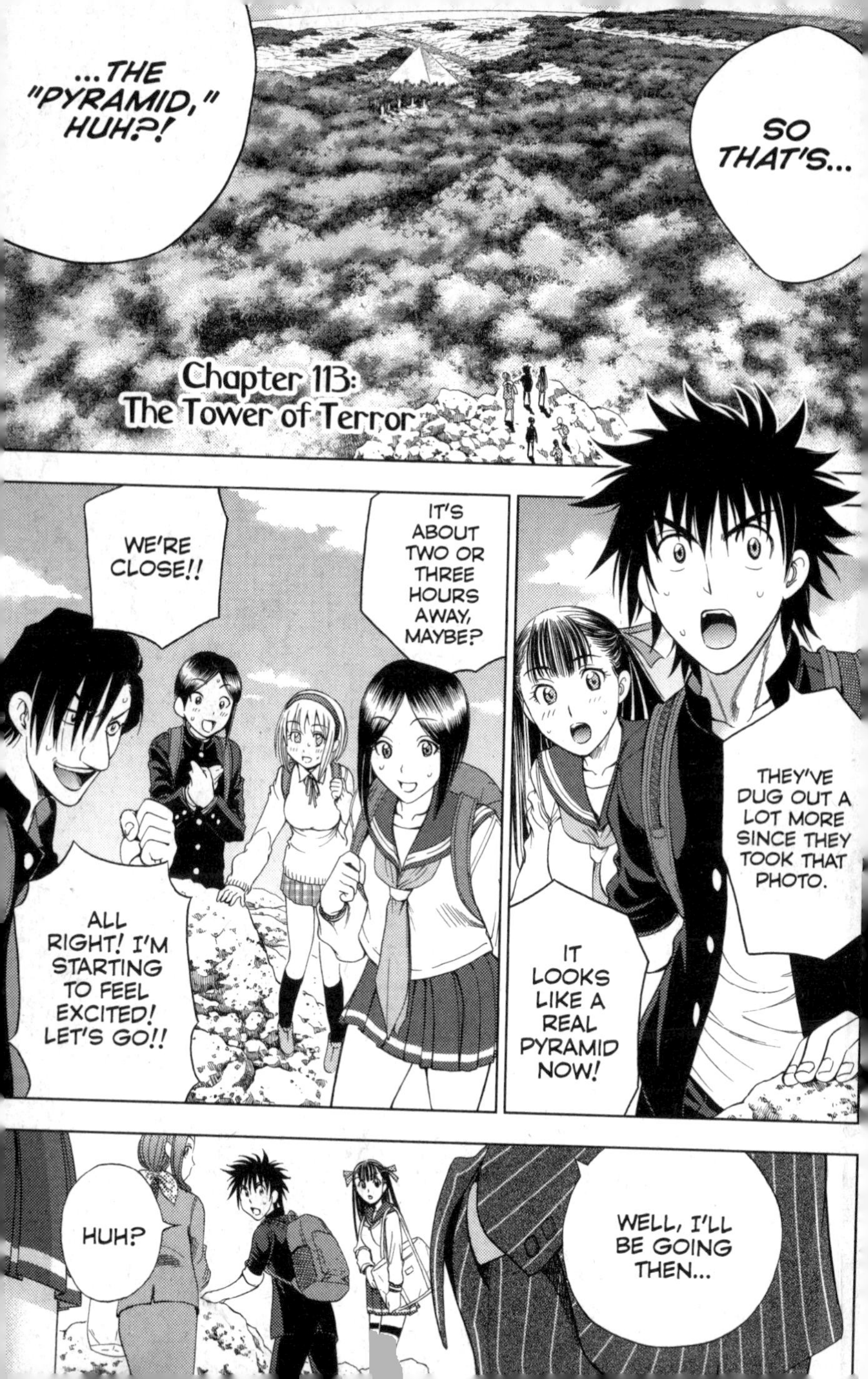
SO THAT'S...
...THE "PYRAMID," HUH?!
Chapter 113: The Tower of Terror
THEY'VE DUG OUT A LOT MORE SINCE THEY TOOK THAT PHOTO.
IT LOOKS LIKE A REAL PYRAMID NOW!
IT'S ABOUT TWO OR THREE HOURS AWAY, MAYBE?
WE'RE CLOSE!!
ALL RIGHT! I'M STARTING TO FEEL EXCITED! LET'S GO!!
WELL, I'LL BE GOING THEN...
HUH?

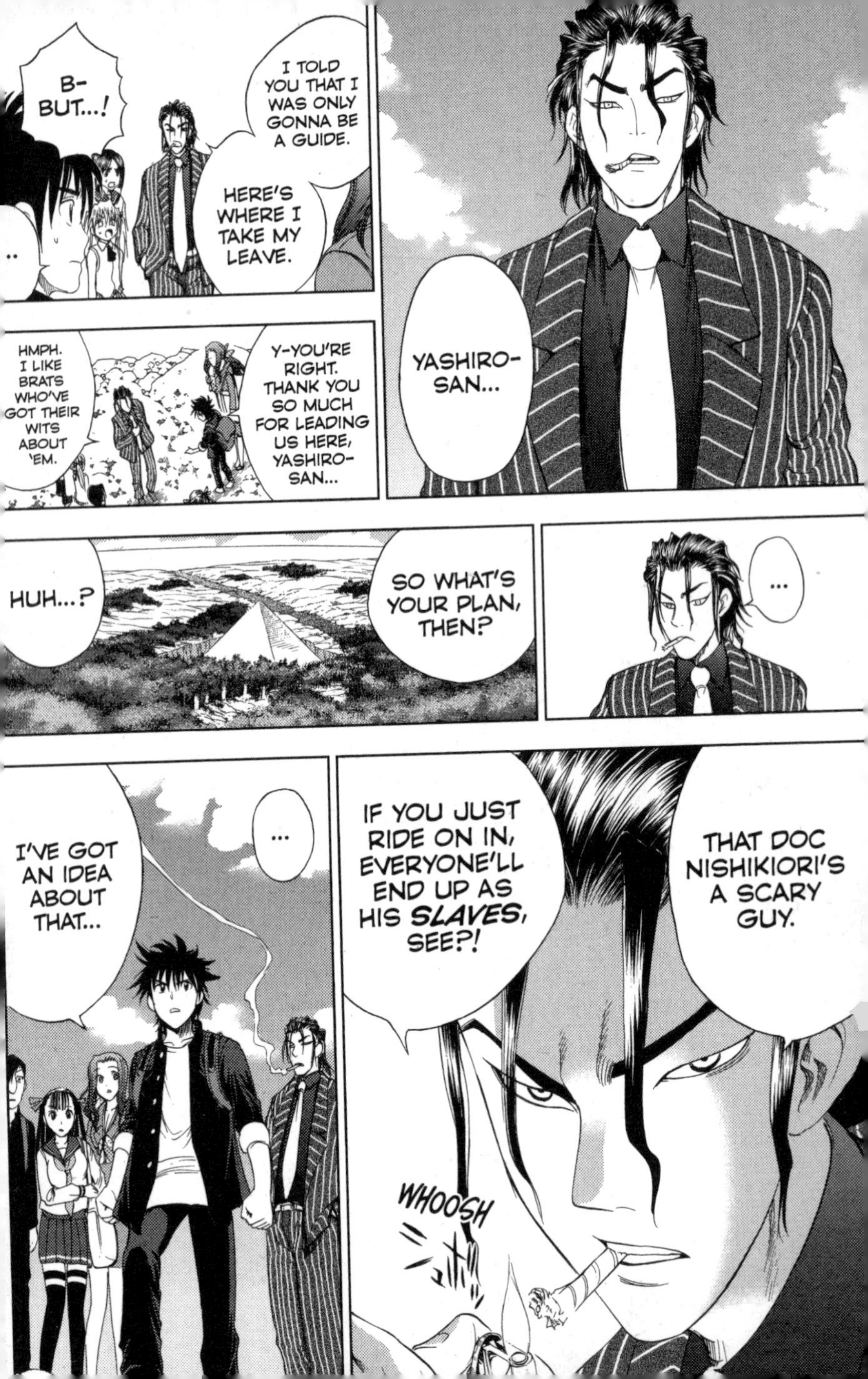
YASHIRO-SAN...
I TOLD YOU THAT I WAS ONLY GONNA BE A GUIDE.
HERE'S WHERE I TAKE MY LEAVE.
B-BUT...!
Y-YOU'RE RIGHT. THANK YOU SO MUCH FOR LEADING US HERE, YASHIRO-SAN...
HMPH. I LIKE BRATS WHO'VE GOT THEIR WITS ABOUT 'EM.
...
SO WHAT'S YOUR PLAN, THEN?
HUH...?
THAT DOC NISHIKIORI'S A SCARY GUY.
IF YOU JUST RIDE ON IN, EVERYONE'LL END UP AS HIS SLAVES, SEE?!
WHOOSH
...
I'VE GOT AN IDEA ABOUT THAT...

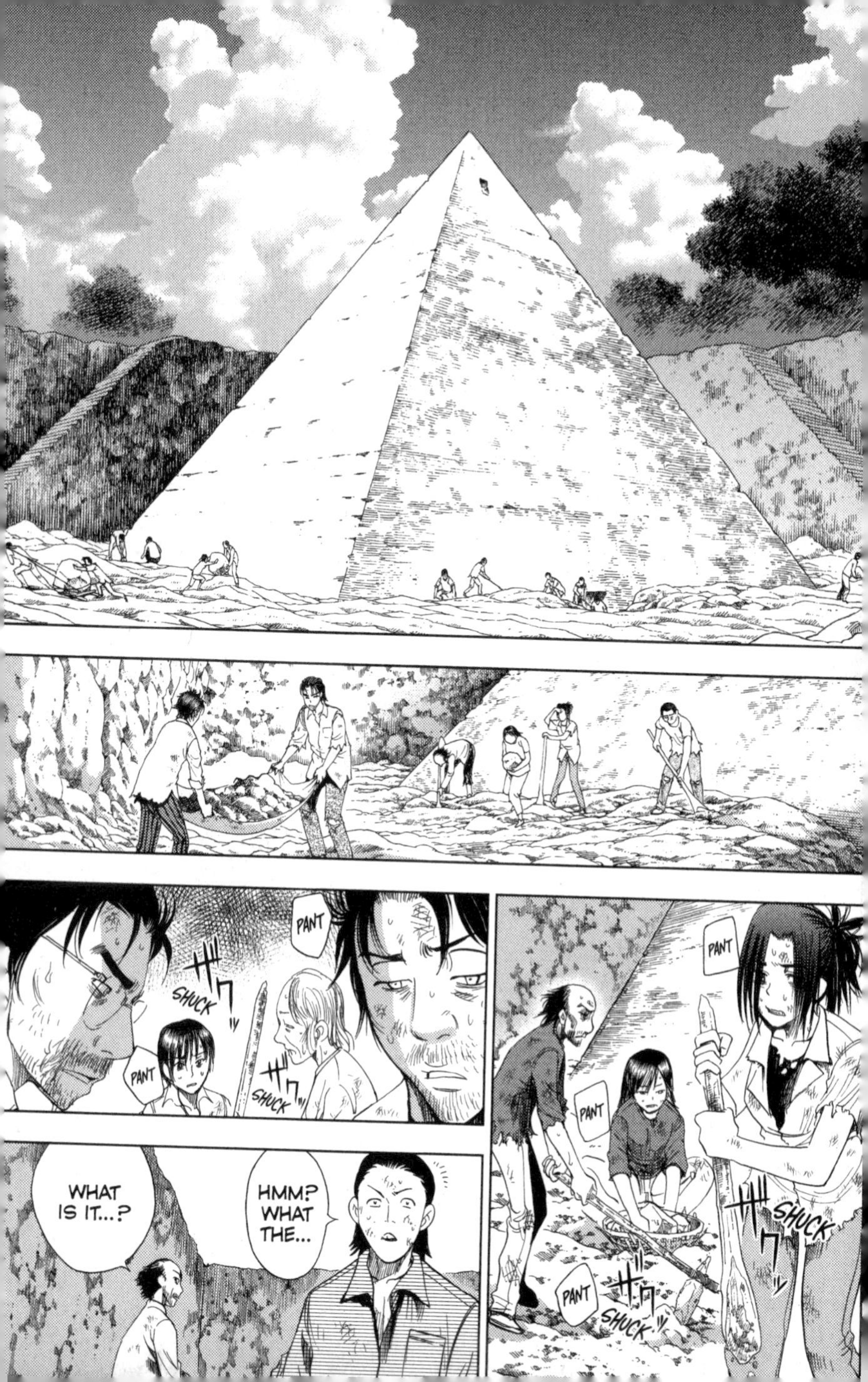
PANT
SHUCK
PANT
PANT
SHUCK
PANT
SHUCK
PANT
SHUCK
HMM? WHAT THE...
WHAT IS IT...?

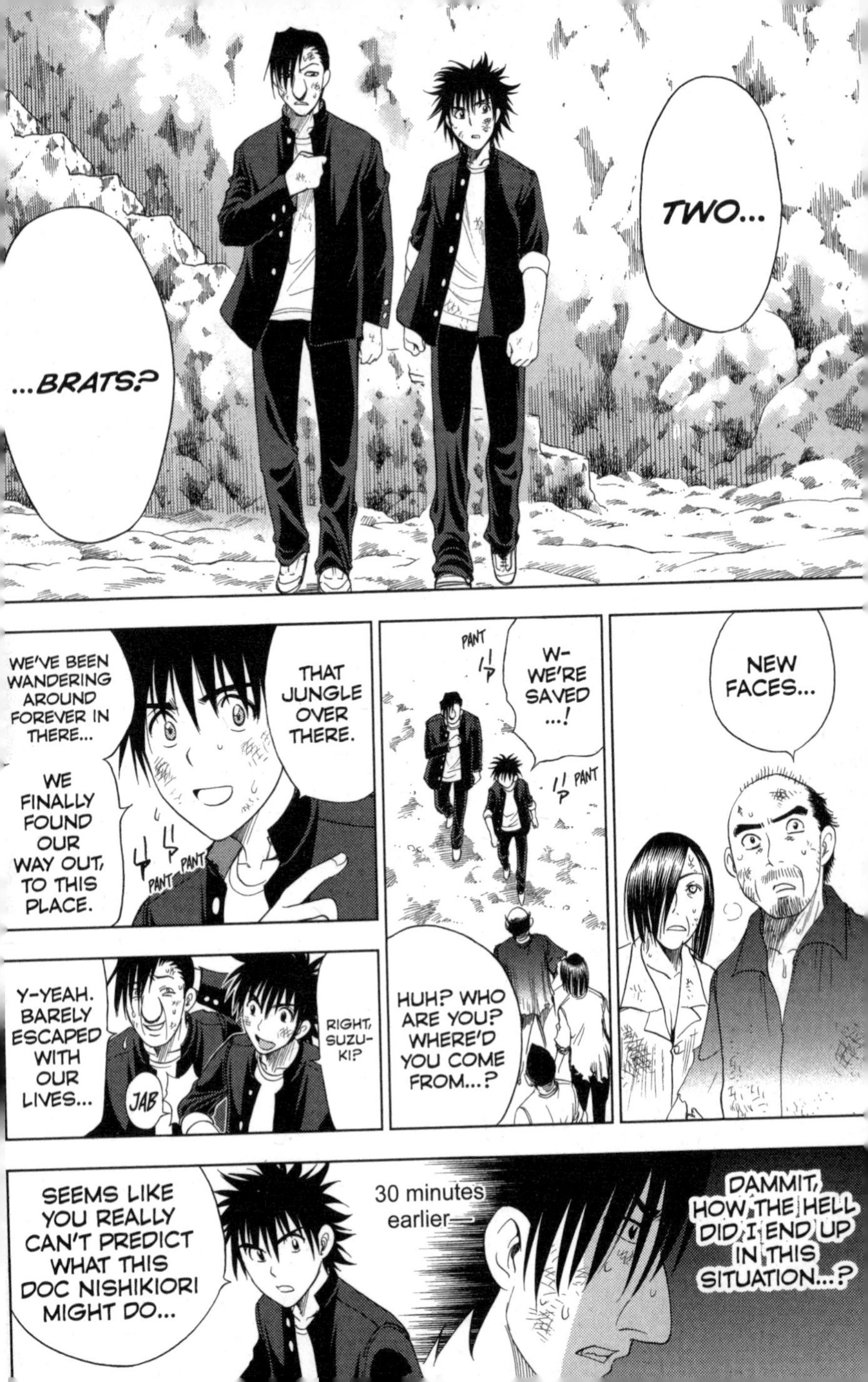
TWO...
...BRATS?
NEW FACES...
PANT
PANT
W- WE'RE SAVED ...!
HUH? WHO ARE YOU? WHERE'D YOU COME FROM...?
THAT JUNGLE OVER THERE.
WE'VE BEEN WANDERING AROUND FOREVER IN THERE...
WE FINALLY FOUND OUR WAY OUT, TO THIS PLACE.
PANT
PANT
RIGHT, SUZUKI?
Y-YEAH. BARELY ESCAPED WITH OUR LIVES...
JAB
DAMMIT, HOW THE HELL DID I END UP IN THIS SITUATION...?
30 minutes earlier—
SEEMS LIKE YOU REALLY CAN'T PREDICT WHAT THIS DOC NISHIKIORI MIGHT DO...

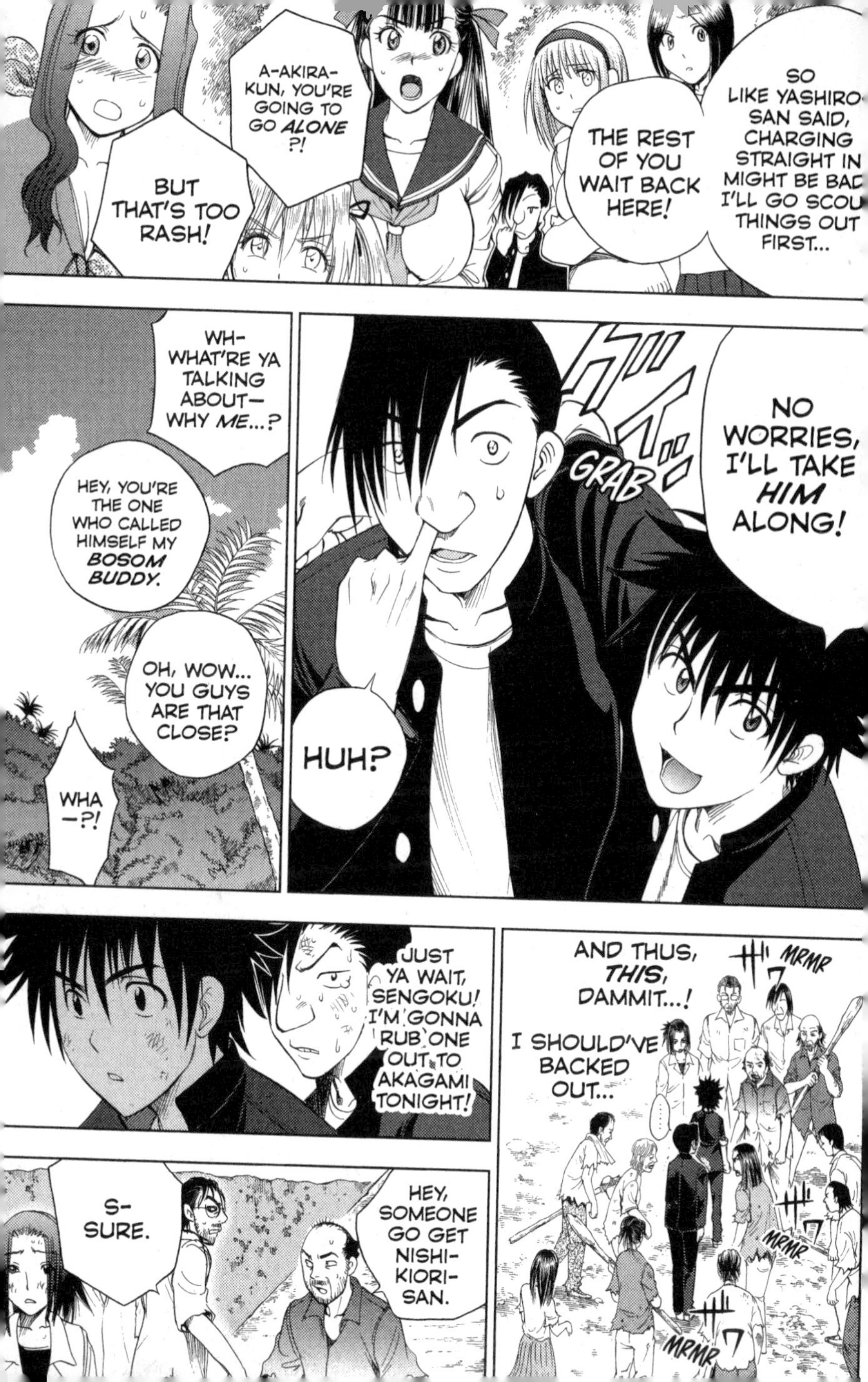
SO LIKE YASHIRO-SAN SAID, CHARGING STRAIGHT IN MIGHT BE BAD I'LL GO SCOU THINGS OUT FIRST...
THE REST OF YOU WAIT BACK HERE!
A-AKIRA-KUN, YOU'RE GOING TO GO *ALONE* ?!
BUT THAT'S TOO RASH!
NO WORRIES, I'LL TAKE *HIM* ALONG!
GRAB
HUH?
WH- WHAT'RE YA TALKING ABOUT— WHY *ME*...?
HEY, YOU'RE THE ONE WHO CALLED HIMSELF MY *BOSOM BUDDY*.
OH, WOW... YOU GUYS ARE THAT CLOSE?
WHA —?!
AND THUS, *THIS*, DAMMIT...!
I SHOULD'VE BACKED OUT...
MRMR
......
MRMR
MRMR
JUST YA WAIT, SENGOKU! I'M GONNA RUB ONE OUT TO AKAGAMI TONIGHT!
HEY, SOMEONE GO GET NISHIKIORI-SAN.
S- SURE.

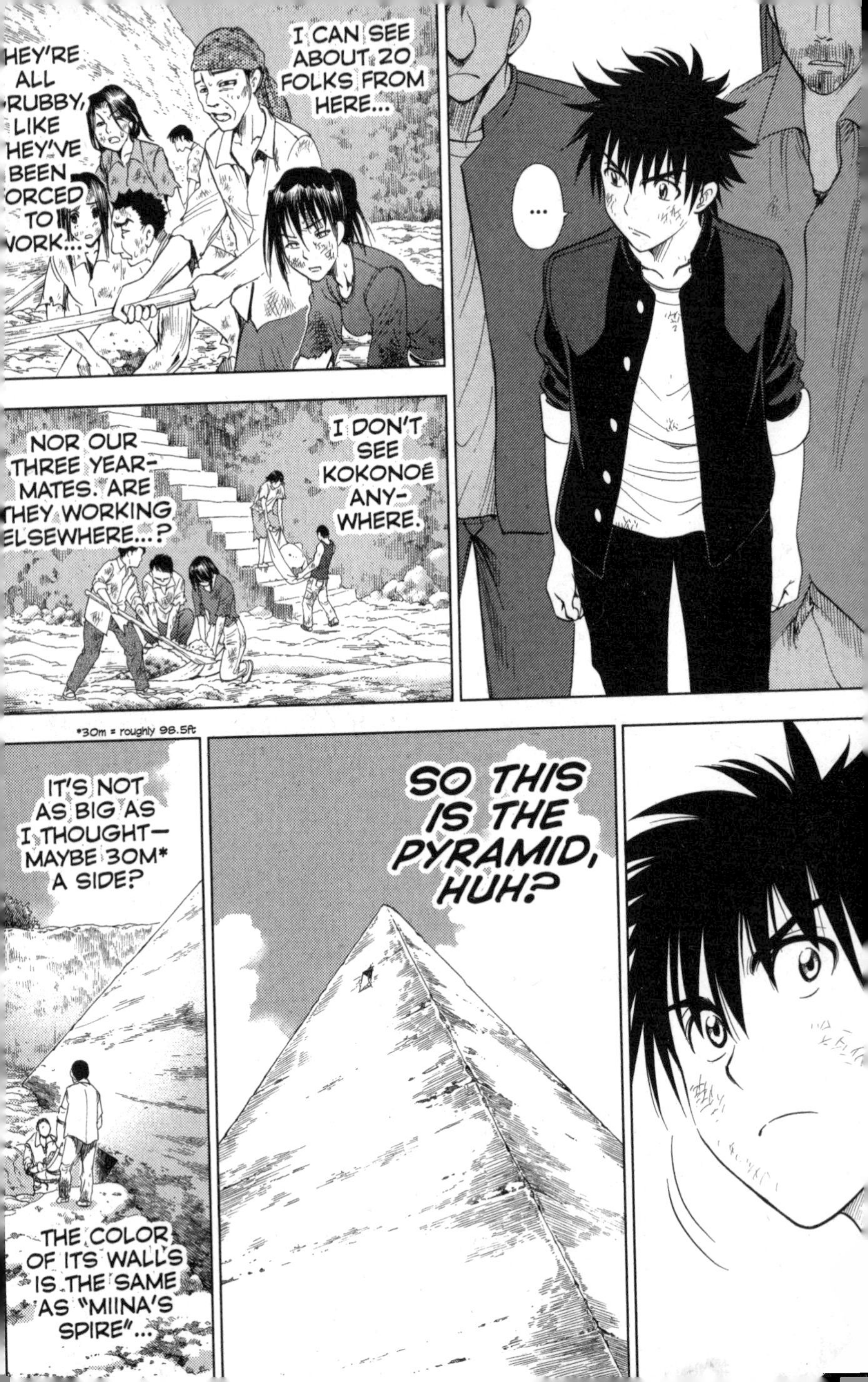
...
I CAN SEE ABOUT 20 FOLKS FROM HERE...
HEY'RE ALL RUBBY, LIKE HEY'VE BEEN ORCED TO ORK...
I DON'T SEE KOKONOE ANY-WHERE.
NOR OUR THREE YEAR-MATES. ARE HEY WORKING LSEWHERE...?
*30m = roughly 98.5ft
SO THIS IS THE PYRAMID, HUH?
IT'S NOT AS BIG AS I THOUGHT—MAYBE 30M* A SIDE?
THE COLOR OF ITS WALLS IS THE SAME AS "MIINA'S SPIRE"...

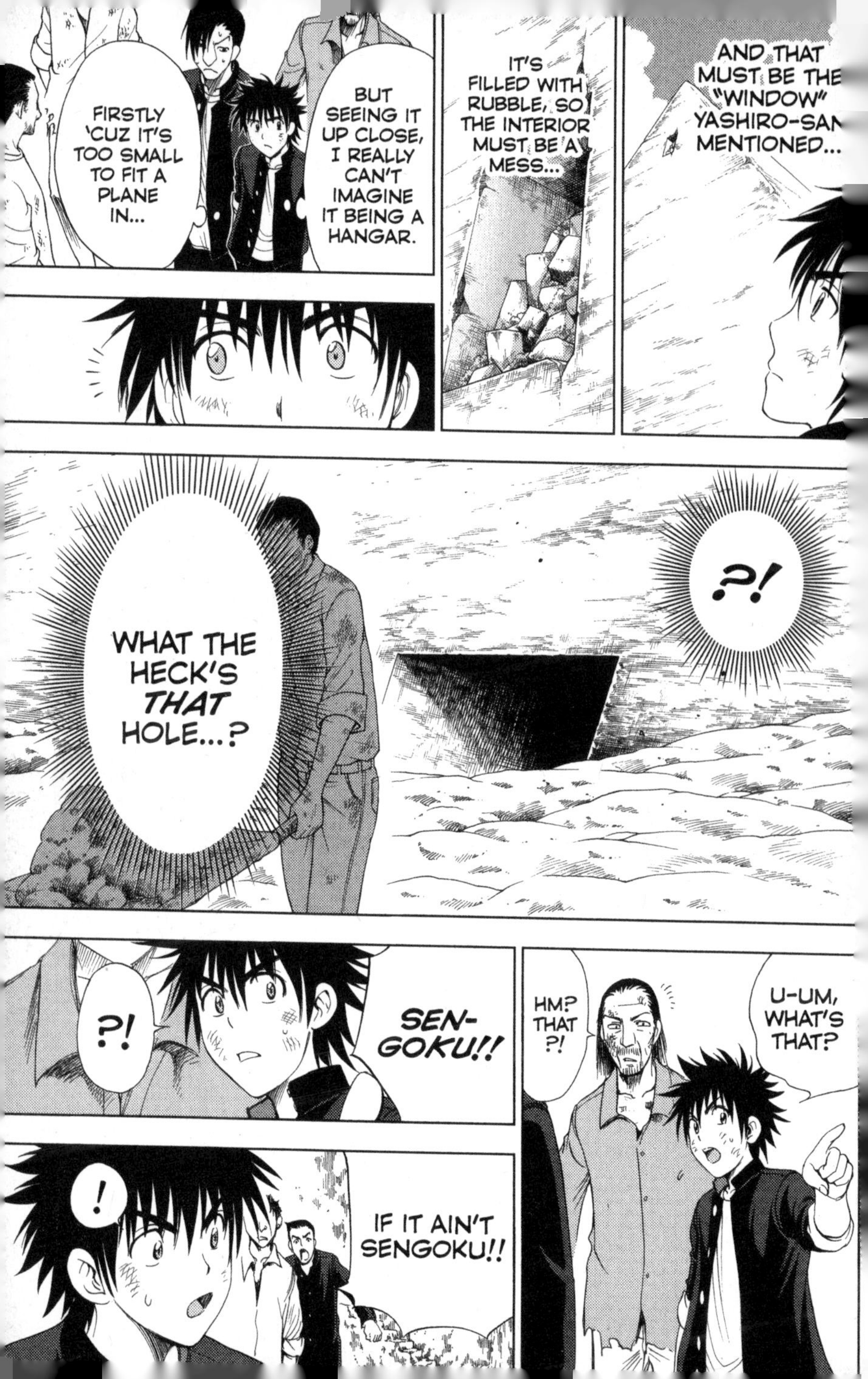
AND THAT MUST BE THE "WINDOW" YASHIRO-SAN MENTIONED...
IT'S FILLED WITH RUBBLE, SO THE INTERIOR MUST BE A MESS...
BUT SEEING IT UP CLOSE, I REALLY CAN'T IMAGINE IT BEING A HANGAR.
FIRSTLY 'CUZ IT'S TOO SMALL TO FIT A PLANE IN...
?!
WHAT THE HECK'S *THAT* HOLE...?
U-UM, WHAT'S THAT?
HM? THAT ?!
SEN-GOKU!!
?!
IF IT AIN'T SENGOKU!!
!

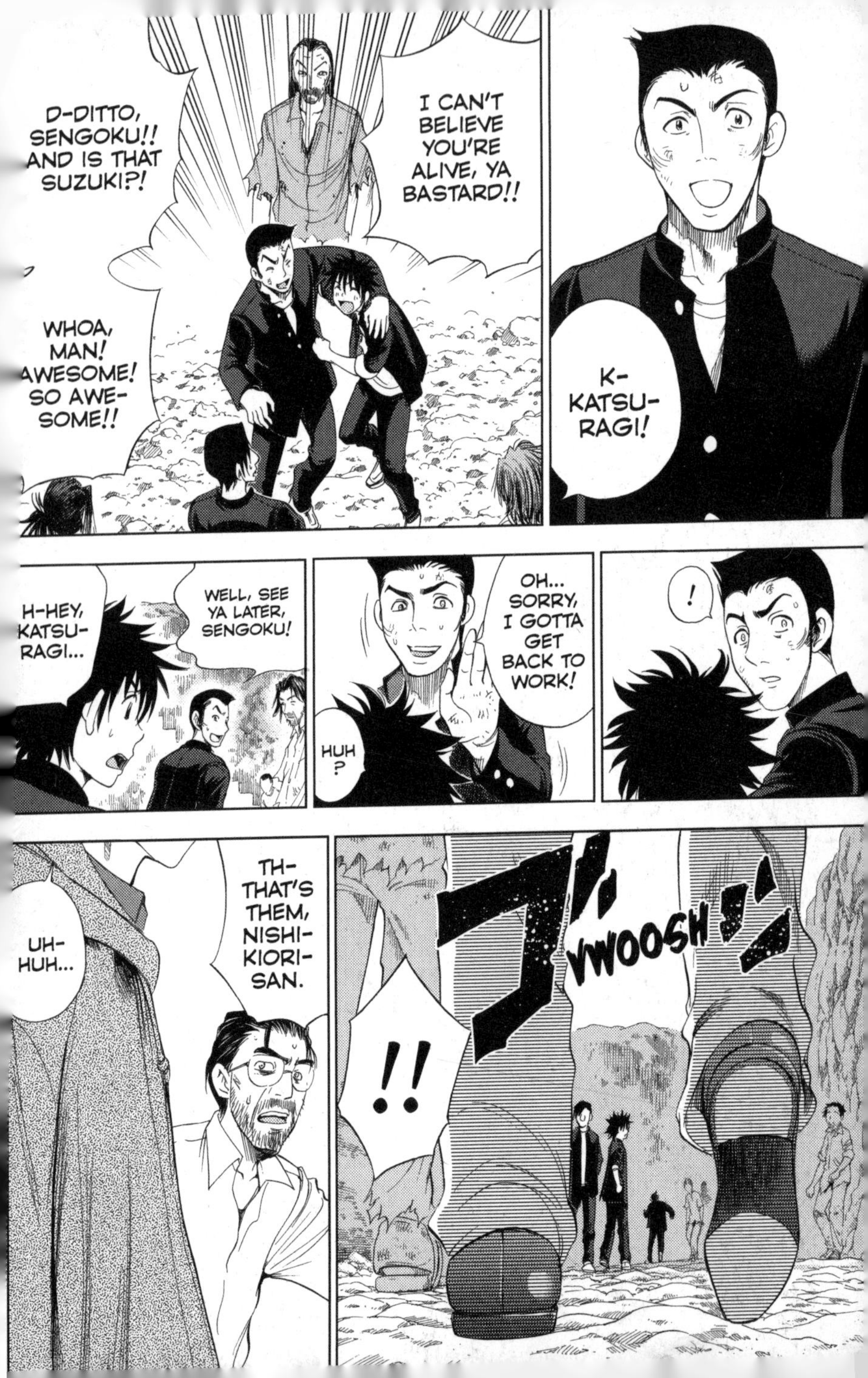
K-KATSURAGI!
I CAN'T BELIEVE YOU'RE ALIVE, YA BASTARD!!
D-DITTO, SENGOKU!! AND IS THAT SUZUKI?!
WHOA, MAN! AWESOME! SO AWE-SOME!!
!
OH... SORRY, I GOTTA GET BACK TO WORK!
HUH?
WELL, SEE YA LATER, SENGOKU!
H-HEY, KATSURAGI...
VWOOSH
!!
TH-THAT'S THEM, NISHIKIORI-SAN.
UH-HUH...

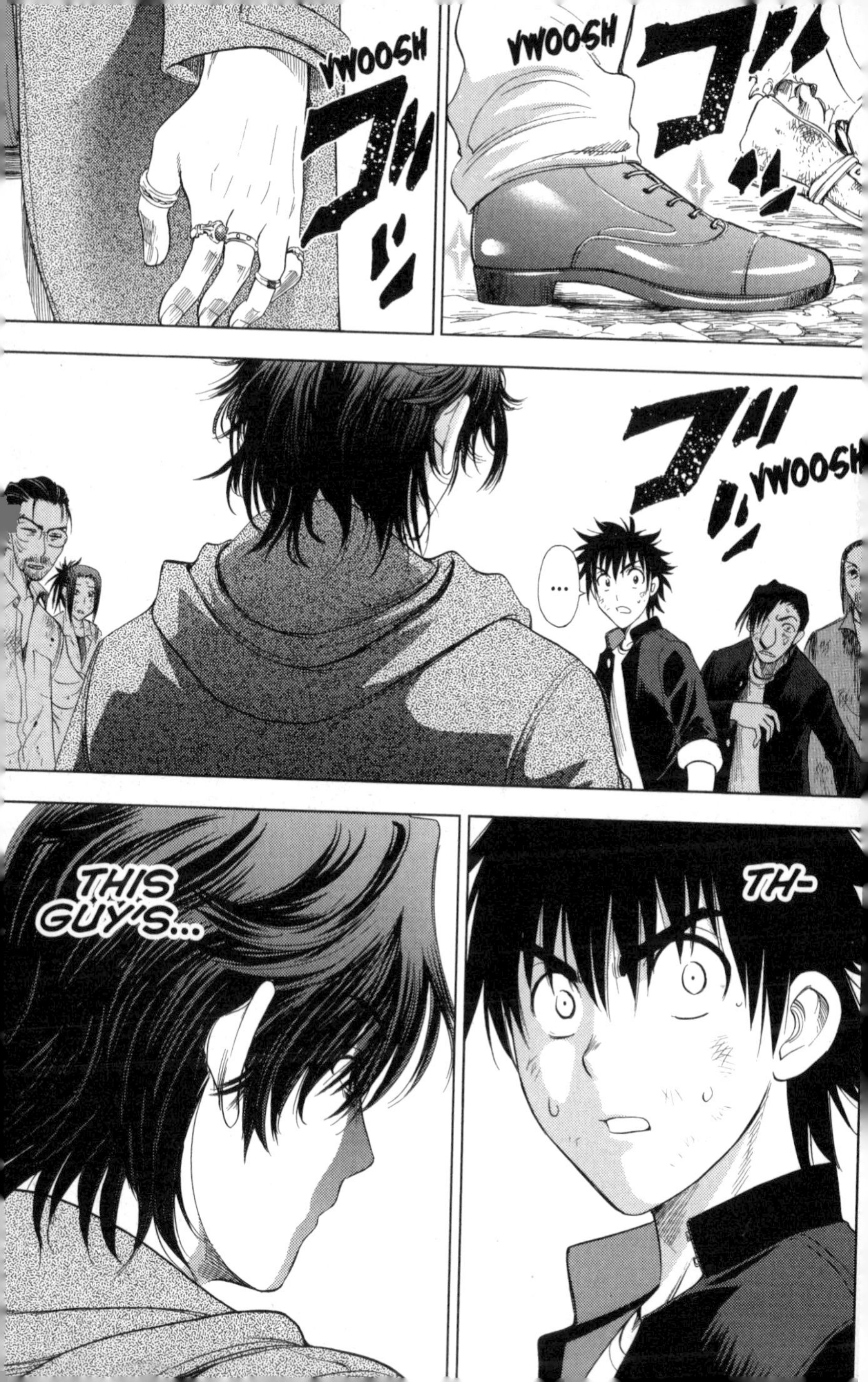
VWOOSH
VWOOSH
VWOOSH
...
TH-
THIS GUY'S...

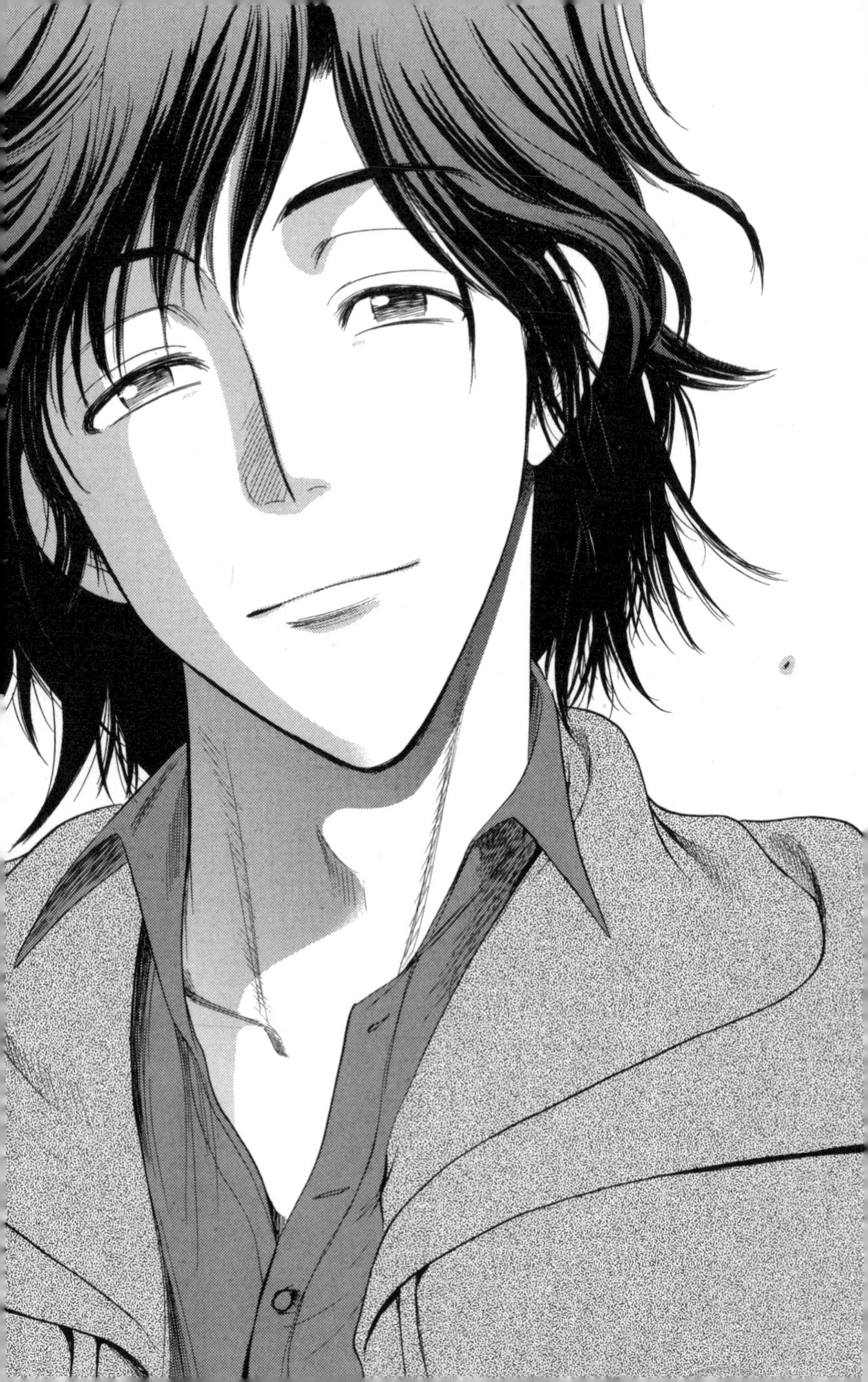

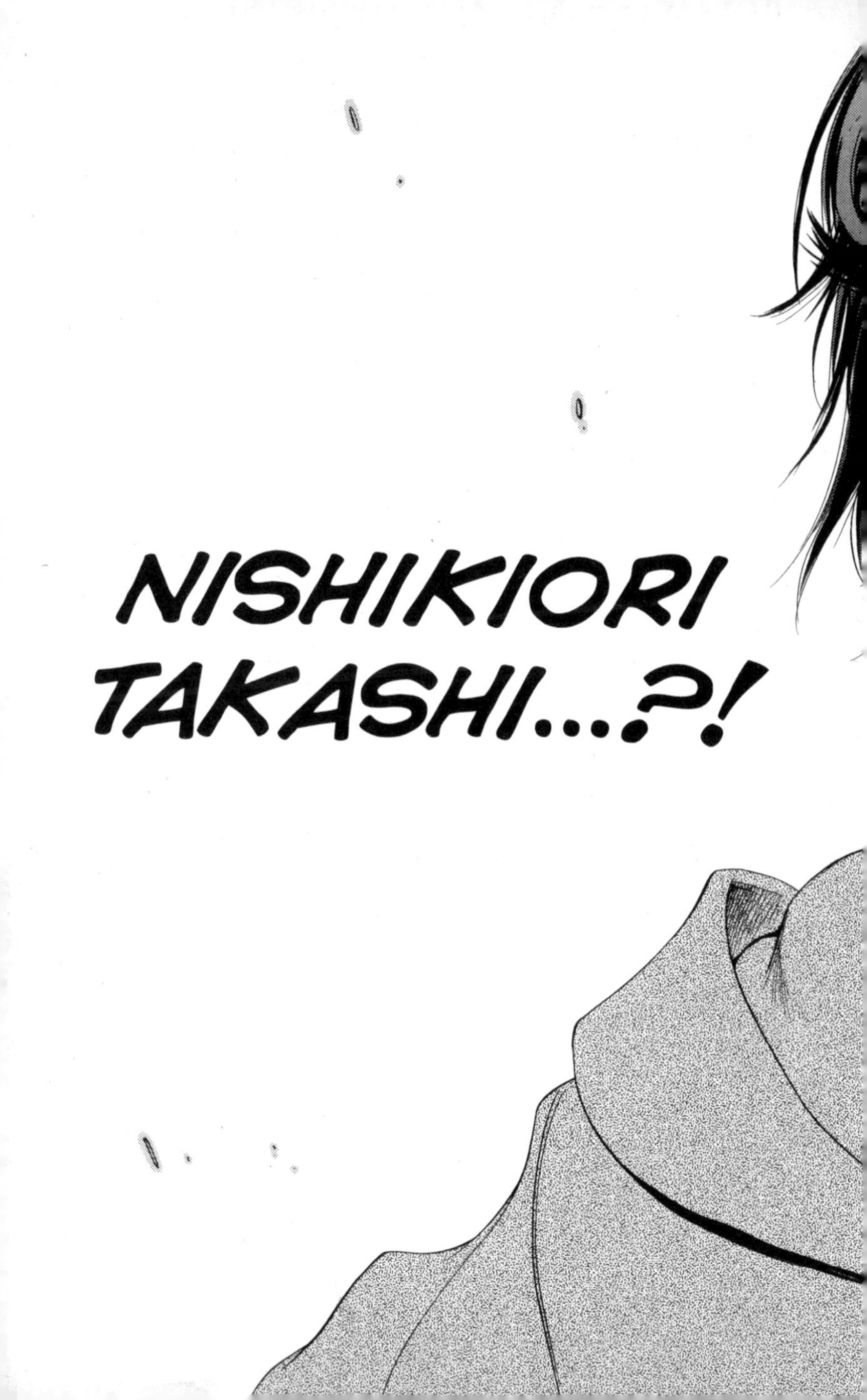
NISHIKIORI TAKASHI...?!

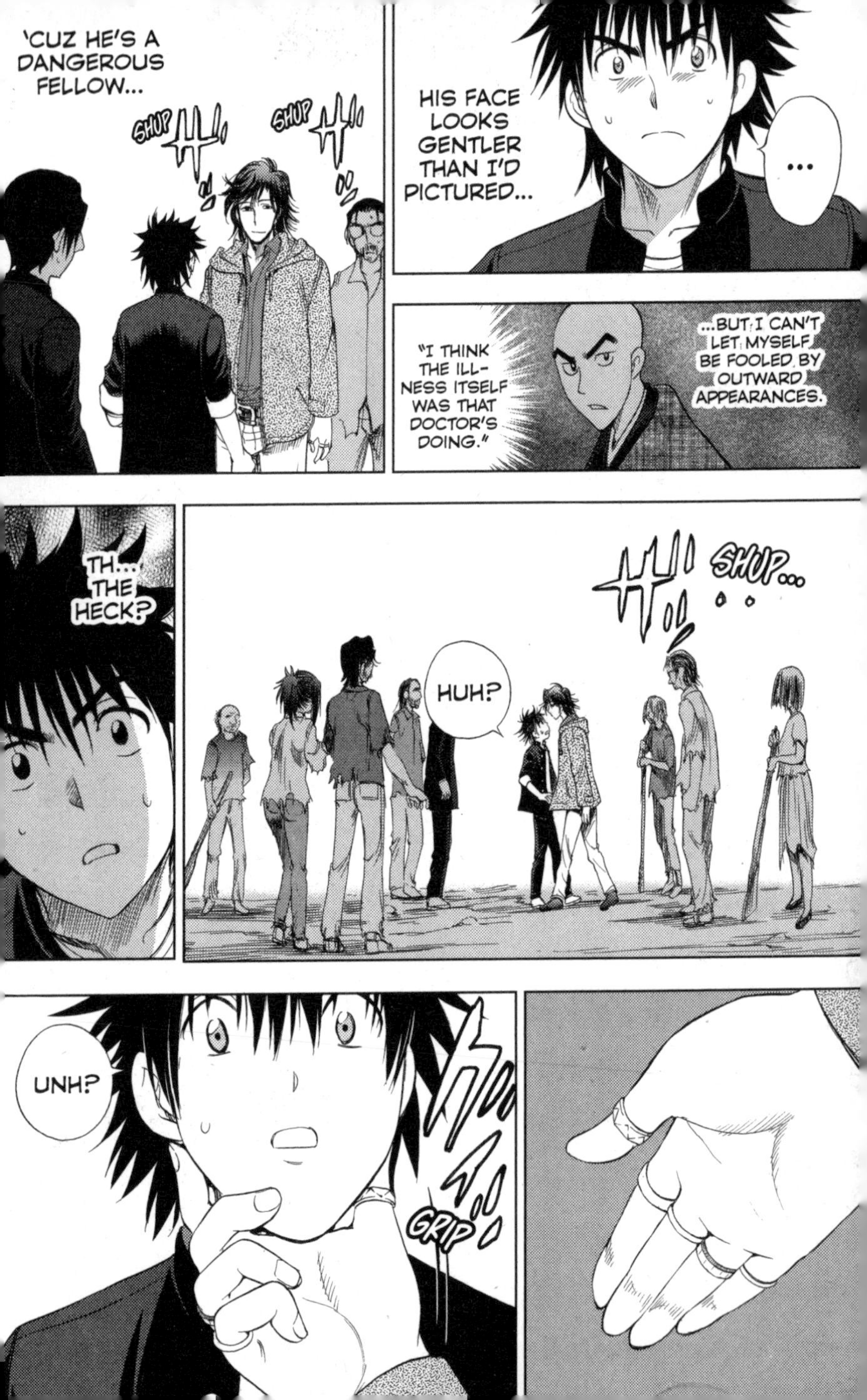
...
HIS FACE LOOKS GENTLER THAN I'D PICTURED...
...BUT I CAN'T LET MYSELF BE FOOLED BY OUTWARD APPEARANCES.
"I THINK THE ILLNESS ITSELF WAS THAT DOCTOR'S DOING."
'CUZ HE'S A DANGEROUS FELLOW...
SHUP
SHUP
SHUP...
HUH?
TH... THE HECK?
UNH?
GRIP

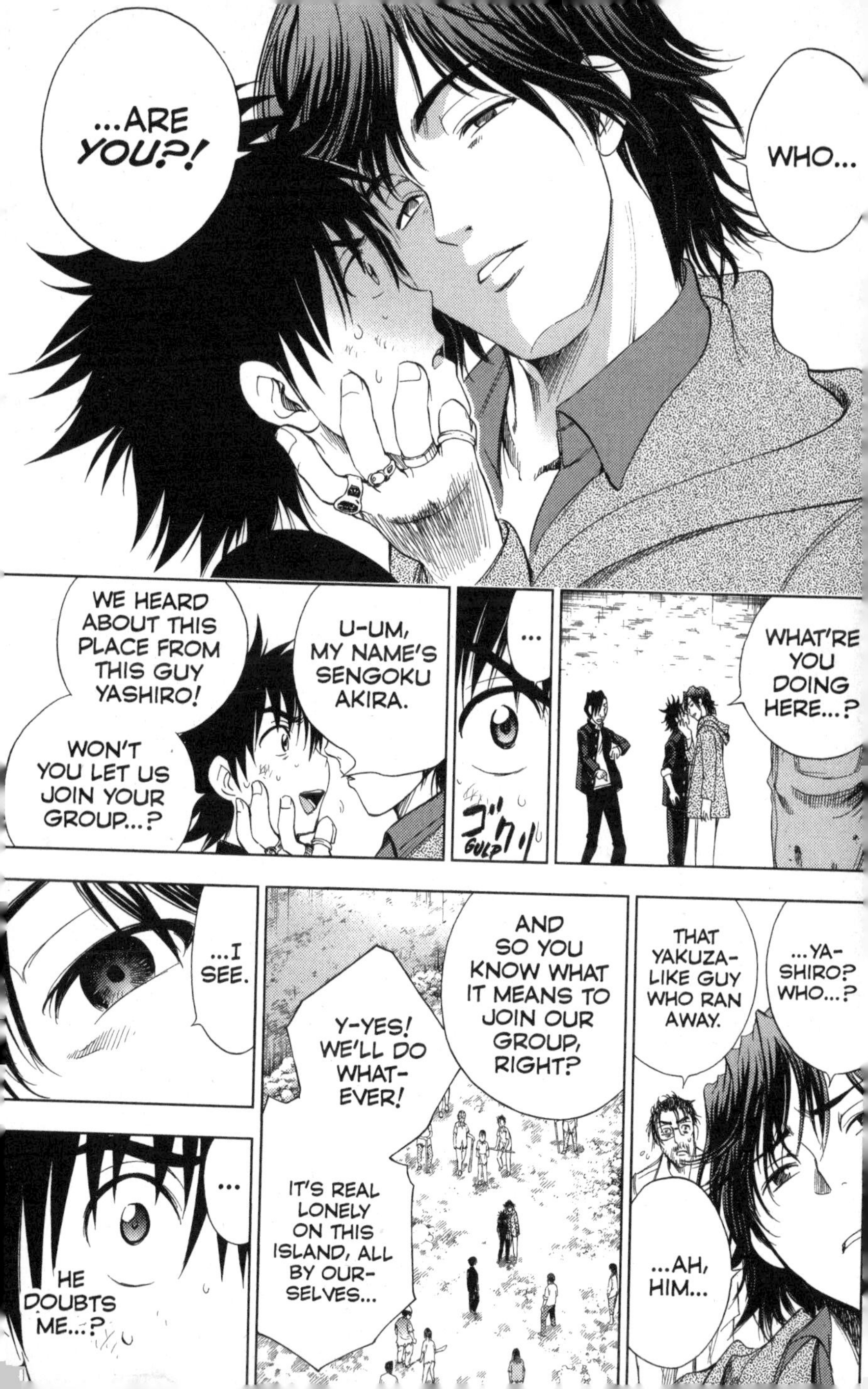
WHO...
...ARE YOU?!
WHAT'RE YOU DOING HERE...?
...
GULP
ゴクリ
U-UM, MY NAME'S SENGOKU AKIRA.
WE HEARD ABOUT THIS PLACE FROM THIS GUY YASHIRO!
WON'T YOU LET US JOIN YOUR GROUP...?
...YA-SHIRO? WHO...?
THAT YAKUZA-LIKE GUY WHO RAN AWAY.
...AH, HIM...
AND SO YOU KNOW WHAT IT MEANS TO JOIN OUR GROUP, RIGHT?
Y-YES! WE'LL DO WHAT-EVER!
IT'S REAL LONELY ON THIS ISLAND, ALL BY OUR-SELVES...
...I SEE.
...
HE DOUBTS ME...?

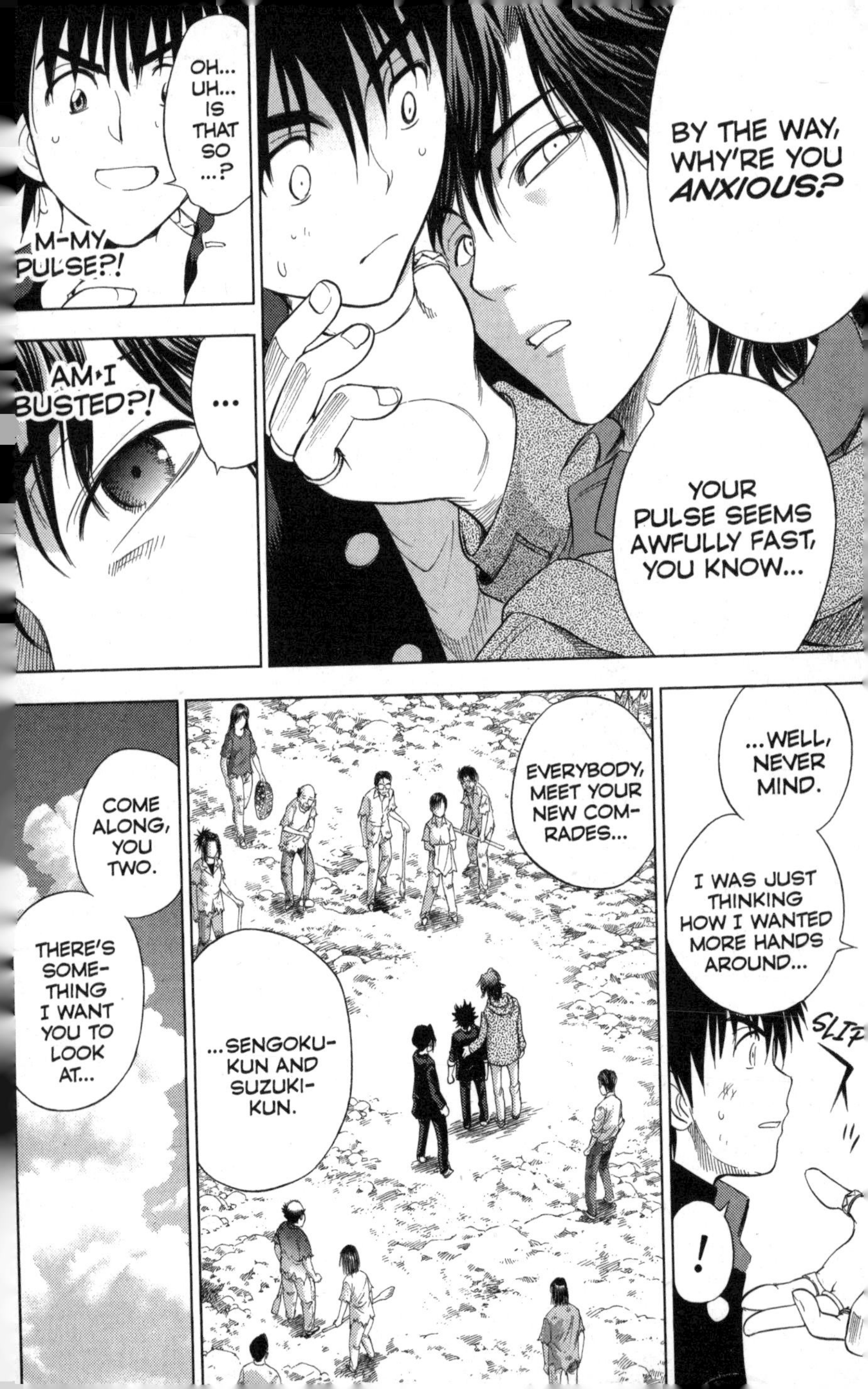
BY THE WAY, WHY'RE YOU ANXIOUS?
YOUR PULSE SEEMS AWFULLY FAST, YOU KNOW...
OH... UH... IS THAT SO...?
M-MY PULSE?!
...
AM I BUSTED?!
...WELL, NEVER MIND.
I WAS JUST THINKING HOW I WANTED MORE HANDS AROUND...
SLIP
!
EVERYBODY, MEET YOUR NEW COMRADES...
...SENGOKU-KUN AND SUZUKI-KUN.
COME ALONG, YOU TWO.
THERE'S SOMETHING I WANT YOU TO LOOK AT...

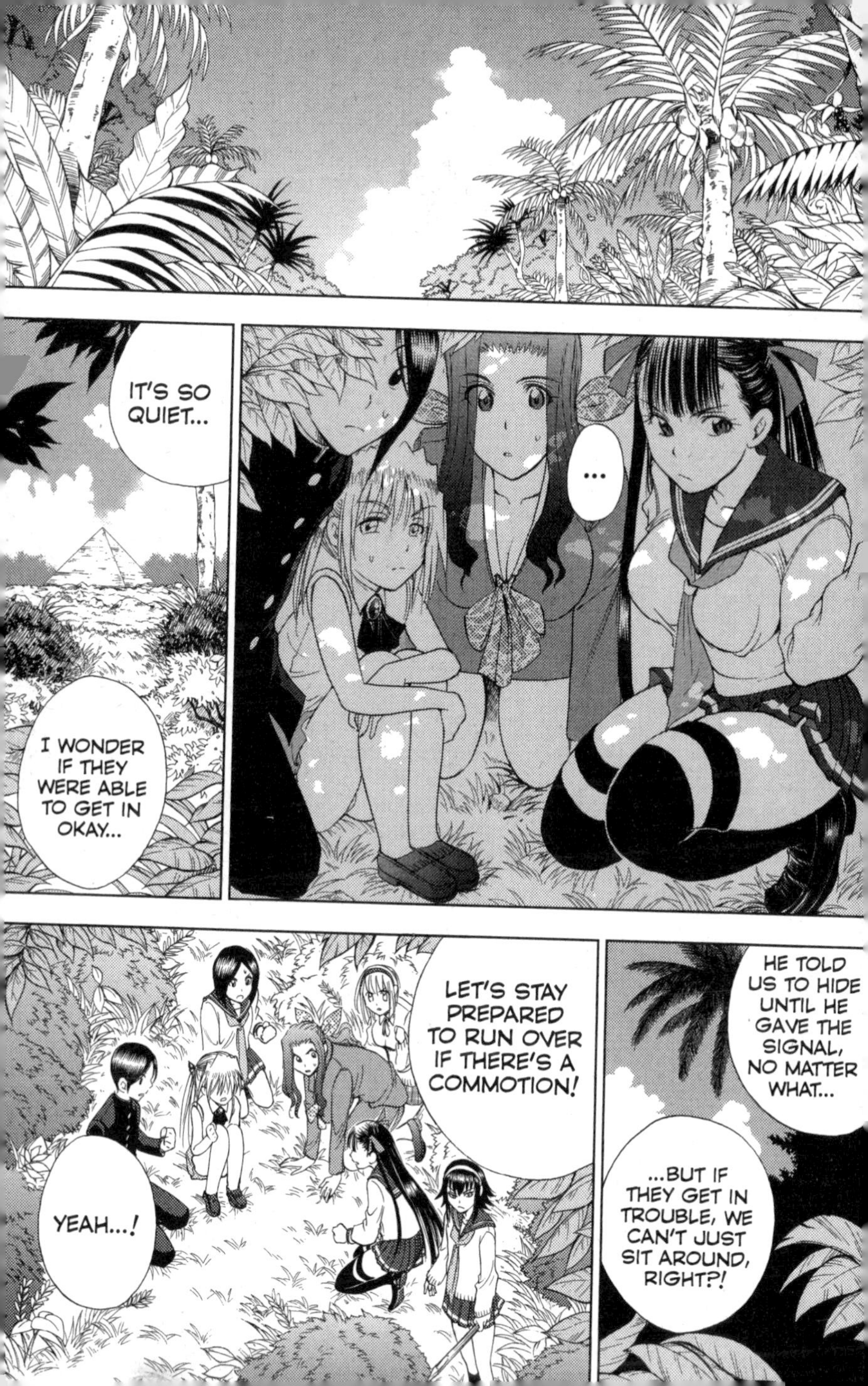
...
IT'S SO QUIET...
I WONDER IF THEY WERE ABLE TO GET IN OKAY...
HE TOLD US TO HIDE UNTIL HE GAVE THE SIGNAL, NO MATTER WHAT...
...BUT IF THEY GET IN TROUBLE, WE CAN'T JUST SIT AROUND, RIGHT?!
LET'S STAY PREPARED TO RUN OVER IF THERE'S A COMMOTION!
YEAH...!

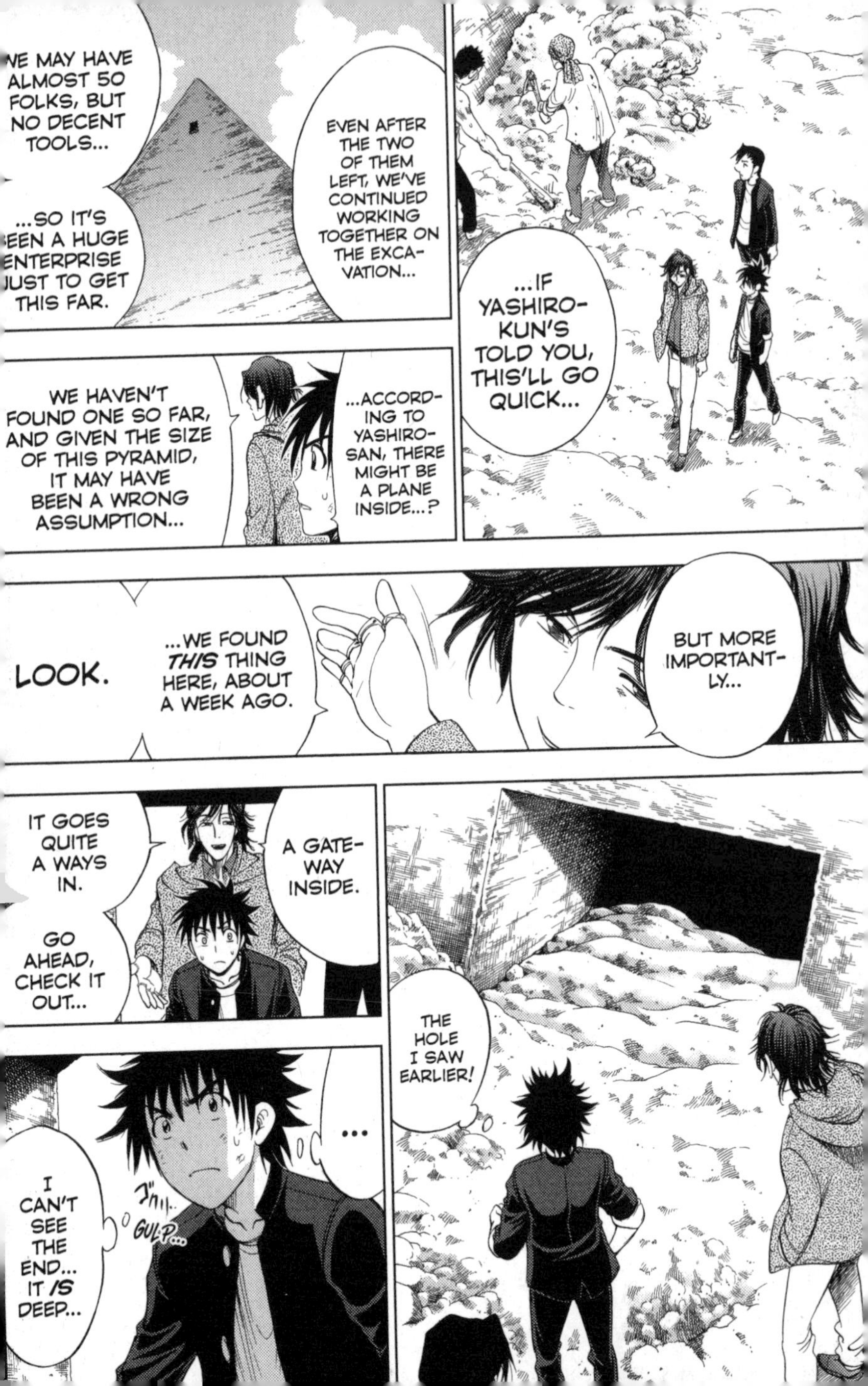
...IF YASHIRO-KUN'S TOLD YOU, THIS'LL GO QUICK...
EVEN AFTER THE TWO OF THEM LEFT, WE'VE CONTINUED WORKING TOGETHER ON THE EXCAVATION...
WE MAY HAVE ALMOST 50 FOLKS, BUT NO DECENT TOOLS...
...SO IT'S BEEN A HUGE ENTERPRISE JUST TO GET THIS FAR.
...ACCORDING TO YASHIRO-SAN, THERE MIGHT BE A PLANE INSIDE...?
WE HAVEN'T FOUND ONE SO FAR, AND GIVEN THE SIZE OF THIS PYRAMID, IT MAY HAVE BEEN A WRONG ASSUMPTION...
BUT MORE IMPORTANTLY...
...WE FOUND *THIS* THING HERE, ABOUT A WEEK AGO.
LOOK.
THE HOLE I SAW EARLIER!
A GATEWAY INSIDE.
IT GOES QUITE A WAYS IN.
GO AHEAD, CHECK IT OUT...
...
GULP...
I CAN'T SEE THE END... IT *IS* DEEP...

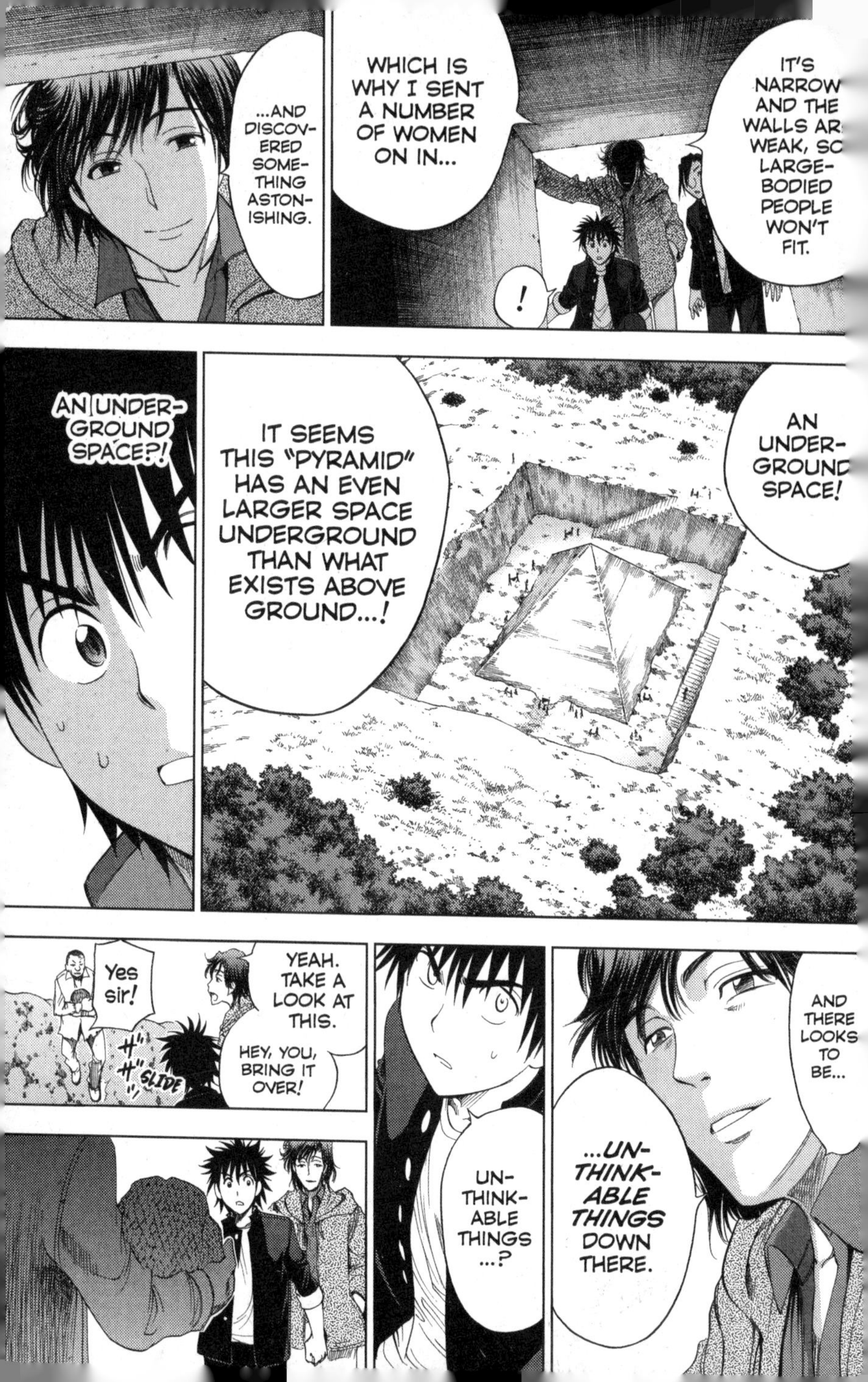
IT'S NARROW AND THE WALLS AR WEAK, SC LARGE-BODIED PEOPLE WON'T FIT.
!
WHICH IS WHY I SENT A NUMBER OF WOMEN ON IN...
...AND DISCOVERED SOMETHING ASTONISHING.
AN UNDERGROUND SPACE!
IT SEEMS THIS "PYRAMID" HAS AN EVEN LARGER SPACE UNDERGROUND THAN WHAT EXISTS ABOVE GROUND...!
AN UNDERGROUND SPACE?!
AND THERE LOOKS TO BE...
...UNTHINKABLE THINGS DOWN THERE.
UNTHINKABLE THINGS...?
YEAH. TAKE A LOOK AT THIS.
HEY, YOU, BRING IT OVER!
Yes sir!
SLIDE

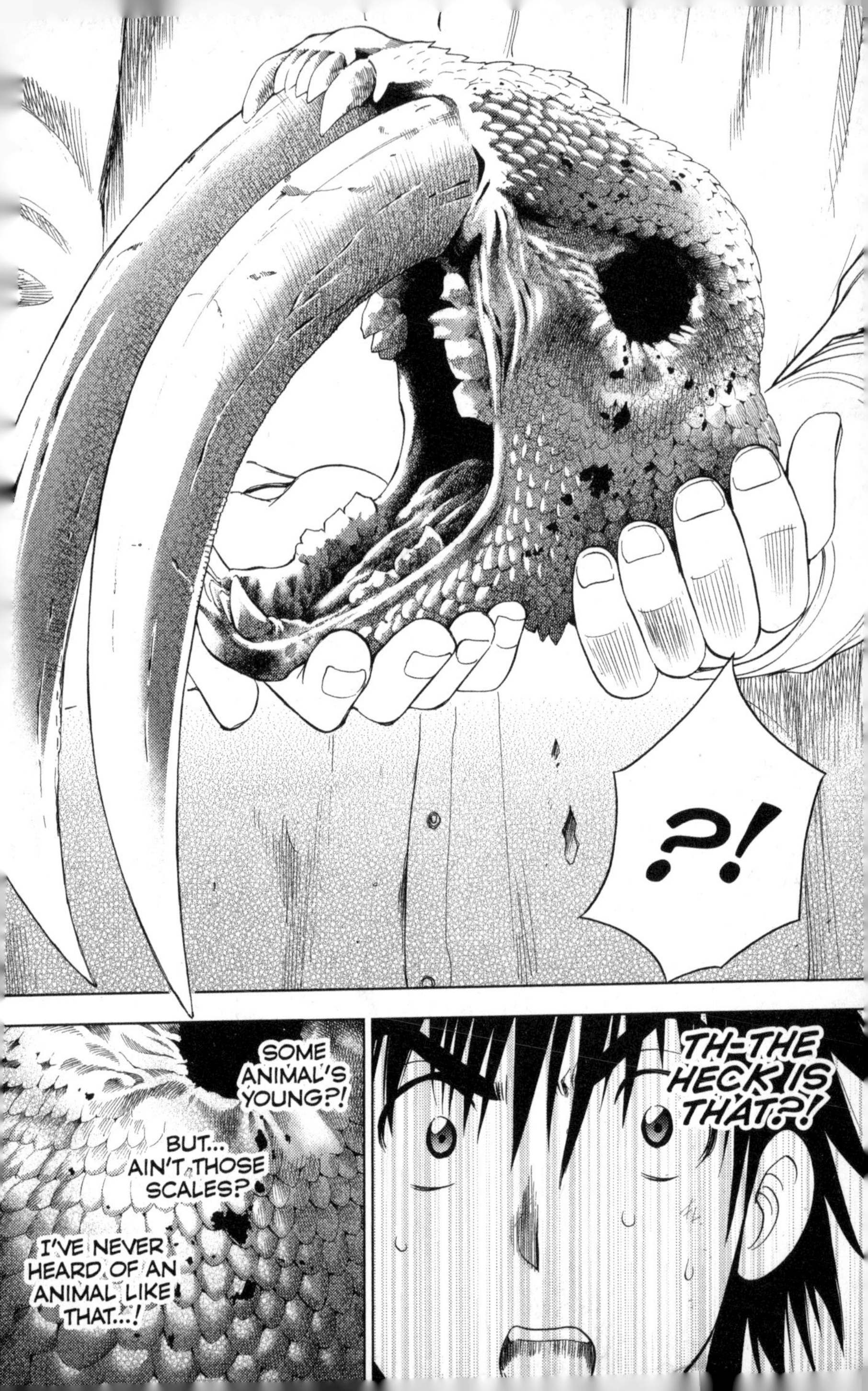
?!
TH-THE HECK IS THAT?!
SOME ANIMAL'S YOUNG?!
BUT... AIN'T THOSE SCALES?
I'VE NEVER HEARD OF AN ANIMAL LIKE THAT...!

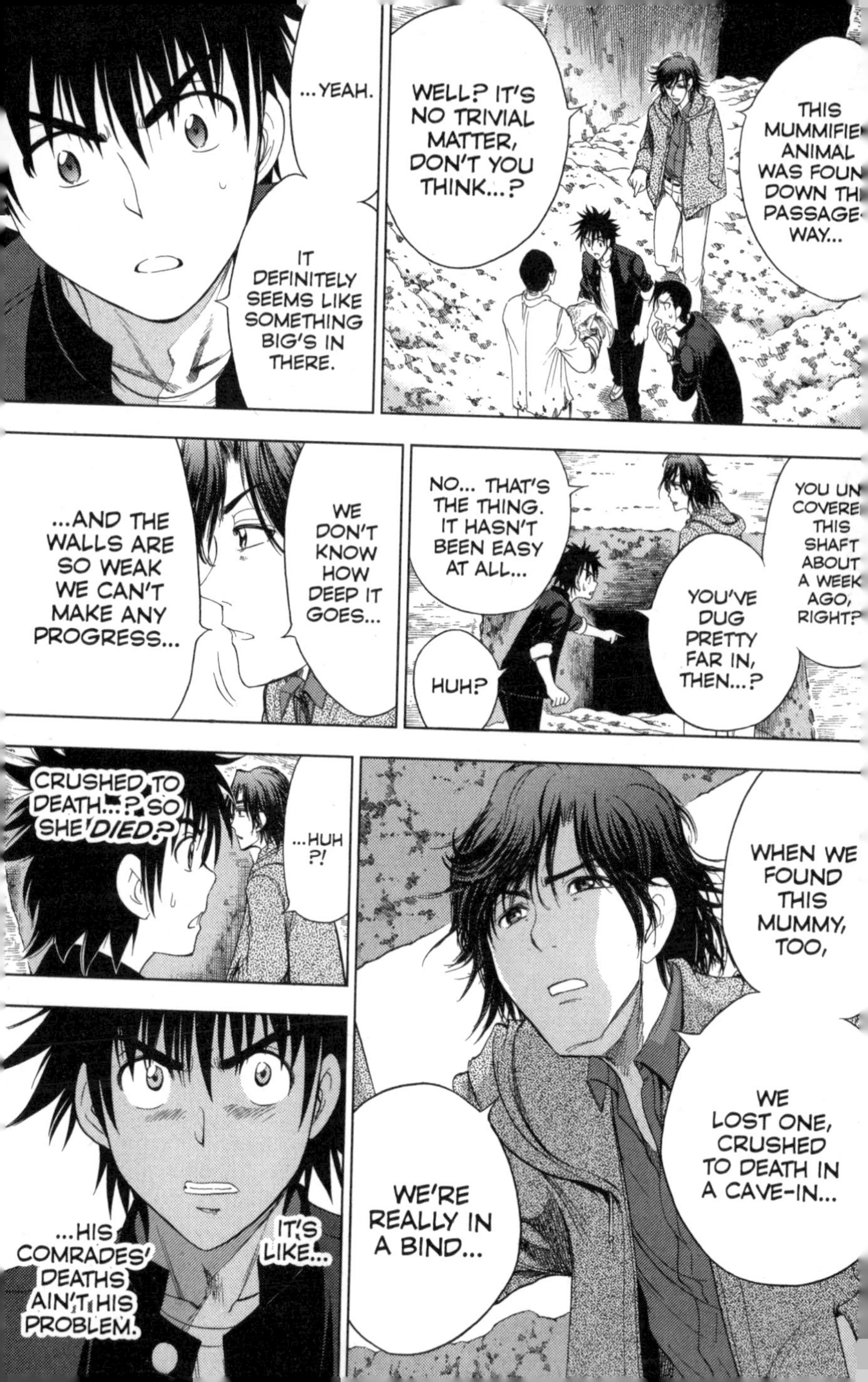
THIS MUMMIFIE ANIMAL WAS FOUN DOWN TH PASSAGE-WAY...
WELL? IT'S NO TRIVIAL MATTER, DON'T YOU THINK...?
...YEAH.
IT DEFINITELY SEEMS LIKE SOMETHING BIG'S IN THERE.
YOU UN COVERE THIS SHAFT ABOUT A WEEK AGO, RIGHT?
YOU'VE DUG PRETTY FAR IN, THEN...?
HUH?
NO... THAT'S THE THING. IT HASN'T BEEN EASY AT ALL...
WE DON'T KNOW HOW DEEP IT GOES...
...AND THE WALLS ARE SO WEAK WE CAN'T MAKE ANY PROGRESS...
WHEN WE FOUND THIS MUMMY, TOO,
WE LOST ONE, CRUSHED TO DEATH IN A CAVE-IN...
WE'RE REALLY IN A BIND...
...HUH ?!
CRUSHED TO DEATH...? SO SHE *DIED*?
IT'S LIKE...
...HIS COMRADES' DEATHS AIN'T HIS PROBLEM.

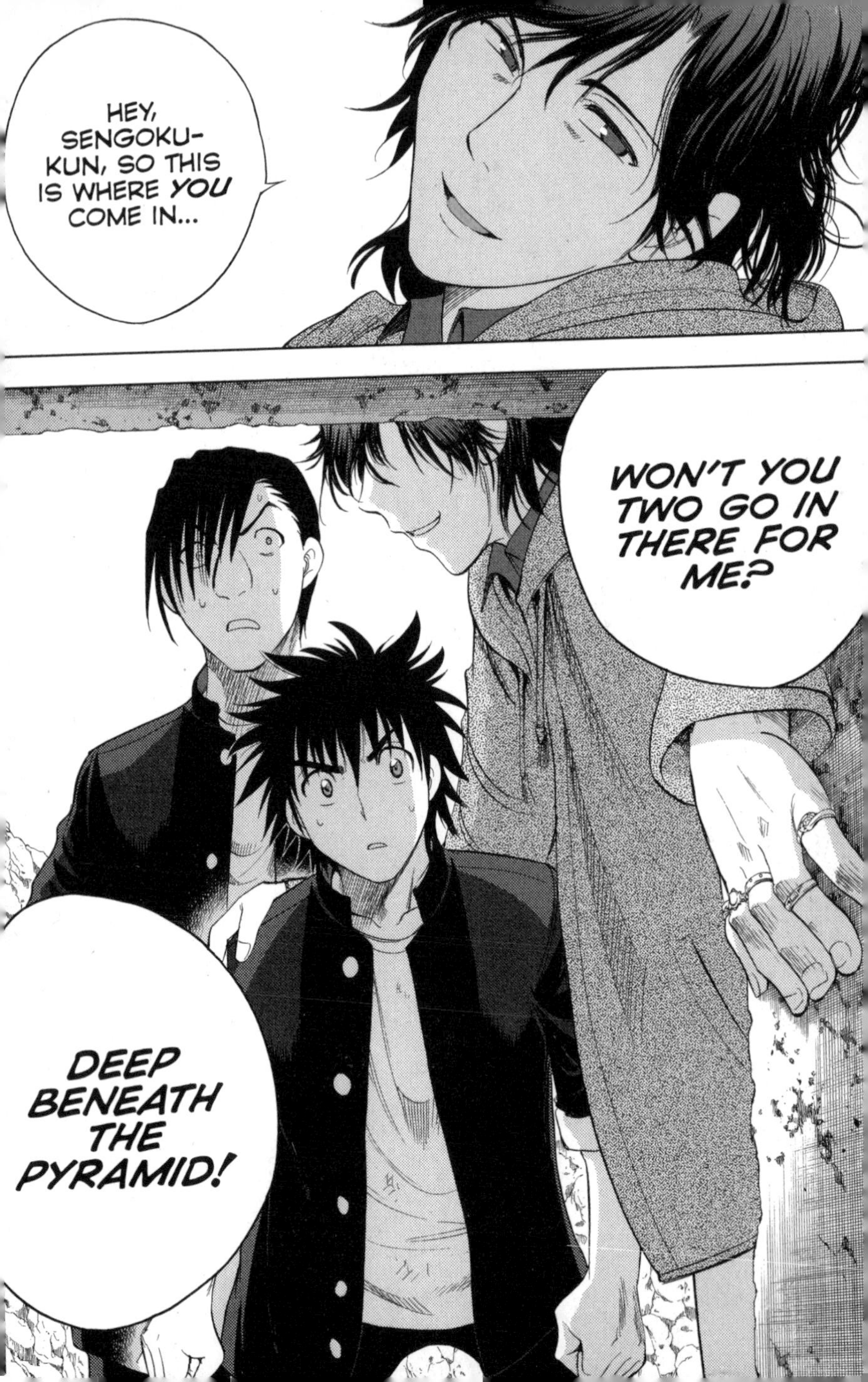
HEY, SENGOKU-KUN, SO THIS IS WHERE *YOU* COME IN...
WON'T YOU TWO GO IN THERE FOR ME?
DEEP BENEATH THE PYRAMID!

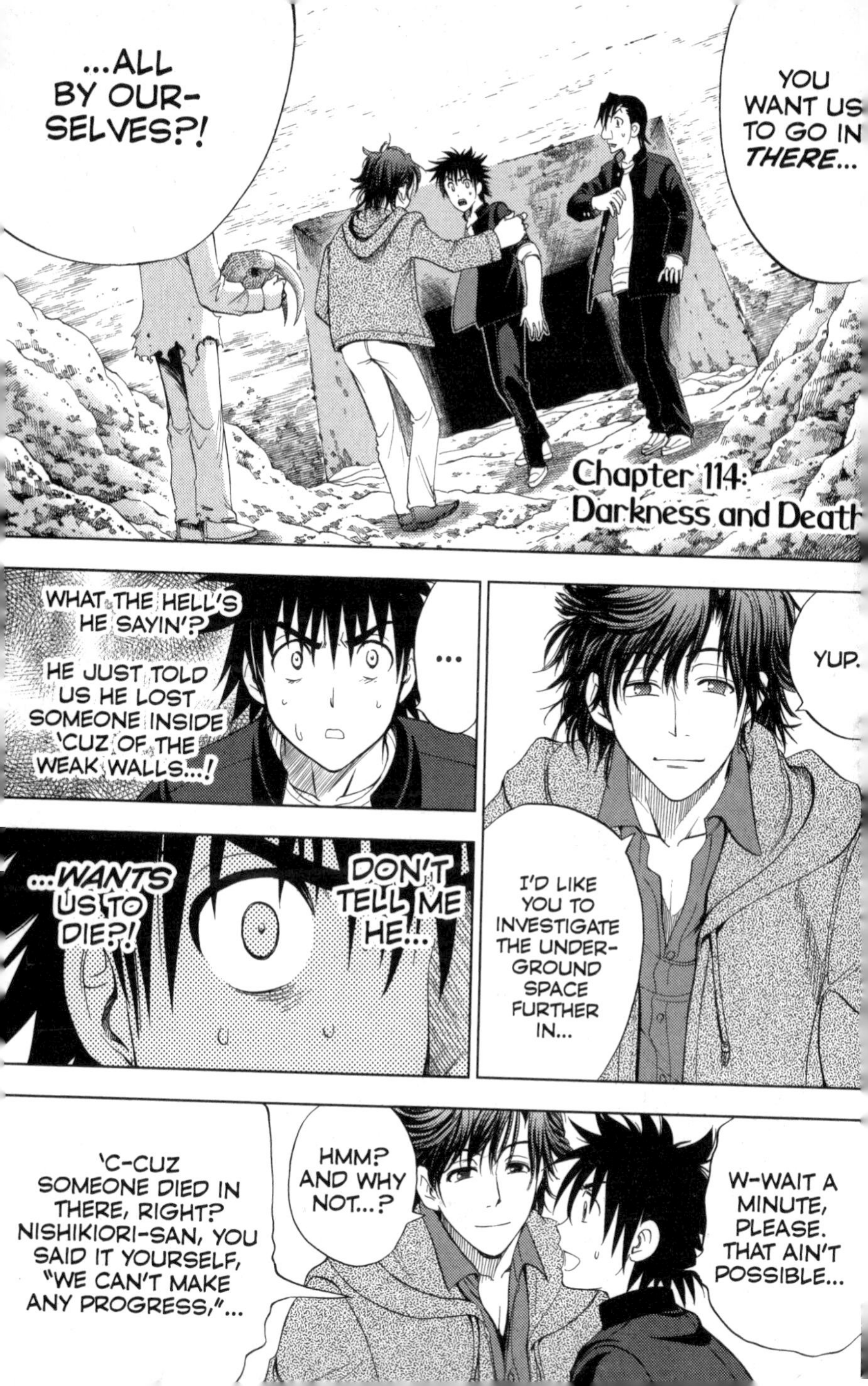
YOU WANT US TO GO IN *THERE*...
...ALL BY OUR-SELVES?!
Chapter 114: Darkness and Death
YUP.
I'D LIKE YOU TO INVESTIGATE THE UNDER-GROUND SPACE FURTHER IN...
...
WHAT THE HELL'S HE SAYIN'?
HE JUST TOLD US HE LOST SOMEONE INSIDE 'CUZ OF THE WEAK WALLS...!
DON'T TELL ME HE...
...*WANTS* US TO DIE?!
W-WAIT A MINUTE, PLEASE. THAT AIN'T POSSIBLE...
HMM? AND WHY NOT...?
'C-CUZ SOMEONE DIED IN THERE, RIGHT? NISHIKIORI-SAN, YOU SAID IT YOURSELF, "WE CAN'T MAKE ANY PROGRESS,"...

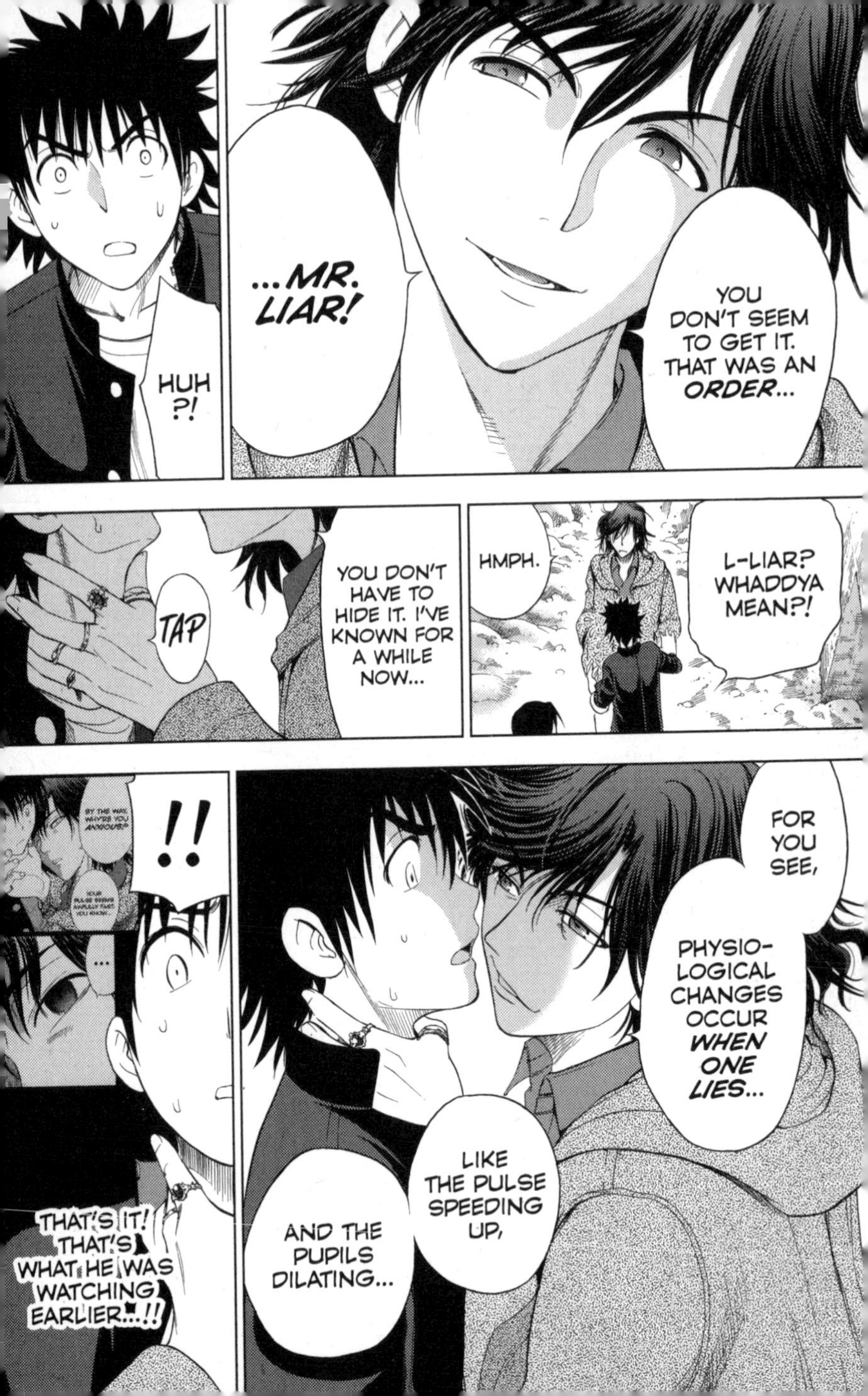
YOU DON'T SEEM TO GET IT. THAT WAS AN ORDER...
...MR. LIAR!
HUH?!
L-LIAR? WHADDYA MEAN?!
HMPH.
YOU DON'T HAVE TO HIDE IT. I'VE KNOWN FOR A WHILE NOW...
TAP
FOR YOU SEE,
PHYSIO-LOGICAL CHANGES OCCUR WHEN ONE LIES...
LIKE THE PULSE SPEEDING UP,
AND THE PUPILS DILATING...
!!
BY THE WAY, WHY'RE YOU ANXIOUS?
YOUR PULSE SEEMS AWFULLY FAST, YOU KNOW...
...
THAT'S IT! THAT'S WHAT HE WAS WATCHING EARLIER...!!

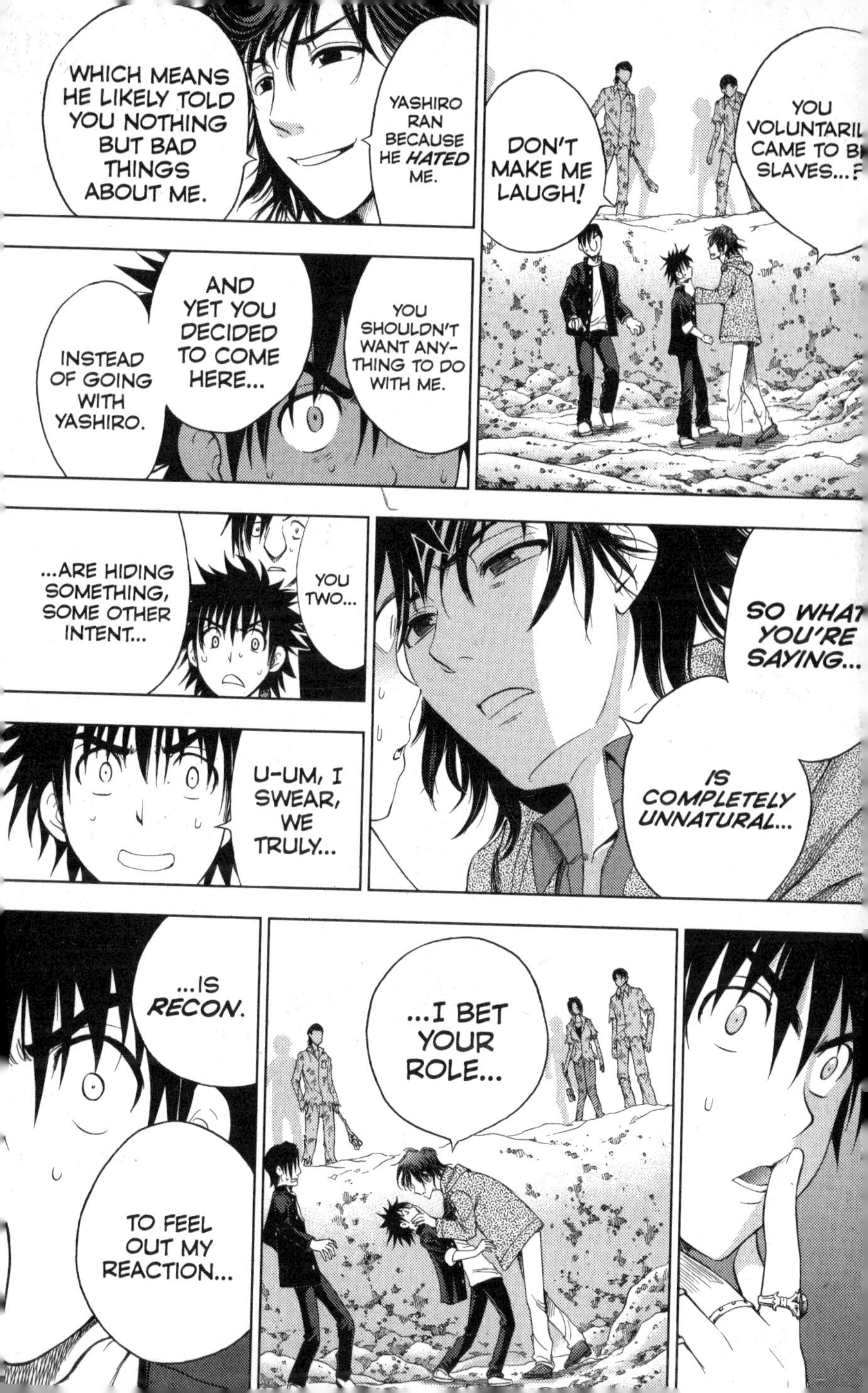
YOU VOLUNTARIL CAME TO B SLAVES...?
DON'T MAKE ME LAUGH!
YASHIRO RAN BECAUSE HE *HATED* ME.
WHICH MEANS HE LIKELY TOLD YOU NOTHING BUT BAD THINGS ABOUT ME.
YOU SHOULDN'T WANT ANY-THING TO DO WITH ME.
AND YET YOU DECIDED TO COME HERE...
INSTEAD OF GOING WITH YASHIRO.
SO WHA YOU'RE SAYING...
IS COMPLETELY UNNATURAL...
YOU TWO...
...ARE HIDING SOMETHING, SOME OTHER INTENT...
U-UM, I SWEAR, WE TRULY...
...I BET YOUR ROLE...
...IS *RECON*.
TO FEEL OUT MY REACTION...

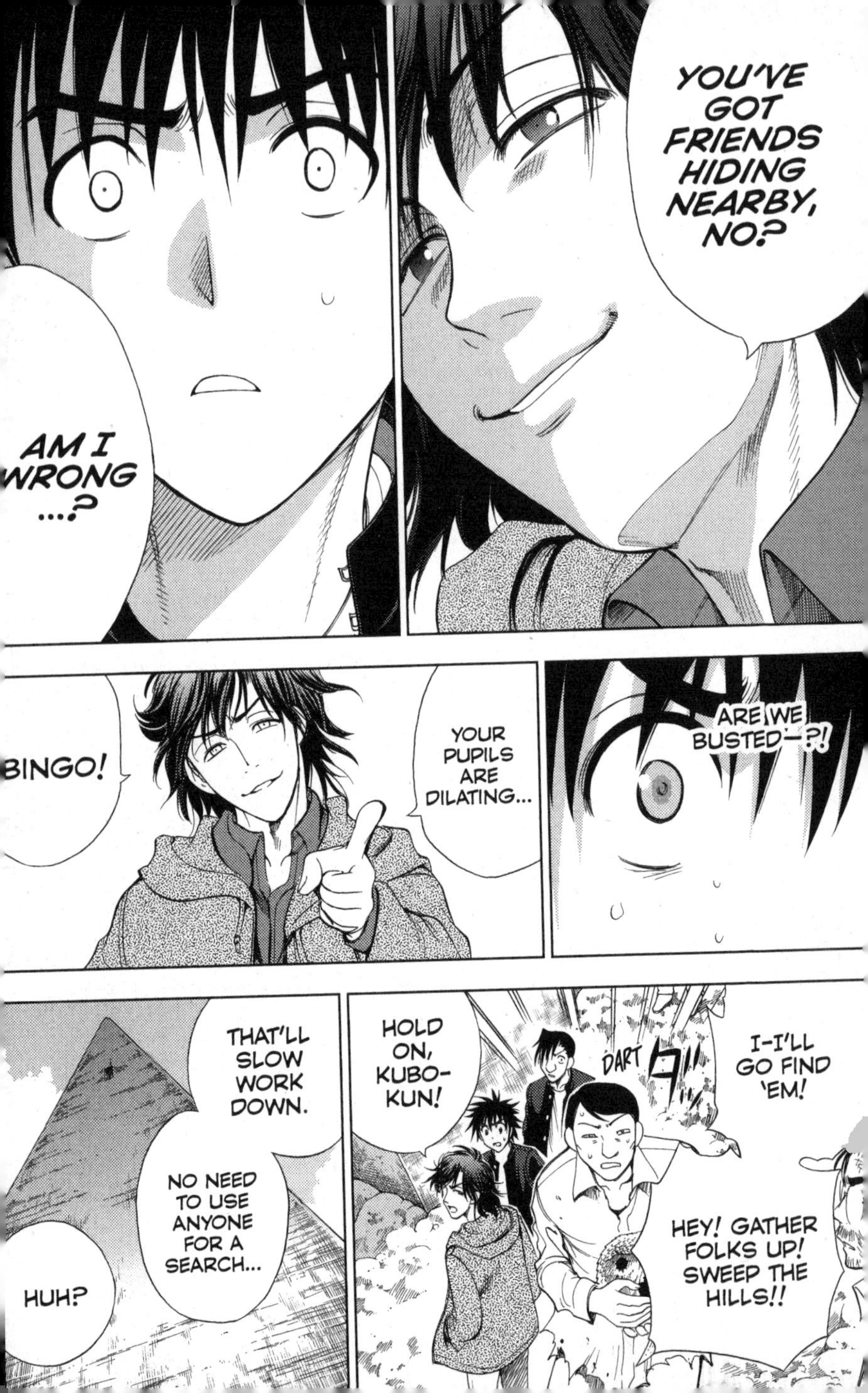
YOU'VE GOT FRIENDS HIDING NEARBY, NO?
AM I WRONG ...?
ARE WE BUSTED—?!
YOUR PUPILS ARE DILATING...
BINGO!
I-I'LL GO FIND 'EM!
DART
HEY! GATHER FOLKS UP! SWEEP THE HILLS!!
HOLD ON, KUBO-KUN!
THAT'LL SLOW WORK DOWN.
NO NEED TO USE ANYONE FOR A SEARCH...
HUH?

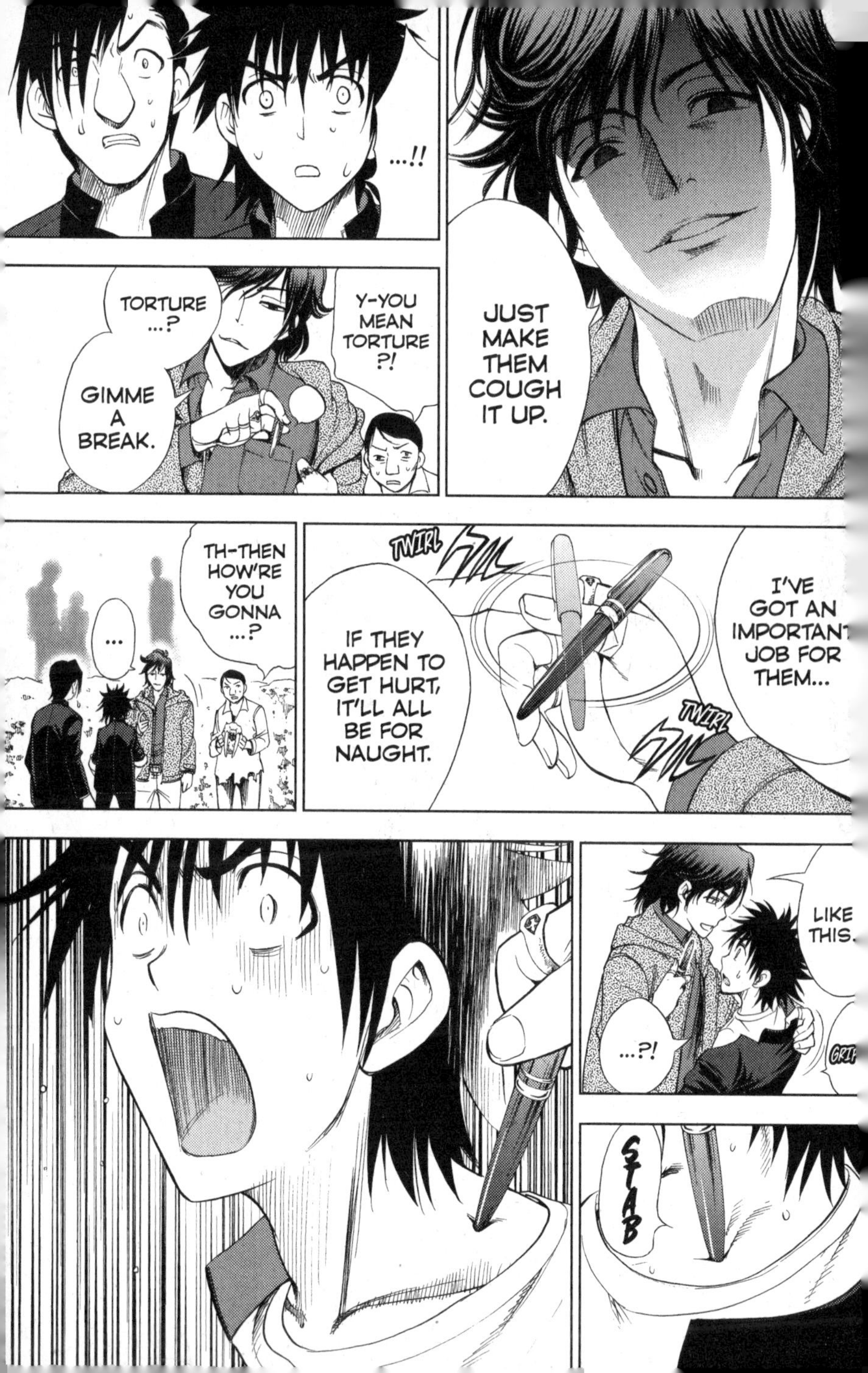
JUST MAKE THEM COUGH IT UP.
...!!
Y-YOU MEAN TORTURE?!
TORTURE...?
GIMME A BREAK.
I'VE GOT AN IMPORTANT JOB FOR THEM...
TWIRL
IF THEY HAPPEN TO GET HURT, IT'LL ALL BE FOR NAUGHT.
TWIRL
TH-THEN HOW'RE YOU GONNA...?
...
LIKE THIS.
GRIP
...?!
STAB

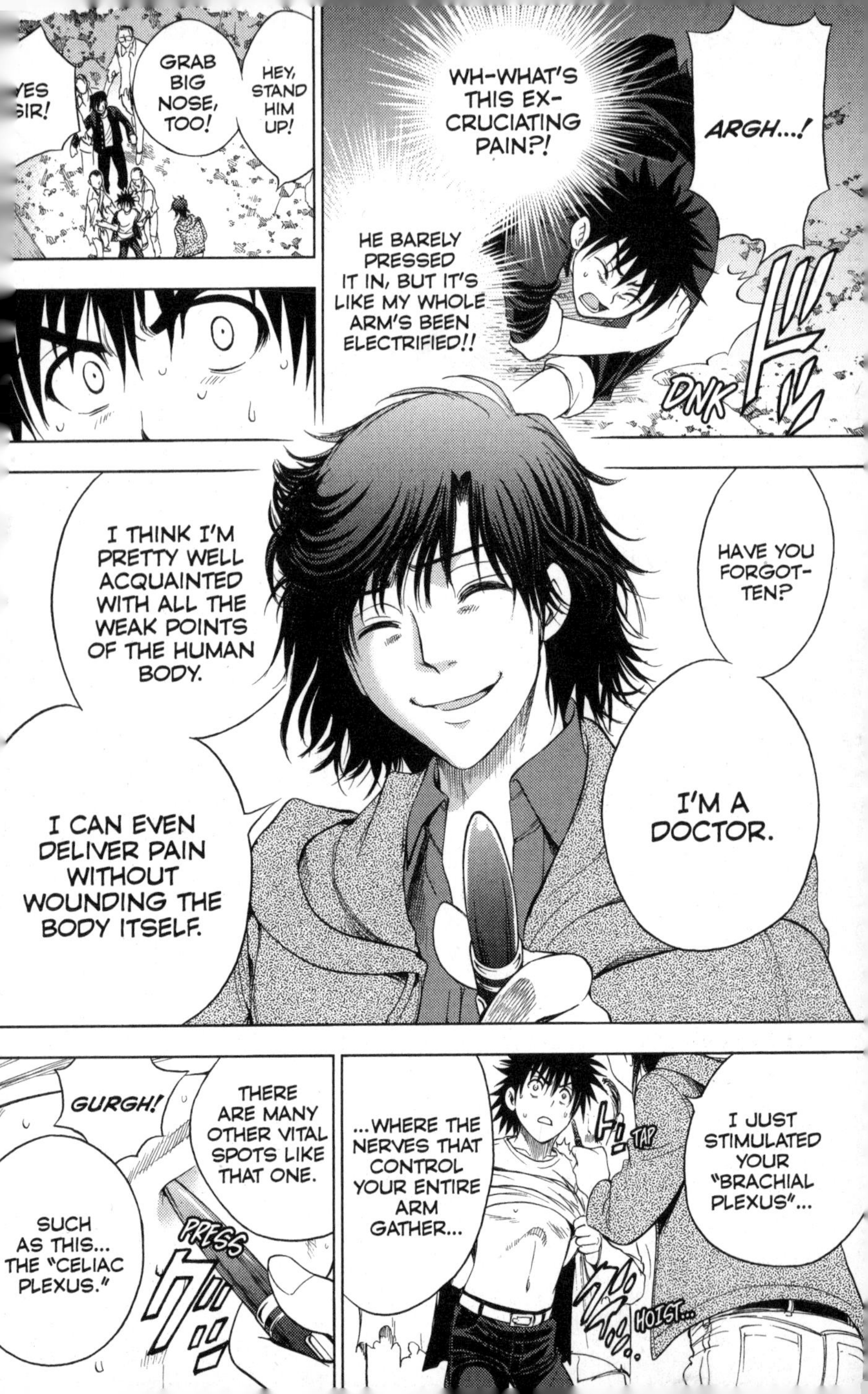
ARGH...!
WH-WHAT'S THIS EX-CRUCIATING PAIN?!
HE BARELY PRESSED IT IN, BUT IT'S LIKE MY WHOLE ARM'S BEEN ELECTRIFIED!!
DNK
HEY, STAND HIM UP!
GRAB BIG NOSE, TOO!
YES SIR!
HAVE YOU FORGOT-TEN?
I'M A DOCTOR.
I THINK I'M PRETTY WELL ACQUAINTED WITH ALL THE WEAK POINTS OF THE HUMAN BODY.
I CAN EVEN DELIVER PAIN WITHOUT WOUNDING THE BODY ITSELF.
I JUST STIMULATED YOUR "BRACHIAL PLEXUS"...
TAP
...WHERE THE NERVES THAT CONTROL YOUR ENTIRE ARM GATHER...
HOIST...
THERE ARE MANY OTHER VITAL SPOTS LIKE THAT ONE.
GURGH!
SUCH AS THIS... THE "CELIAC PLEXUS."
PRESS

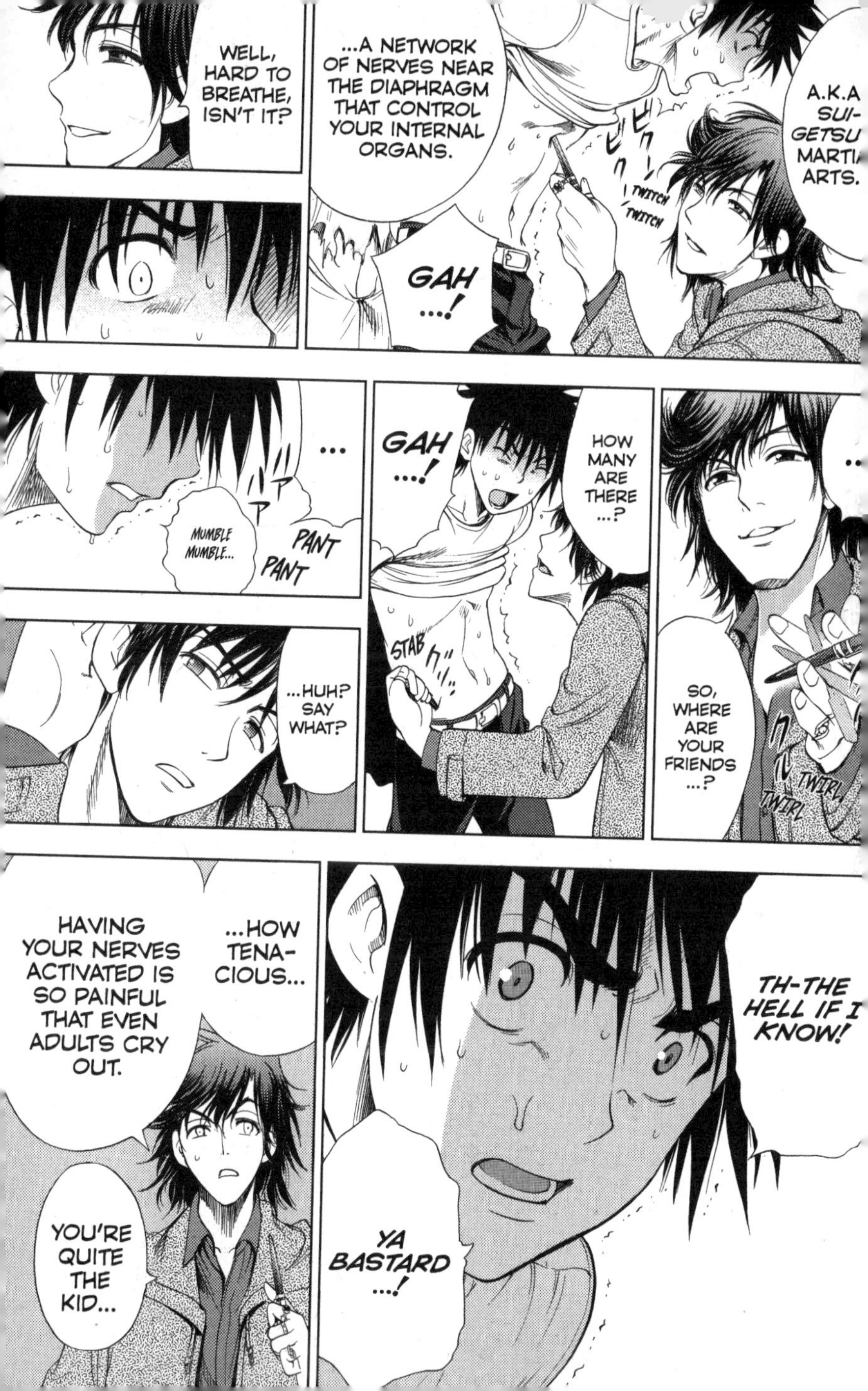
A.K.A
SUI-
GETSU
MARTI
ARTS.
...A NETWORK OF NERVES NEAR THE DIAPHRAGM THAT CONTROL YOUR INTERNAL ORGANS.
TWITCH
TWITCH
GAH ...!
WELL, HARD TO BREATHE, ISN'T IT?
...
SO, WHERE ARE YOUR FRIENDS ...?
TWIRL
TWIRL
HOW MANY ARE THERE ...?
GAH ...!
STAB
...
MUMBLE MUMBLE...
PANT
PANT
...HUH? SAY WHAT?
TH-THE HELL IF I KNOW!
YA BASTARD ...!
...HOW TENA-CIOUS...
HAVING YOUR NERVES ACTIVATED IS SO PAINFUL THAT EVEN ADULTS CRY OUT.
YOU'RE QUITE THE KID...

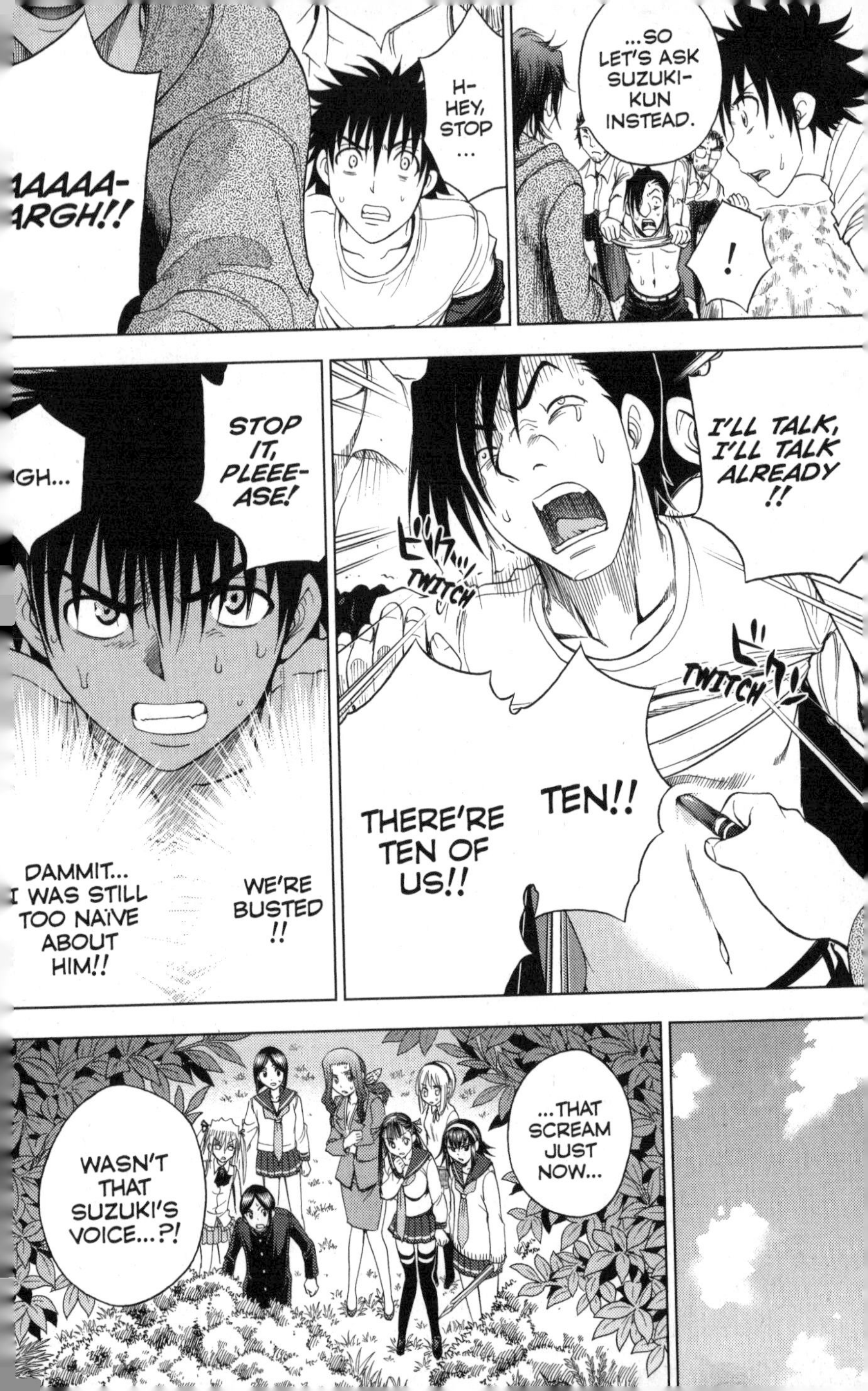
...SO LET'S ASK SUZUKI-KUN INSTEAD.
!
H-HEY, STOP ...
AAAAA-ARGH!!
I'LL TALK, I'LL TALK ALREADY!!
TWITCH
TWITCH
TEN!!
THERE'RE TEN OF US!!
STOP IT, PLEEE-ASE!
GH...
WE'RE BUSTED!!
DAMMIT... I WAS STILL TOO NAÏVE ABOUT HIM!!
...THAT SCREAM JUST NOW...
WASN'T THAT SUZUKI'S VOICE...?!

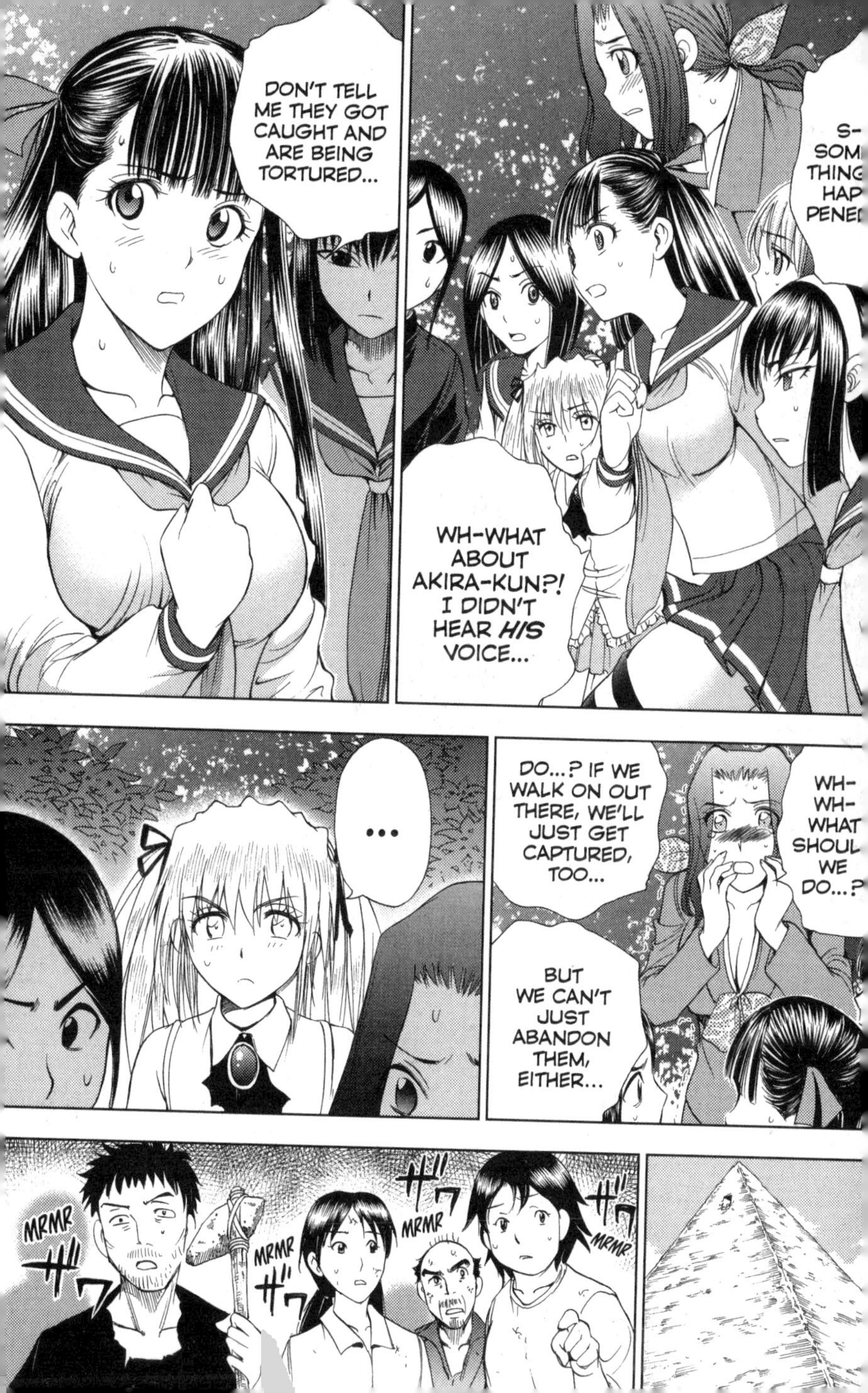

S-SOM THING HAP PENE
WH-WHAT ABOUT AKIRA-KUN?! I DIDN'T HEAR *HIS* VOICE...
DON'T TELL ME THEY GOT CAUGHT AND ARE BEING TORTURED...
WH-WH-WHAT SHOUL WE DO...?
DO...? IF WE WALK ON OUT THERE, WE'LL JUST GET CAPTURED, TOO...
BUT WE CAN'T JUST ABANDON THEM, EITHER...
...
ザワ
MRMR
ザワ
MRMR
MRMR
ザワ
MRMR
MRMR
ザワ

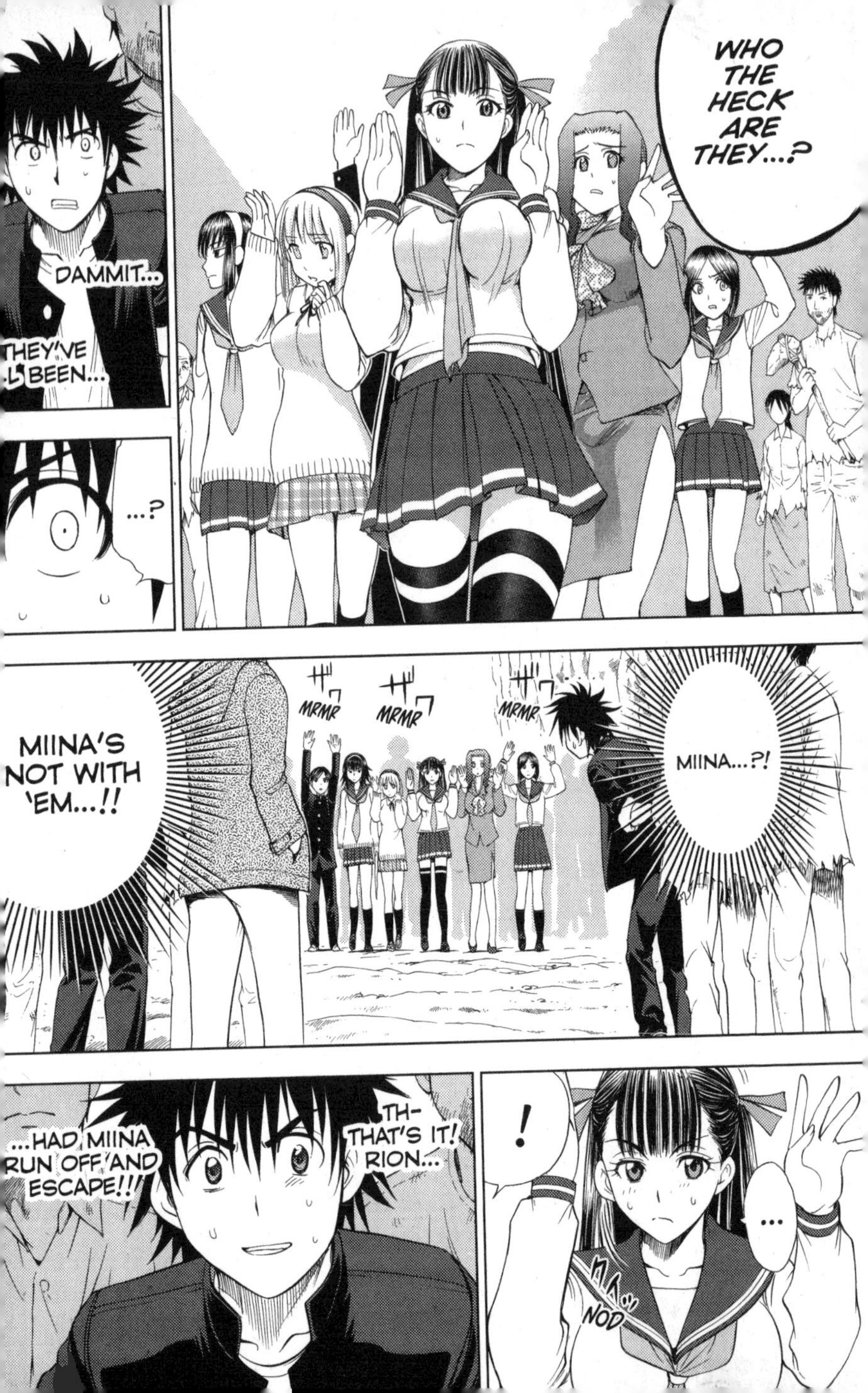
WHO THE HECK ARE THEY...?
DAMMIT...
THEY'VE
BEEN...
...?
MIINA...?!
MRMR
MRMR
MRMR
MIINA'S NOT WITH 'EM...!!
!
...
NOD
TH- THAT'S IT! RION...
...HAD MIINA RUN OFF AND ESCAPE!!!

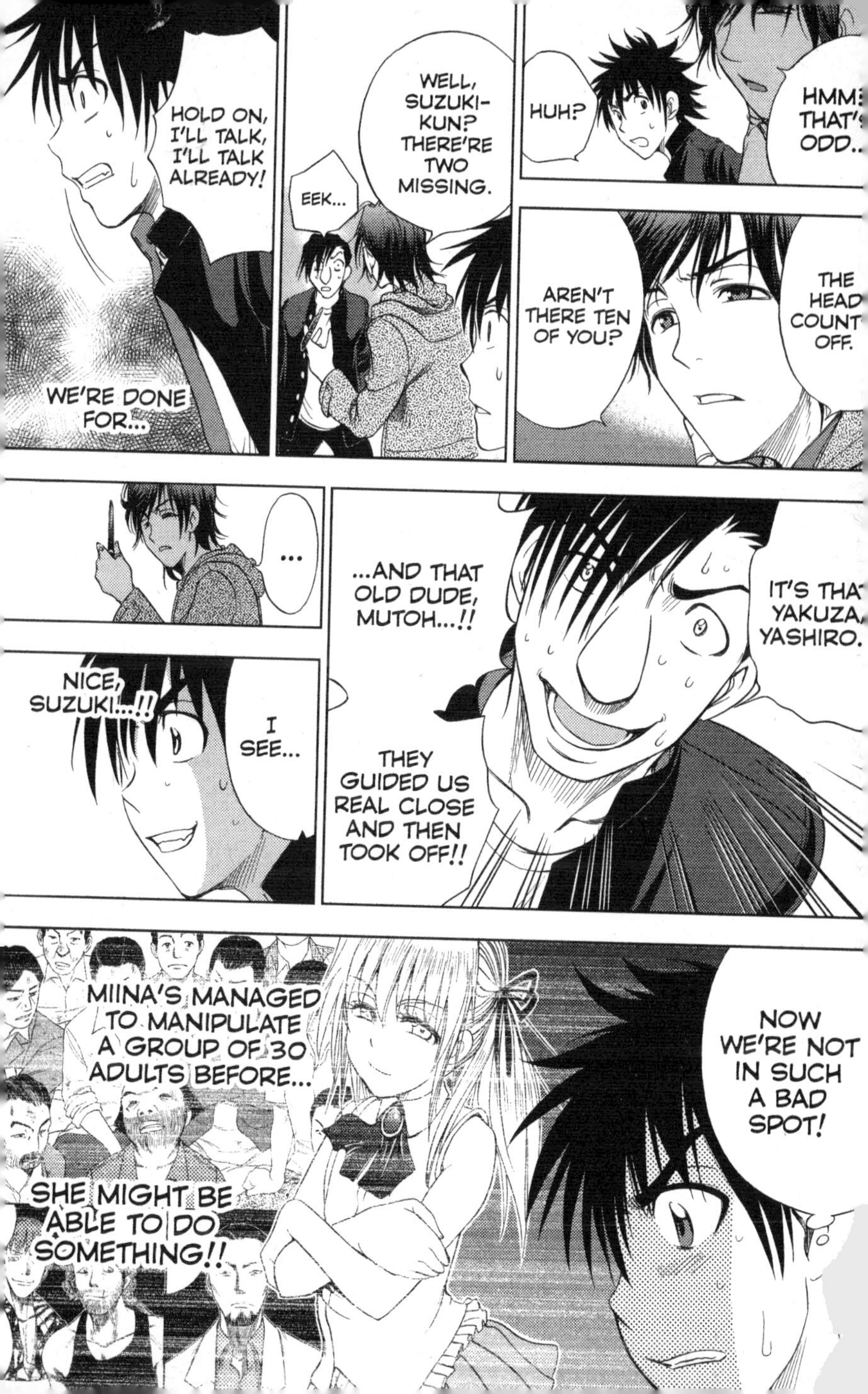
HMM: THAT'S ODD..
HUH?
THE HEAD COUNT OFF.
AREN'T THERE TEN OF YOU?
WELL, SUZUKI-KUN? THERE'RE TWO MISSING.
EEK...
HOLD ON, I'LL TALK, I'LL TALK ALREADY!
WE'RE DONE FOR...
IT'S THA YAKUZA, YASHIRO.
...AND THAT OLD DUDE, MUTOH...!!
THEY GUIDED US REAL CLOSE AND THEN TOOK OFF!!
...
I SEE...
NICE, SUZUKI...!!
NOW WE'RE NOT IN SUCH A BAD SPOT!
MIINA'S MANAGED TO MANIPULATE A GROUP OF 30 ADULTS BEFORE...
SHE MIGHT BE ABLE TO DO SOMETHING!!

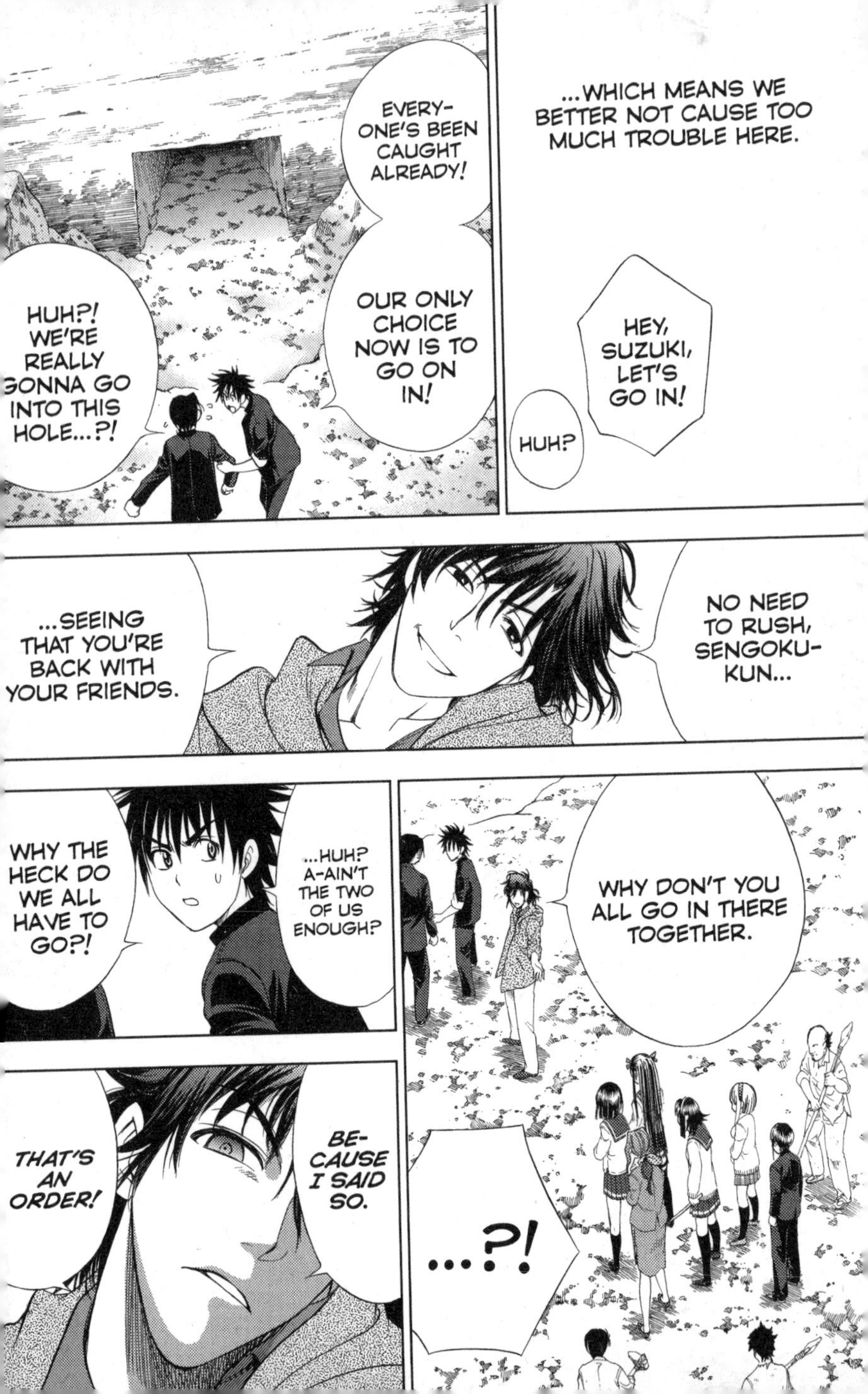
...WHICH MEANS WE BETTER NOT CAUSE TOO MUCH TROUBLE HERE.
HEY, SUZUKI, LET'S GO IN!
HUH?
EVERY-ONE'S BEEN CAUGHT ALREADY!
OUR ONLY CHOICE NOW IS TO GO ON IN!
HUH?! WE'RE REALLY GONNA GO INTO THIS HOLE...?!
NO NEED TO RUSH, SENGOKU-KUN...
...SEEING THAT YOU'RE BACK WITH YOUR FRIENDS.
WHY DON'T YOU ALL GO IN THERE TOGETHER.
...?!
...HUH? A-AIN'T THE TWO OF US ENOUGH?
WHY THE HECK DO WE ALL HAVE TO GO?!
BE-CAUSE I SAID SO.
THAT'S AN ORDER!

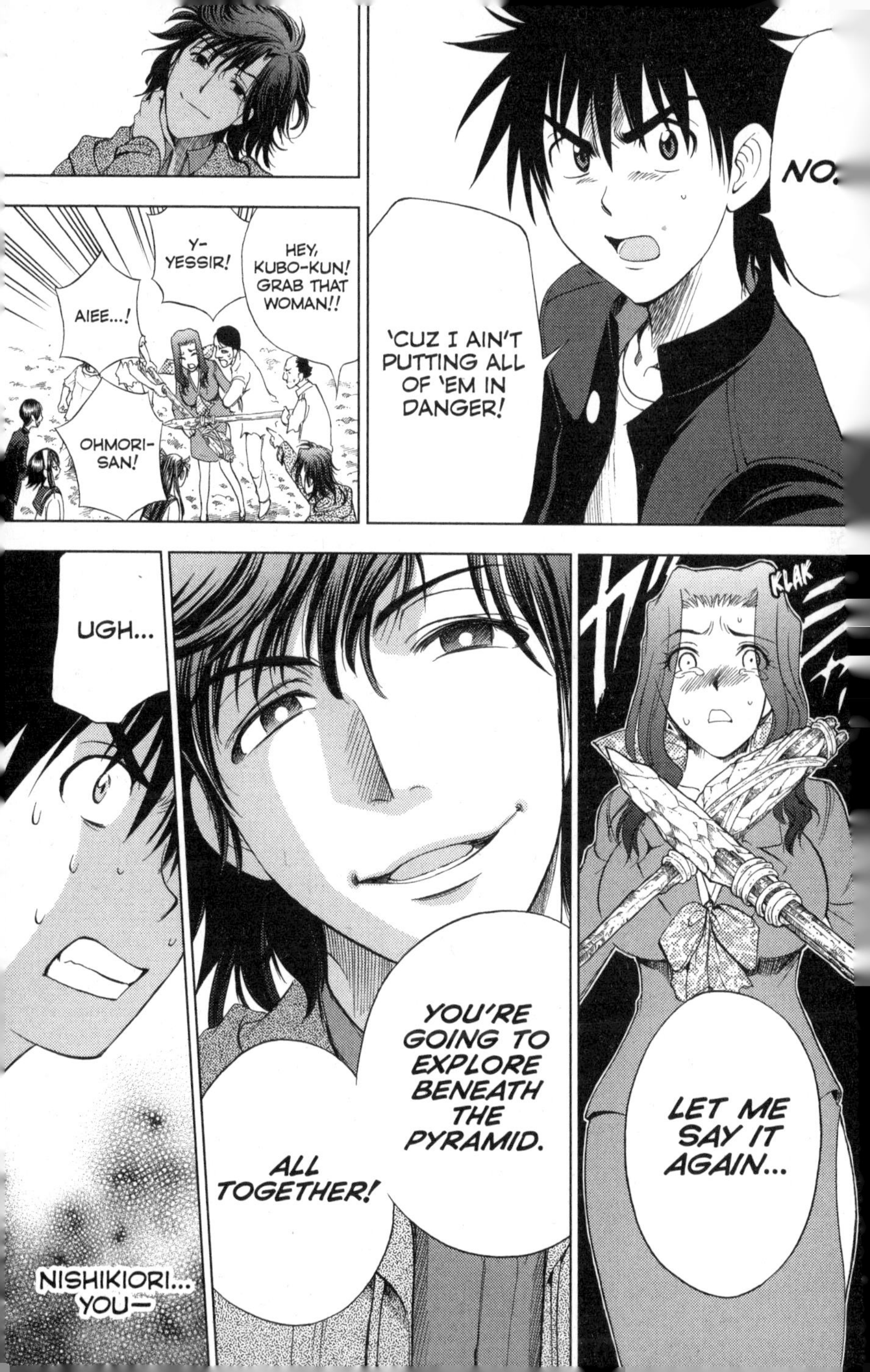
NO.
'CUZ I AIN'T PUTTING ALL OF 'EM IN DANGER!
HEY, KUBO-KUN! GRAB THAT WOMAN!!
Y-YESSIR!
AIEE...!
OHMORI-SAN!
KLAK
LET ME SAY IT AGAIN...
YOU'RE GOING TO EXPLORE BENEATH THE PYRAMID.
ALL TOGETHER!
UGH...
NISHIKIORI... YOU—

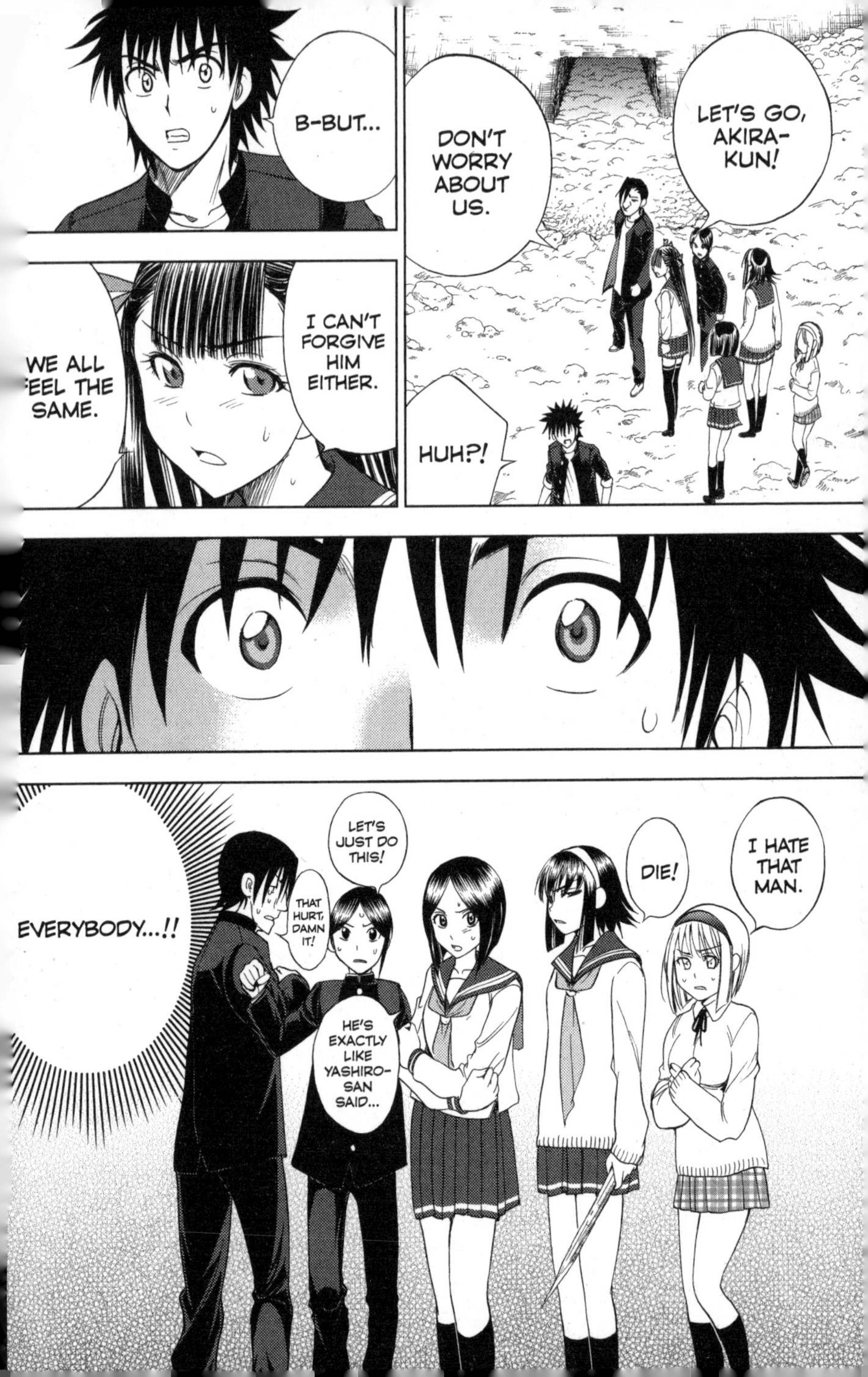
LET'S GO, AKIRA-KUN!
DON'T WORRY ABOUT US.
HUH?!
B-BUT...
I CAN'T FORGIVE HIM EITHER.
WE ALL FEEL THE SAME.
I HATE THAT MAN.
DIE!
LET'S JUST DO THIS!
THAT HURT, DAMN IT!
HE'S EXACTLY LIKE YASHIRO-SAN SAID...
EVERYBODY...!!

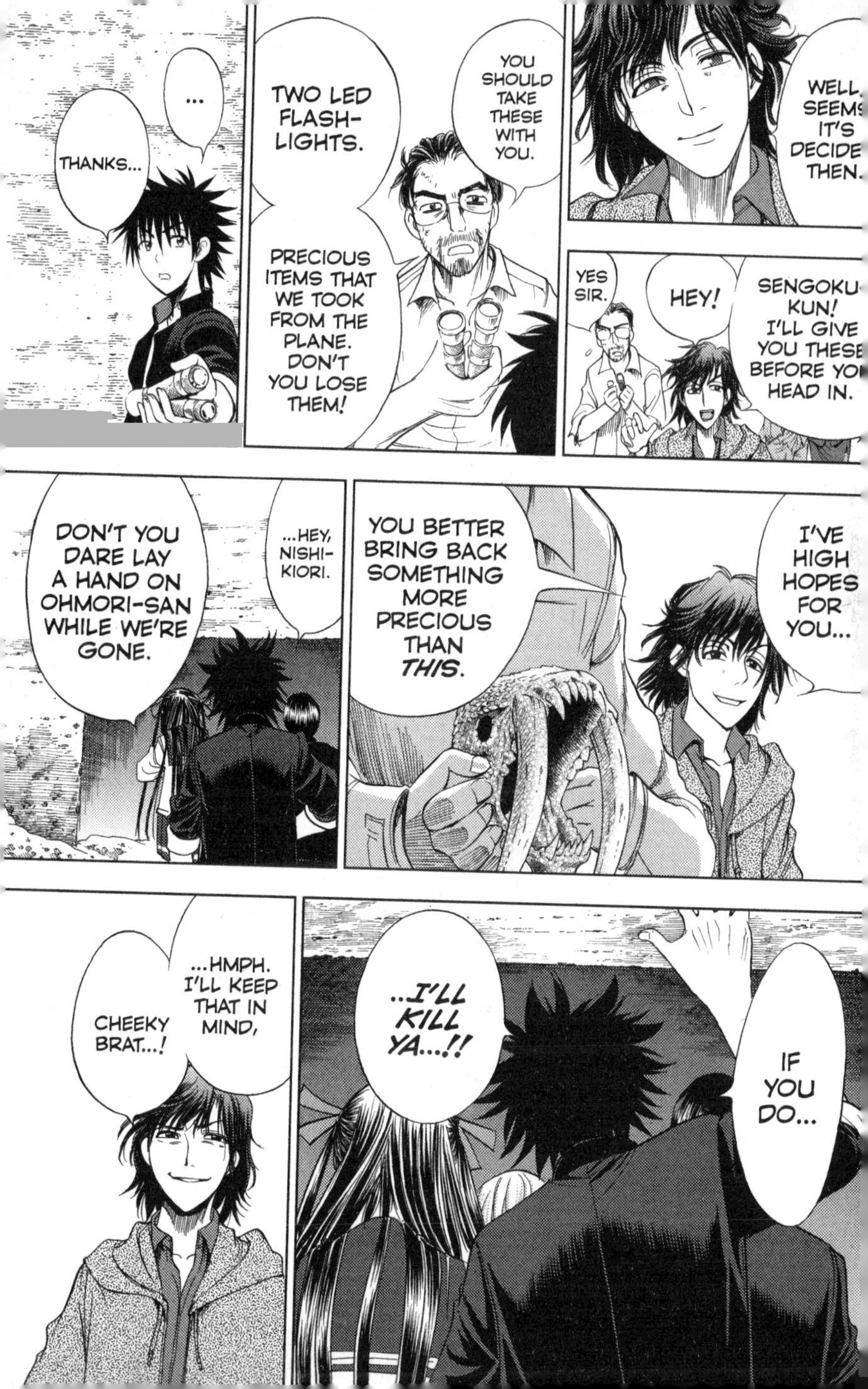
WELL, SEEMS IT'S DECIDE THEN.
SENGOKU-KUN! I'LL GIVE YOU THESE BEFORE YO HEAD IN.
HEY!
YES SIR.
YOU SHOULD TAKE THESE WITH YOU.
TWO LED FLASH-LIGHTS.
PRECIOUS ITEMS THAT WE TOOK FROM THE PLANE. DON'T YOU LOSE THEM!
...
THANKS...
I'VE HIGH HOPES FOR YOU...
YOU BETTER BRING BACK SOMETHING MORE PRECIOUS THAN *THIS*.
...HEY, NISHIKIORI.
DON'T YOU DARE LAY A HAND ON OHMORI-SAN WHILE WE'RE GONE.
IF YOU DO...
...*I'LL KILL YA...!!*
...HMPH. I'LL KEEP THAT IN MIND,
CHEEKY BRAT...!

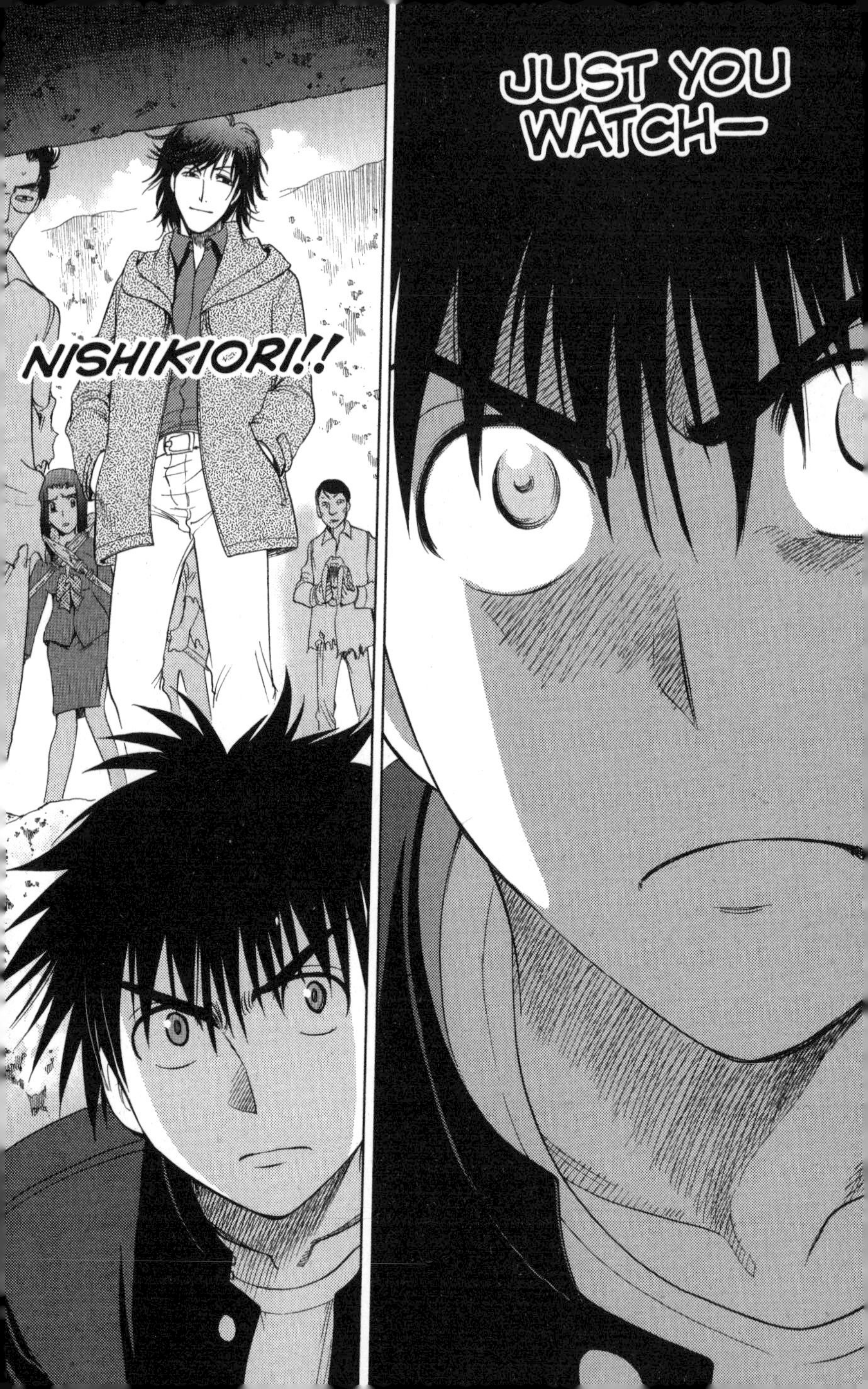
JUST YOU WATCH—
NISHIKIORI!!

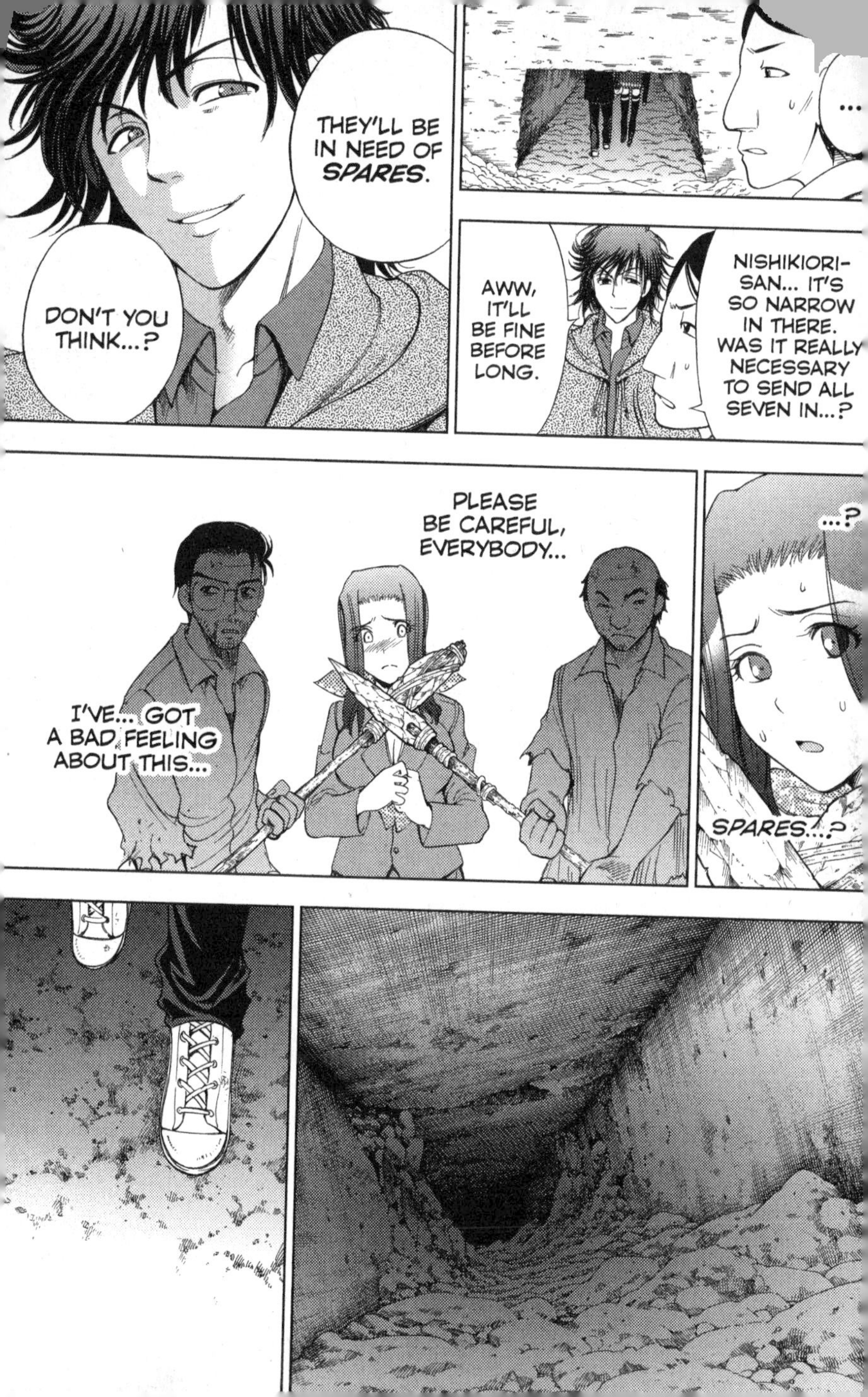
...
NISHIKIORI-SAN... IT'S SO NARROW IN THERE. WAS IT REALLY NECESSARY TO SEND ALL SEVEN IN...?
AWW, IT'LL BE FINE BEFORE LONG.
THEY'LL BE IN NEED OF *SPARES*.
DON'T YOU THINK...?
...?
SPARES...?
PLEASE BE CAREFUL, EVERYBODY...
I'VE... GOT A BAD FEELING ABOUT THIS...

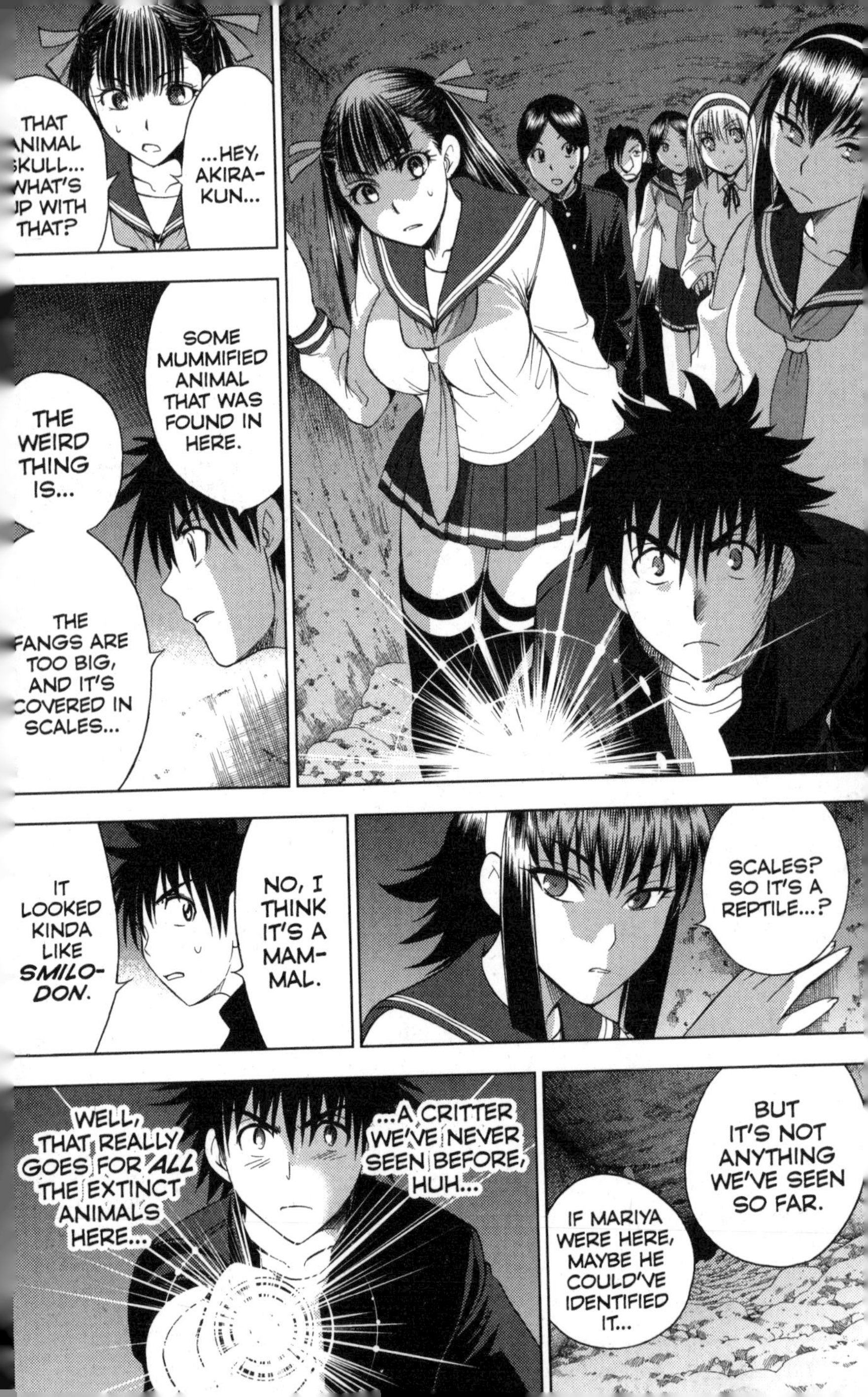
...HEY, AKIRA-KUN...
THAT ANIMAL SKULL... WHAT'S UP WITH THAT?
SOME MUMMIFIED ANIMAL THAT WAS FOUND IN HERE.
THE WEIRD THING IS...
THE FANGS ARE TOO BIG, AND IT'S COVERED IN SCALES...
SCALES? SO IT'S A REPTILE...?
NO, I THINK IT'S A MAM-MAL.
IT LOOKED KINDA LIKE *SMILO-DON*.
BUT IT'S NOT ANYTHING WE'VE SEEN SO FAR.
IF MARIYA WERE HERE, MAYBE HE COULD'VE IDENTIFIED IT...
...A CRITTER WE'VE NEVER SEEN BEFORE, HUH...
WELL, THAT REALLY GOES FOR *ALL* THE EXTINCT ANIMALS HERE...

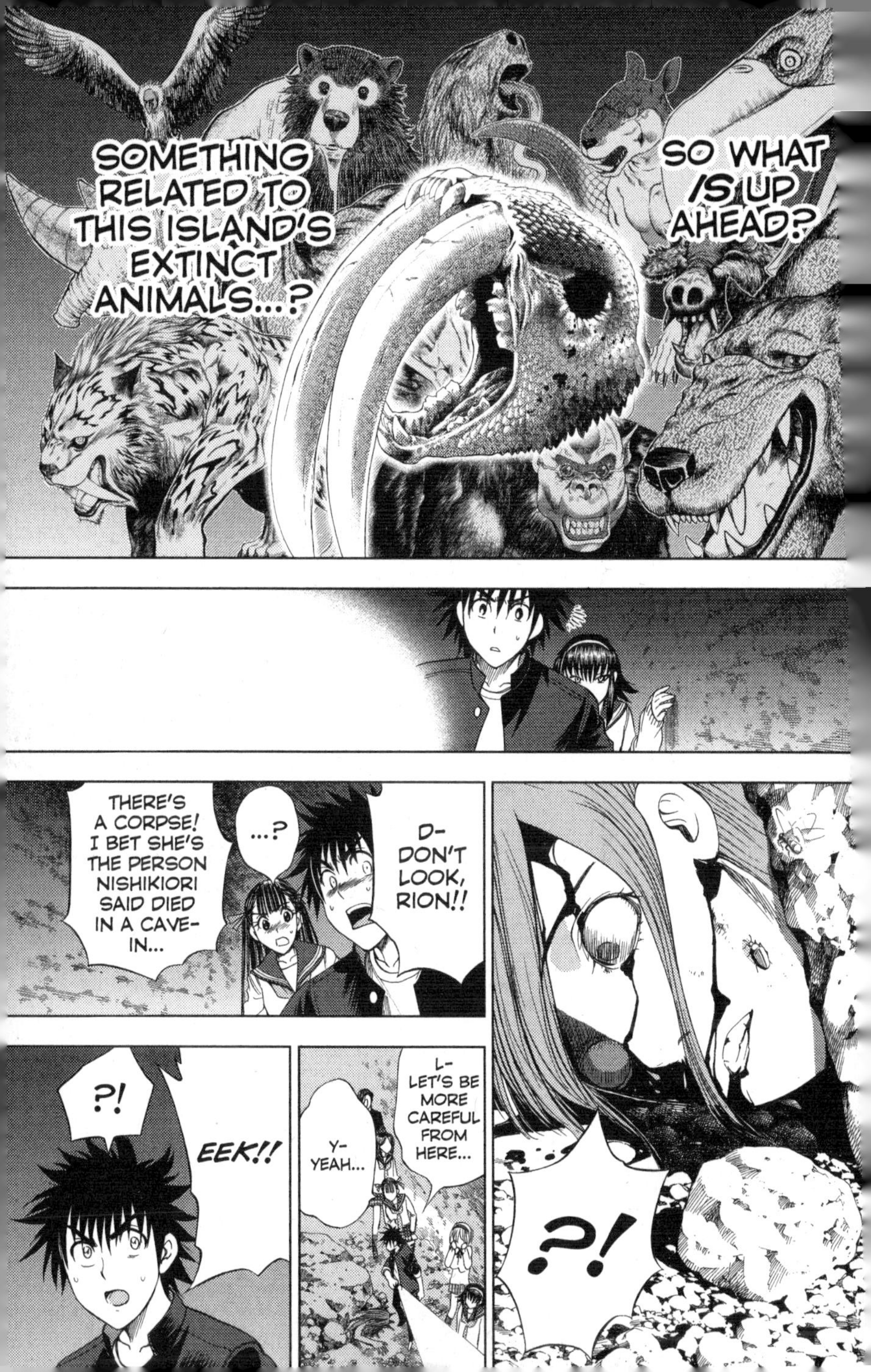
SO WHAT IS UP AHEAD?
SOMETHING RELATED TO THIS ISLAND'S EXTINCT ANIMALS...?
?!
D- DON'T LOOK, RION!!
...?
THERE'S A CORPSE! I BET SHE'S THE PERSON NISHIKIORI SAID DIED IN A CAVE-IN...
L- LET'S BE MORE CAREFUL FROM HERE...
Y- YEAH...
?!
EEK!!

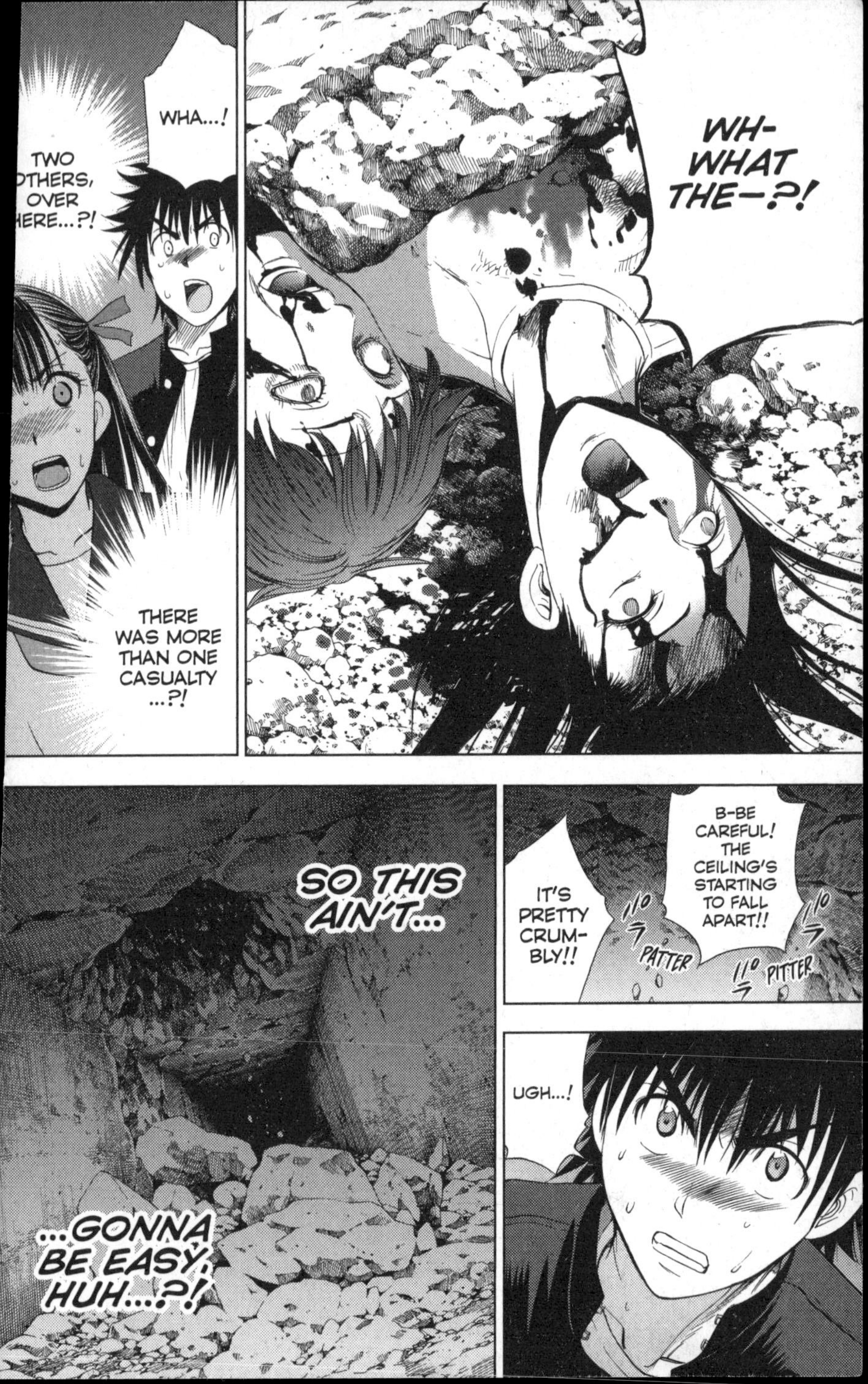
WH- WHAT THE-?!
WHA...!
TWO OTHERS, OVER HERE...?!
THERE WAS MORE THAN ONE CASUALTY ...?!
PITTER
B-BE CAREFUL! THE CEILING'S STARTING TO FALL APART!!
IT'S PRETTY CRUMBLY!!
PATTER
UGH...!
SO THIS AIN'T...
...GONNA BE EASY, HUH...?!

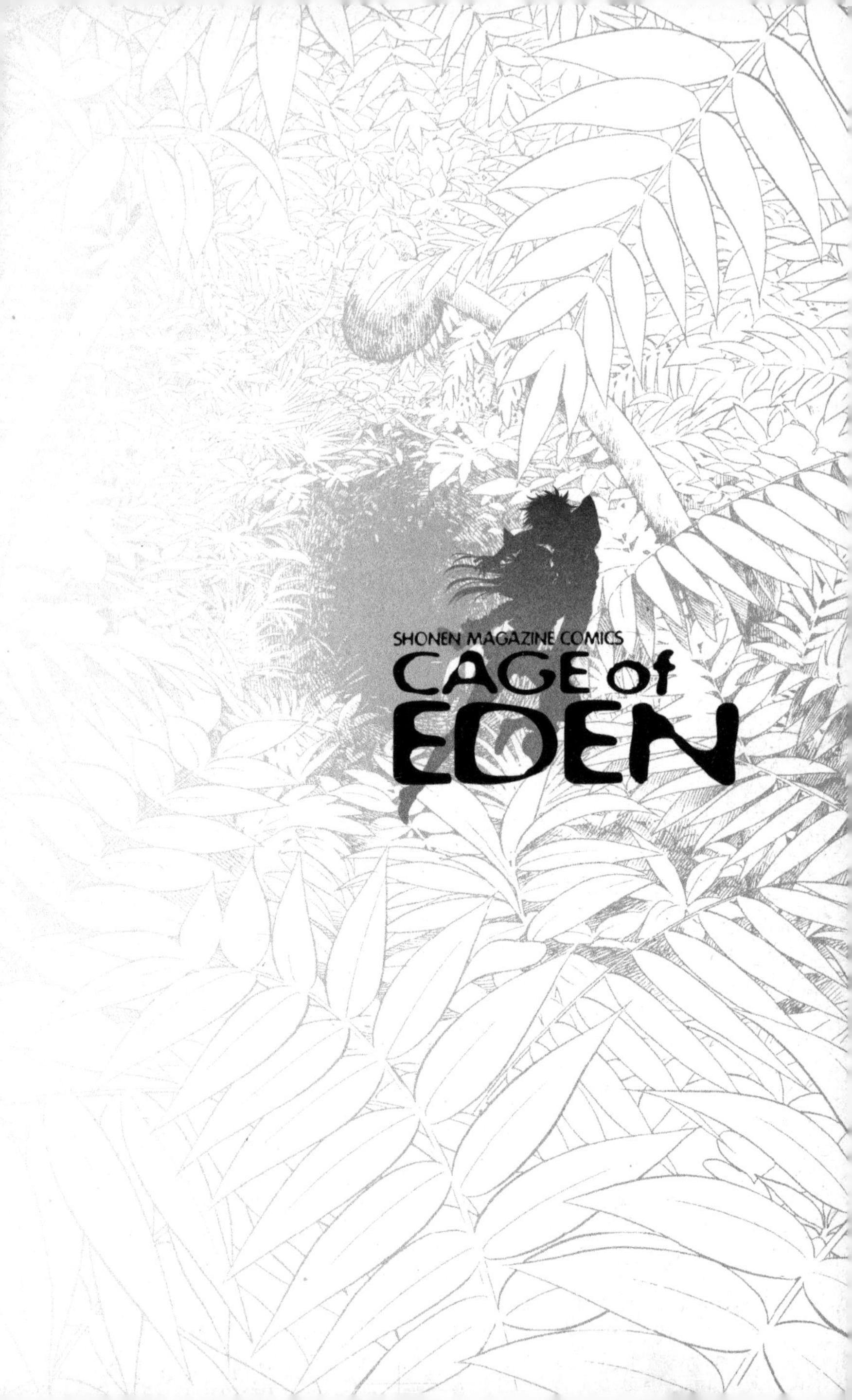
SHONEN MAGAZINE COMICS
CAGE of EDEN

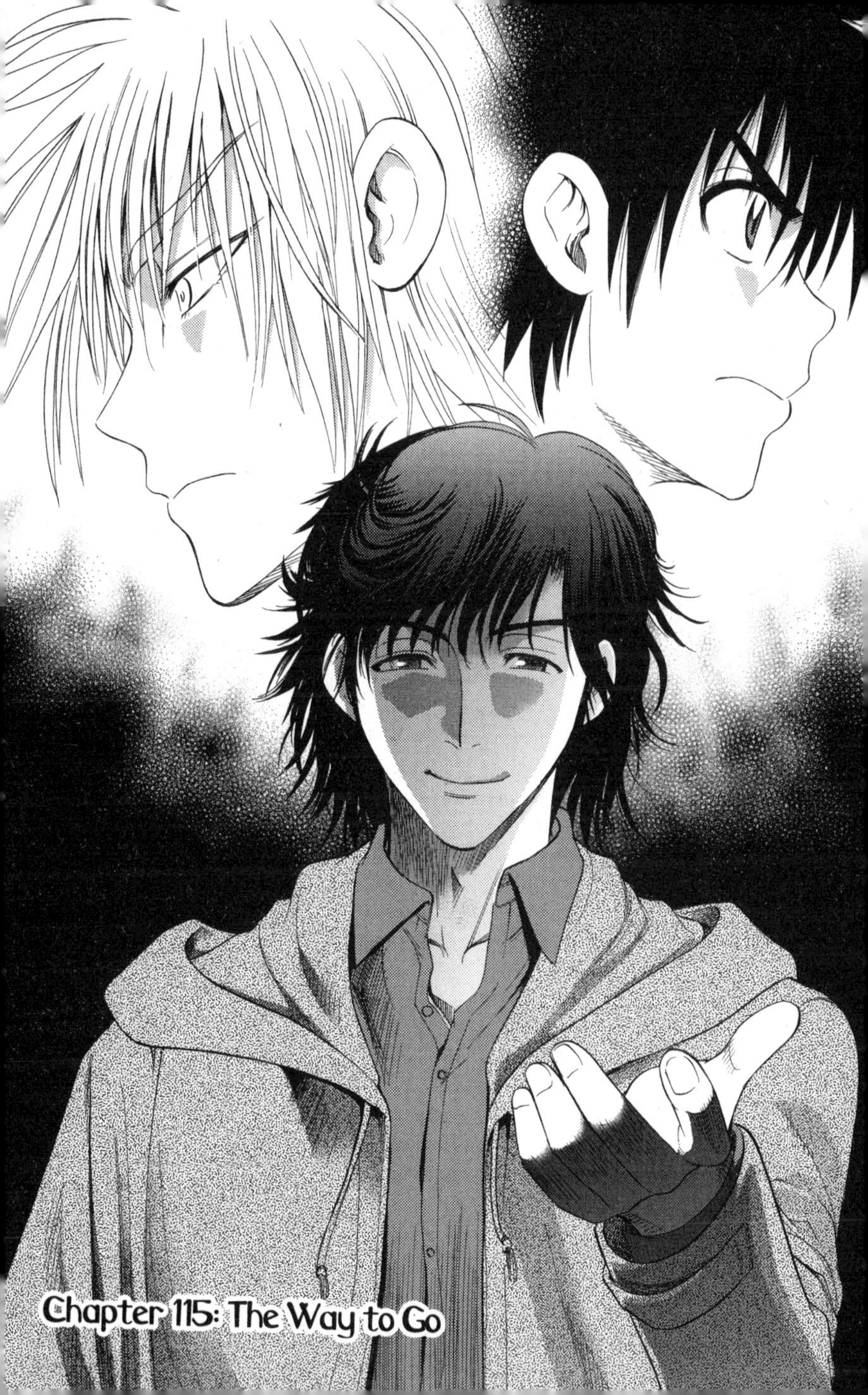
Chapter 115: The Way to Go

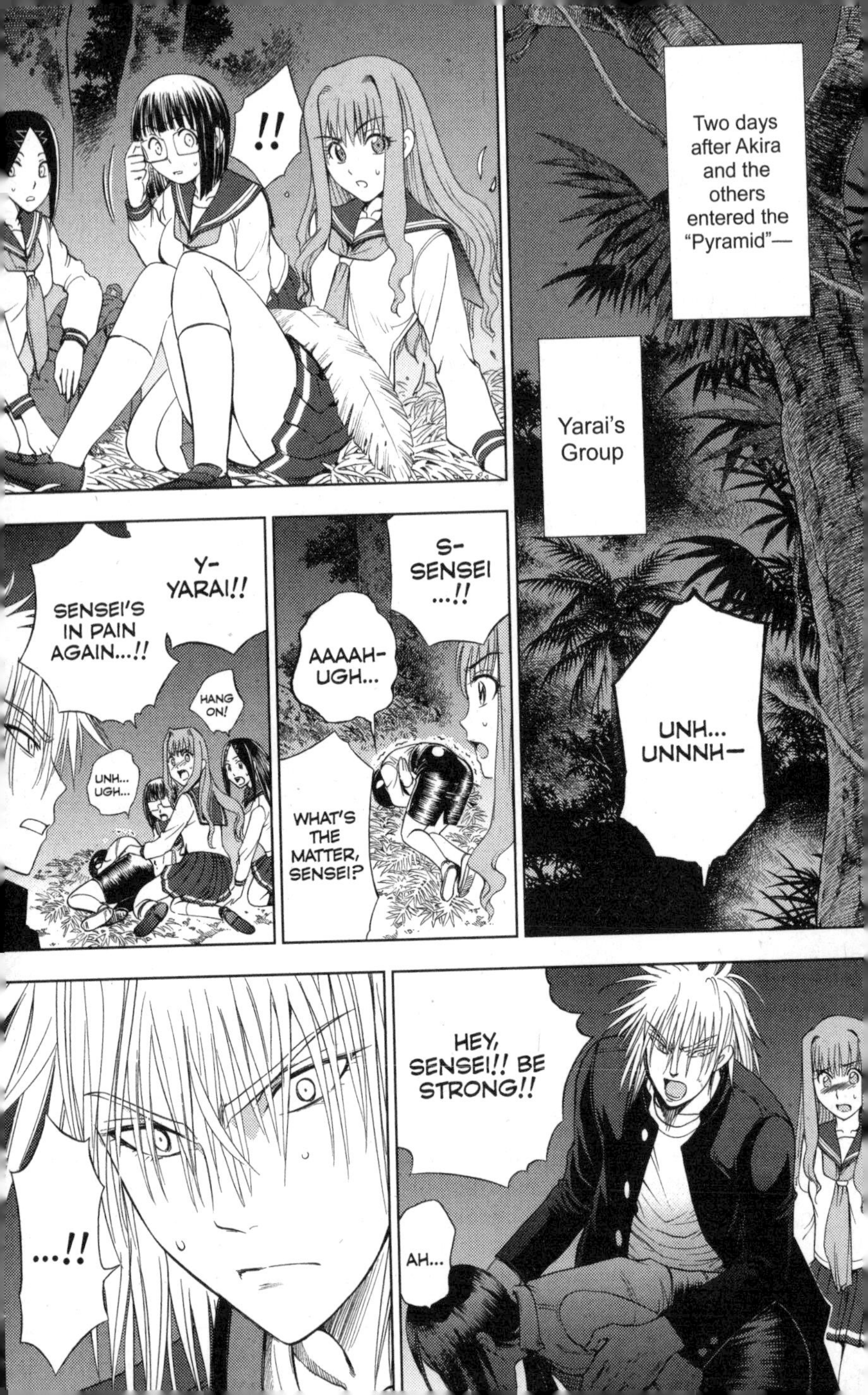
Two days after Akira and the others entered the "Pyramid"—
Yarai's Group
UNH... UNNNH—
!!
S-SENSEI ...!!
AAAAH-UGH...
WHAT'S THE MATTER, SENSEI?
Y-YARAI!!
SENSEI'S IN PAIN AGAIN...!!
HANG ON!
UNH... UGH...
HEY, SENSEI!! BE STRONG!!
AH...
...!!

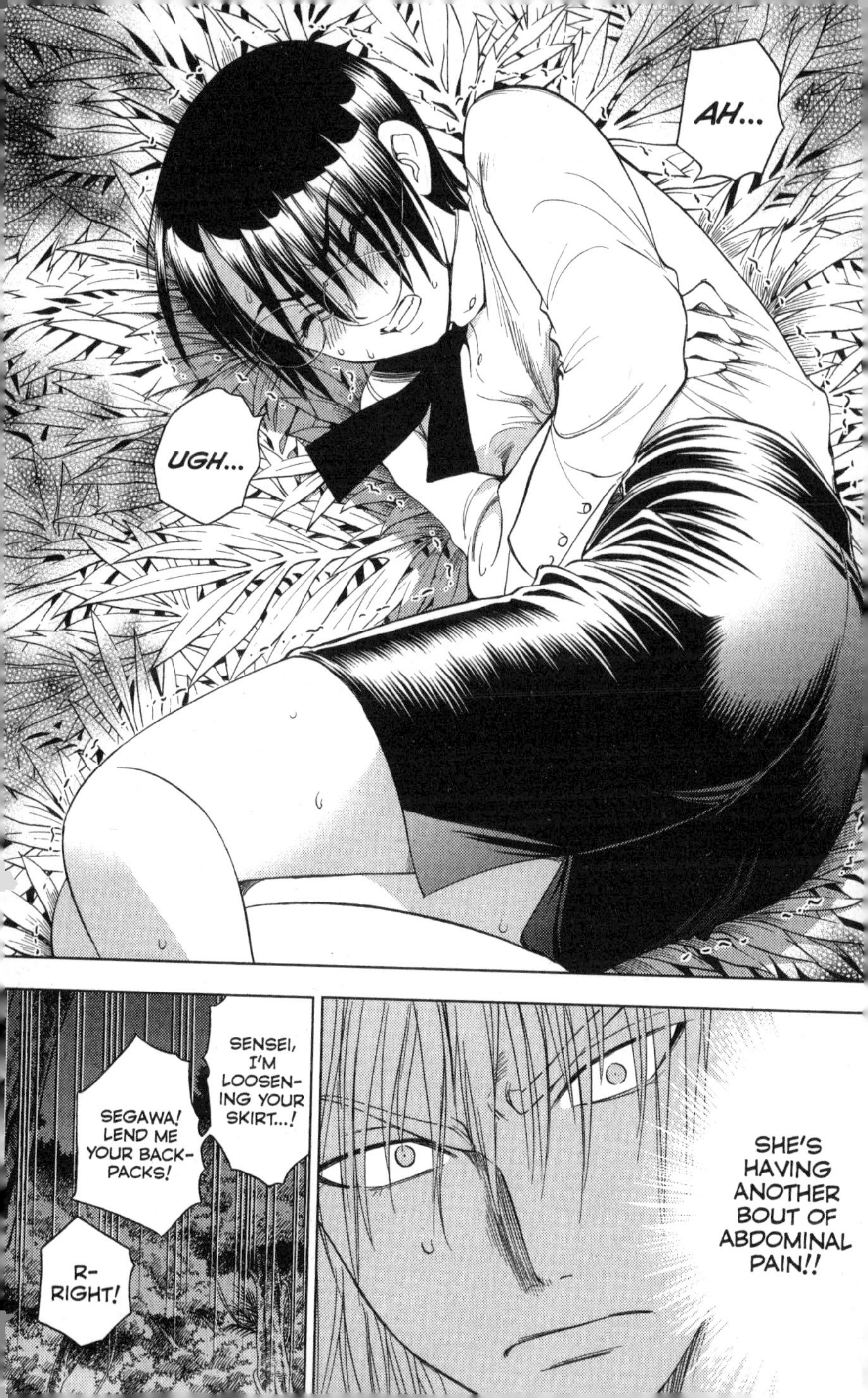
AH...
UGH...
SHE'S HAVING ANOTHER BOUT OF ABDOMINAL PAIN!!
SENSEI, I'M LOOSENING YOUR SKIRT...!
SEGAWA! LEND ME YOUR BACKPACKS!
R-RIGHT!

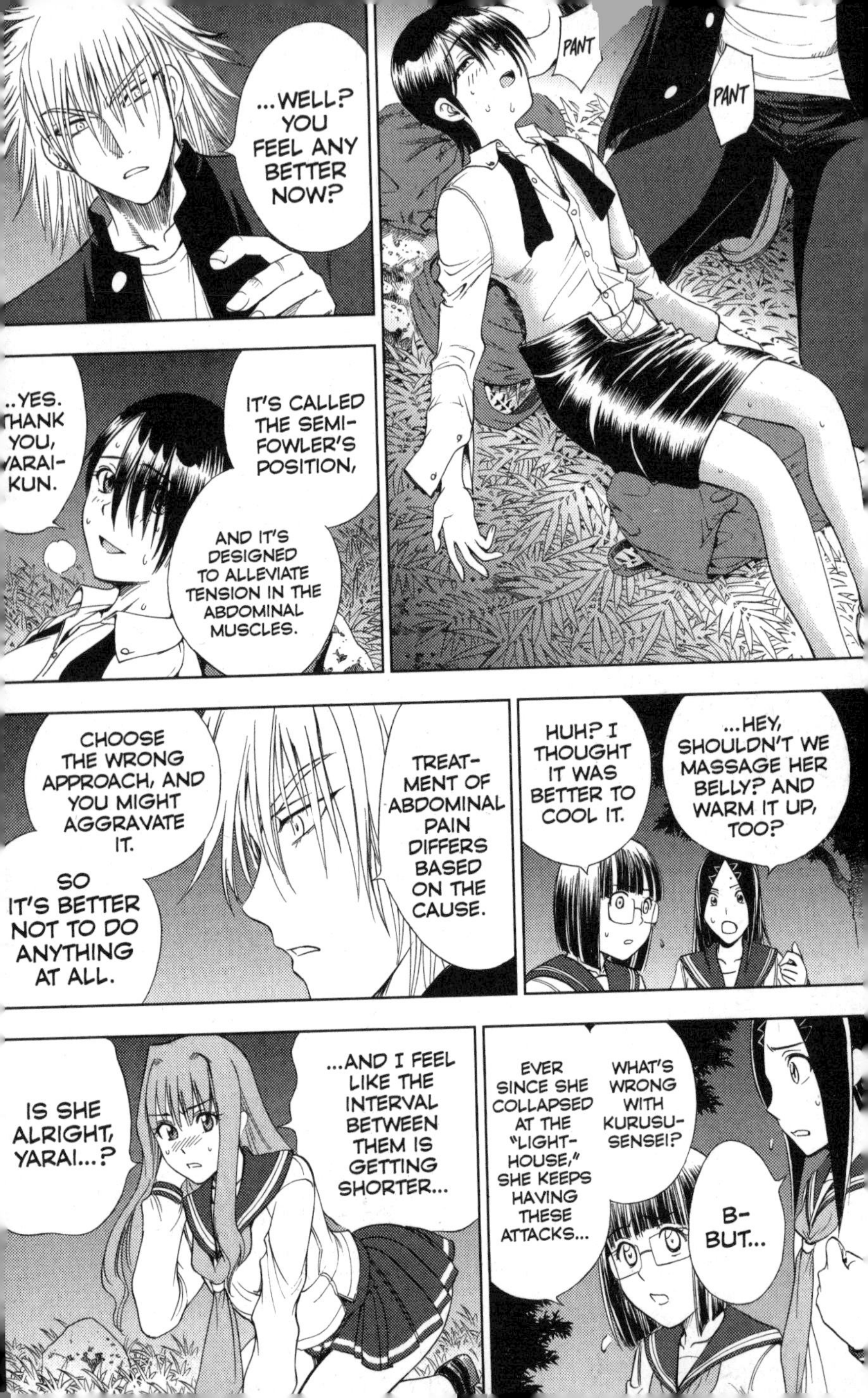
PANT
PANT
...WELL? YOU FEEL ANY BETTER NOW?
IT'S CALLED THE SEMI-FOWLER'S POSITION,
AND IT'S DESIGNED TO ALLEVIATE TENSION IN THE ABDOMINAL MUSCLES.
...YES. THANK YOU, YARAI-KUN.
...HEY, SHOULDN'T WE MASSAGE HER BELLY? AND WARM IT UP, TOO?
HUH? I THOUGHT IT WAS BETTER TO COOL IT.
TREAT-MENT OF ABDOMINAL PAIN DIFFERS BASED ON THE CAUSE.
CHOOSE THE WRONG APPROACH, AND YOU MIGHT AGGRAVATE IT.
SO IT'S BETTER NOT TO DO ANYTHING AT ALL.
WHAT'S WRONG WITH KURUSU-SENSEI?
EVER SINCE SHE COLLAPSED AT THE "LIGHT-HOUSE," SHE KEEPS HAVING THESE ATTACKS...
B-BUT...
...AND I FEEL LIKE THE INTERVAL BETWEEN THEM IS GETTING SHORTER...
IS SHE ALRIGHT, YARAI...?

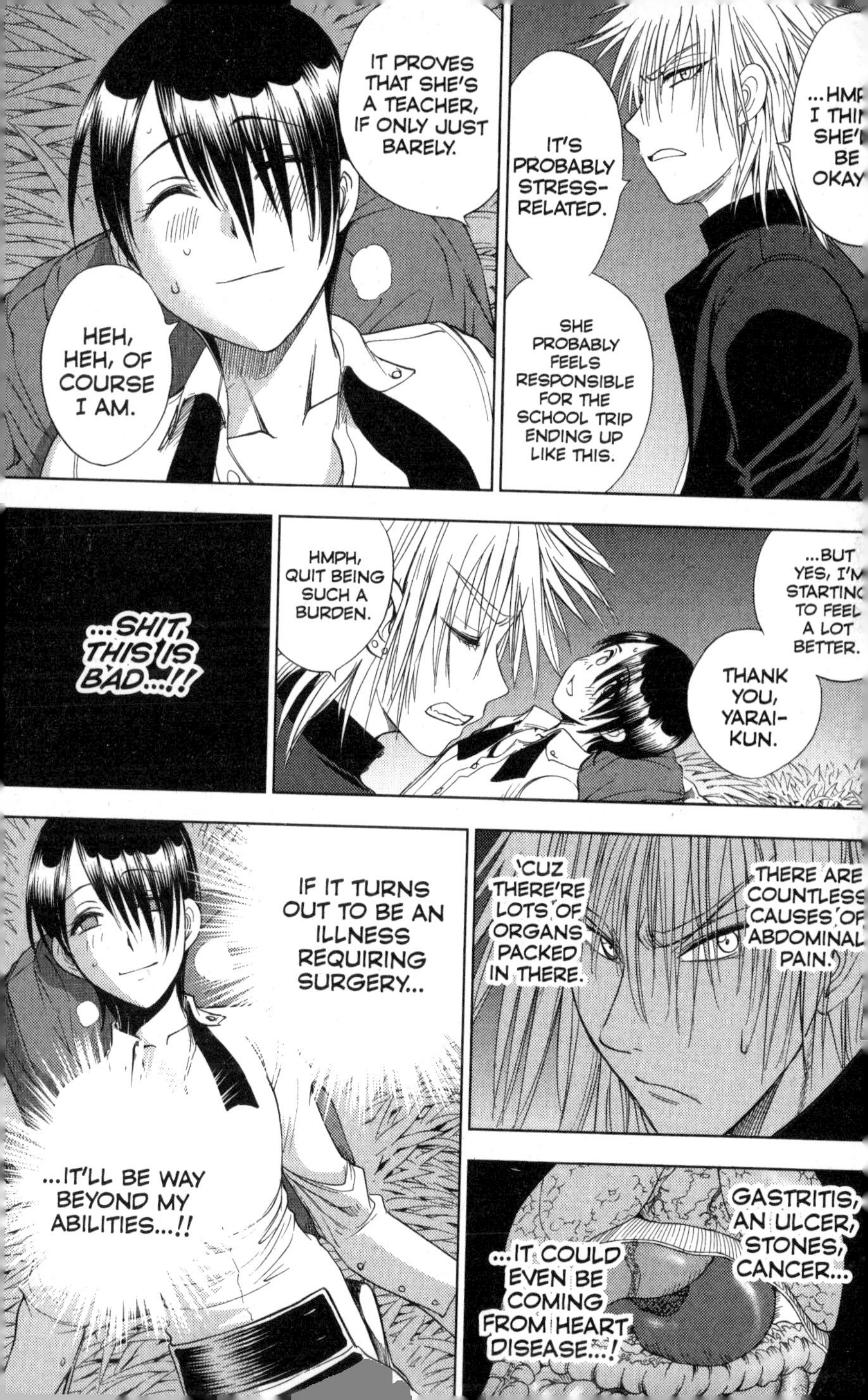
...HM I THI SHE' BE OKAY
IT'S PROBABLY STRESS-RELATED.
SHE PROBABLY FEELS RESPONSIBLE FOR THE SCHOOL TRIP ENDING UP LIKE THIS.
IT PROVES THAT SHE'S A TEACHER, IF ONLY JUST BARELY.
HEH, HEH, OF COURSE I AM.
...BUT YES, I'M STARTING TO FEEL A LOT BETTER.
THANK YOU, YARAI-KUN.
HMPH, QUIT BEING SUCH A BURDEN.
...SHIT, THIS IS BAD...!!
THERE ARE COUNTLES CAUSES OF ABDOMINAL PAIN.
'CUZ THERE'RE LOTS OF ORGANS PACKED IN THERE.
GASTRITIS, AN ULCER, STONES, CANCER...
...IT COULD EVEN BE COMING FROM HEART DISEASE...!
IF IT TURNS OUT TO BE AN ILLNESS REQUIRING SURGERY...
...IT'LL BE WAY BEYOND MY ABILITIES...!!

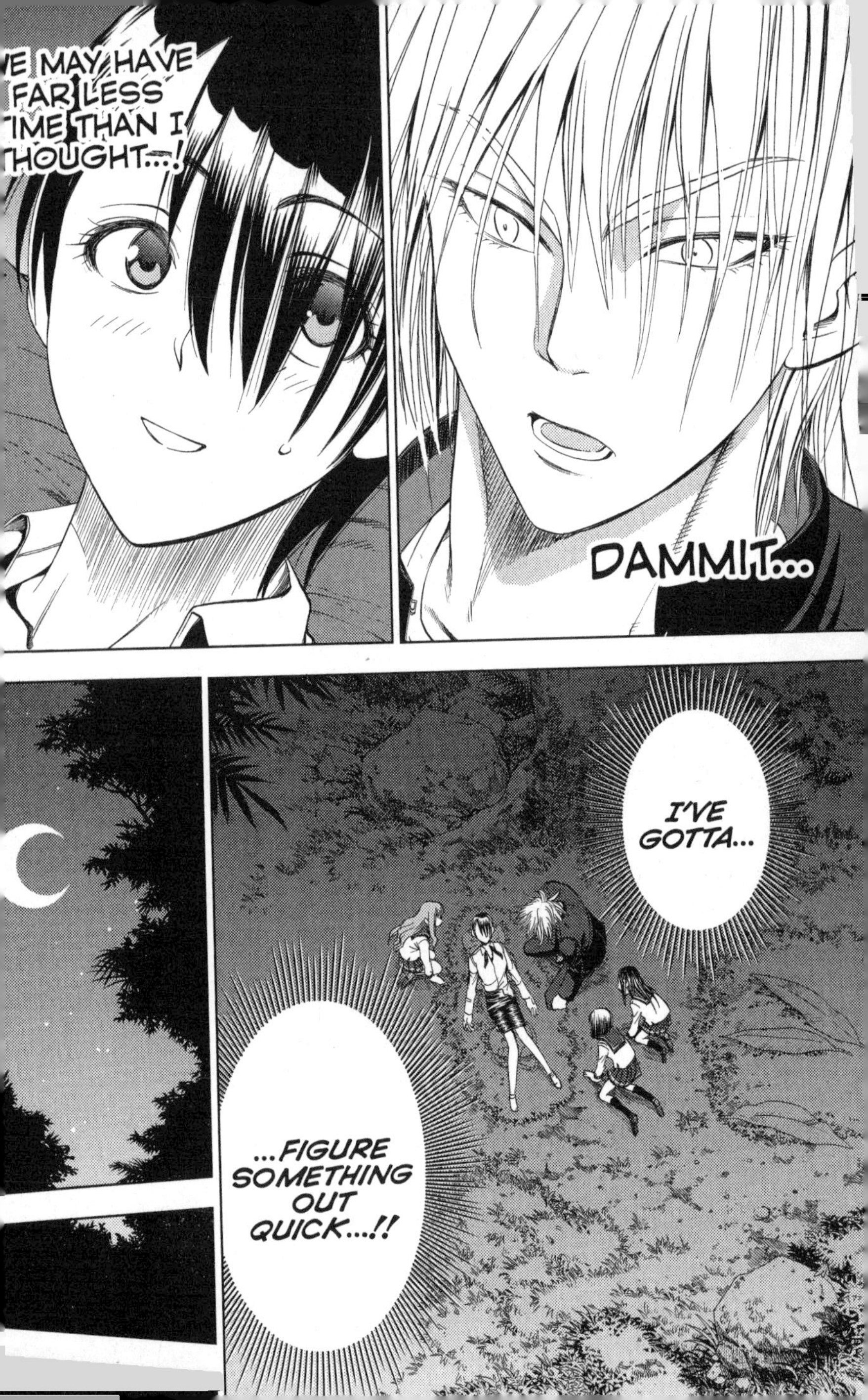
DAMMIT...
E MAY HAVE FAR LESS IME THAN I HOUGHT...!
I'VE GOTTA...
...FIGURE SOMETHING OUT QUICK...!!

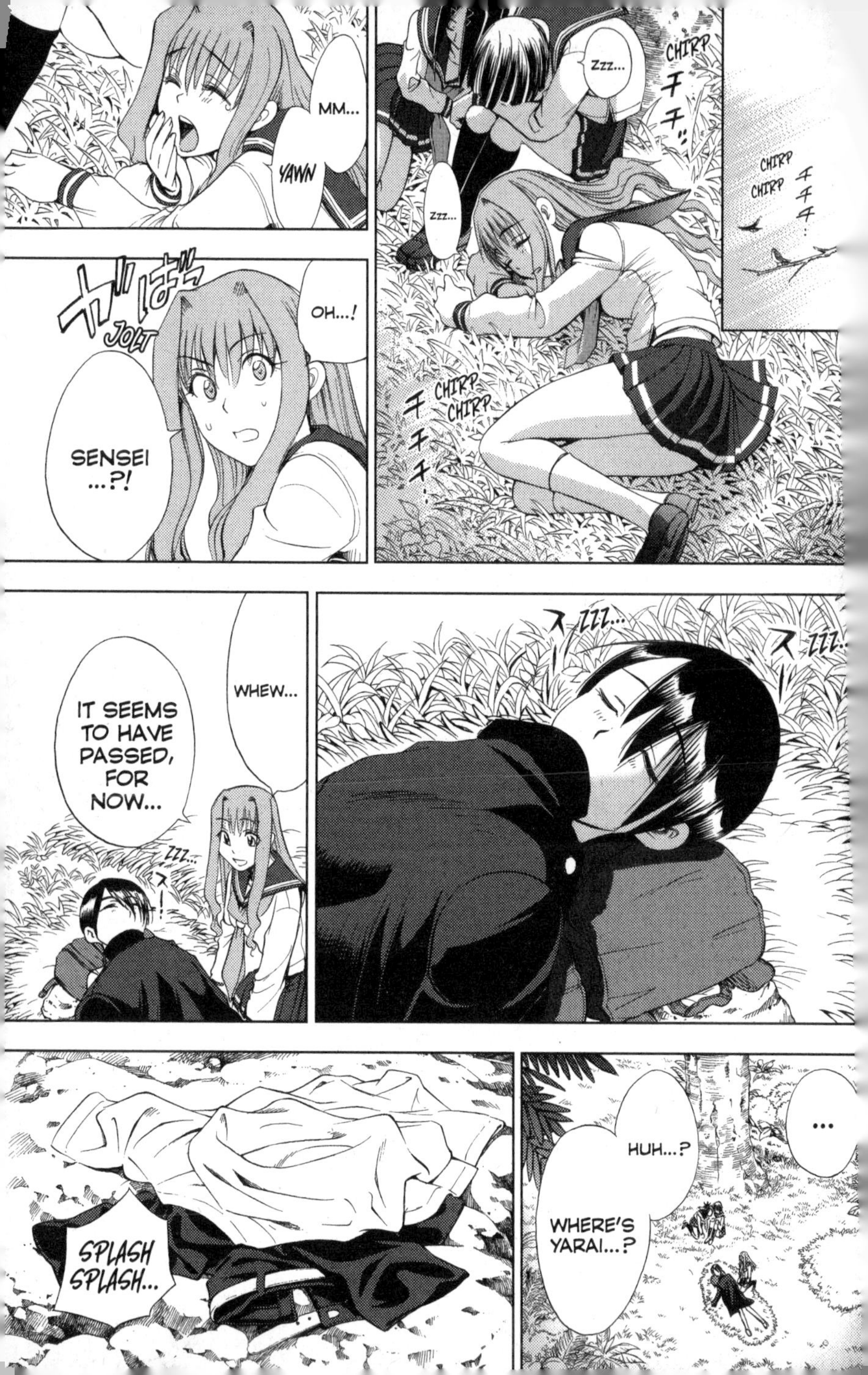
CHIRP CHIRP
チチチ…
Zzz...
CHIRP
チチッ
zzz...
CHIRP CHIRP
チチチ…
MM...
YAWN
OH...!
JOLT
SENSEI ...?!
ス zzz...
ス zzz...
WHEW...
IT SEEMS TO HAVE PASSED, FOR NOW...
zzz...
ス
...
HUH...?
WHERE'S YARAI...?
SPLASH SPLASH...

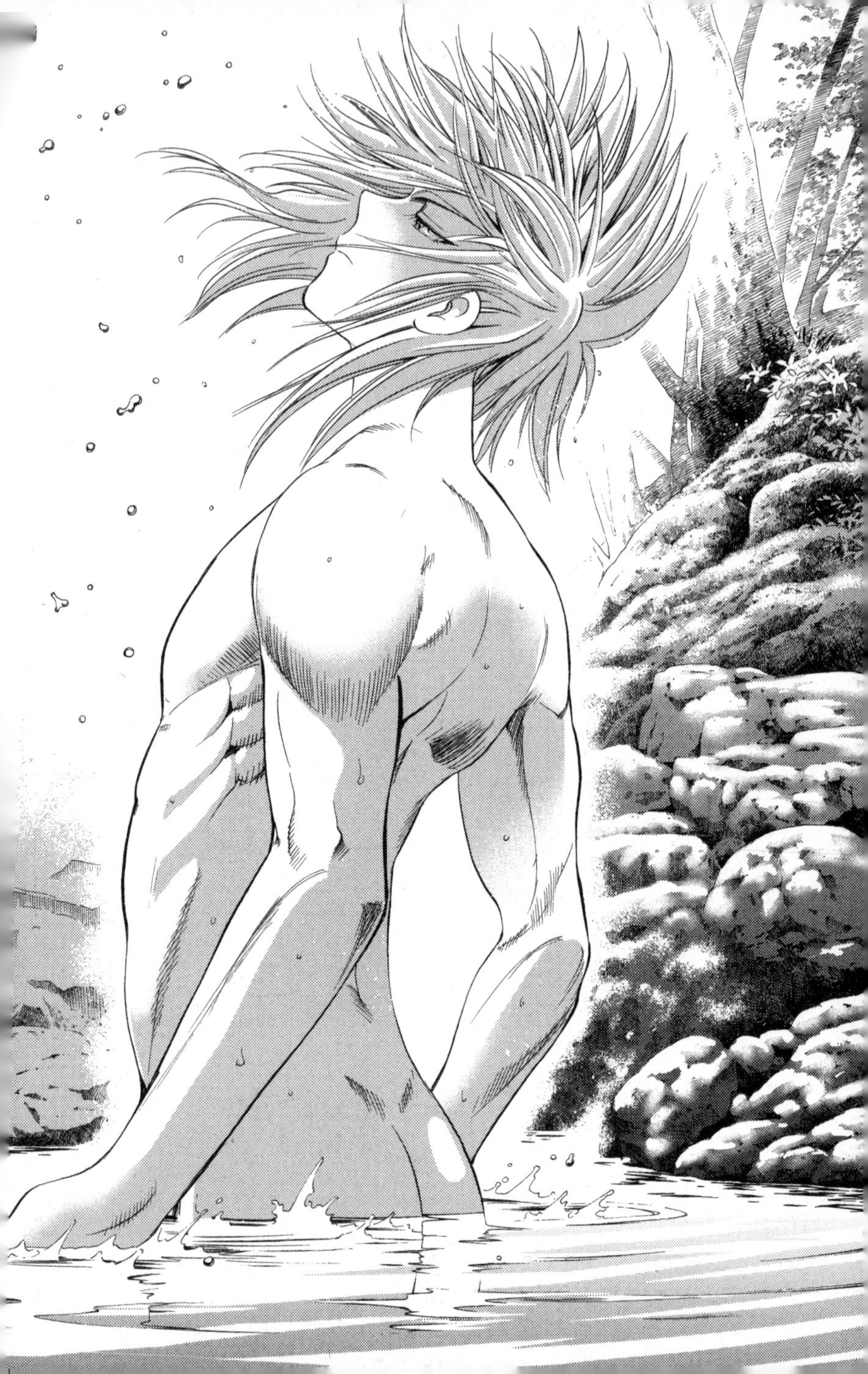

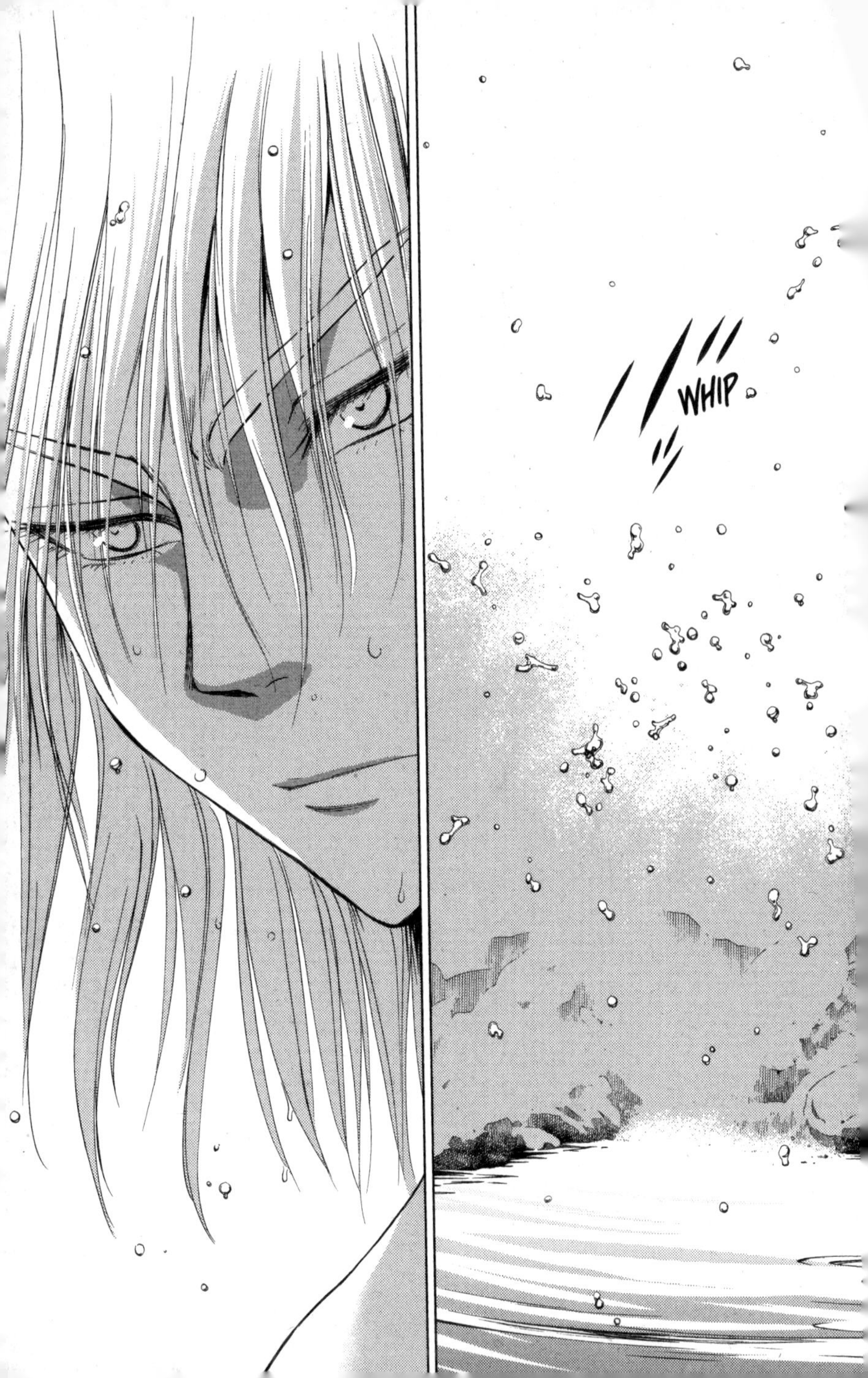
WHIP

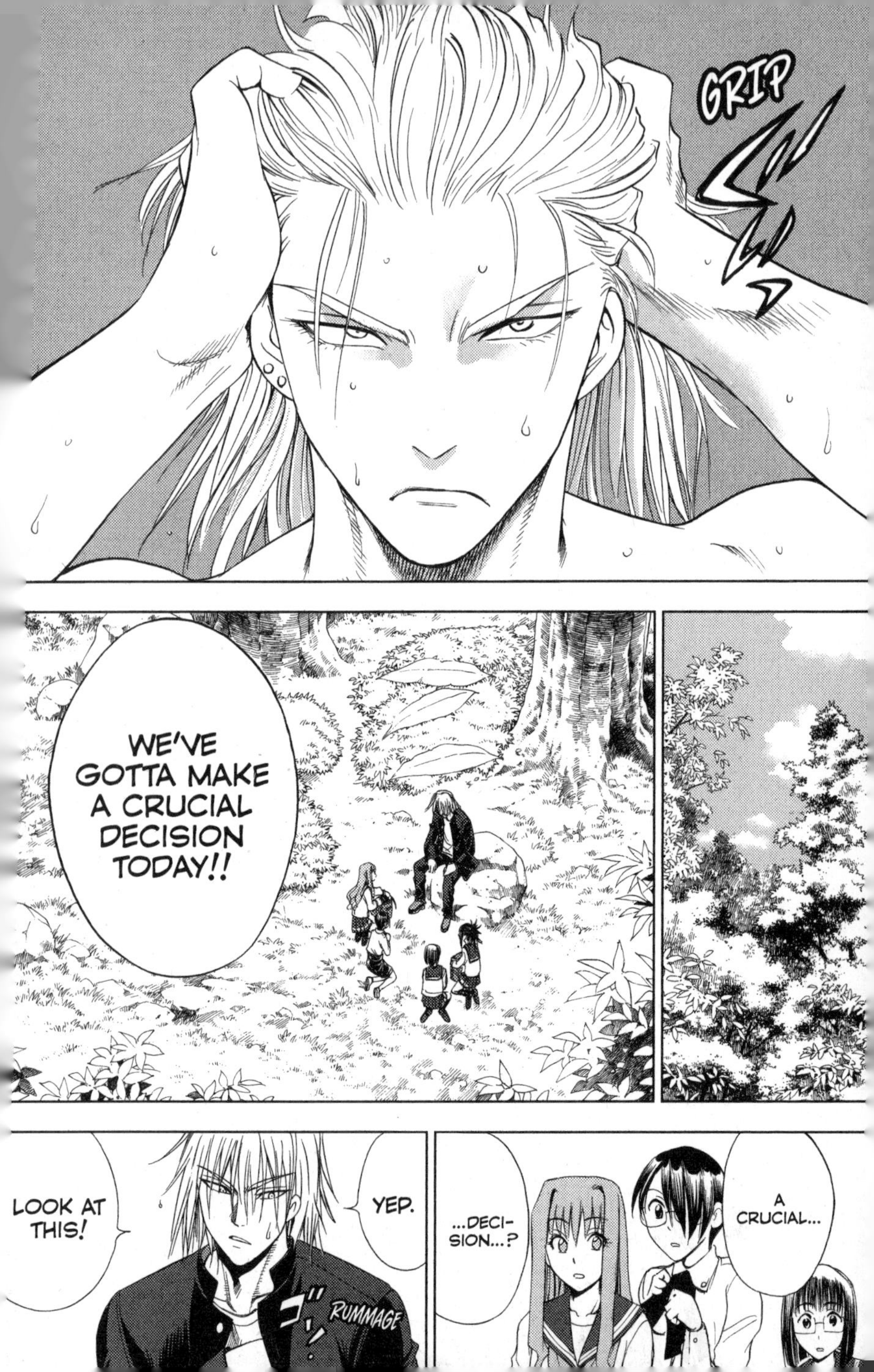
GRIP
WE'VE GOTTA MAKE A CRUCIAL DECISION TODAY!!
A CRUCIAL...
...DECI-SION...?
YEP.
LOOK AT THIS!
RUMMAGE

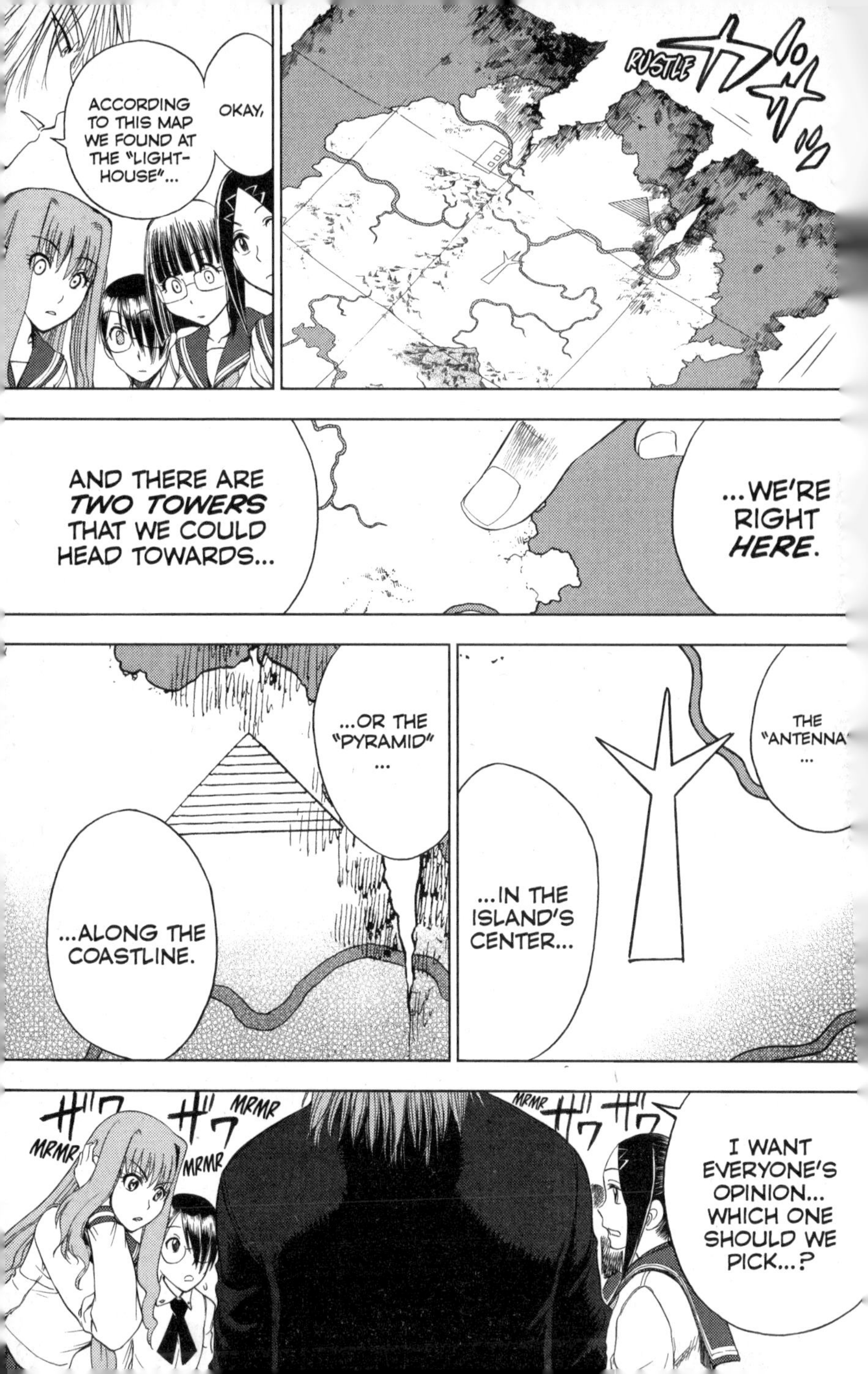
RUSTLE
OKAY,
ACCORDING TO THIS MAP WE FOUND AT THE "LIGHT-HOUSE"...
...WE'RE RIGHT HERE.
AND THERE ARE TWO TOWERS THAT WE COULD HEAD TOWARDS...
THE "ANTENNA" ...
...IN THE ISLAND'S CENTER...
...OR THE "PYRAMID" ...
...ALONG THE COASTLINE.
I WANT EVERYONE'S OPINION... WHICH ONE SHOULD WE PICK...?
MRMR
MRMR
MRMR
MRMR

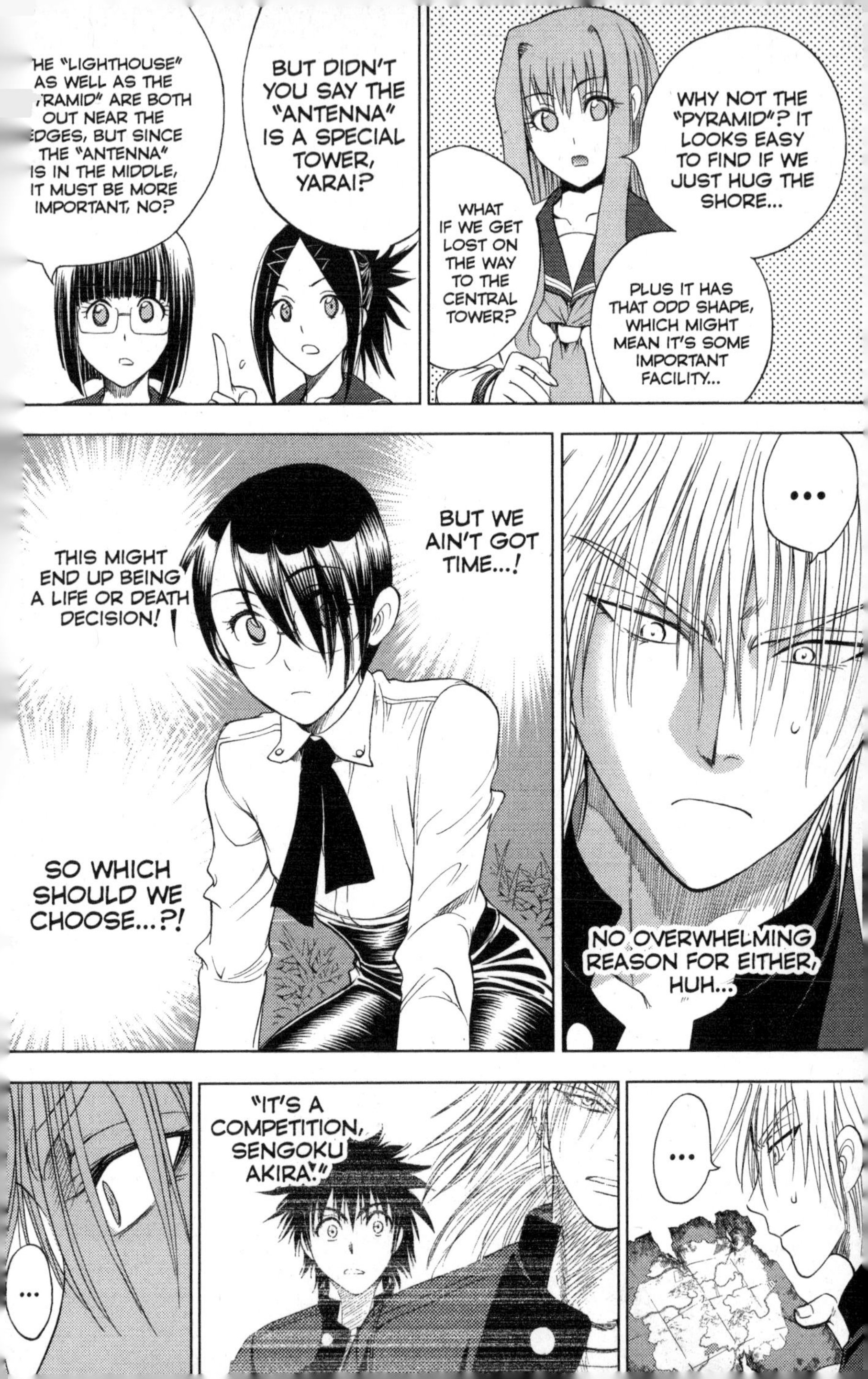

WHY NOT THE "PYRAMID"? IT LOOKS EASY TO FIND IF WE JUST HUG THE SHORE...
PLUS IT HAS THAT ODD SHAPE, WHICH MIGHT MEAN IT'S SOME IMPORTANT FACILITY...
WHAT IF WE GET LOST ON THE WAY TO THE CENTRAL TOWER?
BUT DIDN'T YOU SAY THE "ANTENNA" IS A SPECIAL TOWER, YARAI?
HE "LIGHTHOUSE" AS WELL AS THE "RAMID" ARE BOTH OUT NEAR THE EDGES, BUT SINCE THE "ANTENNA" IS IN THE MIDDLE, IT MUST BE MORE IMPORTANT, NO?
...
NO OVERWHELMING REASON FOR EITHER, HUH...
BUT WE AIN'T GOT TIME...!
THIS MIGHT END UP BEING A LIFE OR DEATH DECISION!
SO WHICH SHOULD WE CHOOSE...?!
...
"IT'S A COMPETITION, SENGOKU AKIRA!"
...

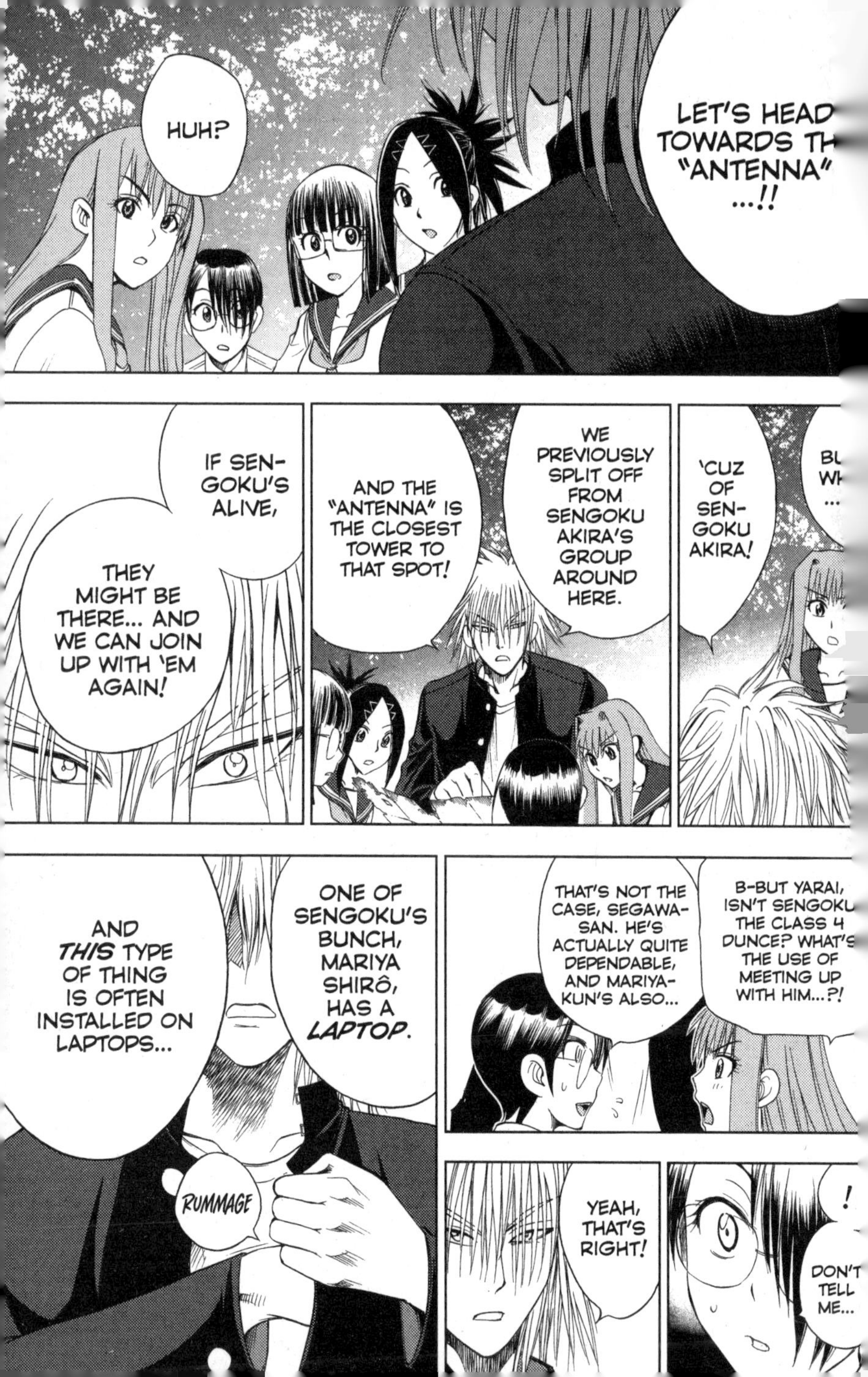
LET'S HEAD TOWARDS TH "ANTENNA" ...!!
HUH?
'CUZ OF SEN-GOKU AKIRA!
WE PREVIOUSLY SPLIT OFF FROM SENGOKU AKIRA'S GROUP AROUND HERE.
AND THE "ANTENNA" IS THE CLOSEST TOWER TO THAT SPOT!
IF SEN-GOKU'S ALIVE,
THEY MIGHT BE THERE... AND WE CAN JOIN UP WITH 'EM AGAIN!
B-BUT YARAI, ISN'T SENGOKU THE CLASS 4 DUNCE? WHAT'S THE USE OF MEETING UP WITH HIM...?!
THAT'S NOT THE CASE, SEGAWA-SAN. HE'S ACTUALLY QUITE DEPENDABLE, AND MARIYA-KUN'S ALSO...
!
DON'T TELL ME...
YEAH, THAT'S RIGHT!
ONE OF SENGOKU'S BUNCH, MARIYA SHIRÔ, HAS A *LAPTOP*.
AND *THIS* TYPE OF THING IS OFTEN INSTALLED ON LAPTOPS...
RUMMAGE

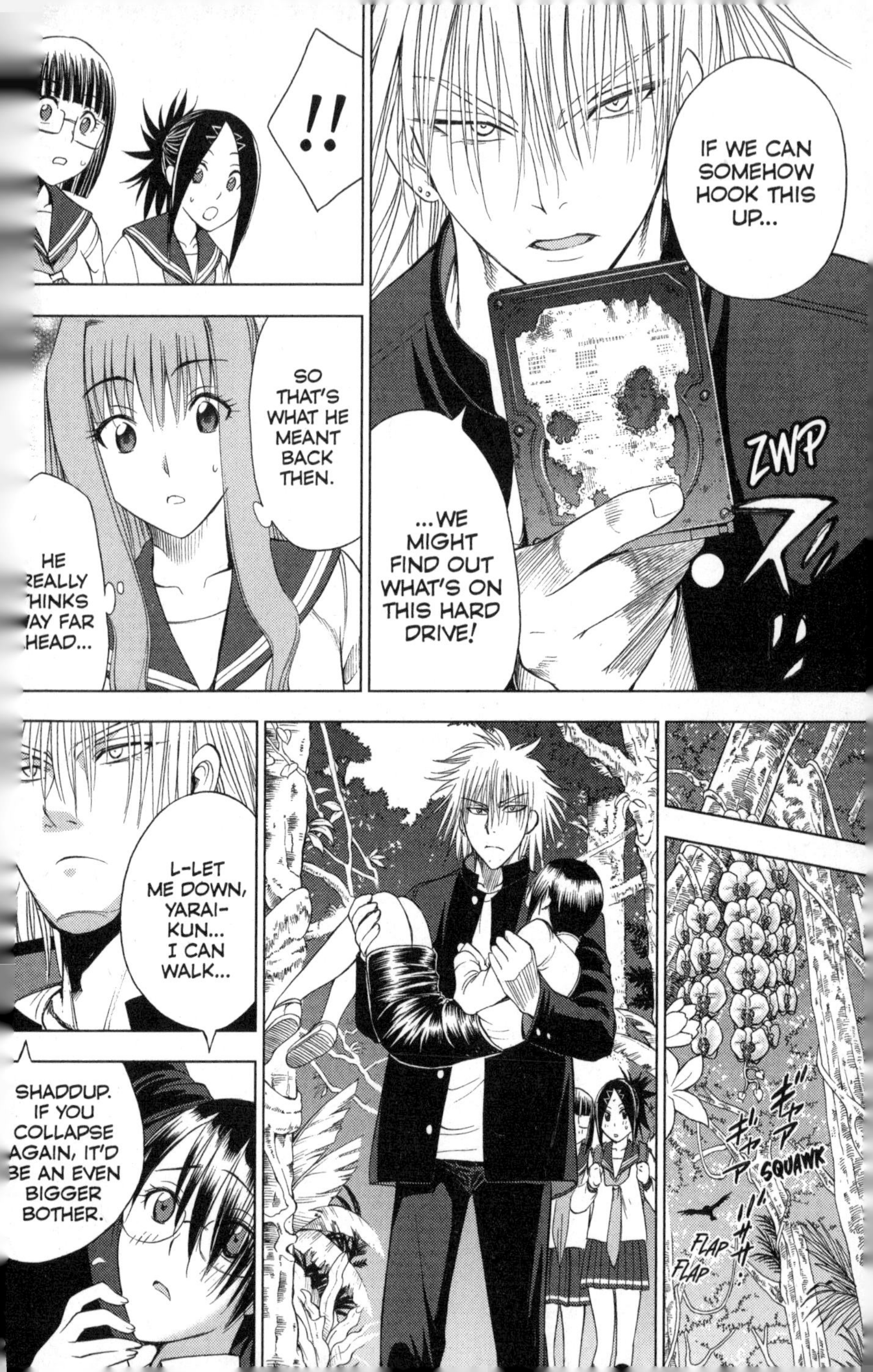
IF WE CAN SOMEHOW HOOK THIS UP...
...WE MIGHT FIND OUT WHAT'S ON THIS HARD DRIVE!
ZWP
!!
SO THAT'S WHAT HE MEANT BACK THEN.
HE REALLY THINKS WAY FAR AHEAD...
SQUAWK
FLAP FLAP
L-LET ME DOWN, YARAI-KUN... I CAN WALK...
SHADDUP. IF YOU COLLAPSE AGAIN, IT'D BE AN EVEN BIGGER BOTHER.

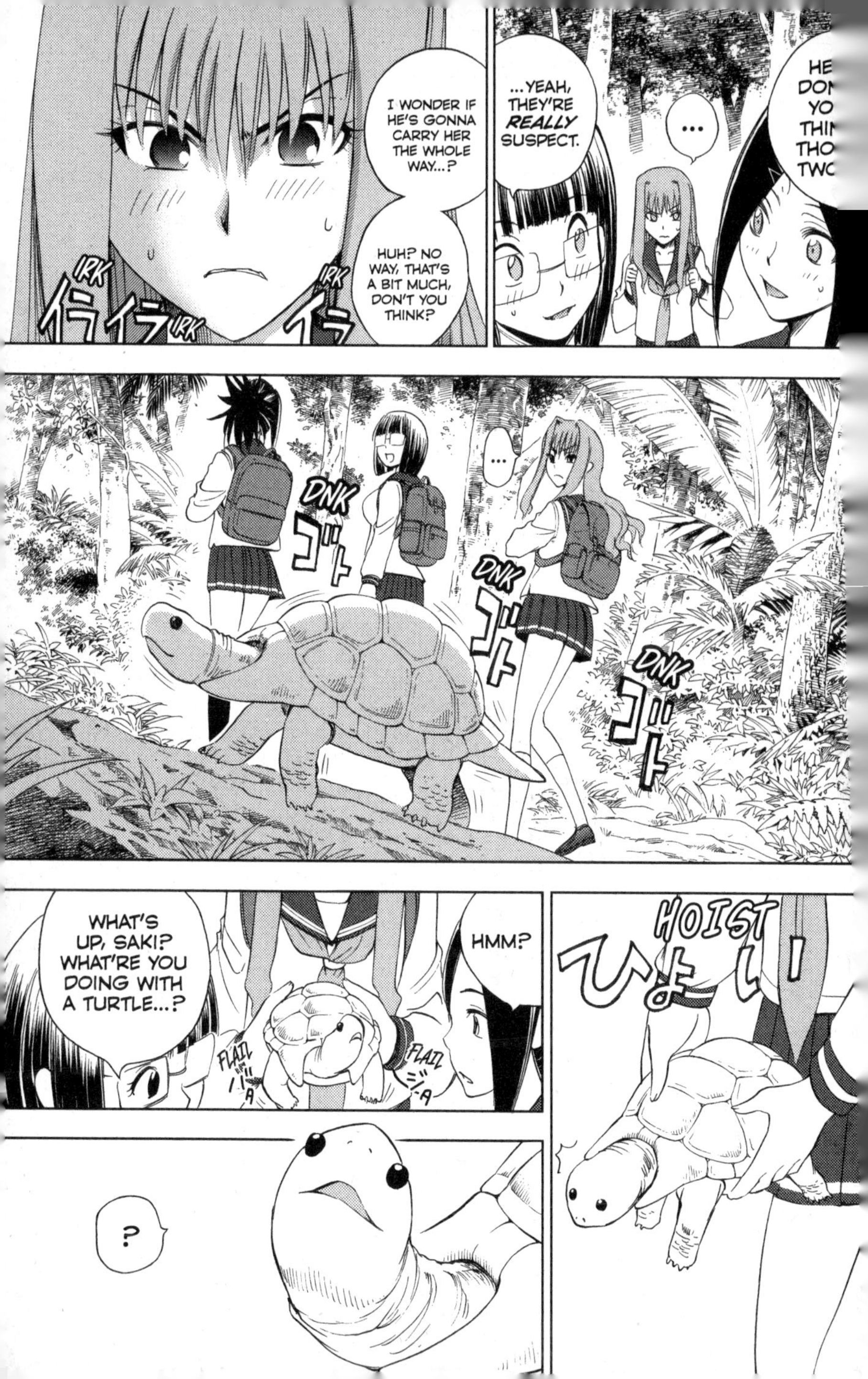
HE DON YO THIN THO TWO
...
...YEAH, THEY'RE *REALLY* SUSPECT.
I WONDER IF HE'S GONNA CARRY HER THE WHOLE WAY...?
HUH? NO WAY, THAT'S A BIT MUCH, DON'T YOU THINK?
IRK
IRK
IRK
...
DNK
DNK
DNK
HOIST
HMM?
WHAT'S UP, SAKI? WHAT'RE YOU DOING WITH A TURTLE...?
FLAIL
FLAIL
?

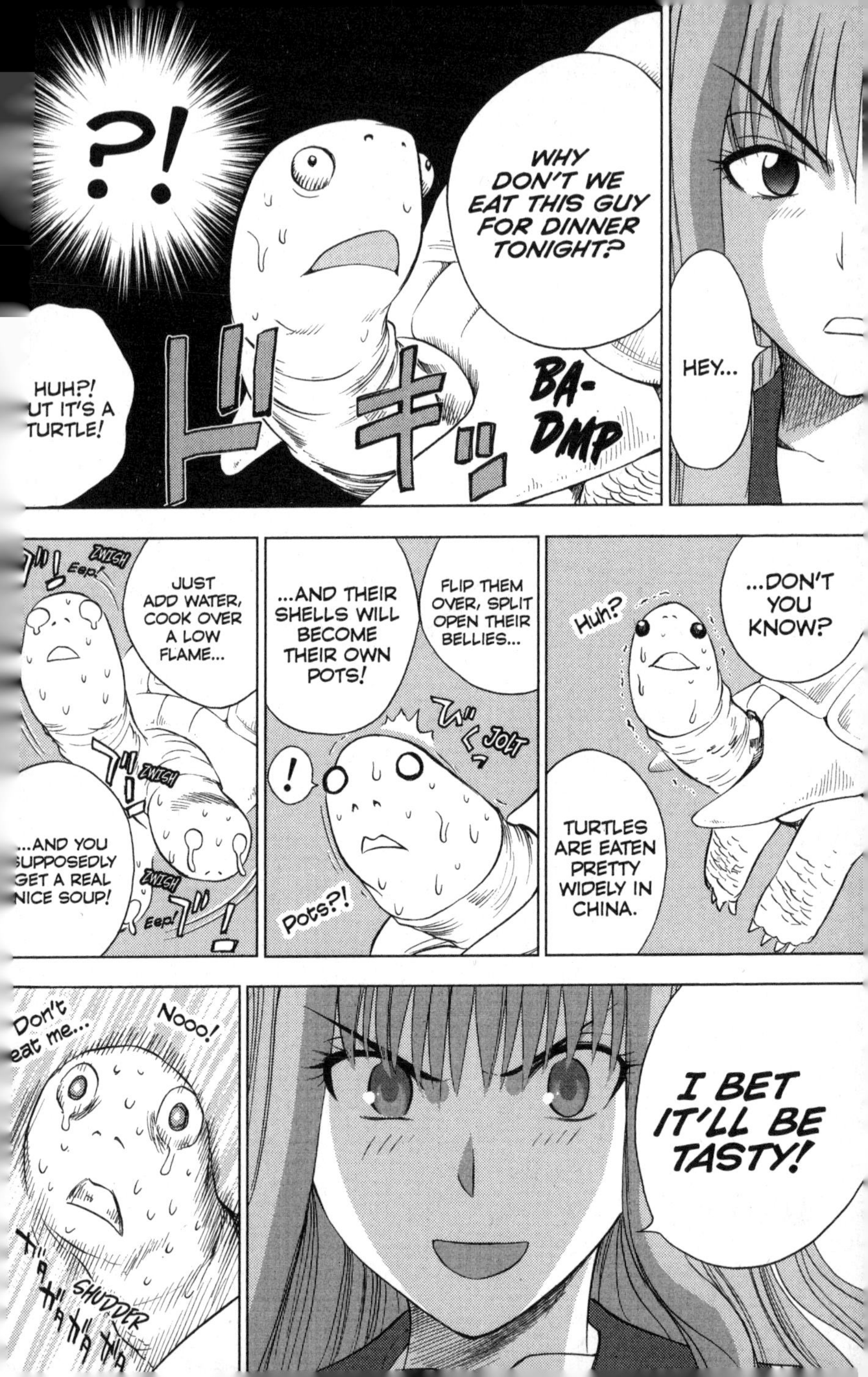
HEY...
WHY DON'T WE EAT THIS GUY FOR DINNER TONIGHT?
BA-DMP
?!
HUH?! UT IT'S A TURTLE!
...DON'T YOU KNOW?
Huh?
TURTLES ARE EATEN PRETTY WIDELY IN CHINA.
FLIP THEM OVER, SPLIT OPEN THEIR BELLIES...
...AND THEIR SHELLS WILL BECOME THEIR OWN POTS!
JOLT
!
Pots?!
JUST ADD WATER, COOK OVER A LOW FLAME...
ZWISH
Eep!
ZWISH
ZWISH
Eep!
...AND YOU SUPPOSEDLY GET A REAL NICE SOUP!
I BET IT'LL BE TASTY!
Nooo!
Don't eat me...
SHUDDER

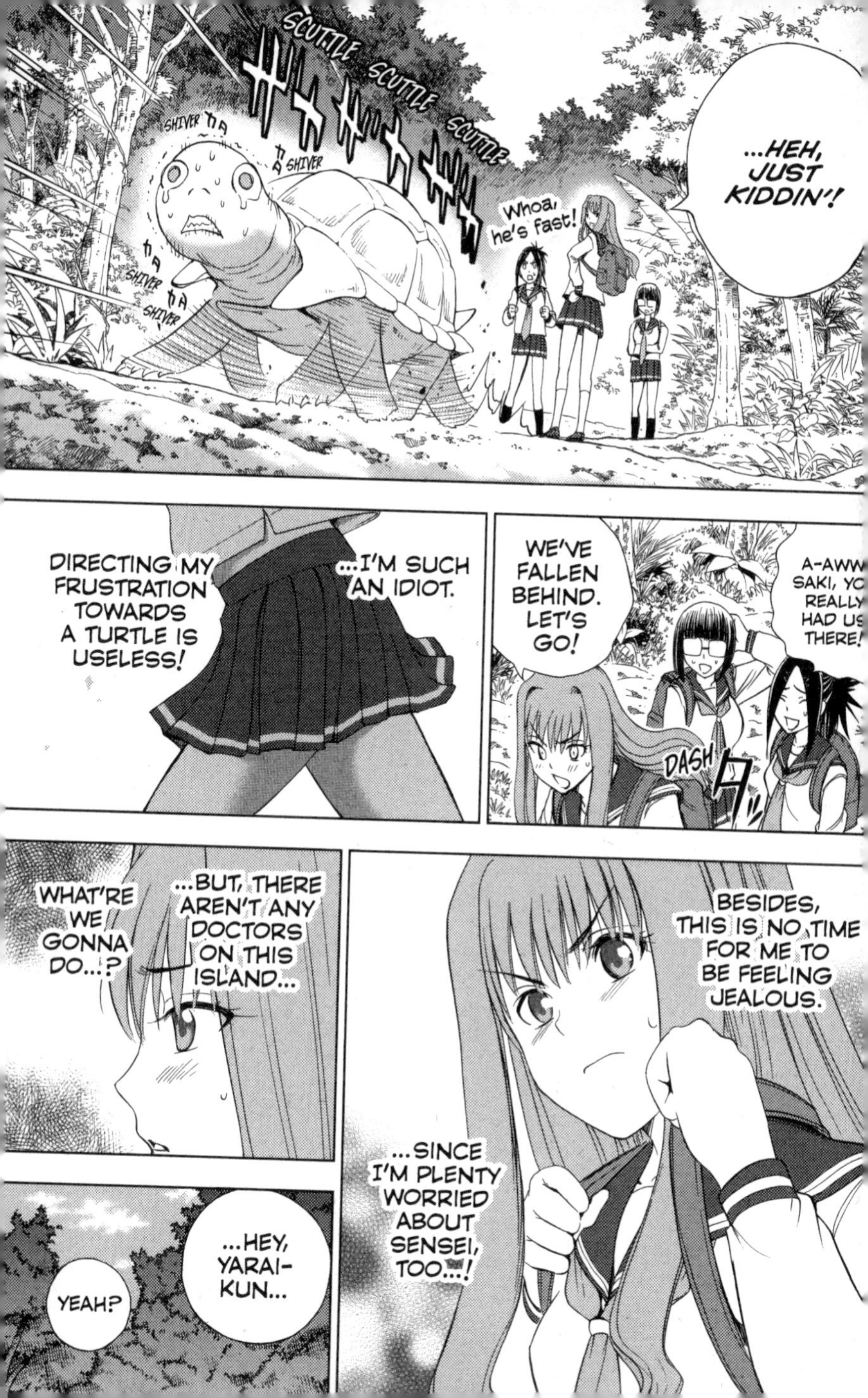
...HEH, JUST KIDDIN'!
SCUTTLE SCUTTLE SCUTTLE
Whoa, he's fast!
SHIVER SHIVER SHIVER SHIVER
A-AWW SAKI, YO REALLY HAD US THERE!
WE'VE FALLEN BEHIND. LET'S GO!
DASH
...I'M SUCH AN IDIOT.
DIRECTING MY FRUSTRATION TOWARDS A TURTLE IS USELESS!
BESIDES, THIS IS NO TIME FOR ME TO BE FEELING JEALOUS.
...SINCE I'M PLENTY WORRIED ABOUT SENSEI, TOO...!
...BUT, THERE AREN'T ANY DOCTORS ON THIS ISLAND...
WHAT'RE WE GONNA DO...?
...HEY, YARAI-KUN...
YEAH?

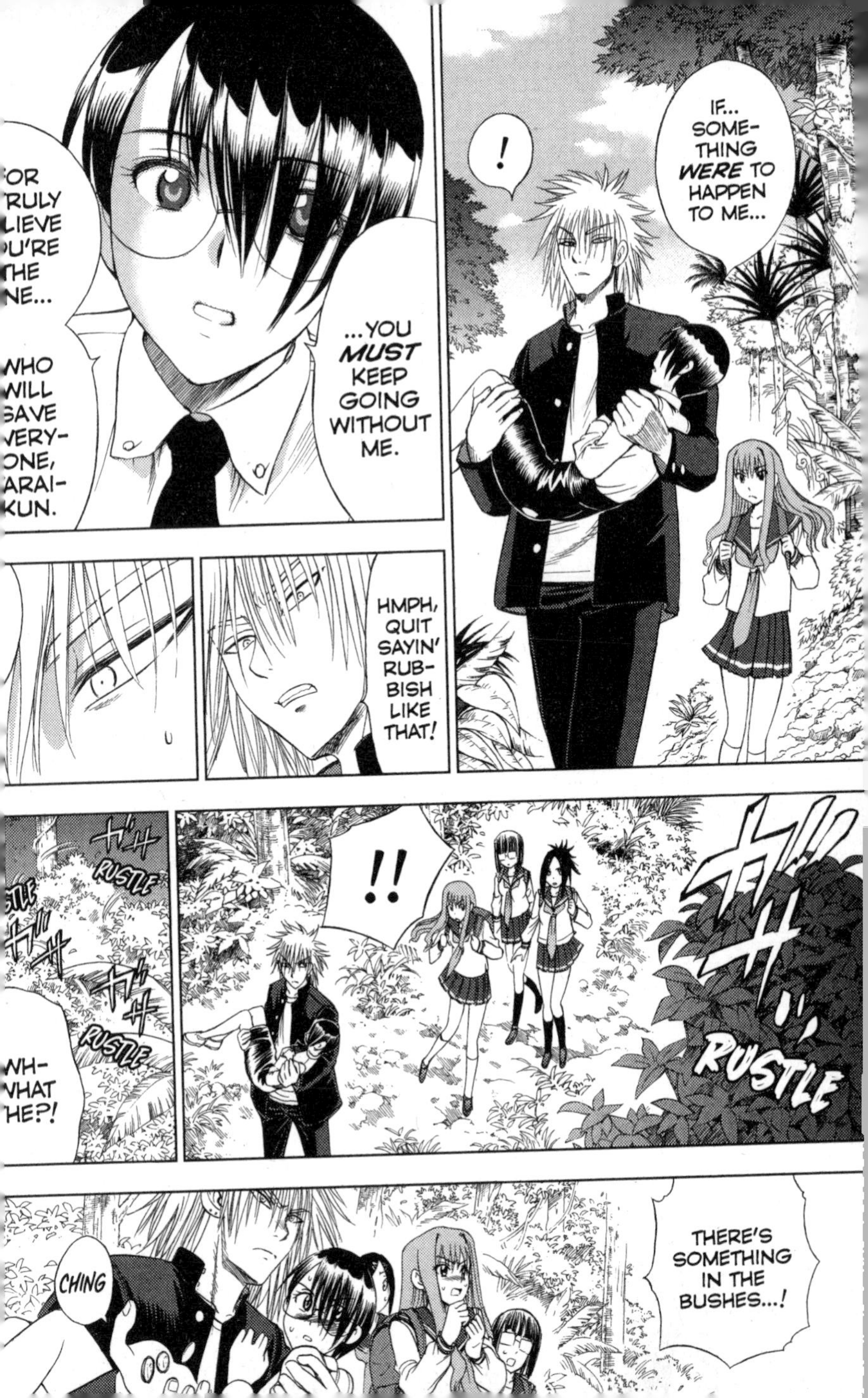
IF... SOMETHING WERE TO HAPPEN TO ME...
!
...YOU MUST KEEP GOING WITHOUT ME.
OR RULY LIEVE U'RE THE NE...
WHO WILL SAVE VERY-ONE, ARAI-KUN.
HMPH, QUIT SAYIN' RUBBISH LIKE THAT!
!!
RUSTLE
RUSTLE
RUSTLE
WH-WHAT HE?!
THERE'S SOMETHING IN THE BUSHES...!
CHING

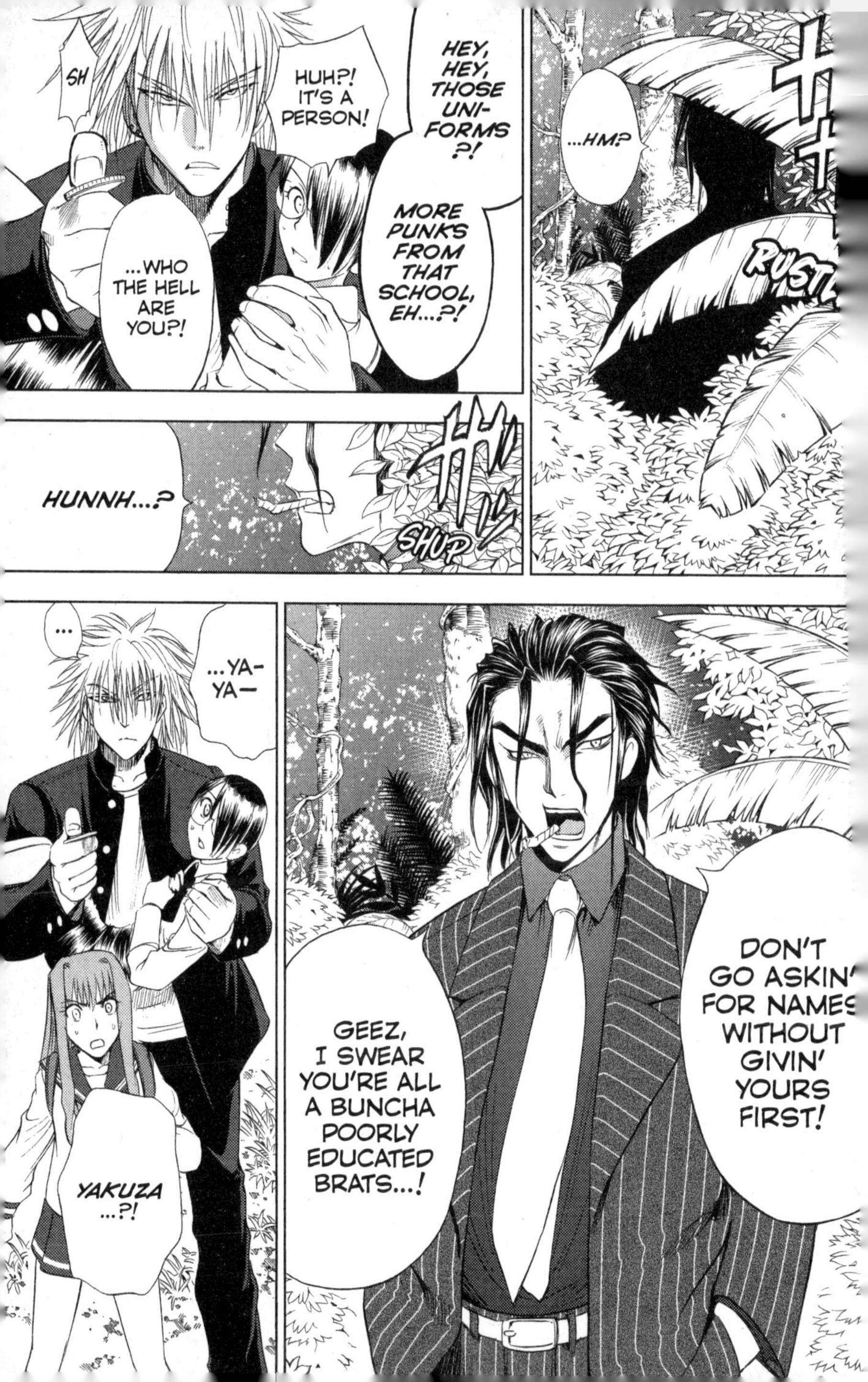
...HM?
RUST
HEY, HEY, THOSE UNI-FORMS?!
MORE PUNKS FROM THAT SCHOOL, EH...?!
HUH?! IT'S A PERSON!
SH
...WHO THE HELL ARE YOU?!
SHUP
HUNNH...?
DON'T GO ASKIN' FOR NAMES WITHOUT GIVIN' YOURS FIRST!
GEEZ, I SWEAR YOU'RE ALL A BUNCHA POORLY EDUCATED BRATS...!
...YA-YA—
...
YAKUZA...?!

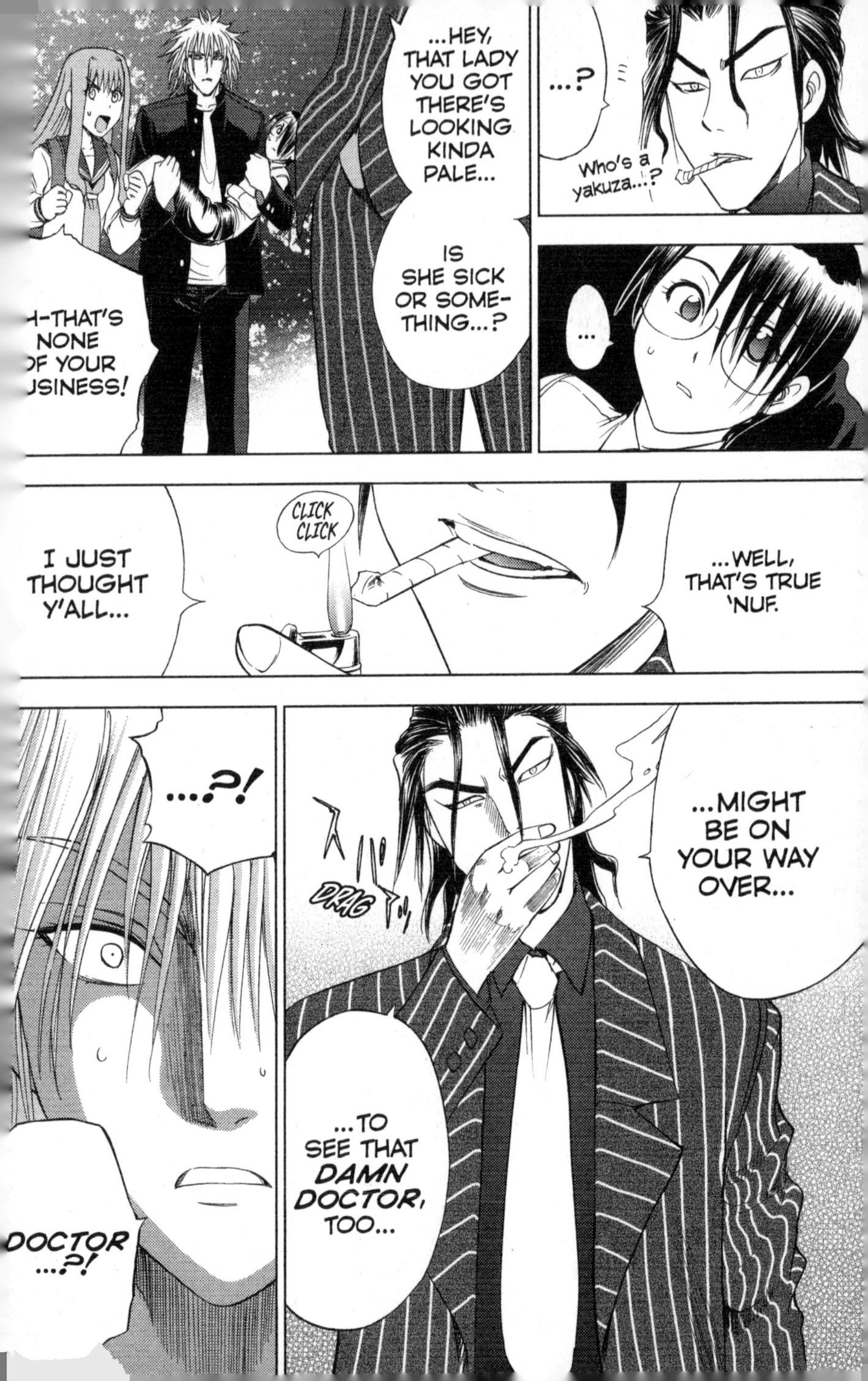
...?
Who's a yakuza...?
...
...HEY, THAT LADY YOU GOT THERE'S LOOKING KINDA PALE...
IS SHE SICK OR SOME-THING...?
H-THAT'S NONE OF YOUR USINESS!
...WELL, THAT'S TRUE 'NUF.
CLICK CLICK
I JUST THOUGHT Y'ALL...
...MIGHT BE ON YOUR WAY OVER...
DRAG
...TO SEE THAT DAMN DOCTOR, TOO...
...?!
DOCTOR ...?!

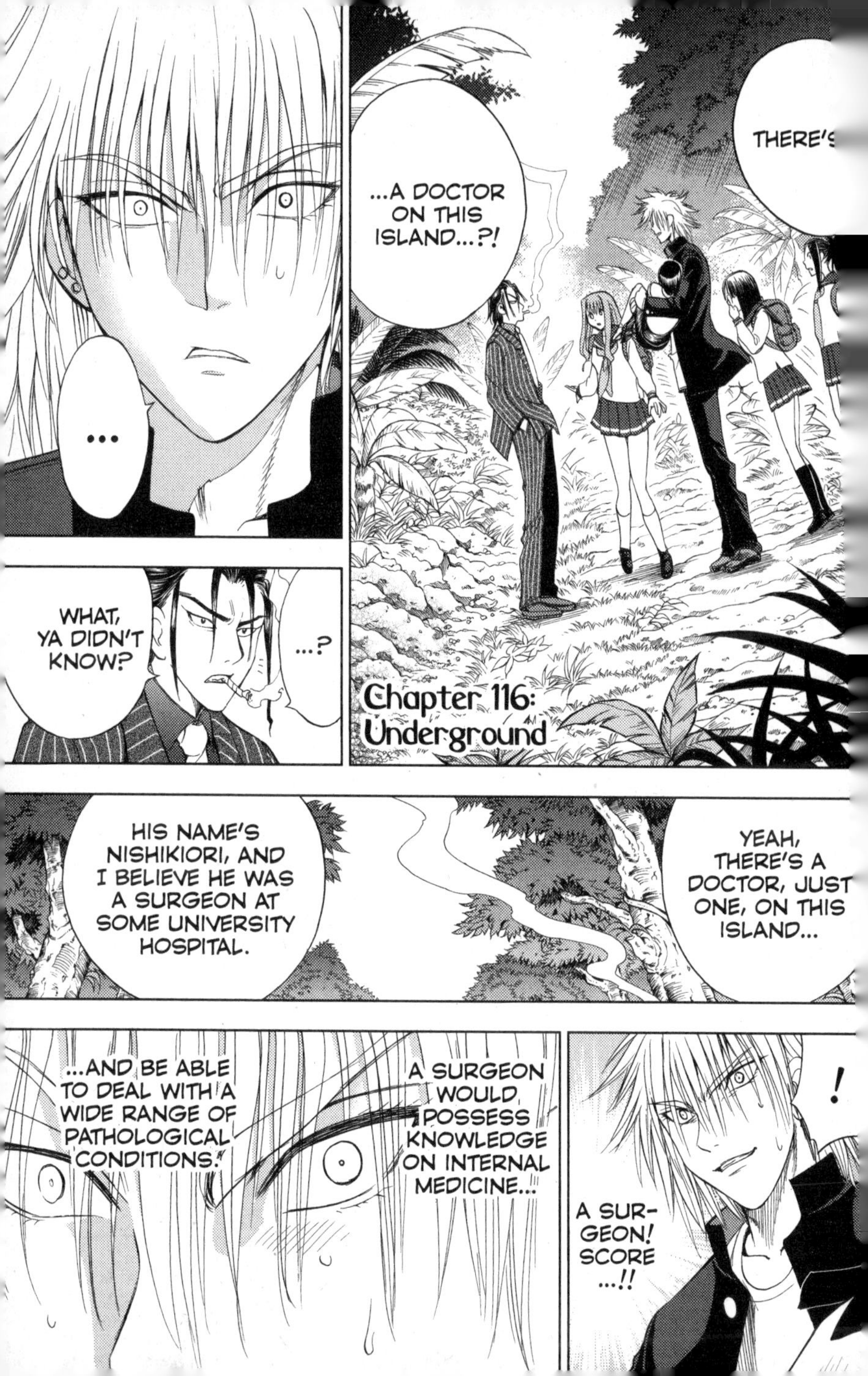
THERE'S
...A DOCTOR ON THIS ISLAND...?!
Chapter 116: Underground
...
WHAT, YA DIDN'T KNOW?
...?
YEAH, THERE'S A DOCTOR, JUST ONE, ON THIS ISLAND...
HIS NAME'S NISHIKIORI, AND I BELIEVE HE WAS A SURGEON AT SOME UNIVERSITY HOSPITAL.
!
A SUR-GEON! SCORE ...!!
A SURGEON WOULD POSSESS KNOWLEDGE ON INTERNAL MEDICINE...
...AND BE ABLE TO DEAL WITH A WIDE RANGE OF PATHOLOGICAL CONDITIONS.

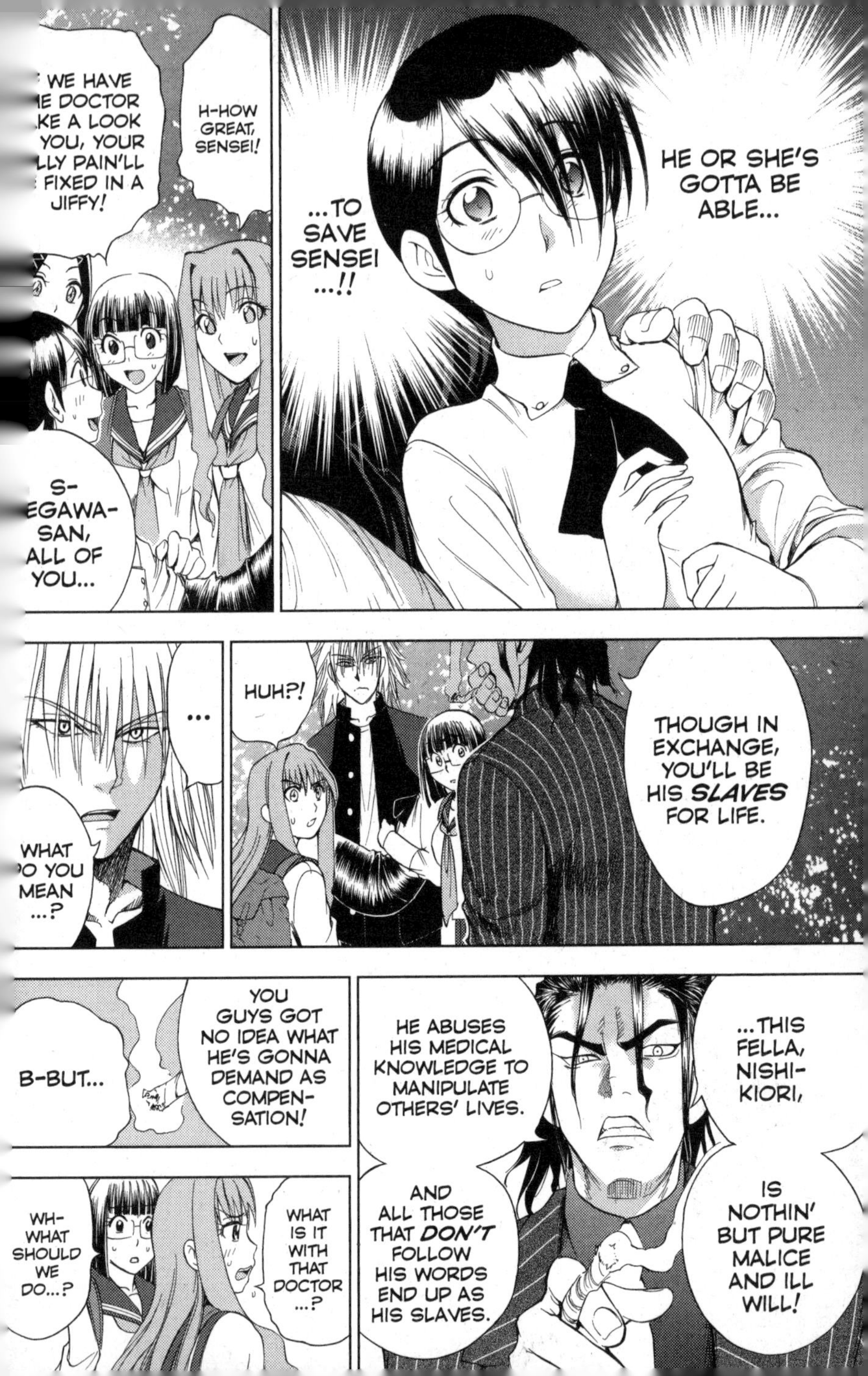
HE OR SHE'S GOTTA BE ABLE...
...TO SAVE SENSEI ...!!
H-HOW GREAT, SENSEI!
WE HAVE E DOCTOR KE A LOOK YOU, YOUR LLY PAIN'LL FIXED IN A JIFFY!
S- EGAWA-SAN, ALL OF YOU...
THOUGH IN EXCHANGE, YOU'LL BE HIS *SLAVES* FOR LIFE.
HUH?!
...
WHAT DO YOU MEAN ...?
...THIS FELLA, NISHIKIORI,
IS NOTHIN' BUT PURE MALICE AND ILL WILL!
HE ABUSES HIS MEDICAL KNOWLEDGE TO MANIPULATE OTHERS' LIVES.
AND ALL THOSE THAT *DON'T* FOLLOW HIS WORDS END UP AS HIS SLAVES.
YOU GUYS GOT NO IDEA WHAT HE'S GONNA DEMAND AS COMPEN-SATION!
B-BUT...
WHAT IS IT WITH THAT DOCTOR ...?
WH-WHAT SHOULD WE DO...?

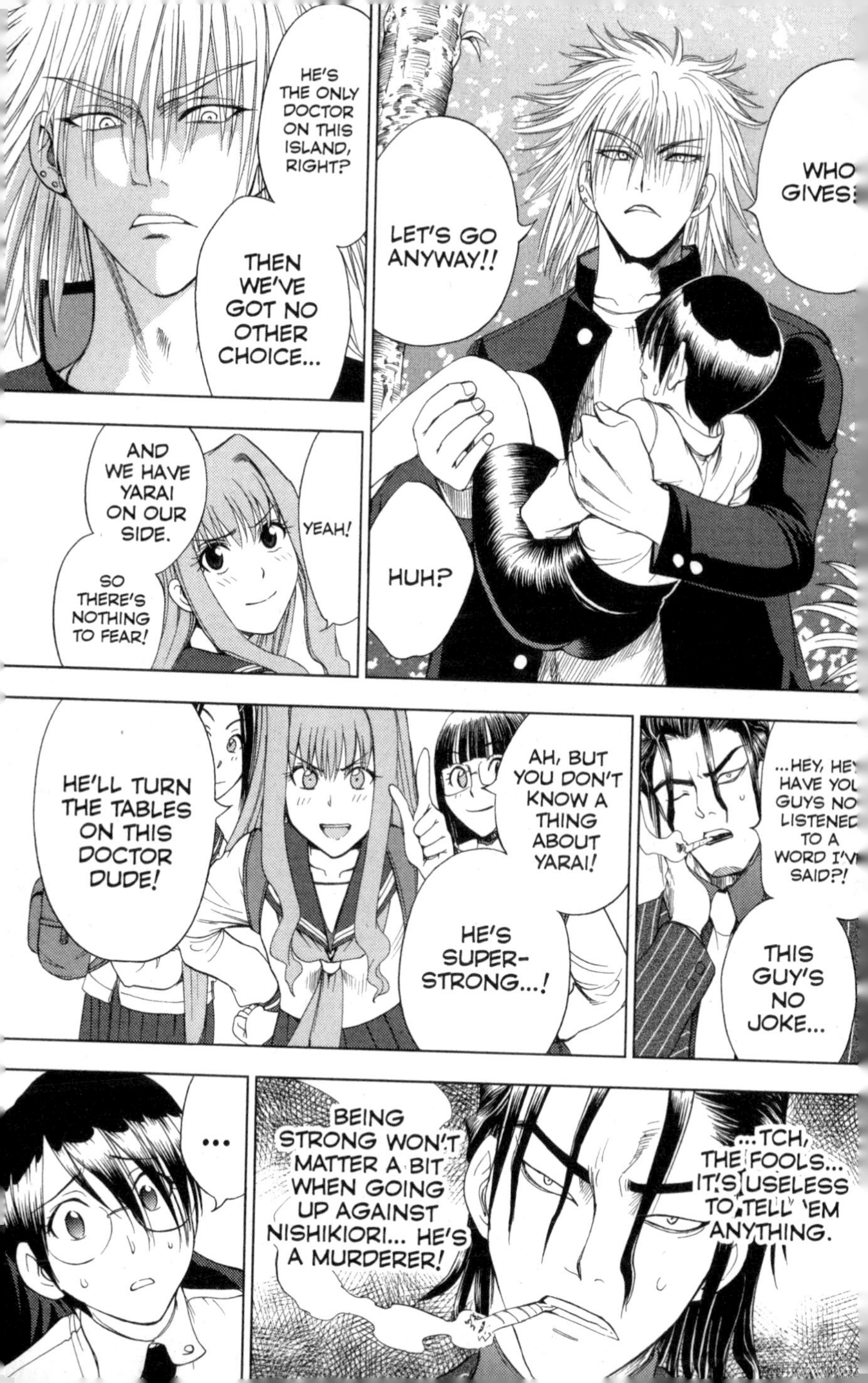
WHO GIVES
LET'S GO ANYWAY!!
HUH?
HE'S THE ONLY DOCTOR ON THIS ISLAND, RIGHT?
THEN WE'VE GOT NO OTHER CHOICE...
YEAH!
AND WE HAVE YARAI ON OUR SIDE.
SO THERE'S NOTHING TO FEAR!
...HEY, HEY HAVE YOU GUYS NOT LISTENED TO A WORD I'VE SAID?!
THIS GUY'S NO JOKE...
AH, BUT YOU DON'T KNOW A THING ABOUT YARAI!
HE'S SUPER-STRONG...!
HE'LL TURN THE TABLES ON THIS DOCTOR DUDE!
...TCH, THE FOOLS... IT'S USELESS TO TELL 'EM ANYTHING.
BEING STRONG WON'T MATTER A BIT WHEN GOING UP AGAINST NISHIKIORI... HE'S A MURDERER!
...

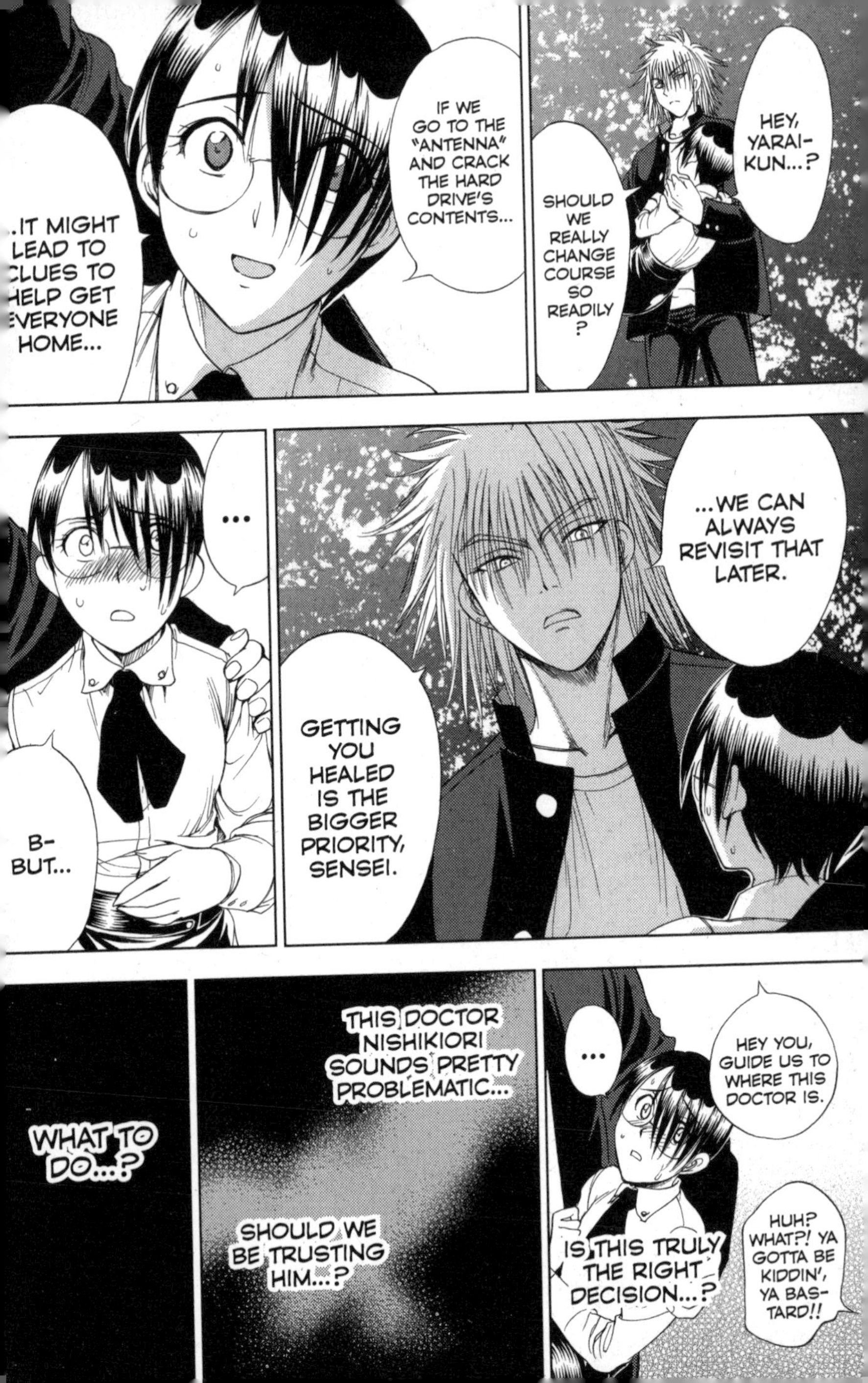
HEY, YARAI-KUN...?
SHOULD WE REALLY CHANGE COURSE SO READILY?
IF WE GO TO THE "ANTENNA" AND CRACK THE HARD DRIVE'S CONTENTS...
.IT MIGHT LEAD TO CLUES TO HELP GET EVERYONE HOME...
...WE CAN ALWAYS REVISIT THAT LATER.
GETTING YOU HEALED IS THE BIGGER PRIORITY, SENSEI.
...
B-BUT...
HEY YOU, GUIDE US TO WHERE THIS DOCTOR IS.
...
HUH? WHAT?! YA GOTTA BE KIDDIN', YA BASTARD!!
IS THIS TRULY THE RIGHT DECISION...?
THIS DOCTOR NISHIKIORI SOUNDS PRETTY PROBLEMATIC...
SHOULD WE BE TRUSTING HIM...?
WHAT TO DO...?

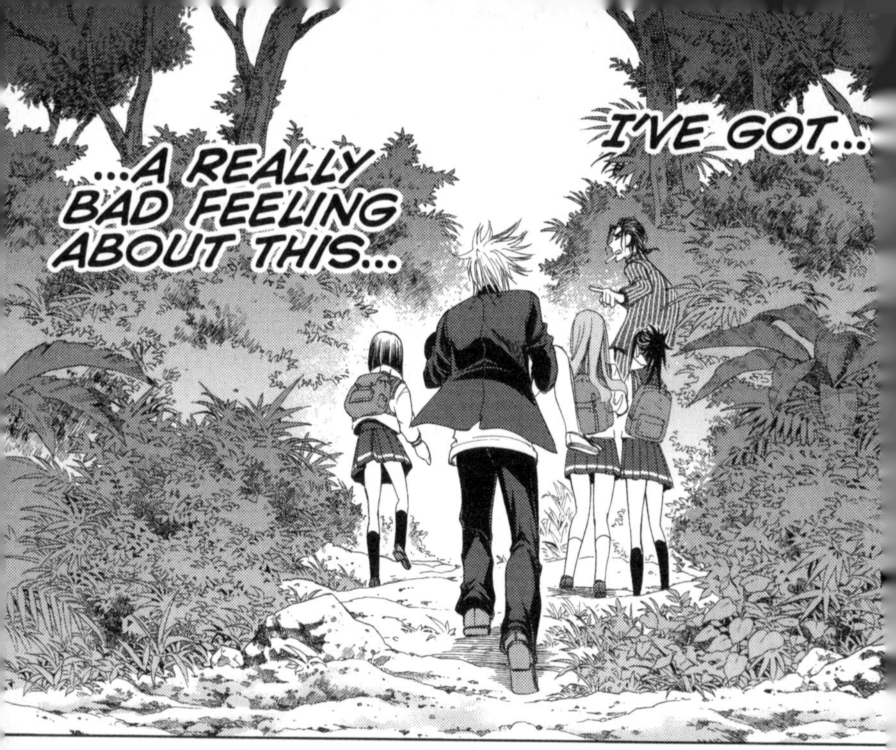
I'VE GOT...
...A REALLY BAD FEELING ABOUT THIS...
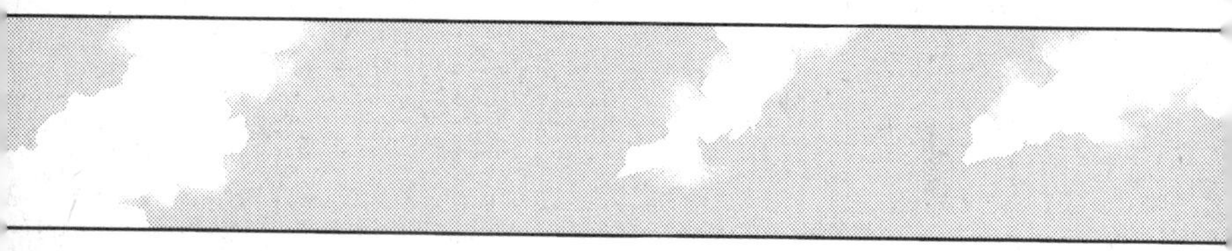
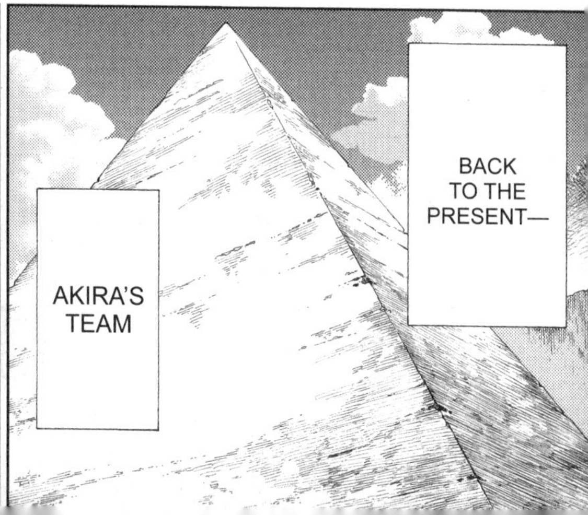
BACK TO THE PRESENT—
AKIRA'S TEAM
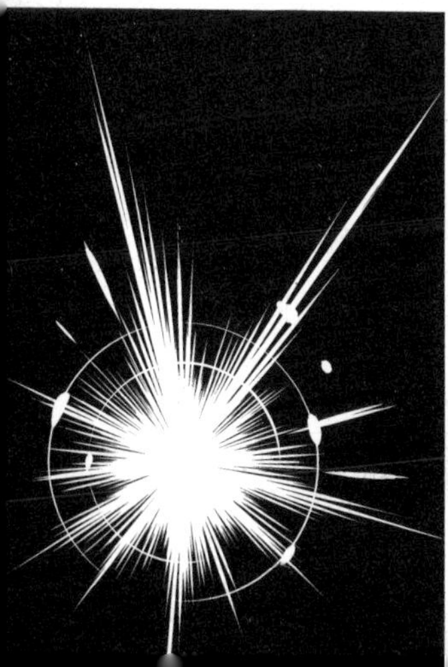

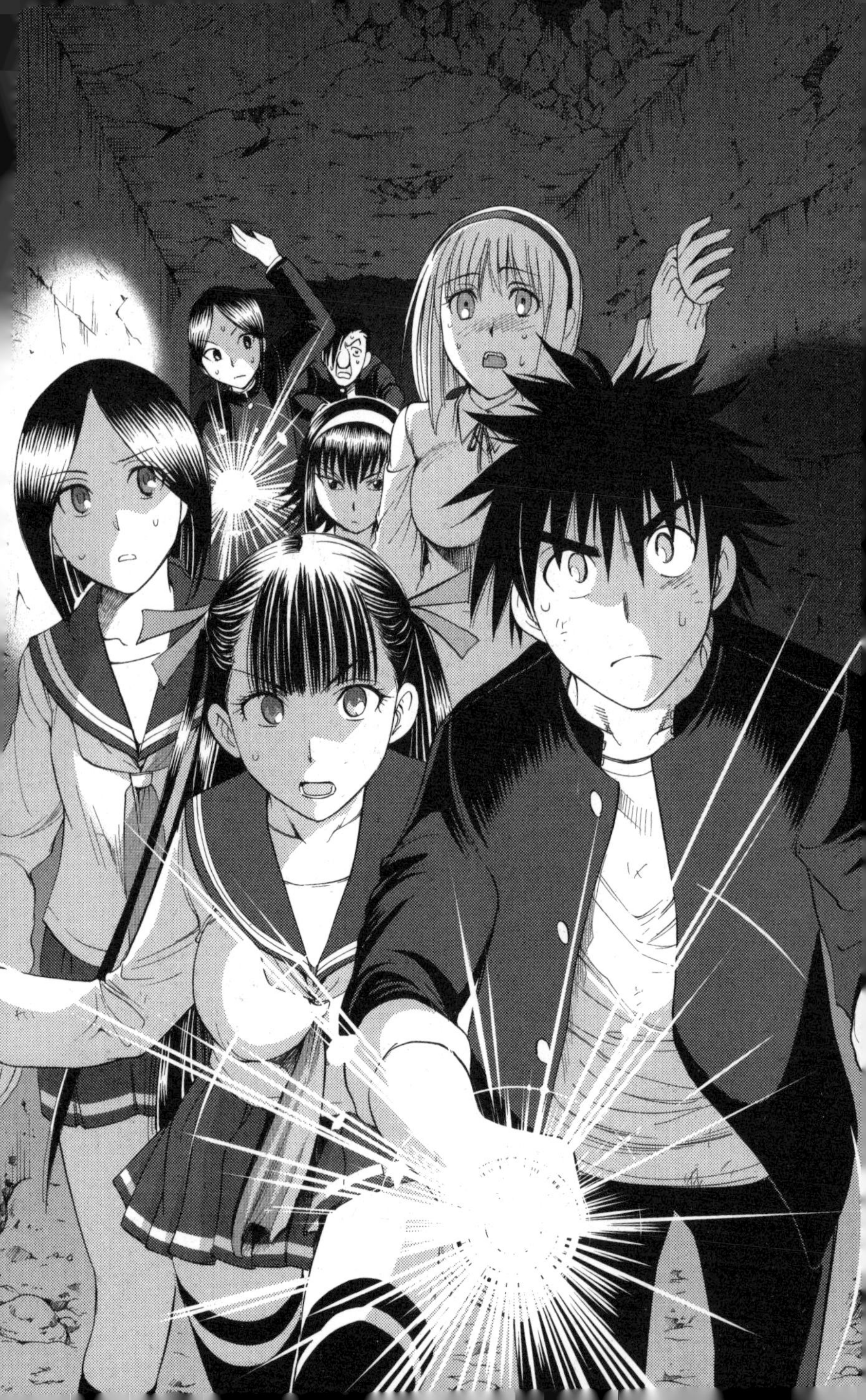

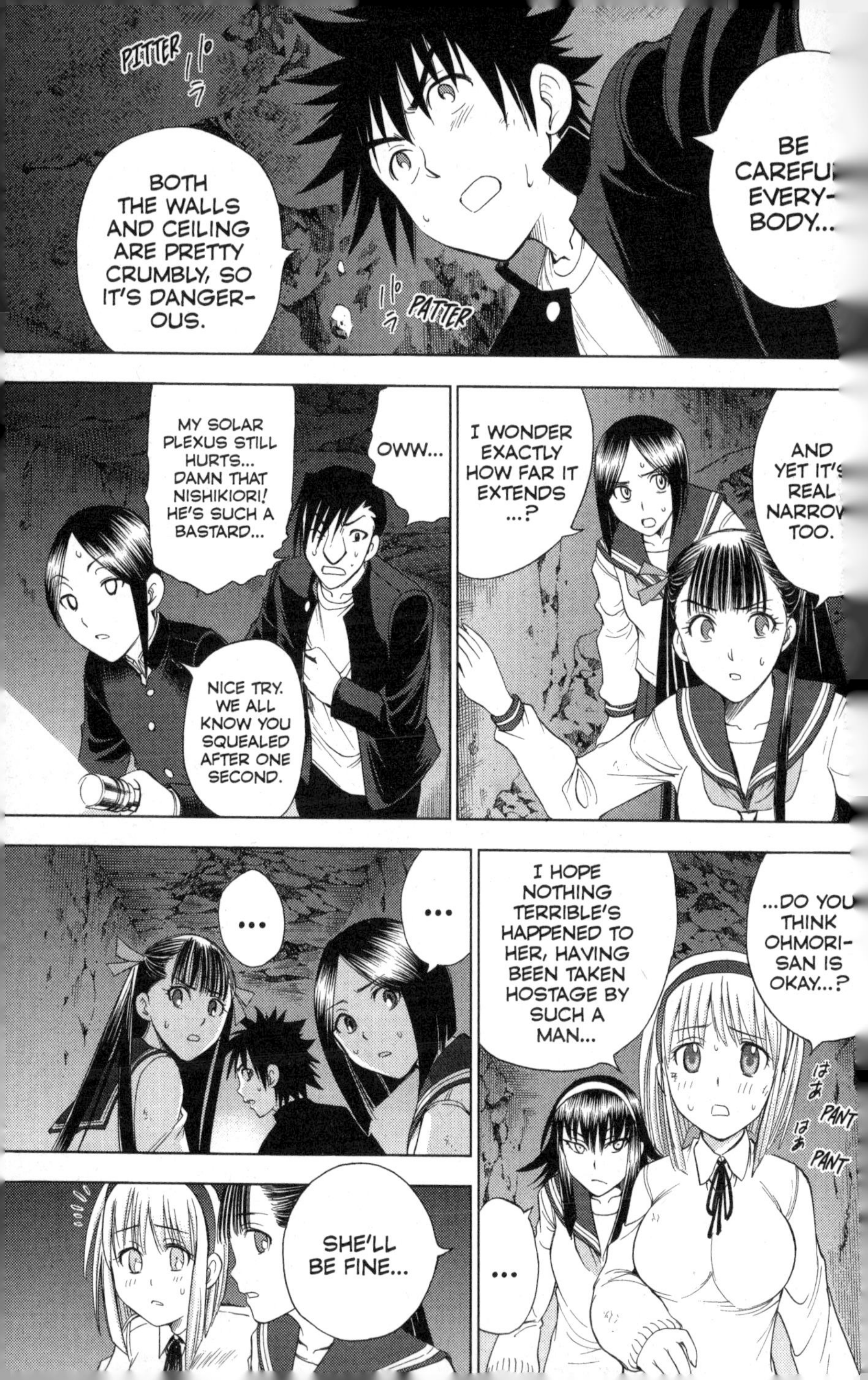
BE CAREFU EVERY-BODY...
PITTER
BOTH THE WALLS AND CEILING ARE PRETTY CRUMBLY, SO IT'S DANGER-OUS.
PATTER
AND YET IT' REAL NARRO TOO.
I WONDER EXACTLY HOW FAR IT EXTENDS ...?
OWW...
MY SOLAR PLEXUS STILL HURTS... DAMN THAT NISHIKIORI! HE'S SUCH A BASTARD...
NICE TRY. WE ALL KNOW YOU SQUEALED AFTER ONE SECOND.
...DO YO THINK OHMORI-SAN IS OKAY...?
I HOPE NOTHING TERRIBLE'S HAPPENED TO HER, HAVING BEEN TAKEN HOSTAGE BY SUCH A MAN...
はぁ PANT
はぁ PANT
...
...
...
SHE'LL BE FINE...

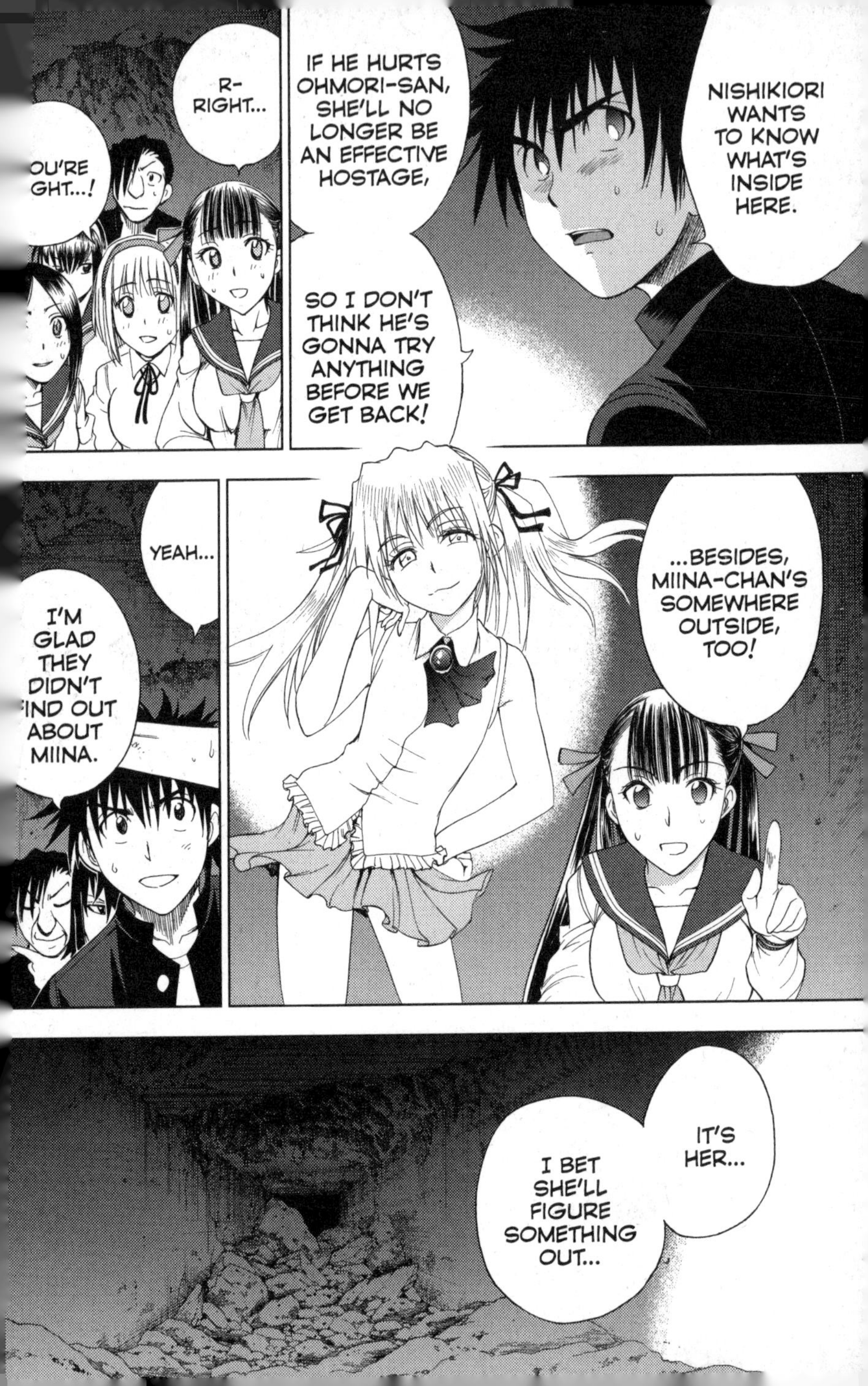
NISHIKIORI WANTS TO KNOW WHAT'S INSIDE HERE.
IF HE HURTS OHMORI-SAN, SHE'LL NO LONGER BE AN EFFECTIVE HOSTAGE,
SO I DON'T THINK HE'S GONNA TRY ANYTHING BEFORE WE GET BACK!
R-RIGHT...
OU'RE GHT...!
...BESIDES, MIINA-CHAN'S SOMEWHERE OUTSIDE, TOO!
YEAH...
I'M GLAD THEY DIDN'T FIND OUT ABOUT MIINA.
IT'S HER...
I BET SHE'LL FIGURE SOMETHING OUT...

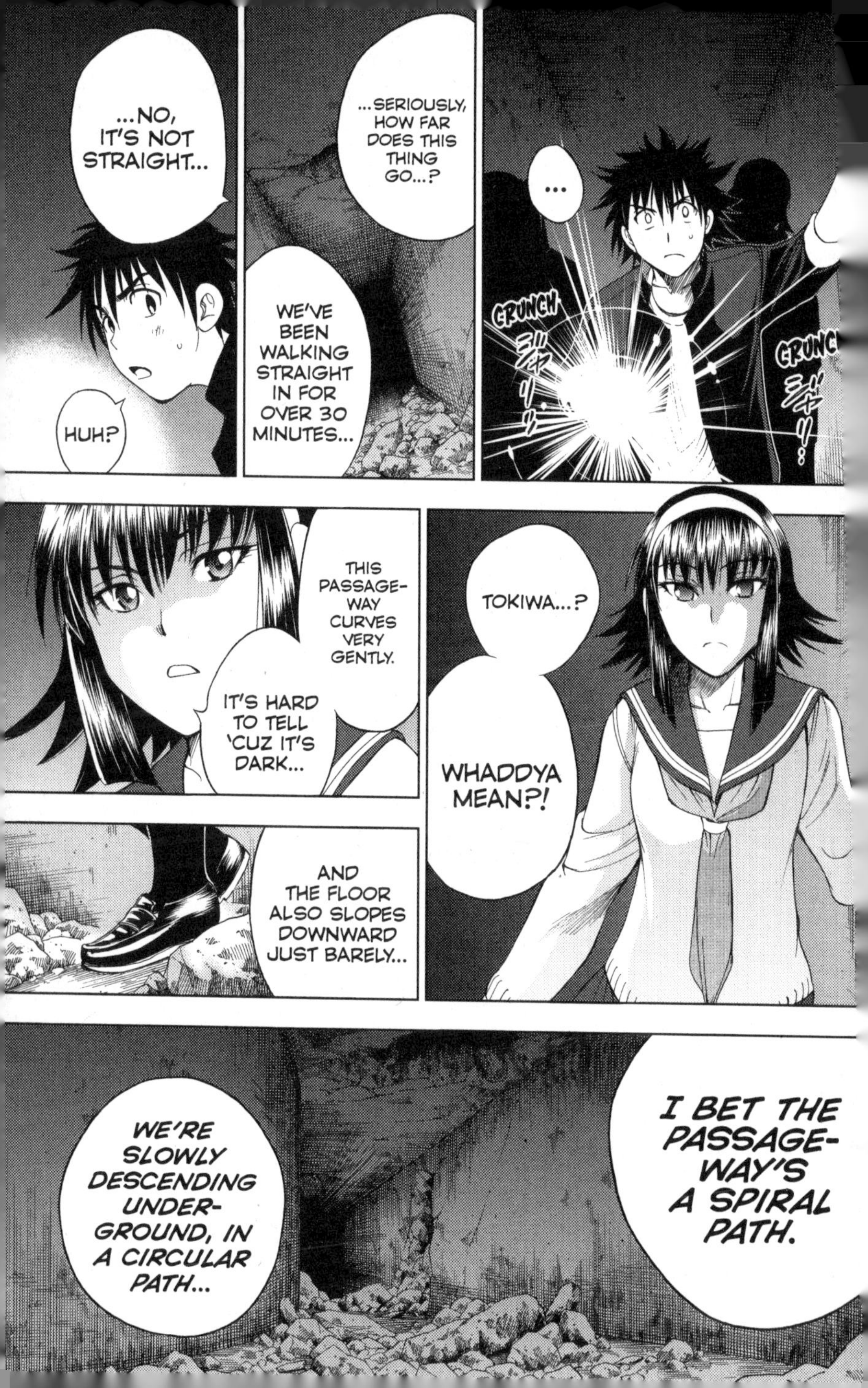
...
CRUNCH
CRUNCH
...SERIOUSLY, HOW FAR DOES THIS THING GO...?
WE'VE BEEN WALKING STRAIGHT IN FOR OVER 30 MINUTES...
...NO, IT'S NOT STRAIGHT...
HUH?
TOKIWA...?
WHADDYA MEAN?!
THIS PASSAGE-WAY CURVES VERY GENTLY.
IT'S HARD TO TELL 'CUZ IT'S DARK...
AND THE FLOOR ALSO SLOPES DOWNWARD JUST BARELY...
I BET THE PASSAGE-WAY'S A SPIRAL PATH.
WE'RE SLOWLY DESCENDING UNDER-GROUND, IN A CIRCULAR PATH...

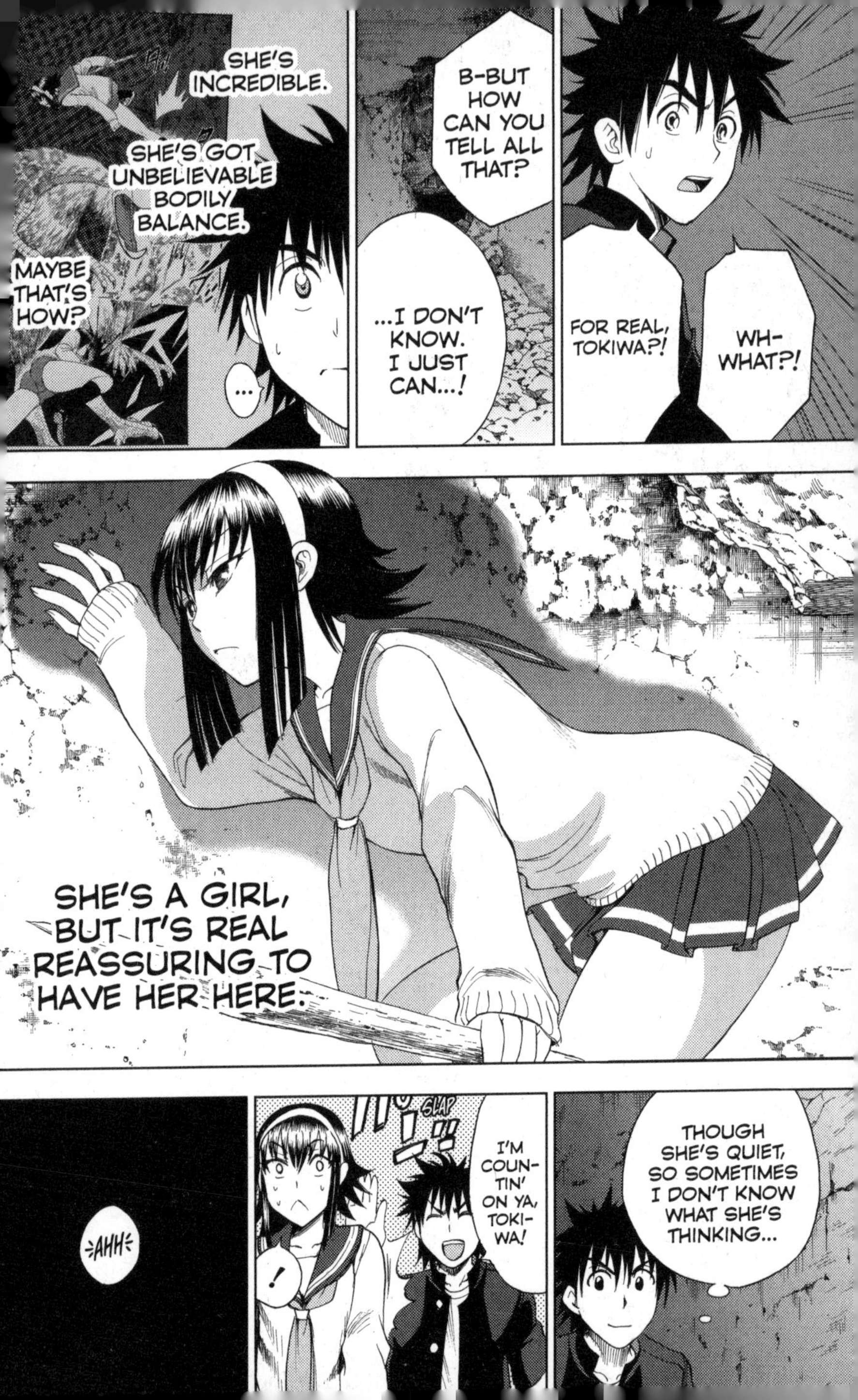
WH- WHAT?!
FOR REAL, TOKIWA?!
B-BUT HOW CAN YOU TELL ALL THAT?
...I DON'T KNOW. I JUST CAN...!
SHE'S INCREDIBLE.
SHE'S GOT UNBELIEVABLE BODILY BALANCE.
MAYBE THAT'S HOW?
...
SHE'S A GIRL, BUT IT'S REAL REASSURING TO HAVE HER HERE.
THOUGH SHE'S QUIET, SO SOMETIMES I DON'T KNOW WHAT SHE'S THINKING...
SLAP
I'M COUNTIN' ON YA, TOKIWA!
!
AHH

...?

HUH?

I-I...

...I SAW THAT!!

...NAH.

...HEY, DID YOU HEAR A STRANGE VOICE JUST NOW?

...

...? WAS IT MY IMAGINA- TION...?

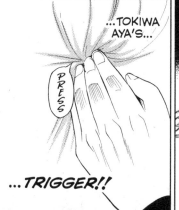

...TOKIWA AYA'S...

PRESS

...TRIGGER!!

...THAT...

IF I'M NOT MISTAKEN...

...SENGOKU JUST HAPPENED TO ACCIDENTALLY HIT...

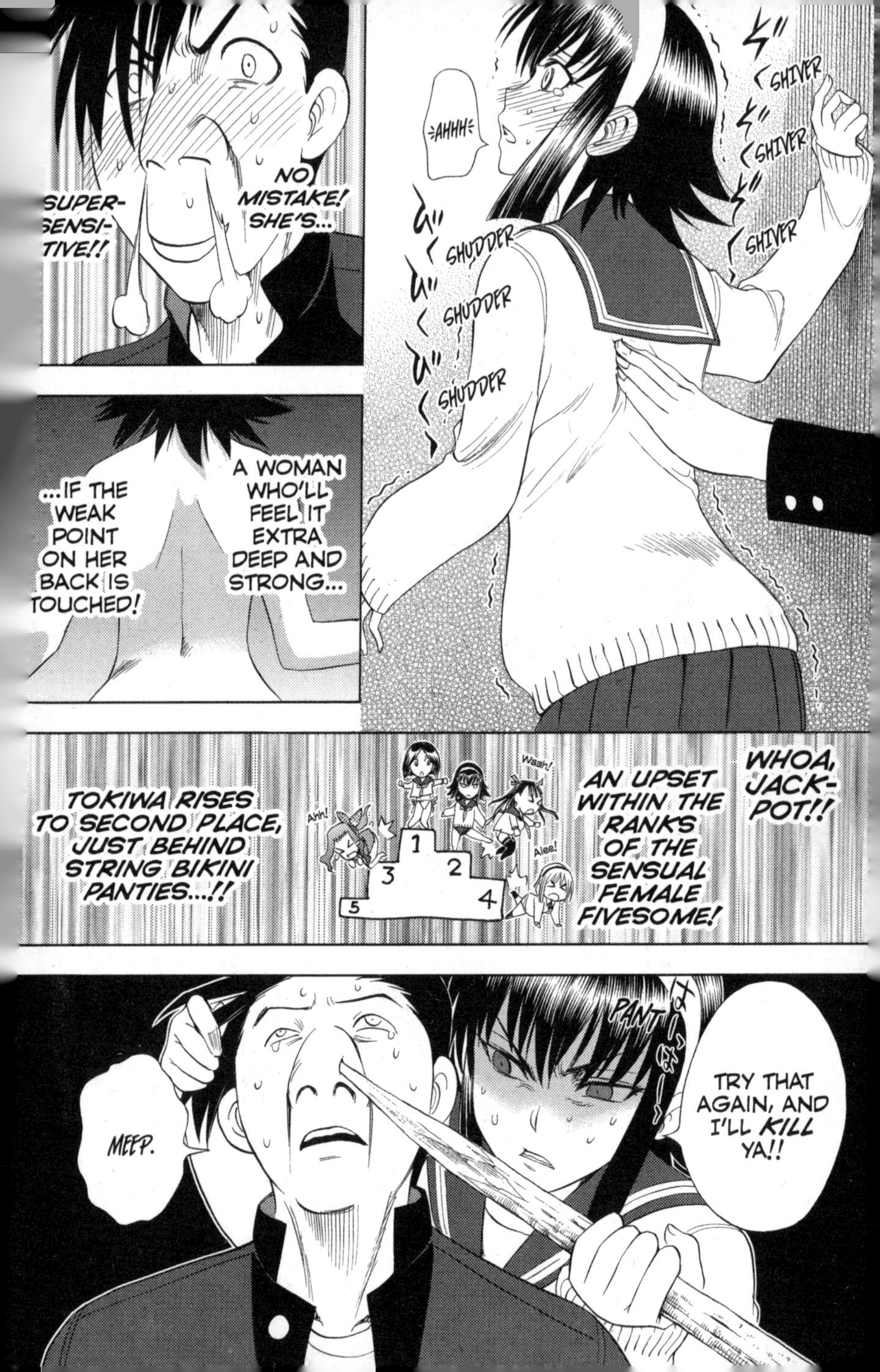
AHHH
SHIVER
SHIVER
SHIVER
SHUDDER
SHUDDER
SHUDDER
NO MISTAKE! SHE'S...
SUPER-SENSITIVE!!
A WOMAN WHO'LL FEEL IT EXTRA DEEP AND STRONG...
...IF THE WEAK POINT ON HER BACK IS TOUCHED!
WHOA, JACKPOT!!
AN UPSET WITHIN THE RANKS OF THE SENSUAL FEMALE FIVESOME!
Waah!
Aiee!
1
2
3
4
5
Ahh!
TOKIWA RISES TO SECOND PLACE, JUST BEHIND STRING BIKINI PANTIES...!!
PANT
TRY THAT AGAIN, AND I'LL *KILL* YA!!
MEEP.

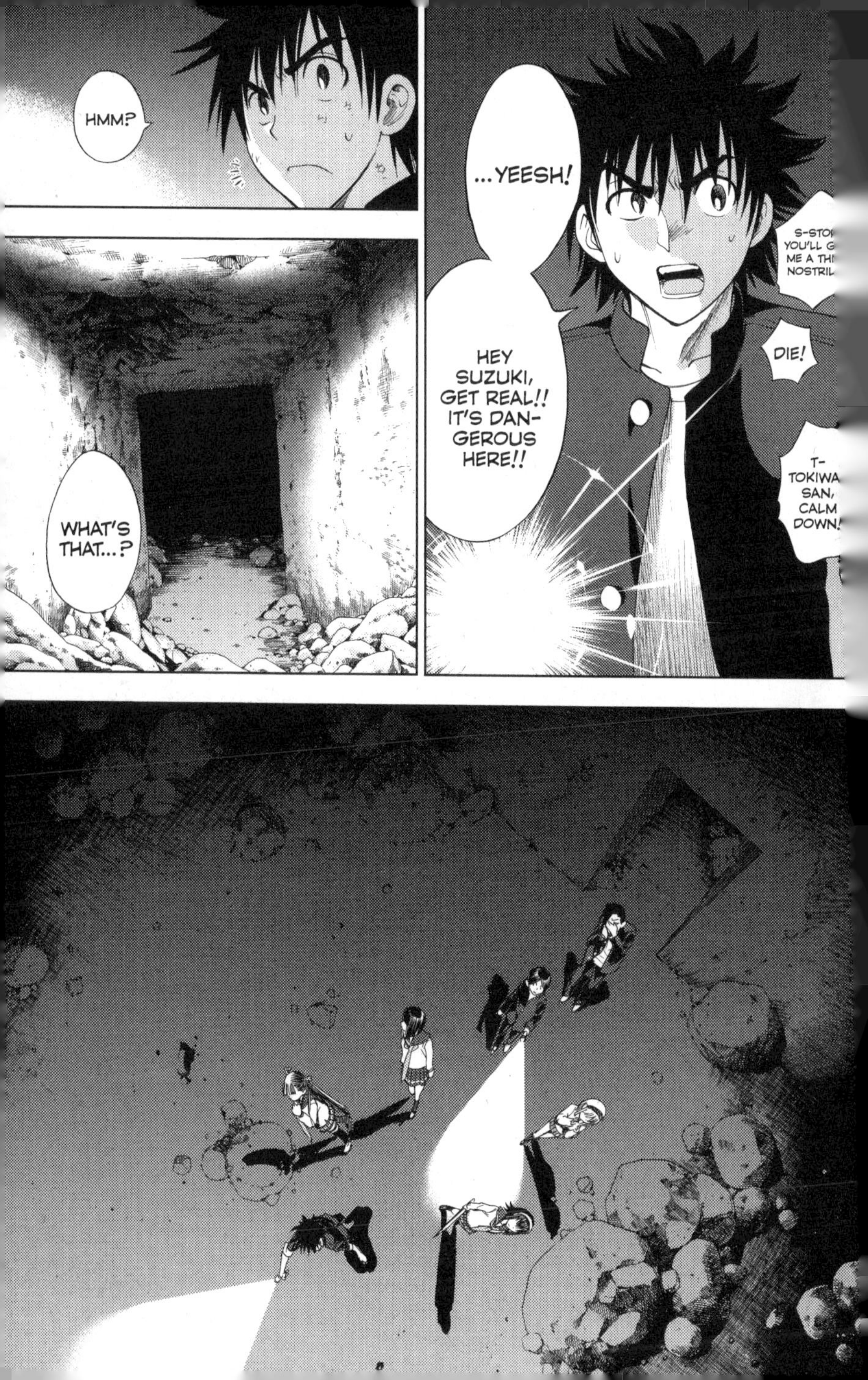
...YEESH!
S-STO
YOU'LL G
ME A THI
NOSTRIL
DIE!
T-
TOKIWA
SAN,
CALM
DOWN!
HEY SUZUKI, GET REAL!! IT'S DAN-GEROUS HERE!!
HMM?
WHAT'S THAT...?

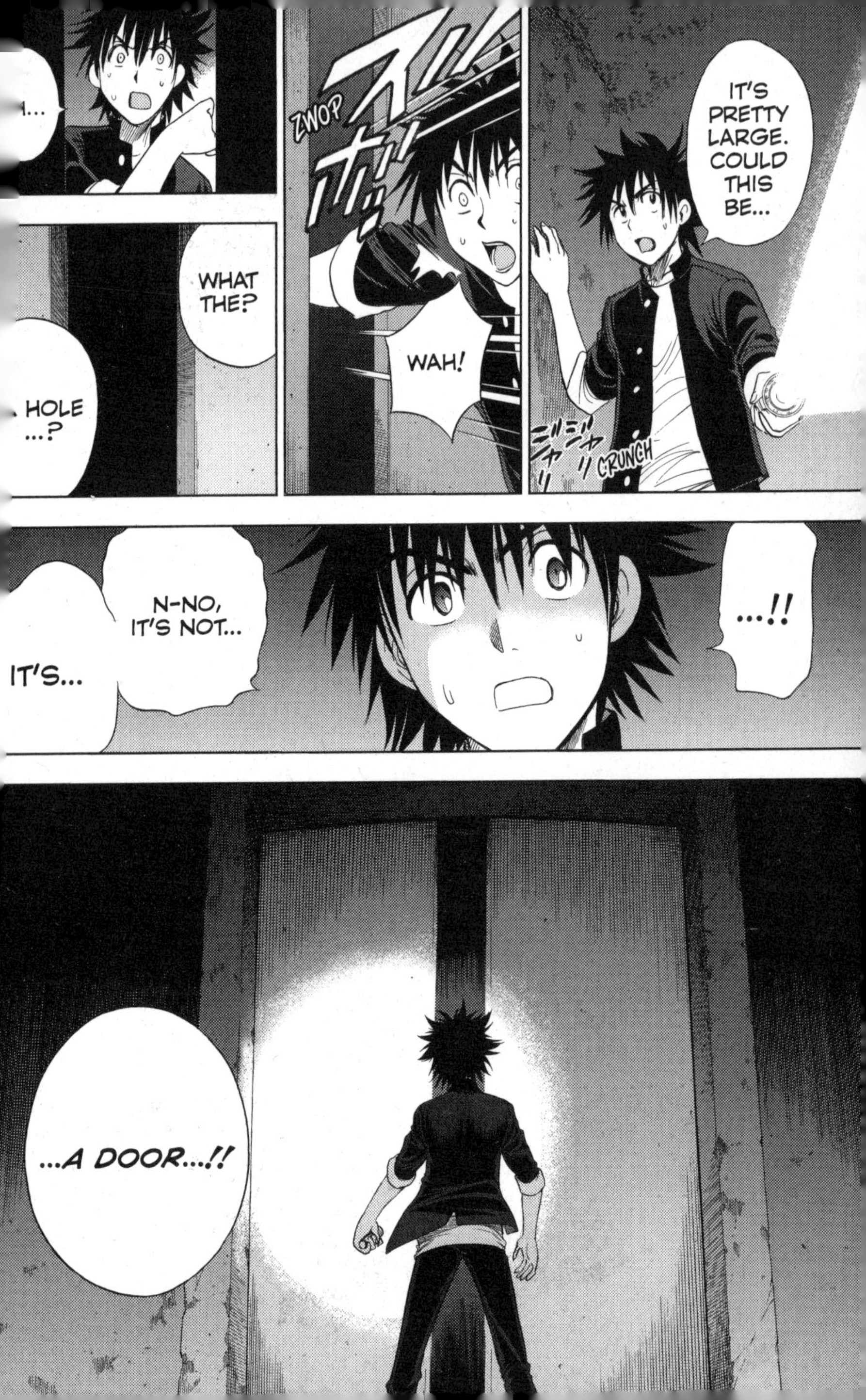
IT'S PRETTY LARGE. COULD THIS BE...
CRUNCH
ZWOP
WAH!
WHAT THE?
HOLE ...?
...!!
N-NO, IT'S NOT...
IT'S...
...A DOOR...!!

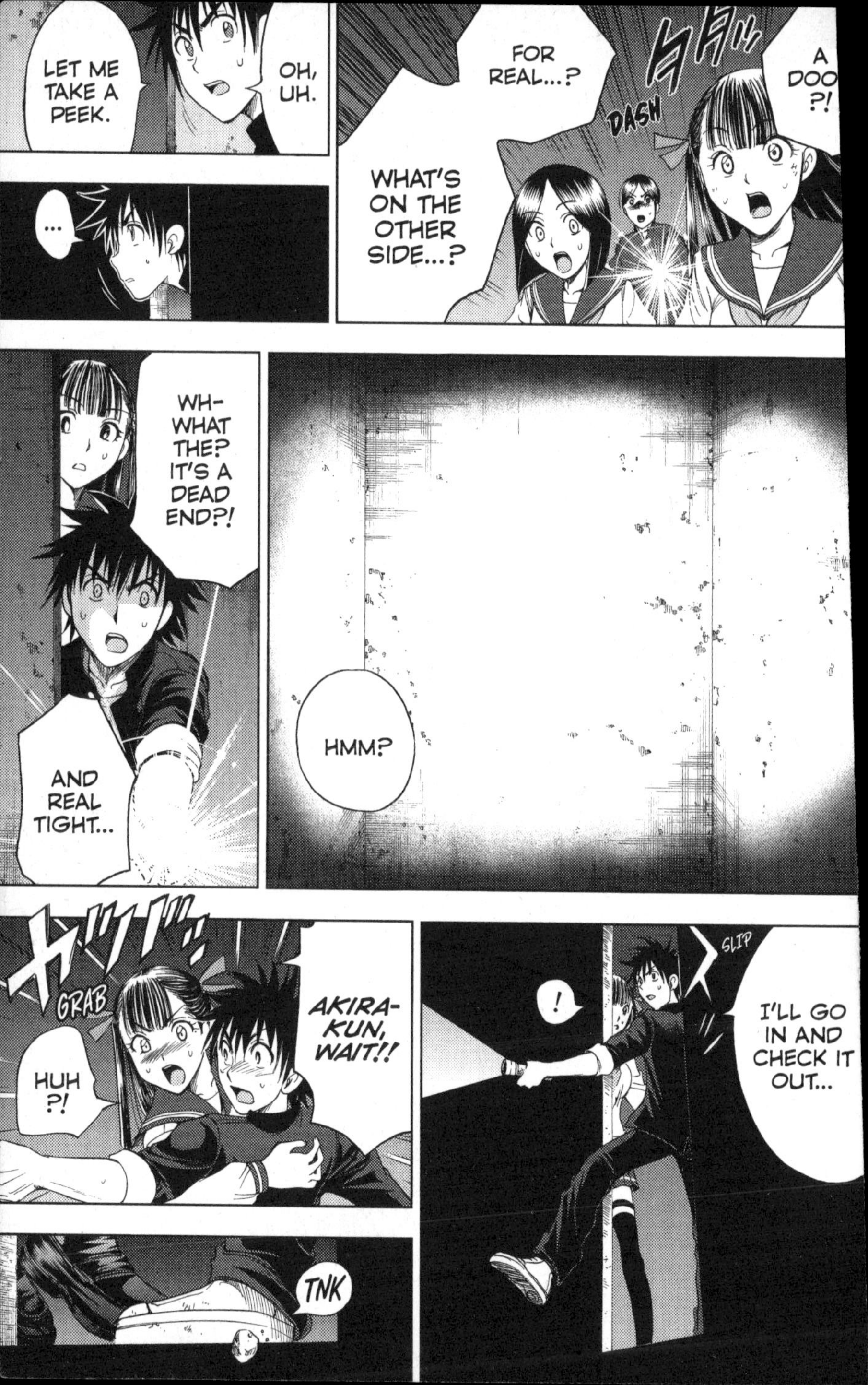
A DOO ?!
DASH
FOR REAL...?
WHAT'S ON THE OTHER SIDE...?
OH, UH.
LET ME TAKE A PEEK.
...
HMM?
WH-WHAT THE? IT'S A DEAD END?!
AND REAL TIGHT...
SLIP
I'LL GO IN AND CHECK IT OUT...
!
AKIRA-KUN, WAIT!!
GRAB
HUH ?!
TNK

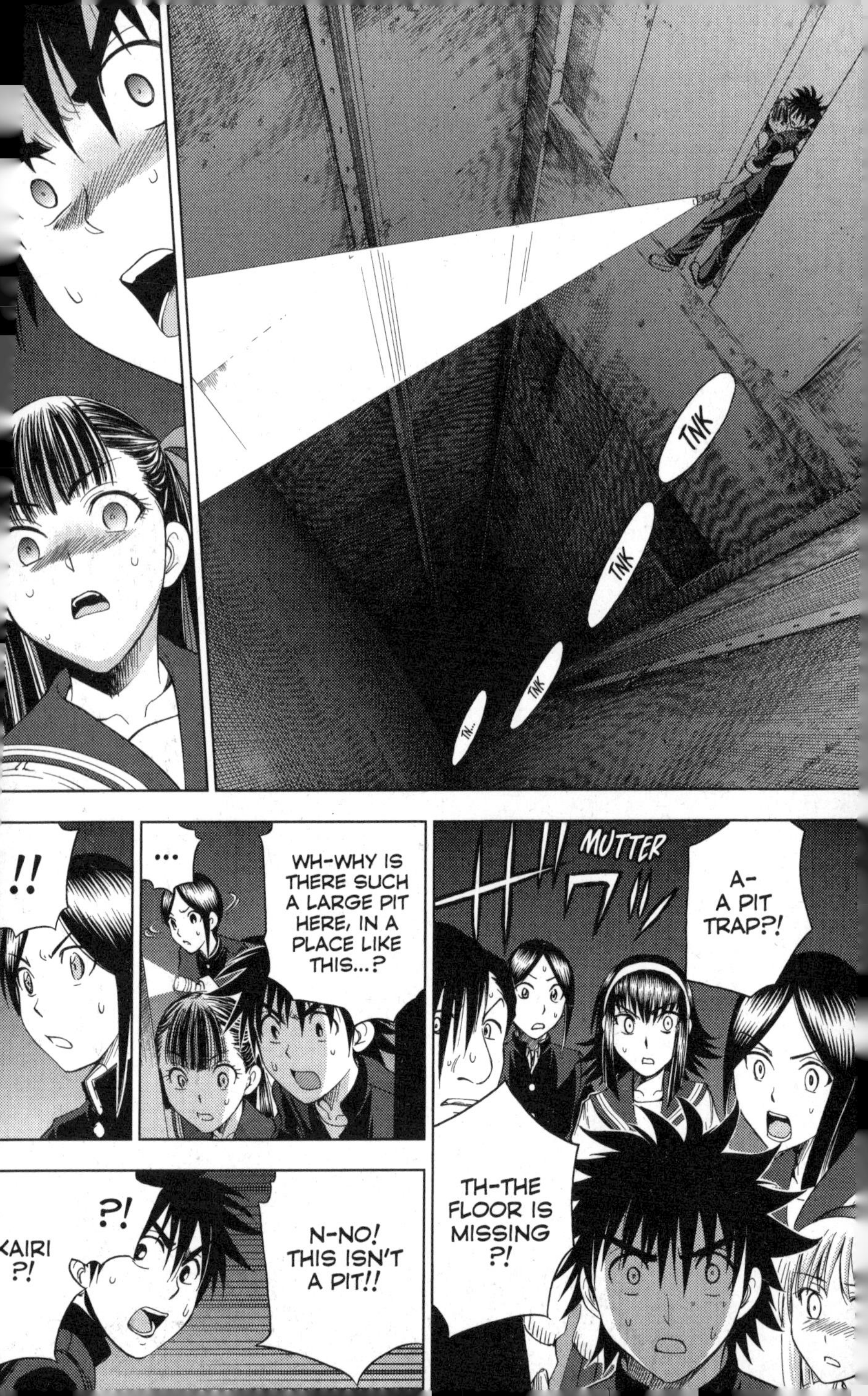
TNK
TNK
TNK
TNK...
A-
A PIT
TRAP?!
MUTTER
TH-THE
FLOOR IS
MISSING
?!
WH-WHY IS
THERE SUCH
A LARGE PIT
HERE, IN A
PLACE LIKE
THIS...?
...
!!
N-NO!
THIS ISN'T
A PIT!!
?!
KAIRI
?!

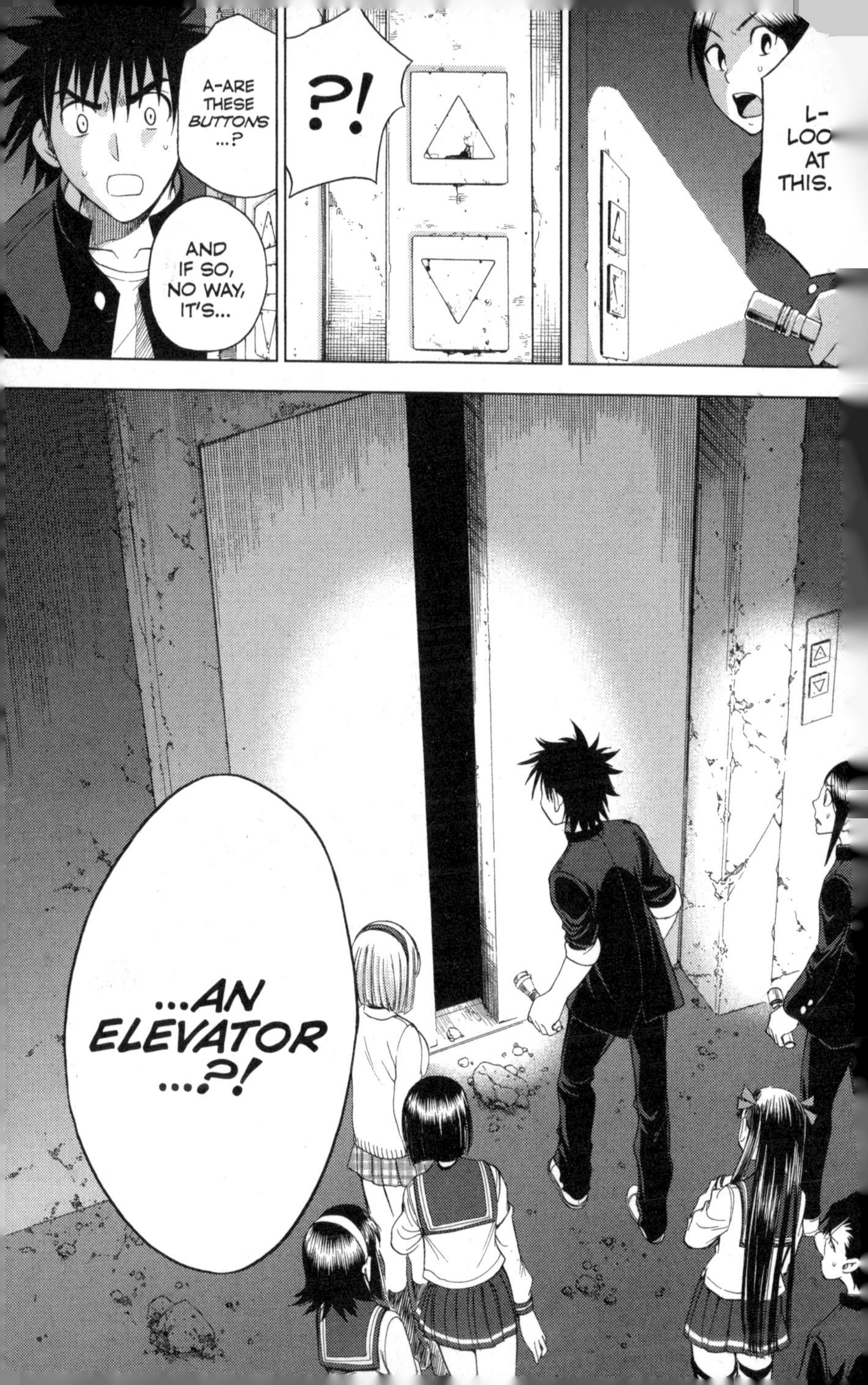
L-LOO[K] AT THIS.
?!
A-ARE THESE *BUTTONS* ...?
AND IF SO, NO WAY, IT'S...
...AN ELEVATOR ...?!

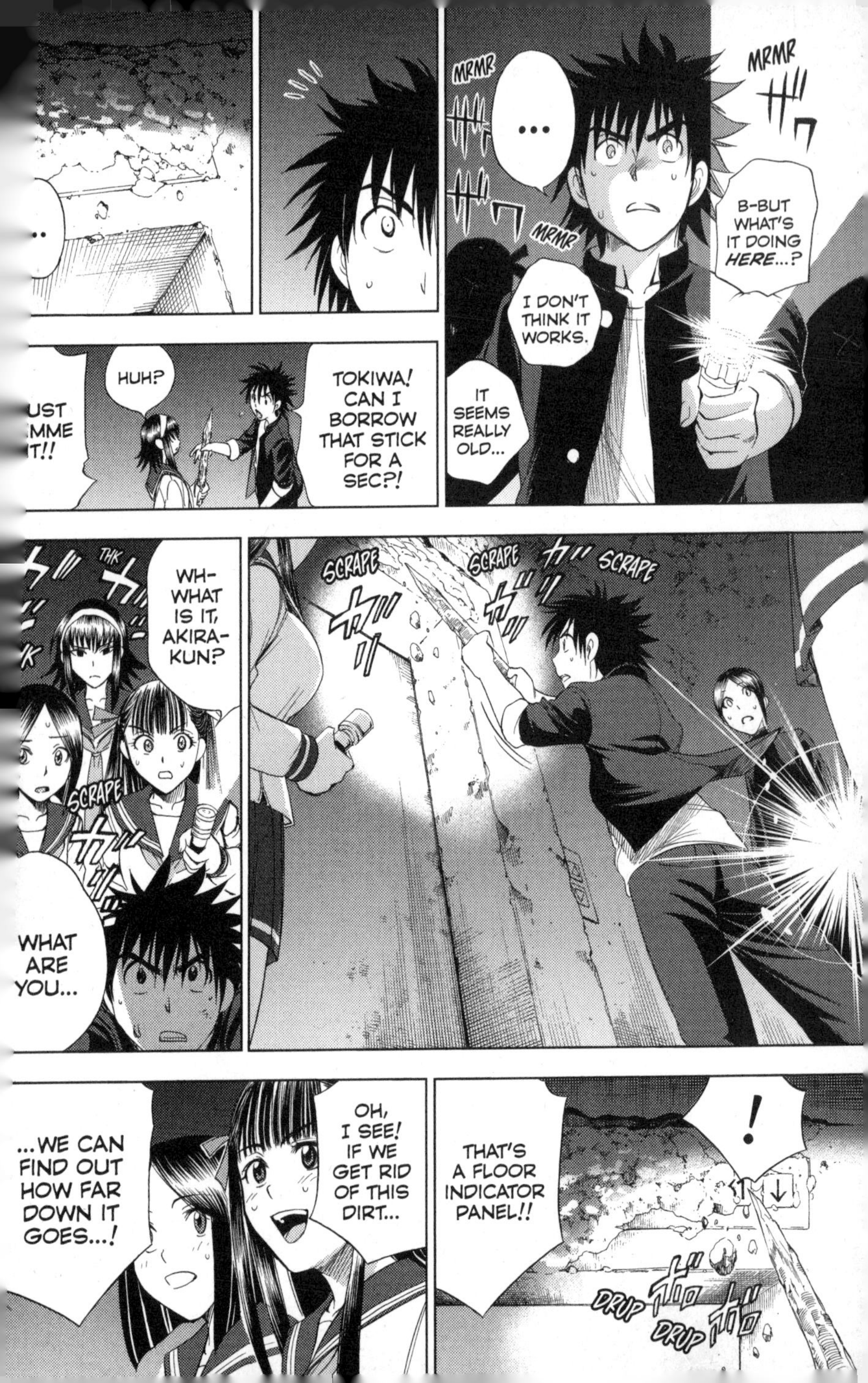
MRMR
B-BUT WHAT'S IT DOING HERE...?
MRMR
...
MRMR
I DON'T THINK IT WORKS.
IT SEEMS REALLY OLD...
...
TOKIWA! CAN I BORROW THAT STICK FOR A SEC?!
HUH?
UST EMME IT!!
SCRAPE
SCRAPE
SCRAPE
THK
WH-WHAT IS IT, AKIRA-KUN?
SCRAPE
WHAT ARE YOU...
!
THAT'S A FLOOR INDICATOR PANEL!!
DRUP
DRUP
OH, I SEE! IF WE GET RID OF THIS DIRT...
...WE CAN FIND OUT HOW FAR DOWN IT GOES...!

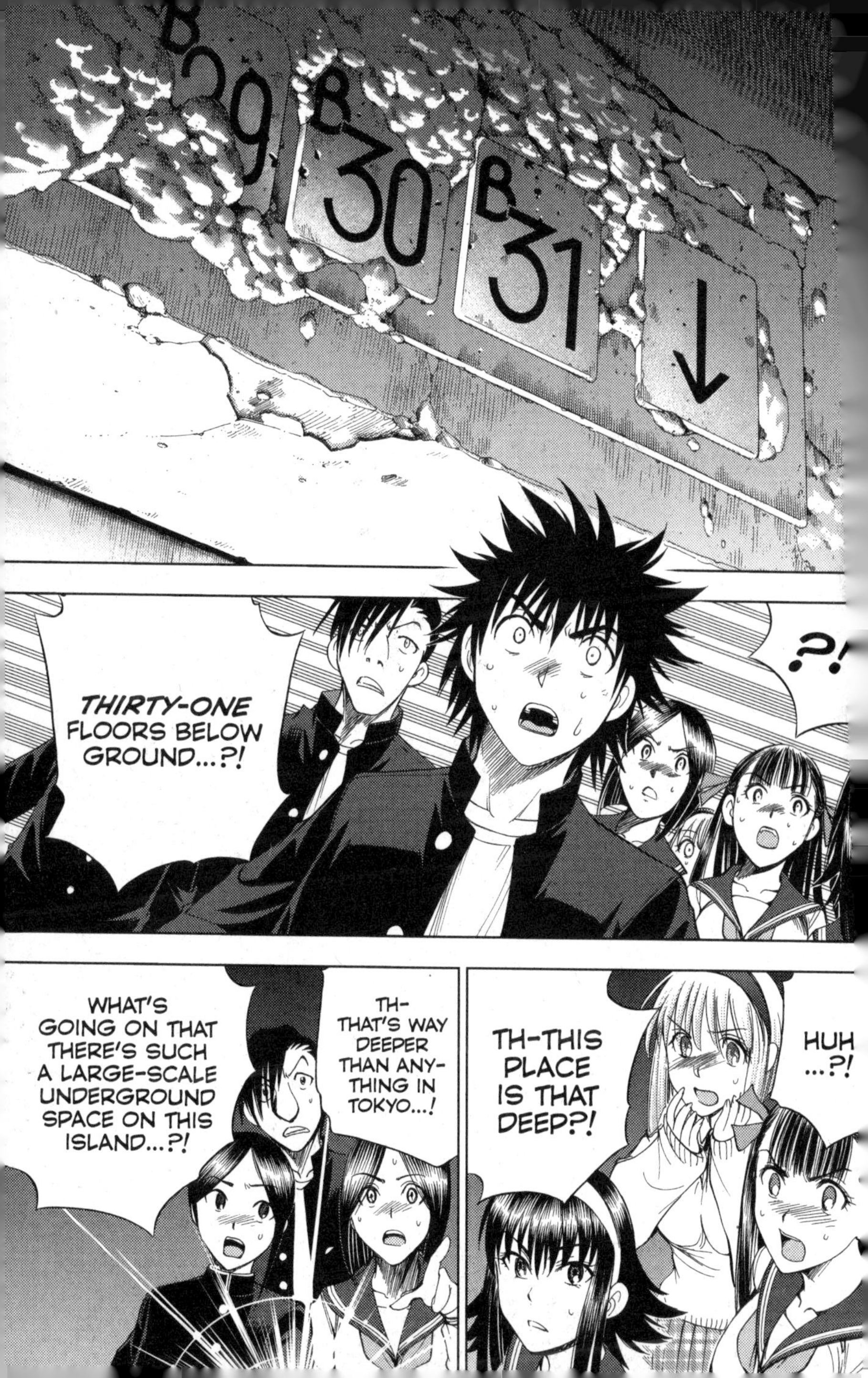
B29
B30
B31
?!
THIRTY-ONE FLOORS BELOW GROUND...?!
HUH ...?!
TH-THIS PLACE IS THAT DEEP?!
TH-THAT'S WAY DEEPER THAN ANYTHING IN TOKYO...!
WHAT'S GOING ON THAT THERE'S SUCH A LARGE-SCALE UNDERGROUND SPACE ON THIS ISLAND...?!

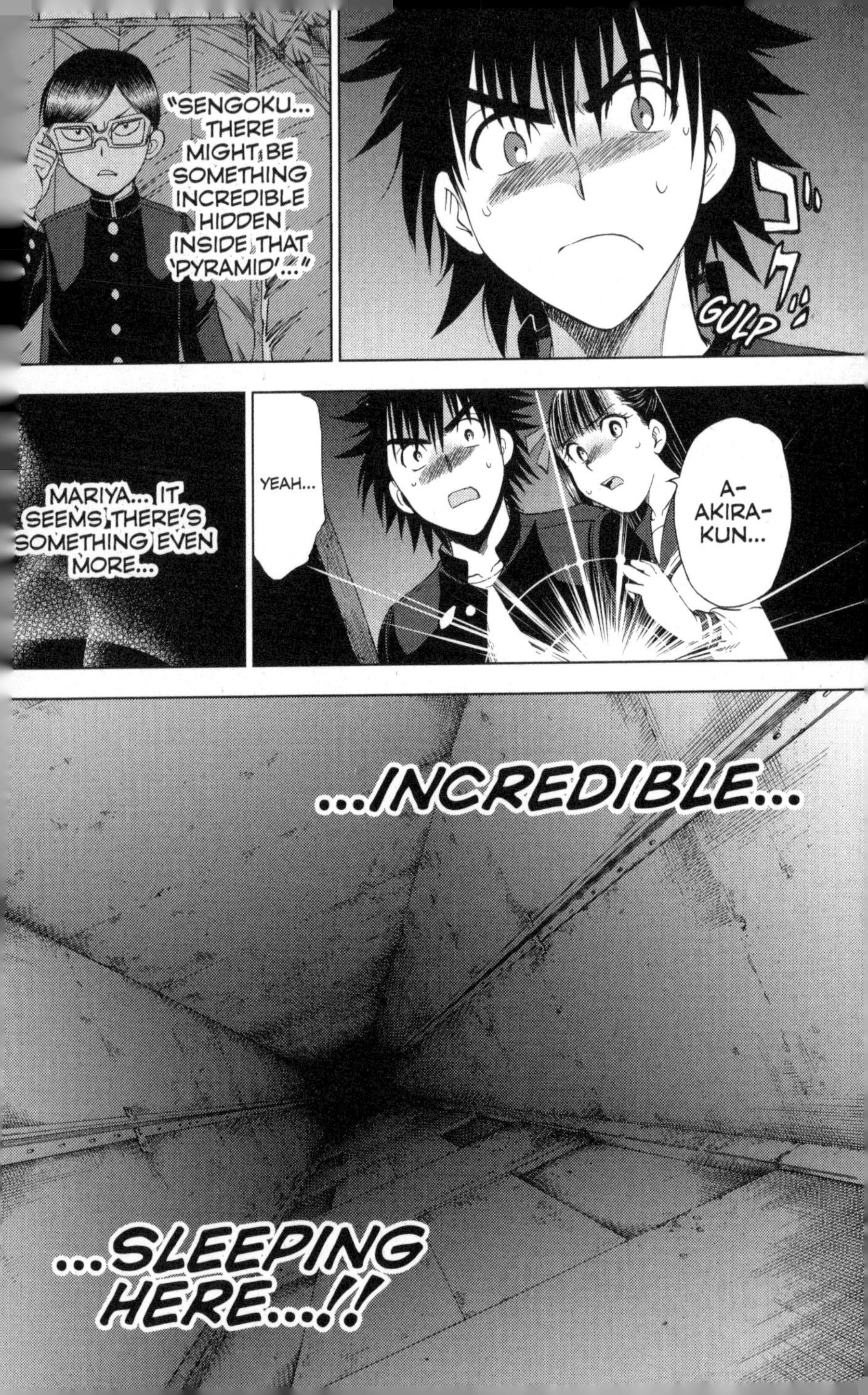
ゴクッ
GULP
"SENGOKU... THERE MIGHT BE SOMETHING INCREDIBLE HIDDEN INSIDE THAT 'PYRAMID'..."
A-AKIRA-KUN...
YEAH...
MARIYA... IT SEEMS THERE'S SOMETHING EVEN MORE...
...INCREDIBLE...
...SLEEPING HERE...!!

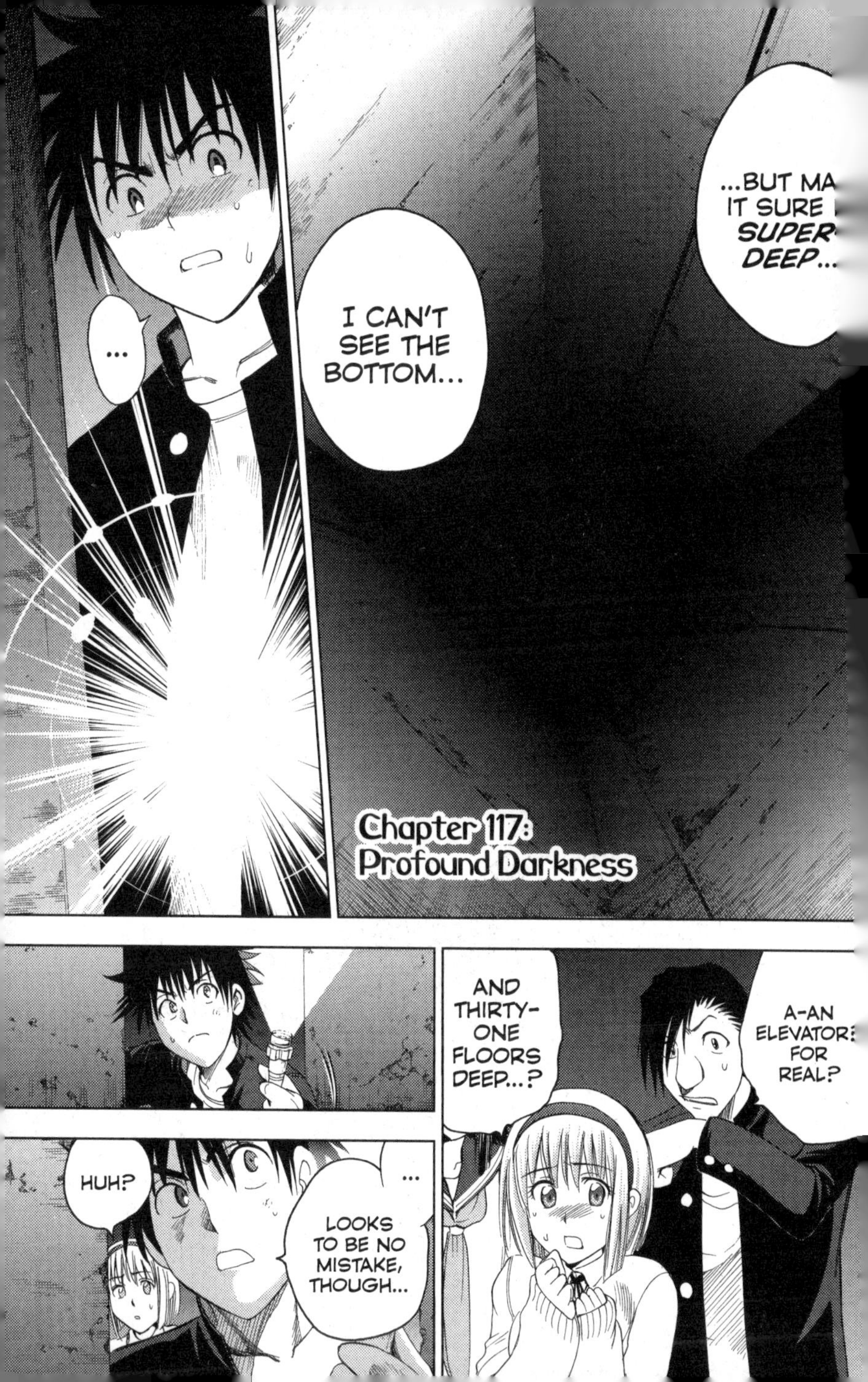
...BUT MA
IT SURE
SUPER
DEEP...
I CAN'T SEE THE BOTTOM...
...
Chapter 117: Profound Darkness
A-AN ELEVATOR? FOR REAL?
AND THIRTY-ONE FLOORS DEEP...?
...
LOOKS TO BE NO MISTAKE, THOUGH...
HUH?

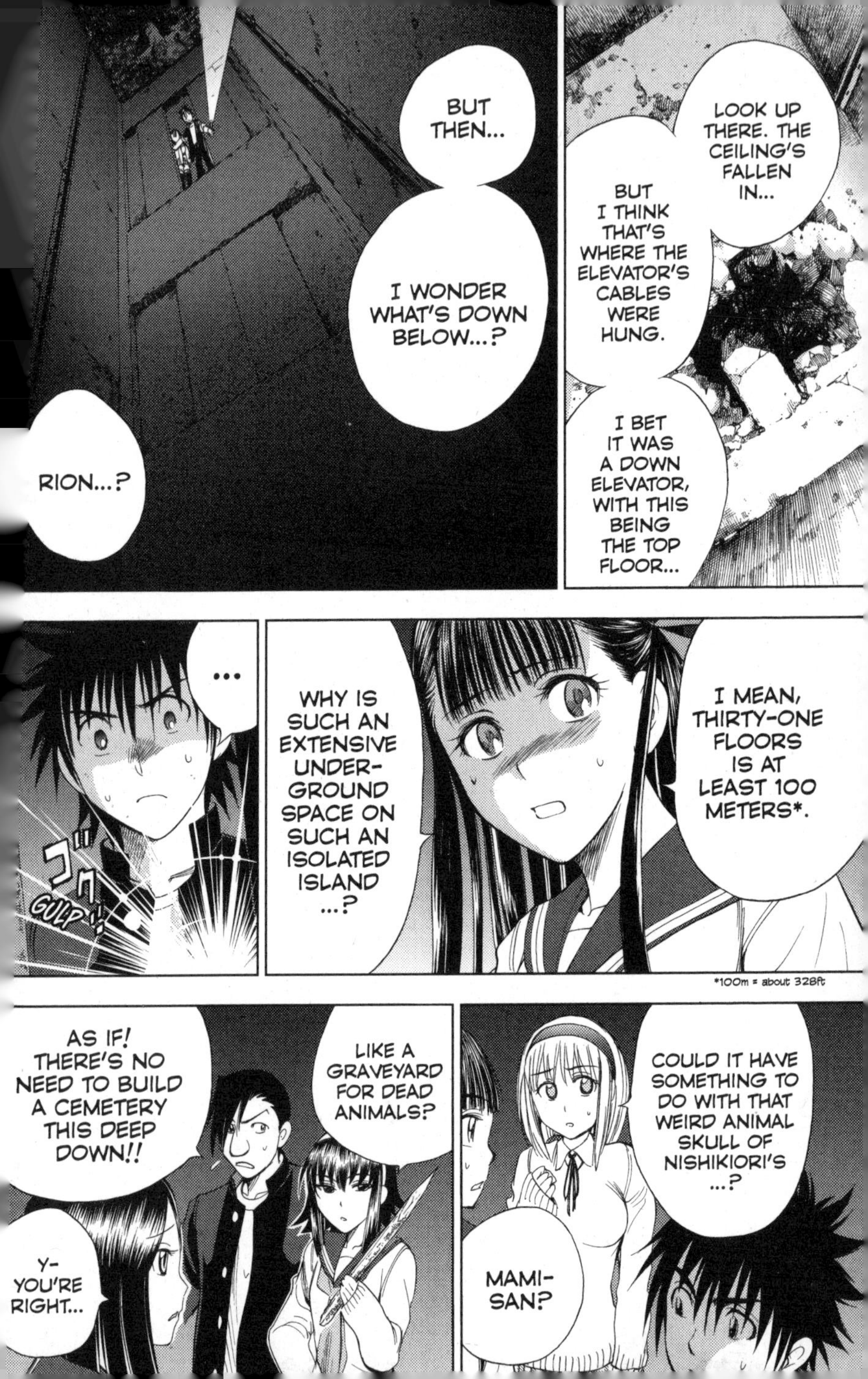
LOOK UP THERE. THE CEILING'S FALLEN IN...
BUT I THINK THAT'S WHERE THE ELEVATOR'S CABLES WERE HUNG.
I BET IT WAS A DOWN ELEVATOR, WITH THIS BEING THE TOP FLOOR...
BUT THEN...
I WONDER WHAT'S DOWN BELOW...?
RION...?
I MEAN, THIRTY-ONE FLOORS IS AT LEAST 100 METERS*.
WHY IS SUCH AN EXTENSIVE UNDER-GROUND SPACE ON SUCH AN ISOLATED ISLAND ...?
...
GULP!!
*100m = about 328ft
COULD IT HAVE SOMETHING TO DO WITH THAT WEIRD ANIMAL SKULL OF NISHIKIORI'S ...?
MAMI-SAN?
LIKE A GRAVEYARD FOR DEAD ANIMALS?
AS IF! THERE'S NO NEED TO BUILD A CEMETERY THIS DEEP DOWN!!
Y-YOU'RE RIGHT...

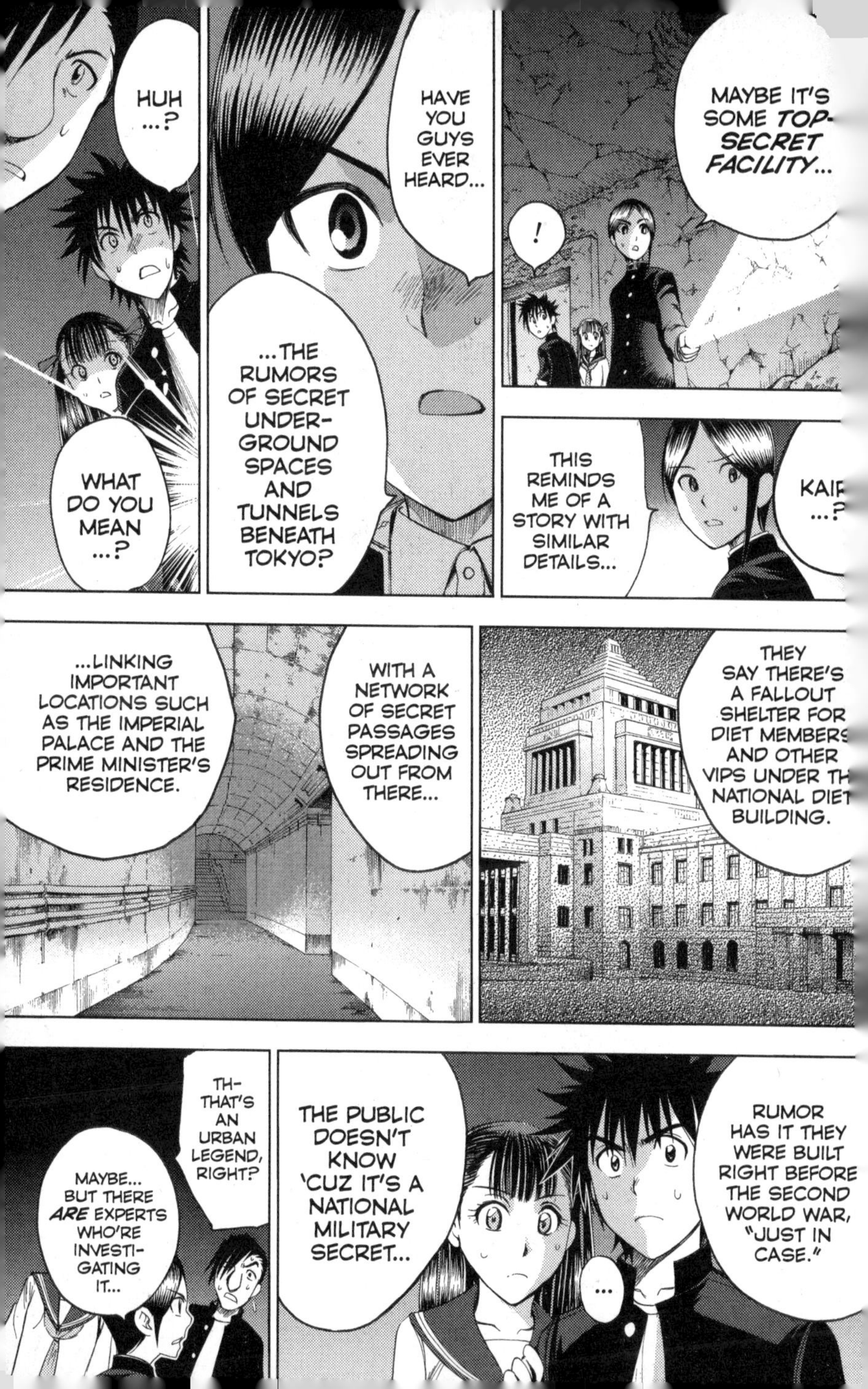
MAYBE IT'S SOME TOP-SECRET FACILITY...
!
KAIR ...?
THIS REMINDS ME OF A STORY WITH SIMILAR DETAILS...
HAVE YOU GUYS EVER HEARD...
...THE RUMORS OF SECRET UNDERGROUND SPACES AND TUNNELS BENEATH TOKYO?
HUH ...?
WHAT DO YOU MEAN ...?
THEY SAY THERE'S A FALLOUT SHELTER FOR DIET MEMBERS AND OTHER VIPS UNDER TH NATIONAL DIET BUILDING.
WITH A NETWORK OF SECRET PASSAGES SPREADING OUT FROM THERE...
...LINKING IMPORTANT LOCATIONS SUCH AS THE IMPERIAL PALACE AND THE PRIME MINISTER'S RESIDENCE.
RUMOR HAS IT THEY WERE BUILT RIGHT BEFORE THE SECOND WORLD WAR, "JUST IN CASE."
THE PUBLIC DOESN'T KNOW 'CUZ IT'S A NATIONAL MILITARY SECRET...
...
TH-THAT'S AN URBAN LEGEND, RIGHT?
MAYBE... BUT THERE ARE EXPERTS WHO'RE INVESTIGATING IT...

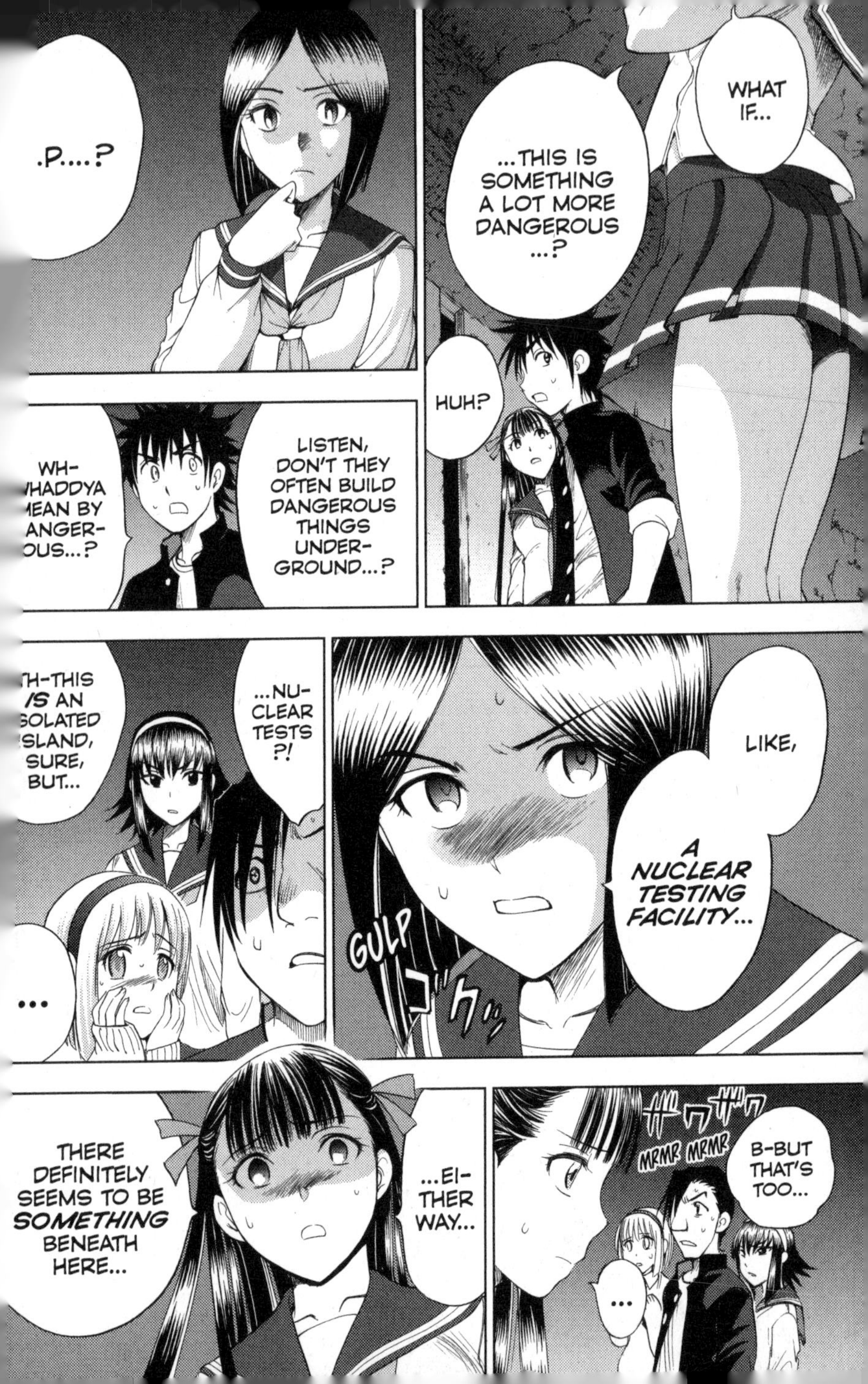
WHAT IF...
...THIS IS SOMETHING A LOT MORE DANGEROUS ...?
HUH?
.P....?
LISTEN, DON'T THEY OFTEN BUILD DANGEROUS THINGS UNDER-GROUND...?
WH- HADDYA IEAN BY ANGER- OUS...?
LIKE,
A NUCLEAR TESTING FACILITY...
GULP
ゴクッ
...NU-CLEAR TESTS?!
H-THIS IS AN SOLATED SLAND, SURE, BUT...
...
ザワザワ
MRMR MRMR
B-BUT THAT'S TOO...
...
...EI-THER WAY...
THERE DEFINITELY SEEMS TO BE SOMETHING BENEATH HERE...

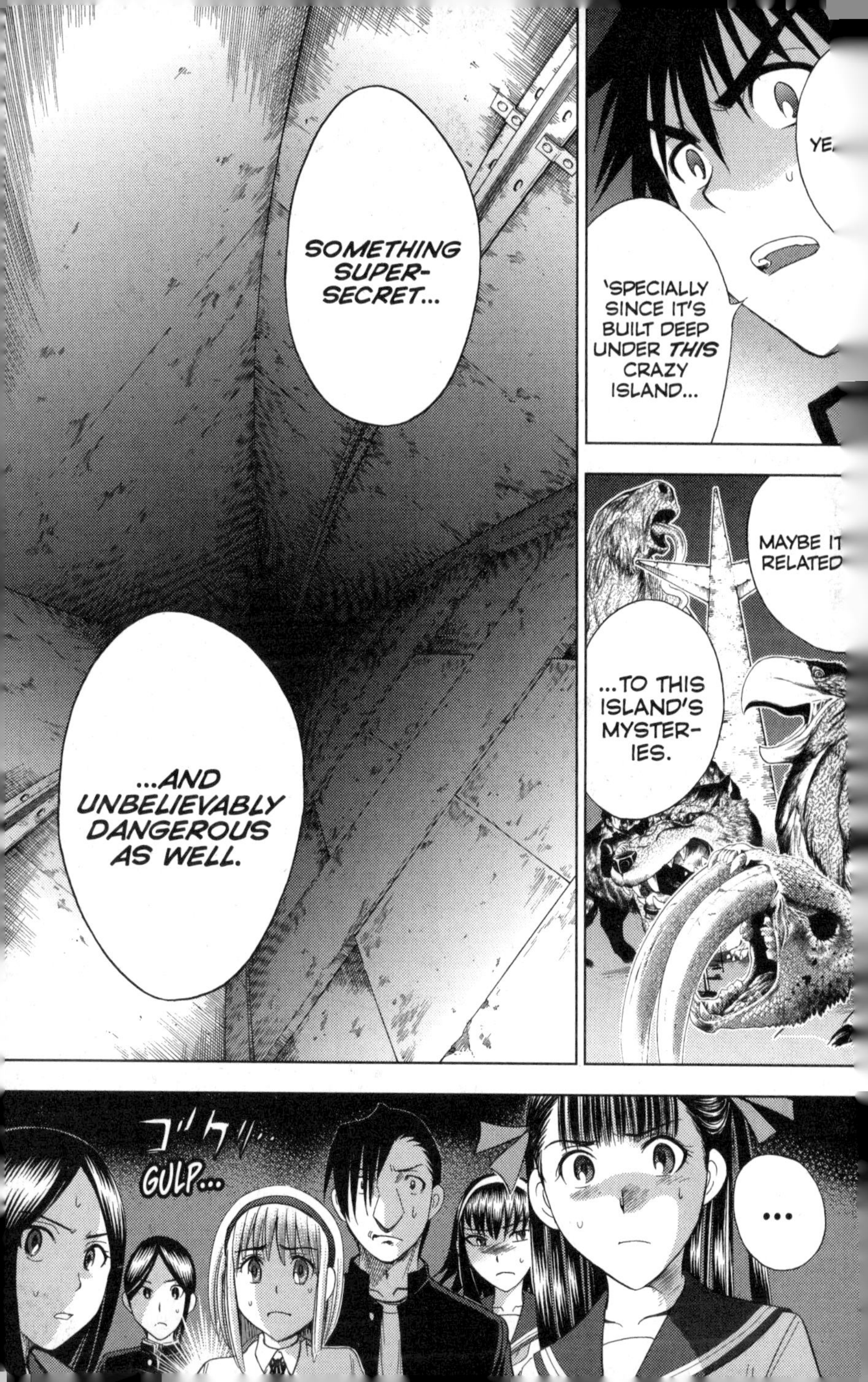
YE
'SPECIALLY SINCE IT'S BUILT DEEP UNDER *THIS* CRAZY ISLAND...
MAYBE IT RELATED
...TO THIS ISLAND'S MYSTER-IES.
SOMETHING SUPER-SECRET...
...AND UNBELIEVABLY DANGEROUS AS WELL.
...
ゴクッ…
GULP...

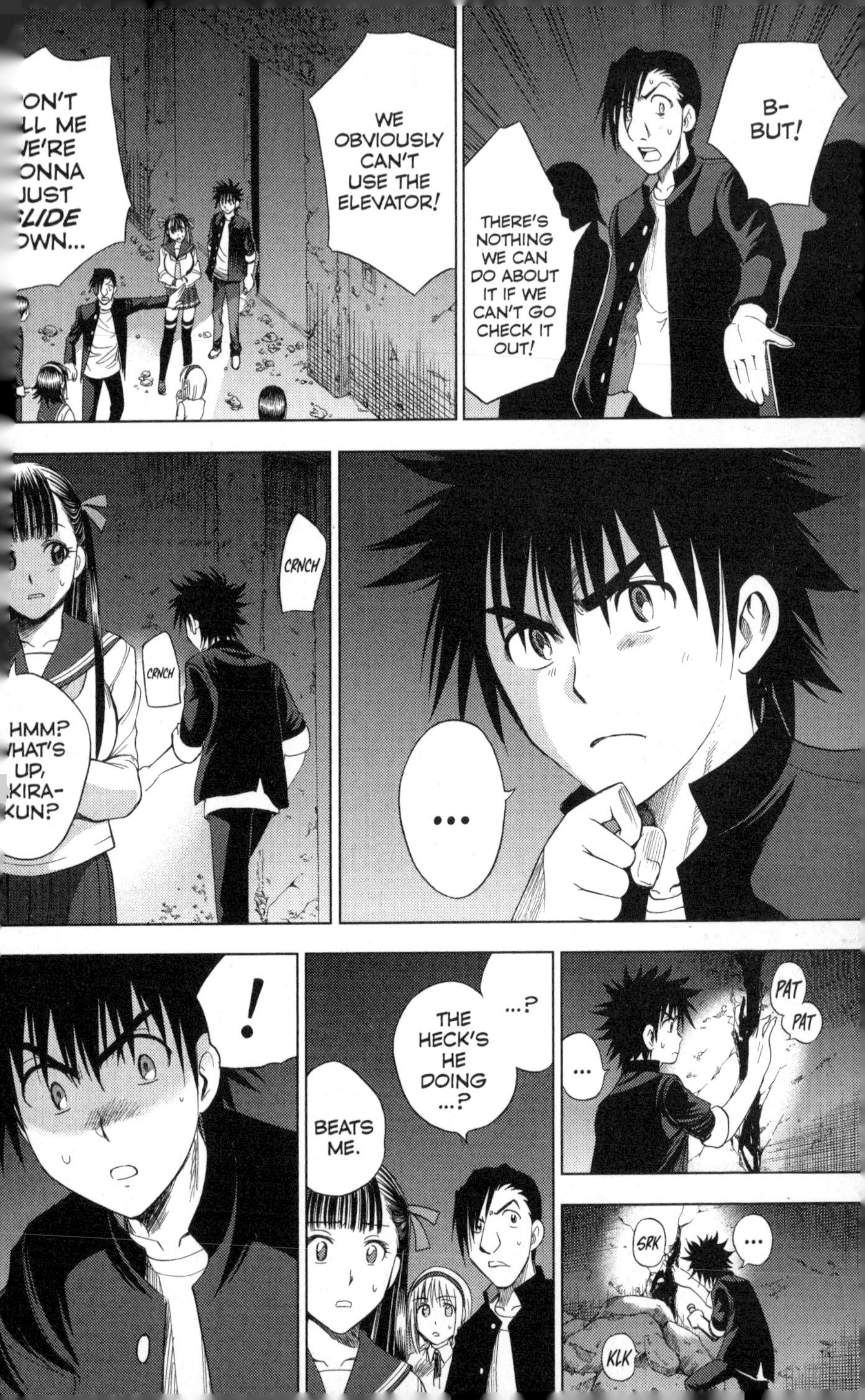
B- BUT!
THERE'S NOTHING WE CAN DO ABOUT IT IF WE CAN'T GO CHECK IT OUT!
WE OBVIOUSLY CAN'T USE THE ELEVATOR!
ON'T LL ME E'RE ONNA JUST *SLIDE* OWN...
...
CRNCH
CRNCH
HMM? HAT'S UP, KIRA-KUN?
PAT
PAT
...
...
SRK
KLK
...?
THE HECK'S HE DOING ...?
BEATS ME.
!

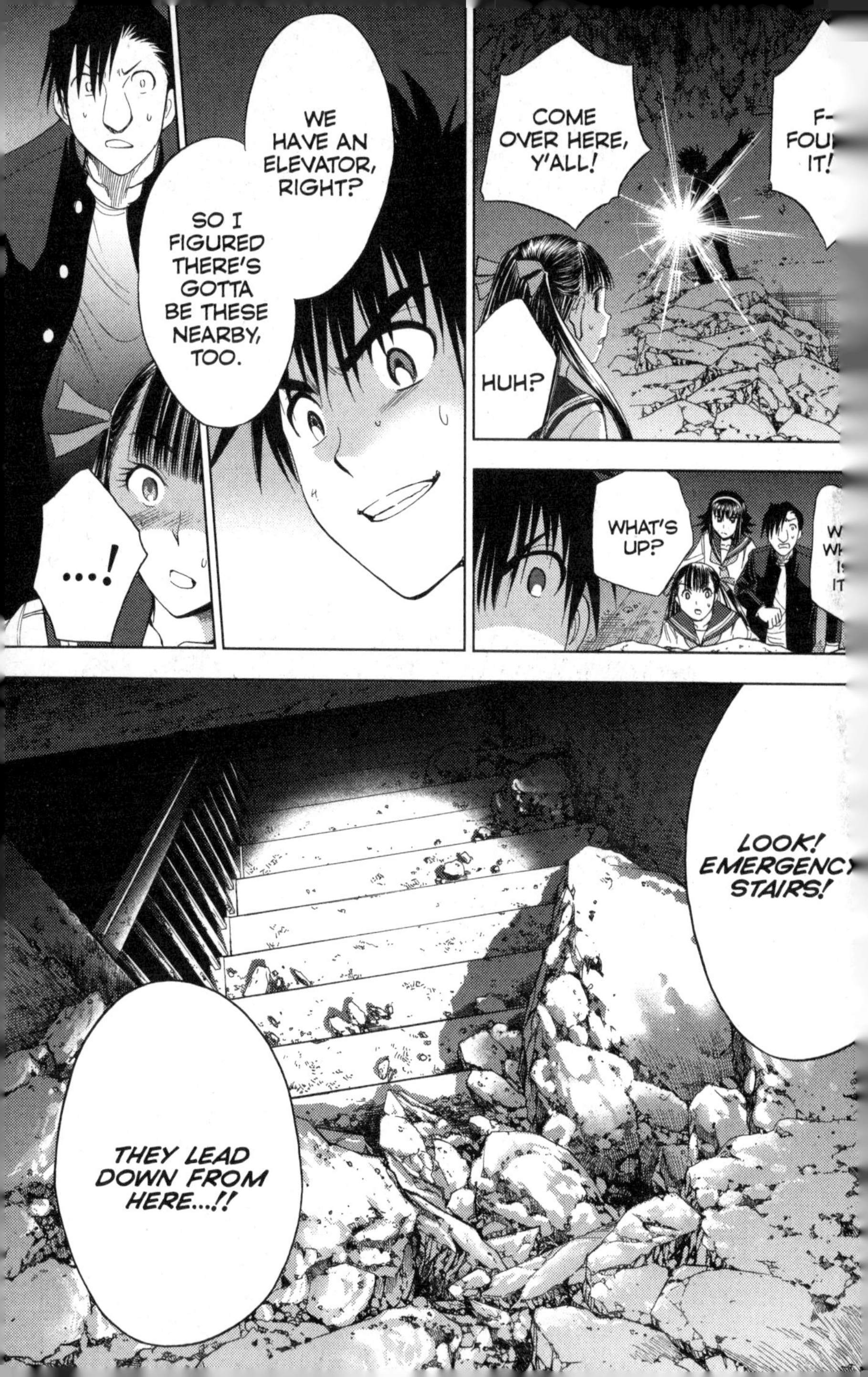
F- FOU IT!
COME OVER HERE, Y'ALL!
HUH?
W WH IS IT
WHAT'S UP?
WE HAVE AN ELEVATOR, RIGHT?
SO I FIGURED THERE'S GOTTA BE THESE NEARBY, TOO.
...!
LOOK! EMERGENCY STAIRS!
THEY LEAD DOWN FROM HERE...!!

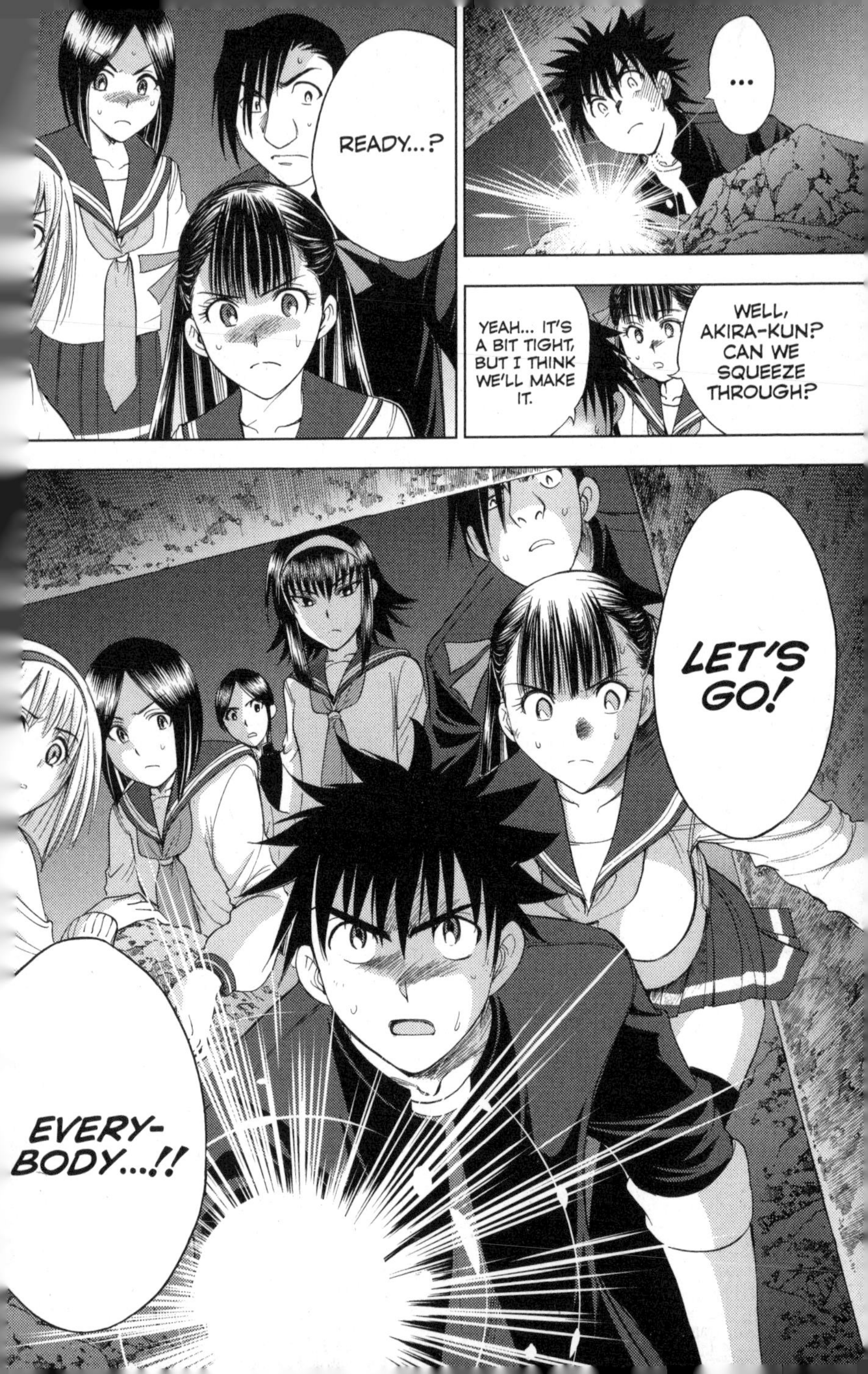
...
WELL, AKIRA-KUN? CAN WE SQUEEZE THROUGH?
YEAH... IT'S A BIT TIGHT, BUT I THINK WE'LL MAKE IT.
READY...?
LET'S GO!
EVERY-BODY...!!

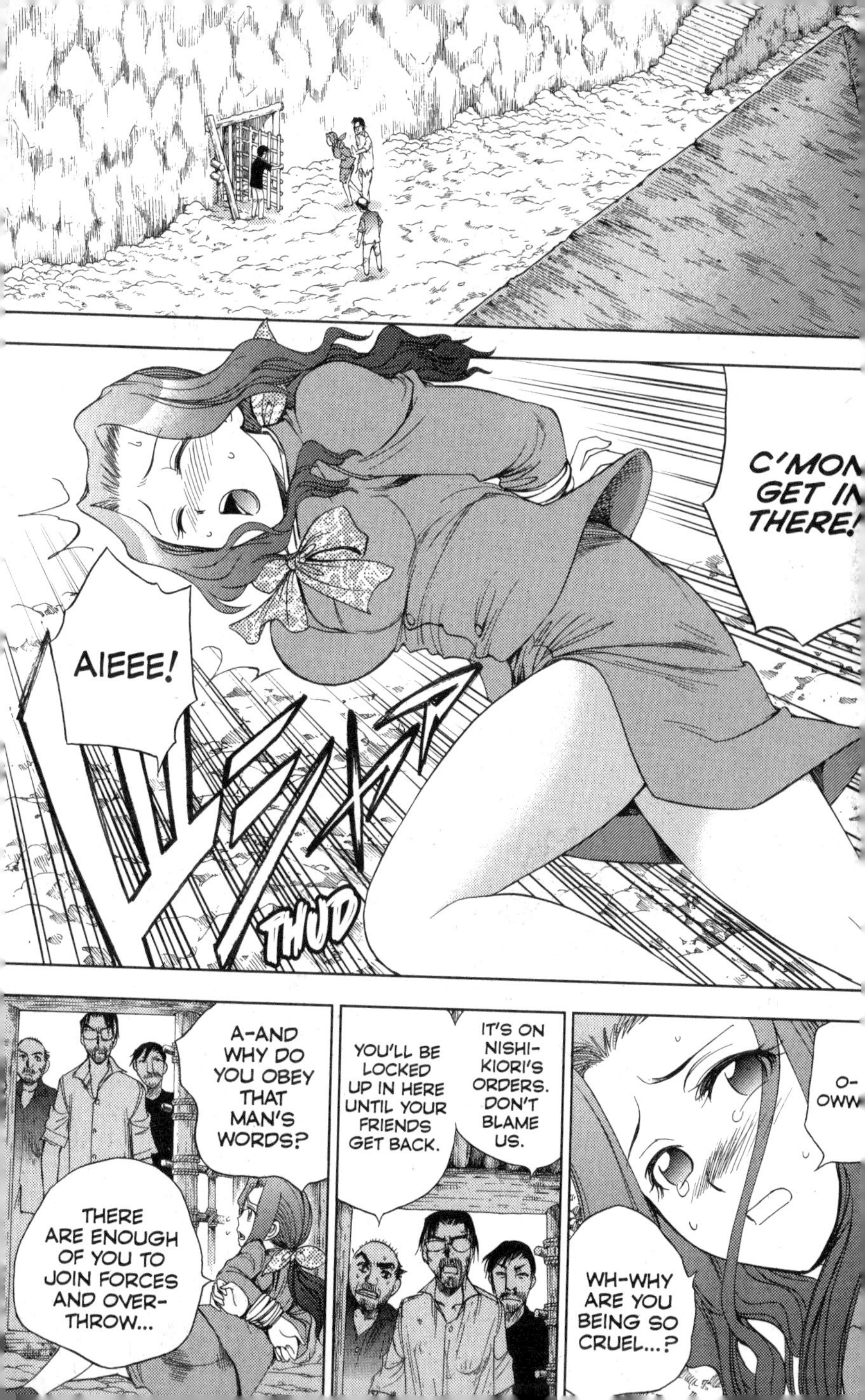
C'MON GET IN THERE!
AIEEE!
WHAM
THUD
O-OWW
WH-WHY ARE YOU BEING SO CRUEL...?
IT'S ON NISHI-KIORI'S ORDERS. DON'T BLAME US.
YOU'LL BE LOCKED UP IN HERE UNTIL YOUR FRIENDS GET BACK.
A-AND WHY DO YOU OBEY THAT MAN'S WORDS?
THERE ARE ENOUGH OF YOU TO JOIN FORCES AND OVER-THROW...

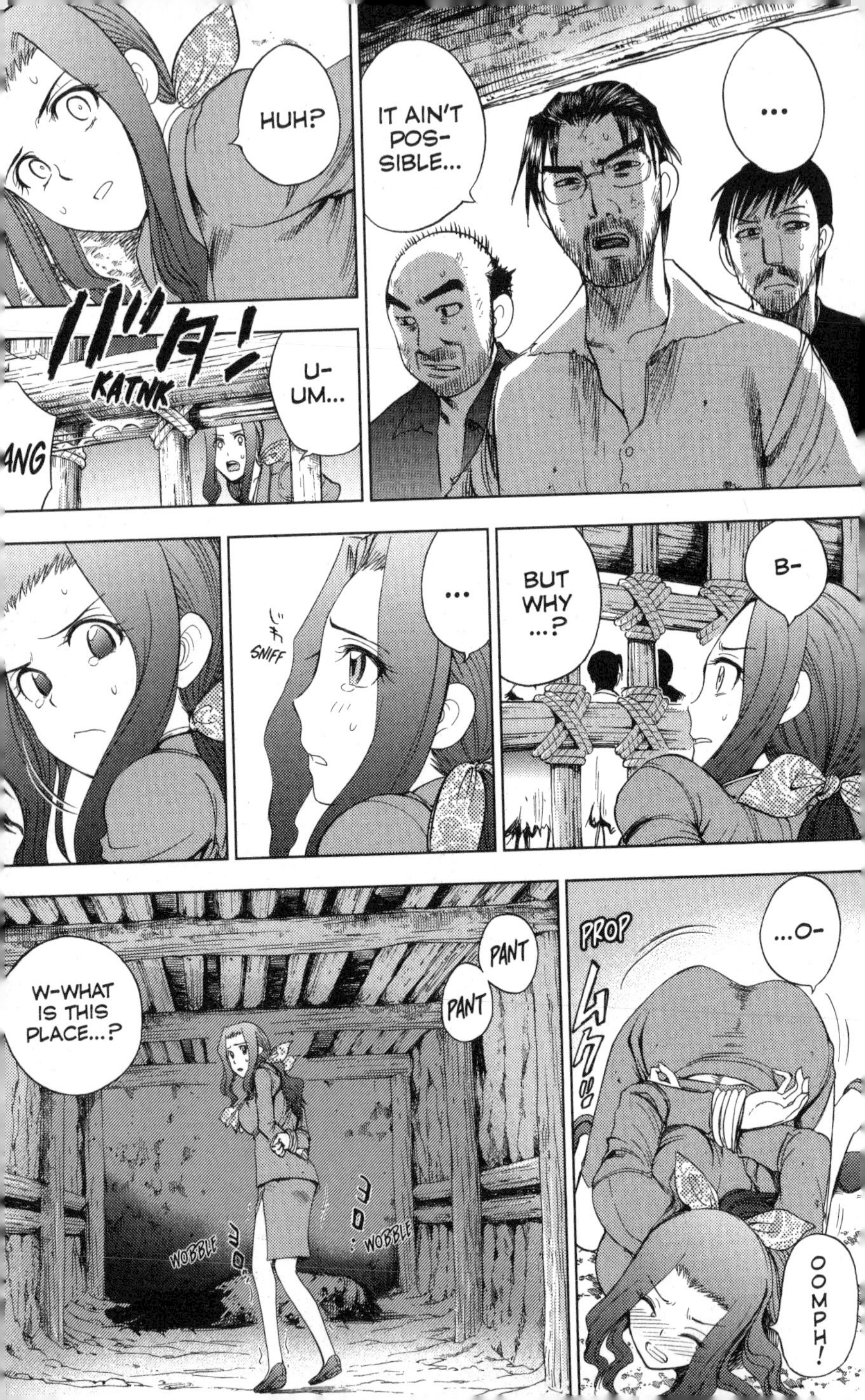
...
IT AIN'T POS-SIBLE...
HUH?
バタン!
KATNK
ANG
U-UM...
B-
BUT WHY ...?
...
じわ
SNIFF
...O-
PROP
ムクッ
OOMPH!
PANT
PANT
W-WHAT IS THIS PLACE...?
ヨロ…
WOBBLE
ヨロ…
WOBBLE

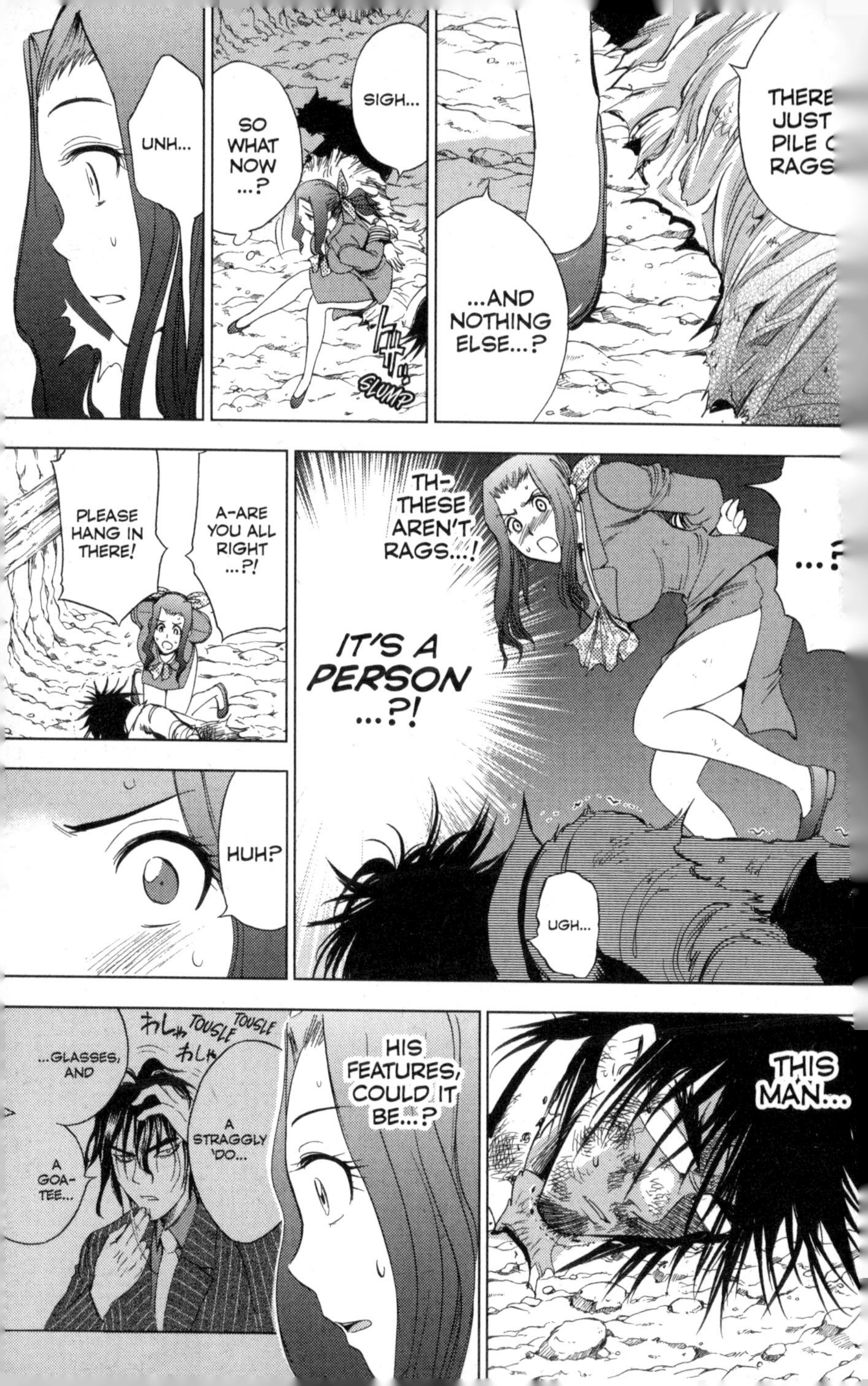
THERE JUST PILE O RAGS
SIGH...
...AND NOTHING ELSE...?
SO WHAT NOW ...?
SLUMP
UNH...
...?
TH-THESE AREN'T RAGS...!
IT'S A PERSON ...?!
UGH...
A-ARE YOU ALL RIGHT ...?!
PLEASE HANG IN THERE!
HUH?
THIS MAN...
HIS FEATURES, COULD IT BE...?
わしゃ TOUSLE
わしゃ TOUSLE
A STRAGGLY 'DO...
...GLASSES, AND
A GOA-TEE...

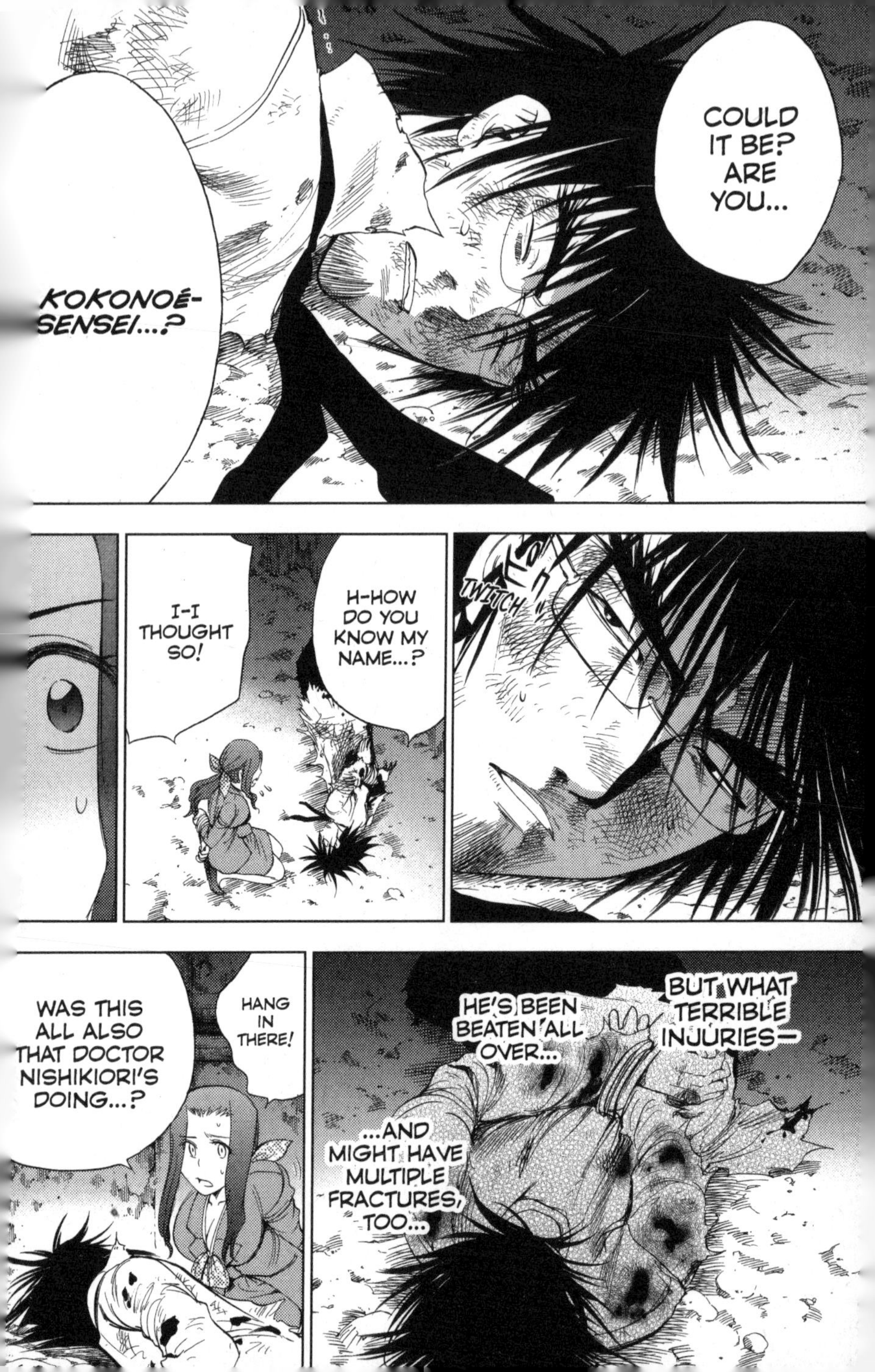
COULD IT BE? ARE YOU...
KOKONOÉ-SENSEI...?
TWITCH
H-HOW DO YOU KNOW MY NAME...?
I-I THOUGHT SO!
BUT WHAT TERRIBLE INJURIES—
HE'S BEEN BEATEN ALL OVER...
...AND MIGHT HAVE MULTIPLE FRACTURES, TOO...
HANG IN THERE!
WAS THIS ALL ALSO THAT DOCTOR NISHIKIORI'S DOING...?

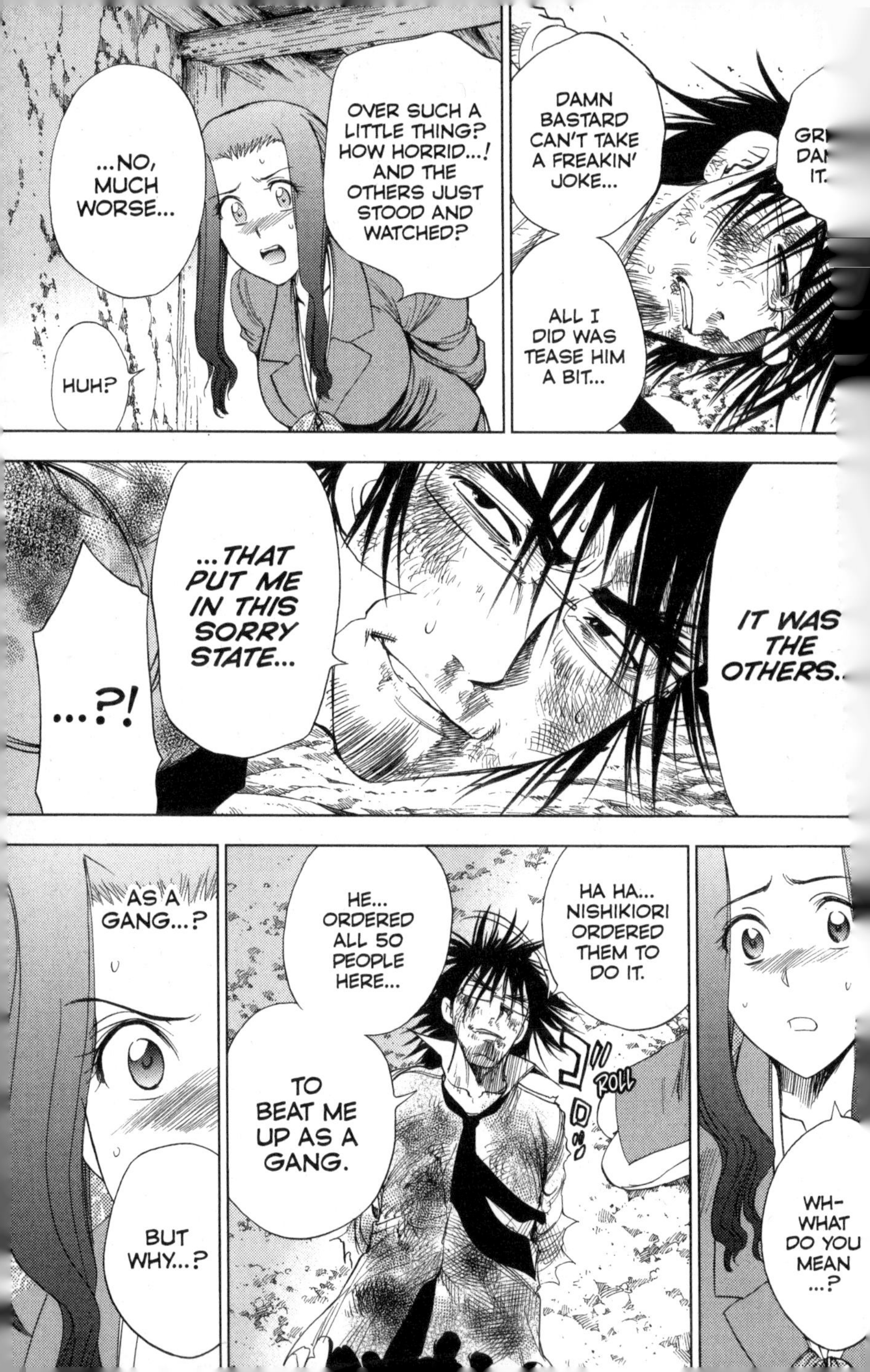
DAMN BASTARD CAN'T TAKE A FREAKIN' JOKE...
ALL I DID WAS TEASE HIM A BIT...
OVER SUCH A LITTLE THING? HOW HORRID...! AND THE OTHERS JUST STOOD AND WATCHED?
...NO, MUCH WORSE...
HUH?
IT WAS THE OTHERS..
...THAT PUT ME IN THIS SORRY STATE...
...?!
WH-WHAT DO YOU MEAN ...?
HA HA... NISHIKIORI ORDERED THEM TO DO IT.
HE... ORDERED ALL 50 PEOPLE HERE...
TO BEAT ME UP AS A GANG.
ROLL
AS A GANG...?
BUT WHY...?

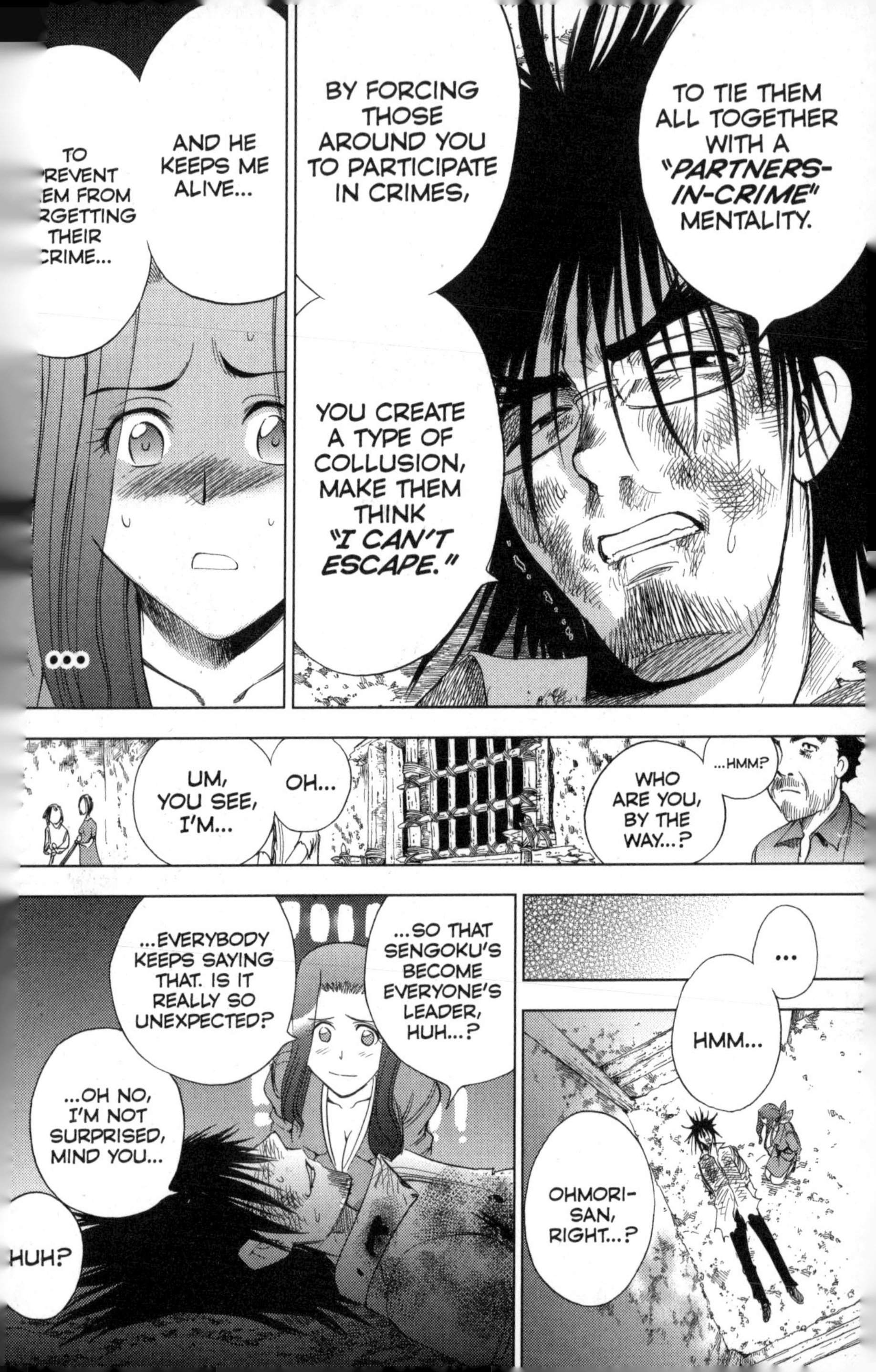
TO TIE THEM ALL TOGETHER WITH A "PARTNERS-IN-CRIME" MENTALITY.
BY FORCING THOSE AROUND YOU TO PARTICIPATE IN CRIMES,
YOU CREATE A TYPE OF COLLUSION, MAKE THEM THINK "I CAN'T ESCAPE."
AND HE KEEPS ME ALIVE...
TO REVENT EM FROM RGETTING THEIR CRIME...
...HMM?
WHO ARE YOU, BY THE WAY...?
OH...
UM, YOU SEE, I'M...
...
HMM...
OHMORI-SAN, RIGHT...?
...SO THAT SENGOKU'S BECOME EVERYONE'S LEADER, HUH...?
...EVERYBODY KEEPS SAYING THAT. IS IT REALLY SO UNEXPECTED?
...OH NO, I'M NOT SURPRISED, MIND YOU...
HUH?

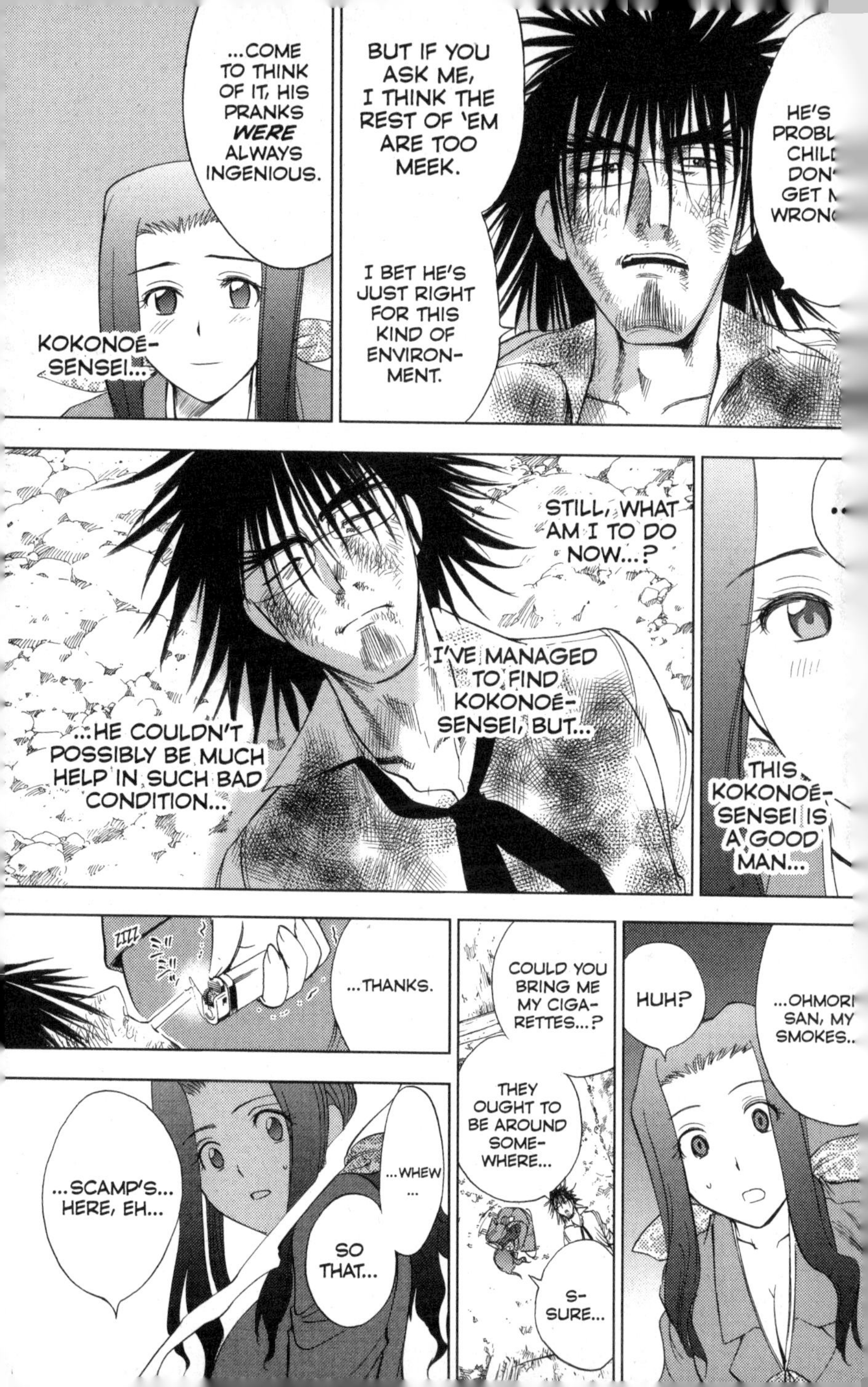
HE'S PROBL CHILD DON' GET M WRONG
BUT IF YOU ASK ME, I THINK THE REST OF 'EM ARE TOO MEEK.
I BET HE'S JUST RIGHT FOR THIS KIND OF ENVIRON-MENT.
...COME TO THINK OF IT, HIS PRANKS *WERE* ALWAYS INGENIOUS.
KOKONOE-SENSEI...
THIS KOKONOE-SENSEI IS A GOOD MAN...
STILL, WHAT AM I TO DO NOW...?
I'VE MANAGED TO FIND KOKONOE-SENSEI, BUT...
...HE COULDN'T POSSIBLY BE MUCH HELP IN SUCH BAD CONDITION...
...OHMORI SAN, MY SMOKES...
HUH?
COULD YOU BRING ME MY CIGA-RETTES...?
THEY OUGHT TO BE AROUND SOME-WHERE...
S-SURE...
ZIII
...THANKS.
...WHEW...
SO THAT...
...SCAMP'S... HERE, EH...

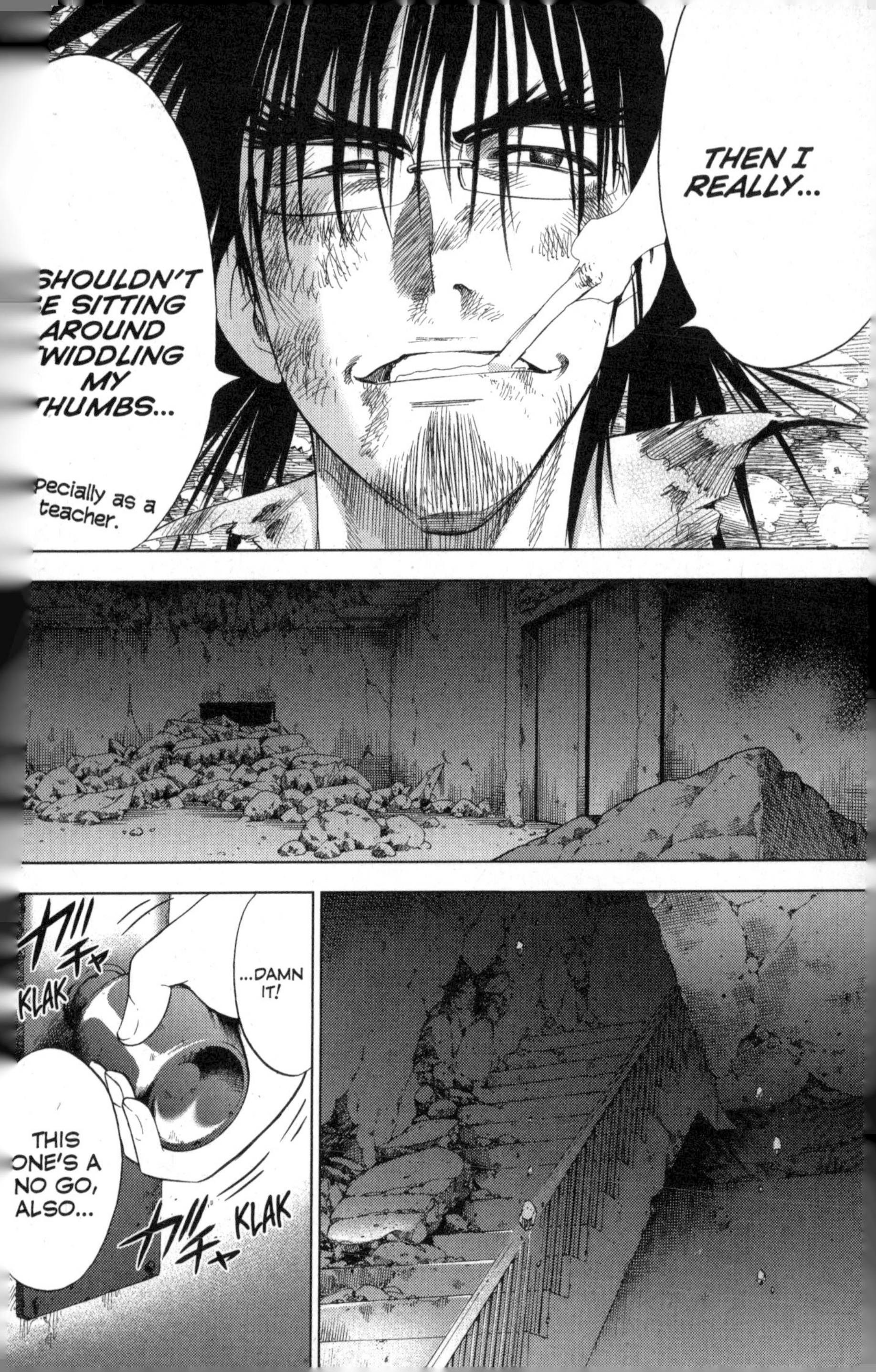
THEN I REALLY...
SHOULDN'T E SITTING AROUND WIDDLING MY THUMBS...
pecially as a teacher.
...DAMN IT!
ガチャ
KLAK
THIS ONE'S A NO GO, ALSO...
ガチャ
KLAK

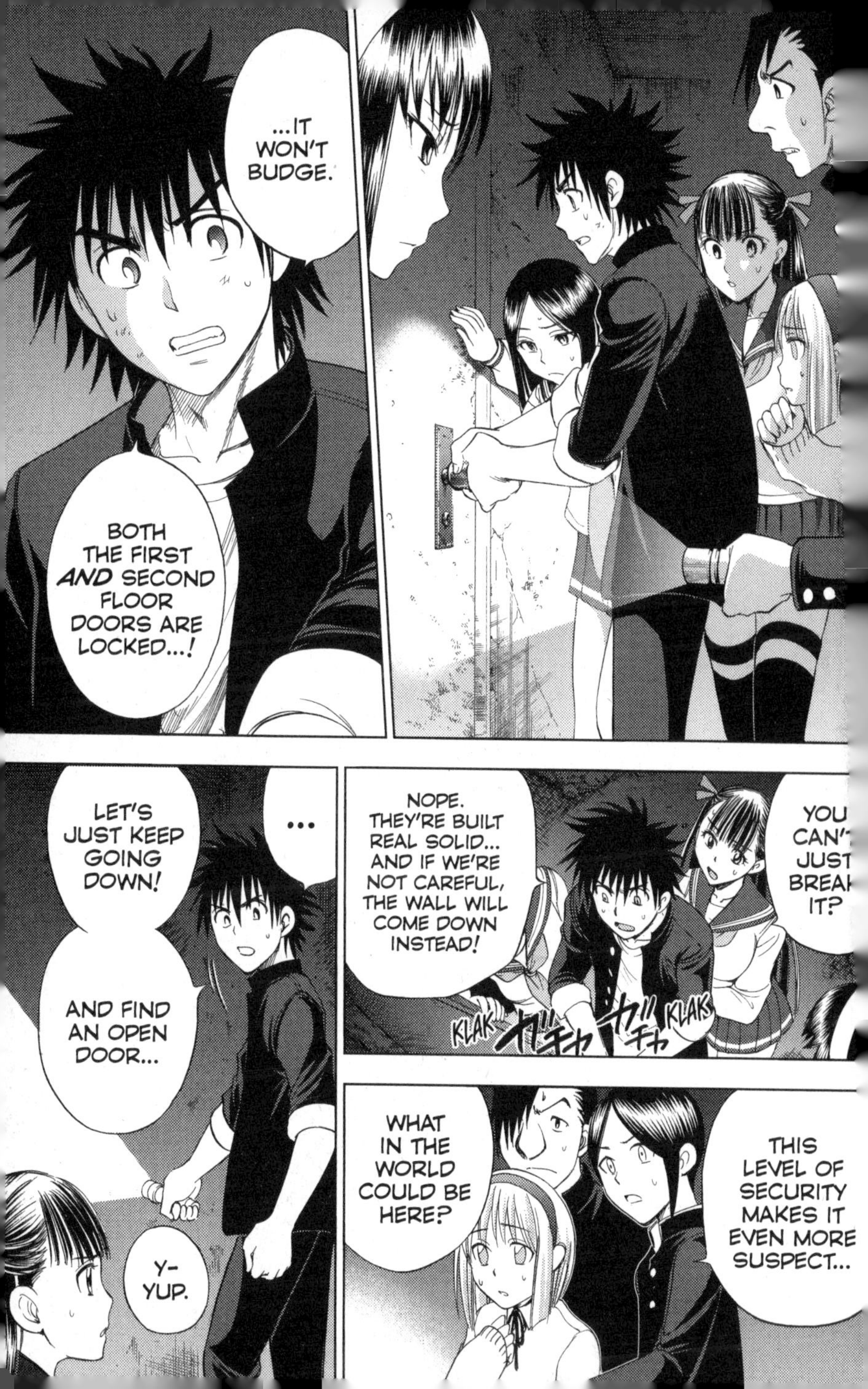
...IT WON'T BUDGE.
BOTH THE FIRST *AND* SECOND FLOOR DOORS ARE LOCKED...!
YOU CAN'T JUST BREAK IT?
NOPE. THEY'RE BUILT REAL SOLID... AND IF WE'RE NOT CAREFUL, THE WALL WILL COME DOWN INSTEAD!
KLAKS
ガチャ
ガチャ
KLAK
THIS LEVEL OF SECURITY MAKES IT EVEN MORE SUSPECT...
WHAT IN THE WORLD COULD BE HERE?
...
LET'S JUST KEEP GOING DOWN!
AND FIND AN OPEN DOOR...
Y- YUP.

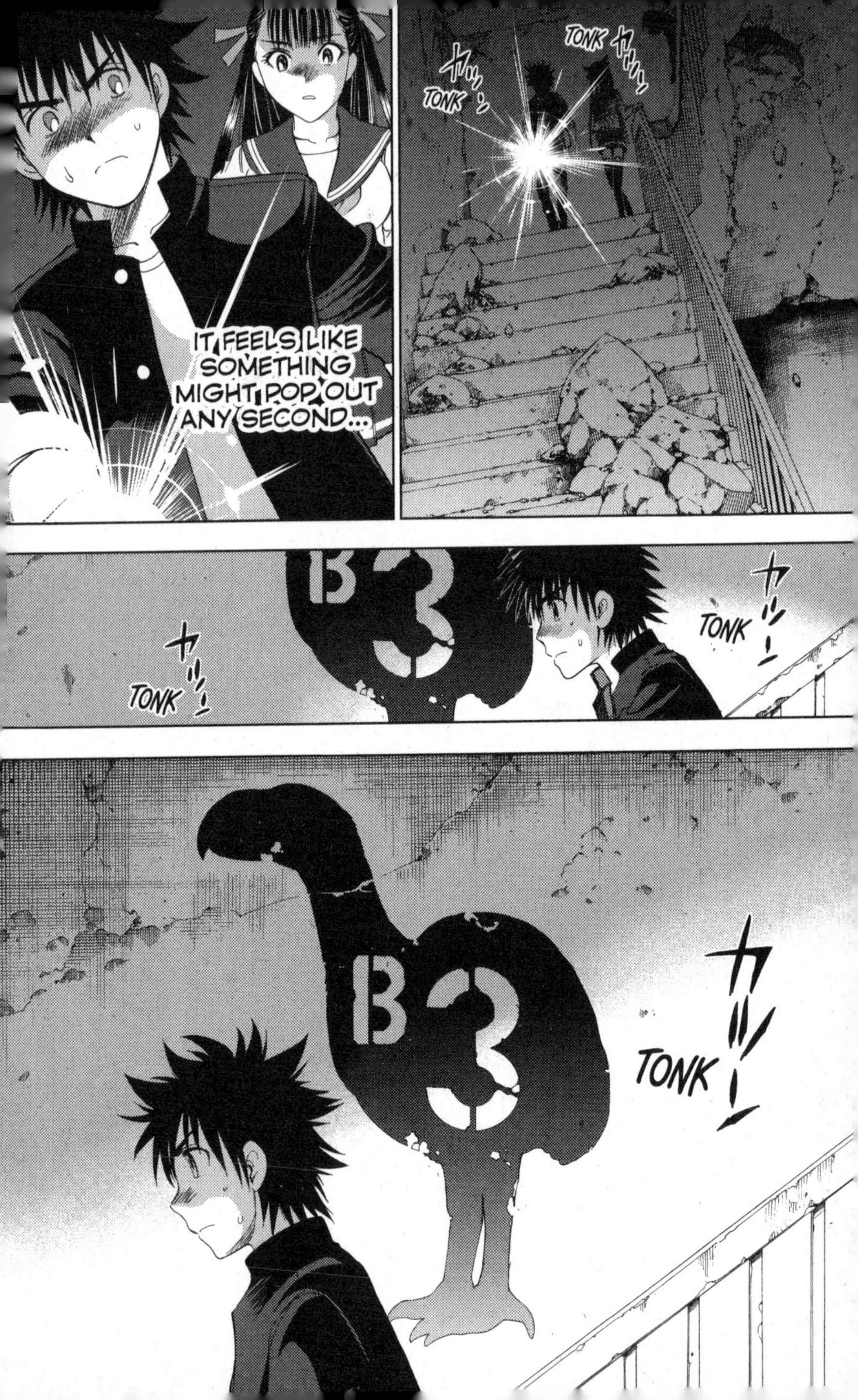
TONK
TONK
IT FEELS LIKE SOMETHING MIGHT POP OUT ANY SECOND...
TONK
TONK
TONK

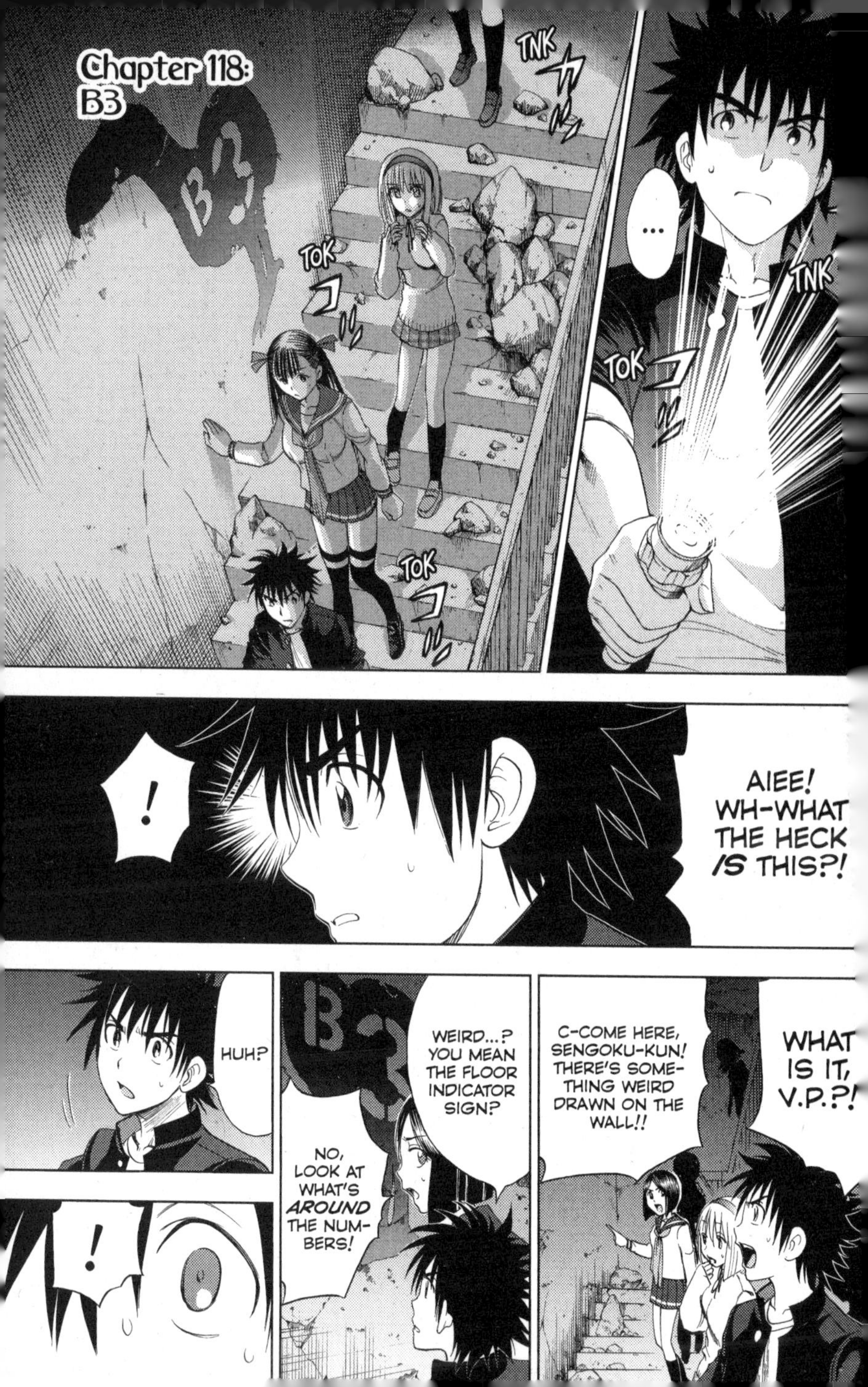
...
TNK
TOK
Chapter 118: B3
TNK
TOK
TOK
AIEE! WH-WHAT THE HECK *IS* THIS?!
!
WHAT IS IT, V.P.?!
C-COME HERE, SENGOKU-KUN! THERE'S SOME-THING WEIRD DRAWN ON THE WALL!!
WEIRD...? YOU MEAN THE FLOOR INDICATOR SIGN?
NO, LOOK AT WHAT'S *AROUND* THE NUM-BERS!
HUH?
!

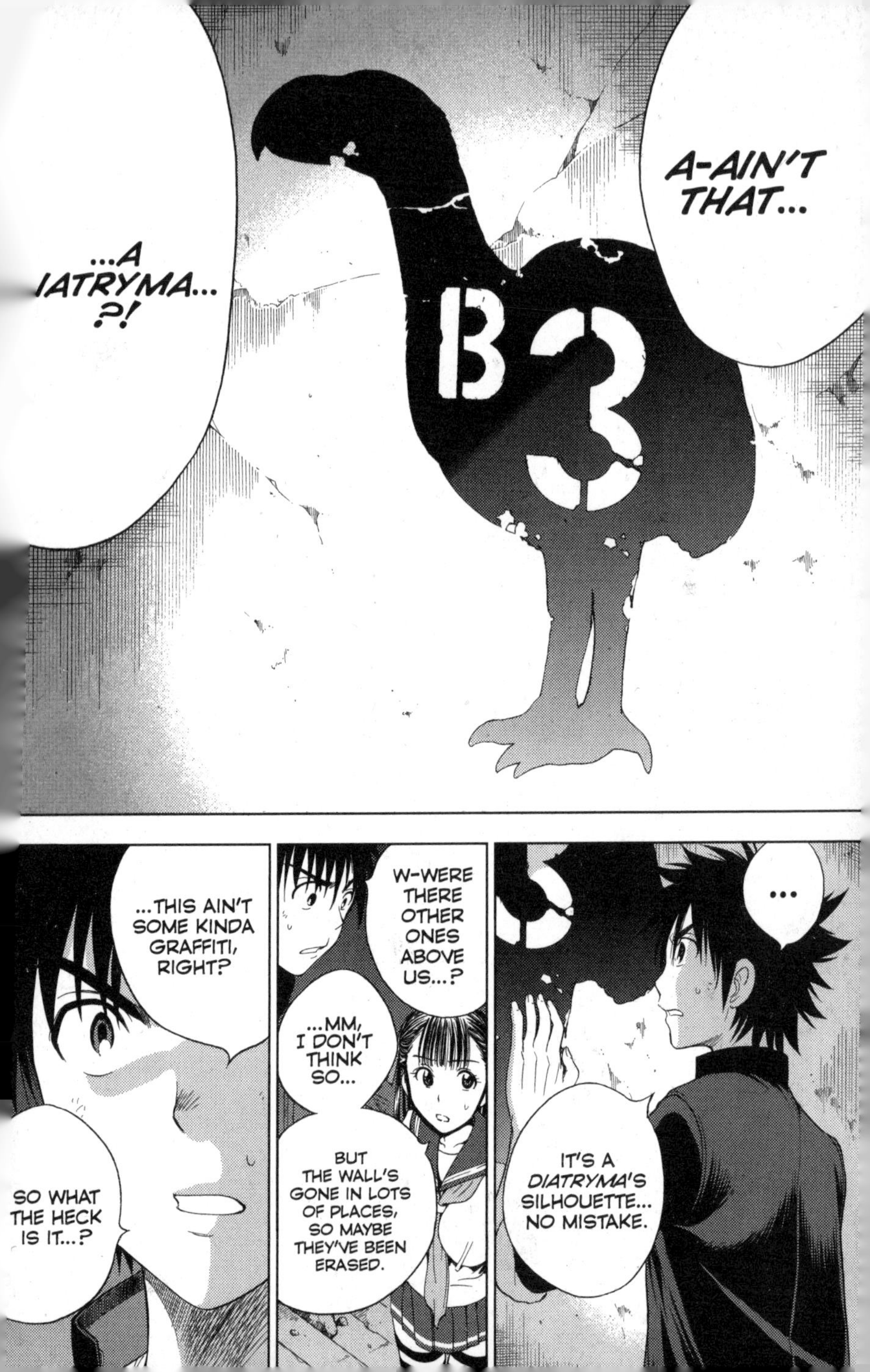
A-AIN'T THAT...
...A IATRYMA...?!
...
IT'S A DIATRYMA'S SILHOUETTE... NO MISTAKE.
W-WERE THERE OTHER ONES ABOVE US...?
...MM, I DON'T THINK SO...
BUT THE WALL'S GONE IN LOTS OF PLACES, SO MAYBE THEY'VE BEEN ERASED.
...THIS AIN'T SOME KINDA GRAFFITI, RIGHT?
SO WHAT THE HECK IS IT...?

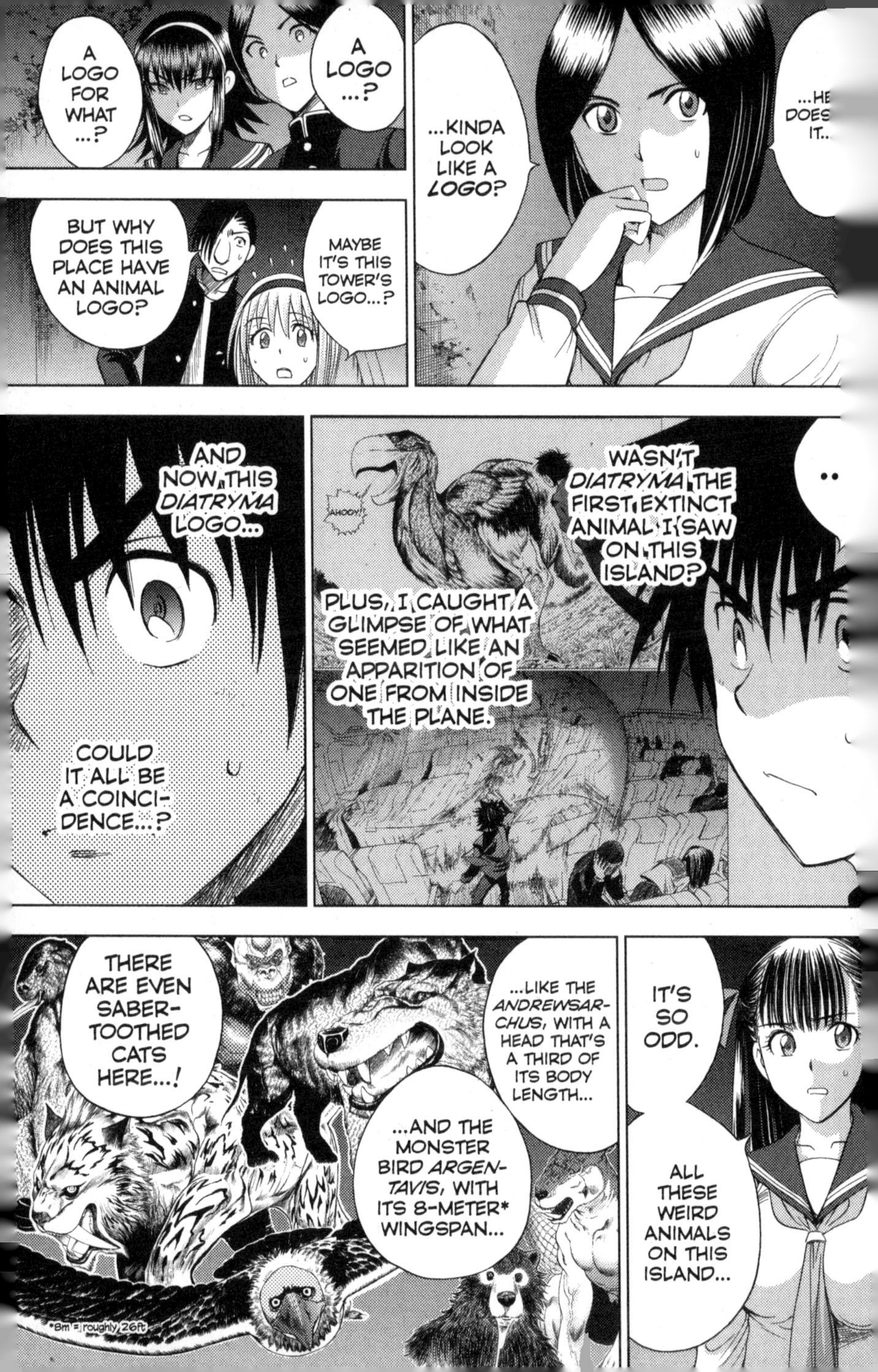
...HE DOES IT...
...KINDA LOOK LIKE A *LOGO*?
A LOGO...?
A LOGO FOR WHAT...?
MAYBE IT'S THIS TOWER'S LOGO...?
BUT WHY DOES THIS PLACE HAVE AN ANIMAL LOGO?
..
WASN'T *DIATRYMA* THE FIRST EXTINCT ANIMAL I SAW ON THIS ISLAND?
AHOOY!
PLUS, I CAUGHT A GLIMPSE OF WHAT SEEMED LIKE AN APPARITION OF ONE FROM INSIDE THE PLANE.
AND NOW THIS *DIATRYMA* LOGO...
COULD IT ALL BE A COINCIDENCE...?
IT'S SO ODD.
ALL THESE WEIRD ANIMALS ON THIS ISLAND...
...LIKE THE *ANDREWSARCHUS*, WITH A HEAD THAT'S A THIRD OF ITS BODY LENGTH...
THERE ARE EVEN SABER-TOOTHED CATS HERE...!
...AND THE MONSTER BIRD *ARGENTAVIS*, WITH ITS 8-METER* WINGSPAN...
*8m = roughly 26ft

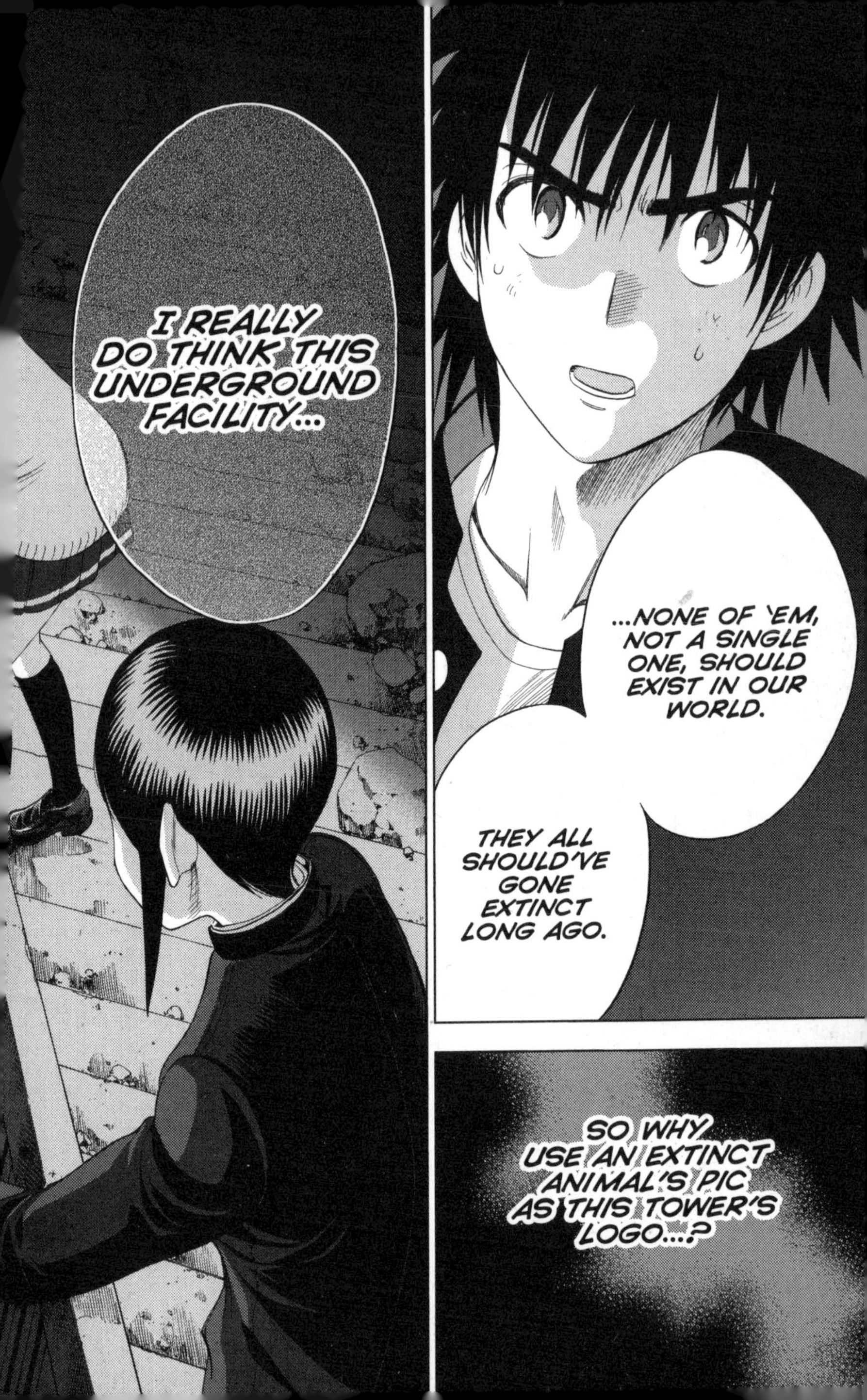
...NONE OF 'EM, NOT A SINGLE ONE, SHOULD EXIST IN OUR WORLD.
THEY ALL SHOULD'VE GONE EXTINCT LONG AGO.
SO WHY USE AN EXTINCT ANIMAL'S PIC AS THIS TOWER'S LOGO...?
I REALLY DO THINK THIS UNDERGROUND FACILITY...

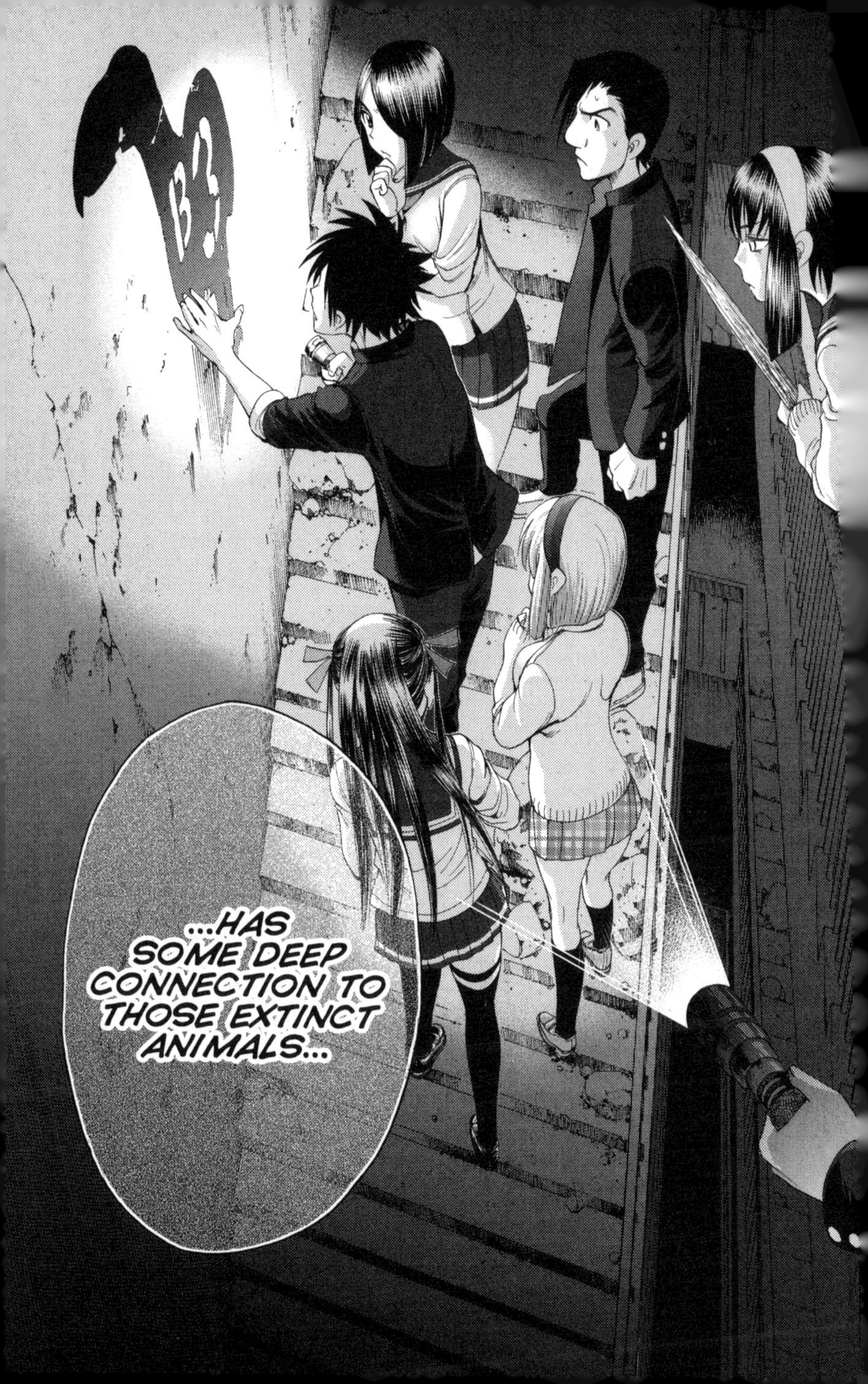
...HAS SOME DEEP CONNECTION TO THOSE EXTINCT ANIMALS...

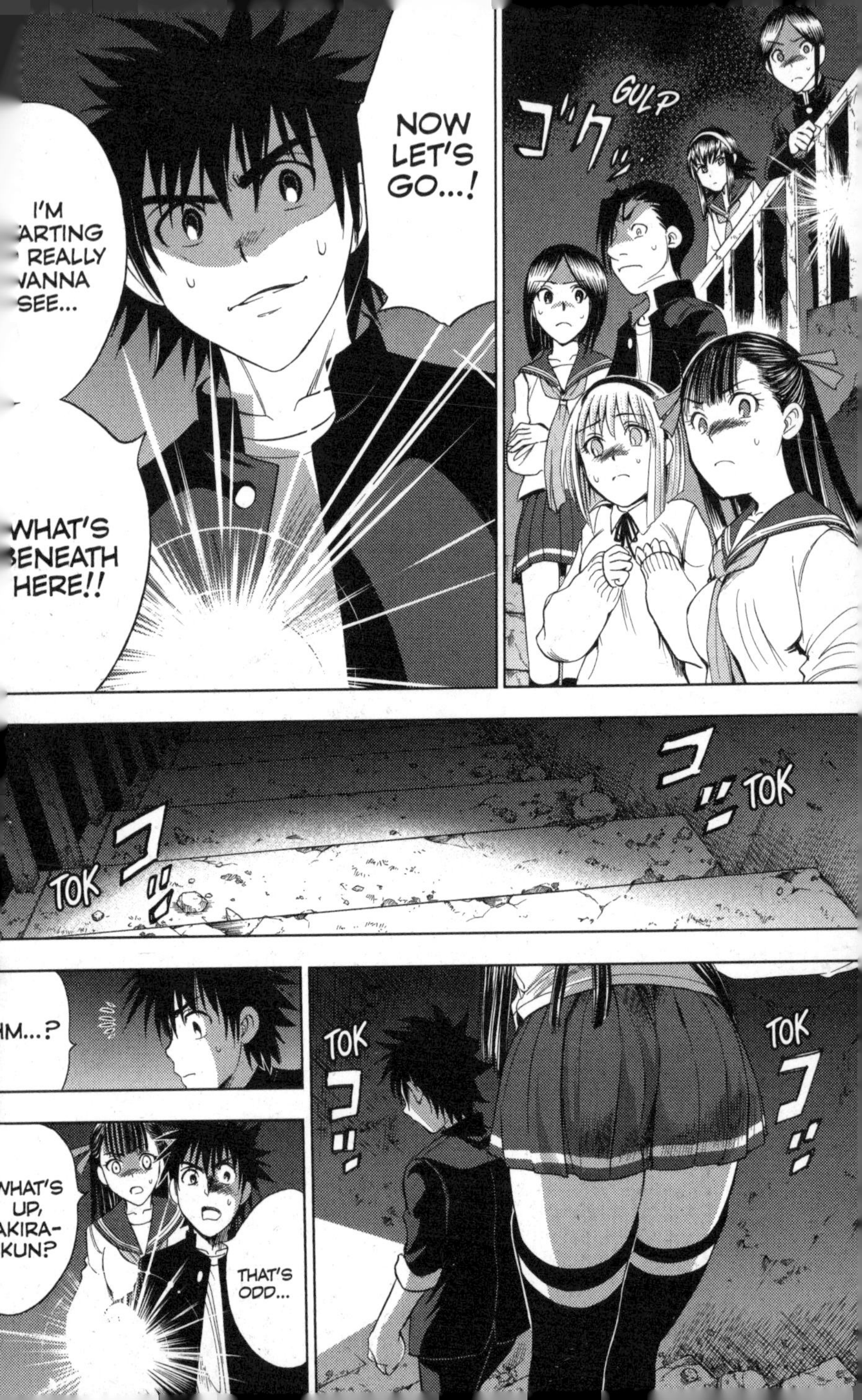

ゴクッ
GULP
NOW LET'S GO...!
I'M
ARTING
REALLY
VANNA
SEE...
WHAT'S
BENEATH
HERE!!
TOK
TOK
TOK
TOK
HM...?
WHAT'S UP, AKIRA-KUN?
THAT'S ODD...

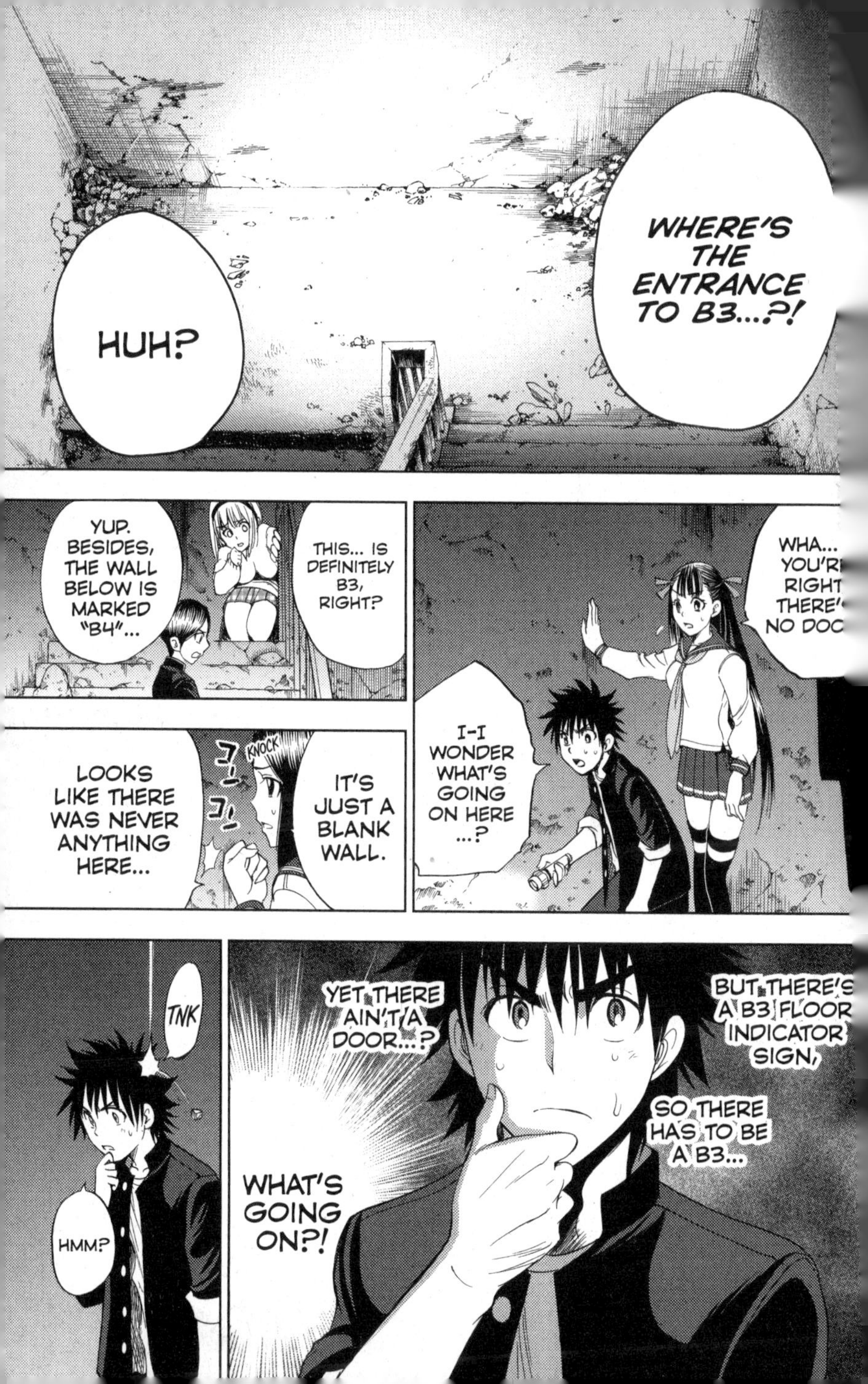
WHERE'S THE ENTRANCE TO B3...?!
HUH?
WHA... YOU'R RIGHT THERE' NO DO
I-I WONDER WHAT'S GOING ON HERE ...?
THIS... IS DEFINITELY B3, RIGHT?
YUP. BESIDES, THE WALL BELOW IS MARKED "B4"...
KNOCK
IT'S JUST A BLANK WALL.
LOOKS LIKE THERE WAS NEVER ANYTHING HERE...
BUT THERE'S A B3 FLOOR INDICATOR SIGN,
SO THERE HAS TO BE A B3...
YET THERE AIN'T A DOOR...?
WHAT'S GOING ON?!
TNK
HMM?

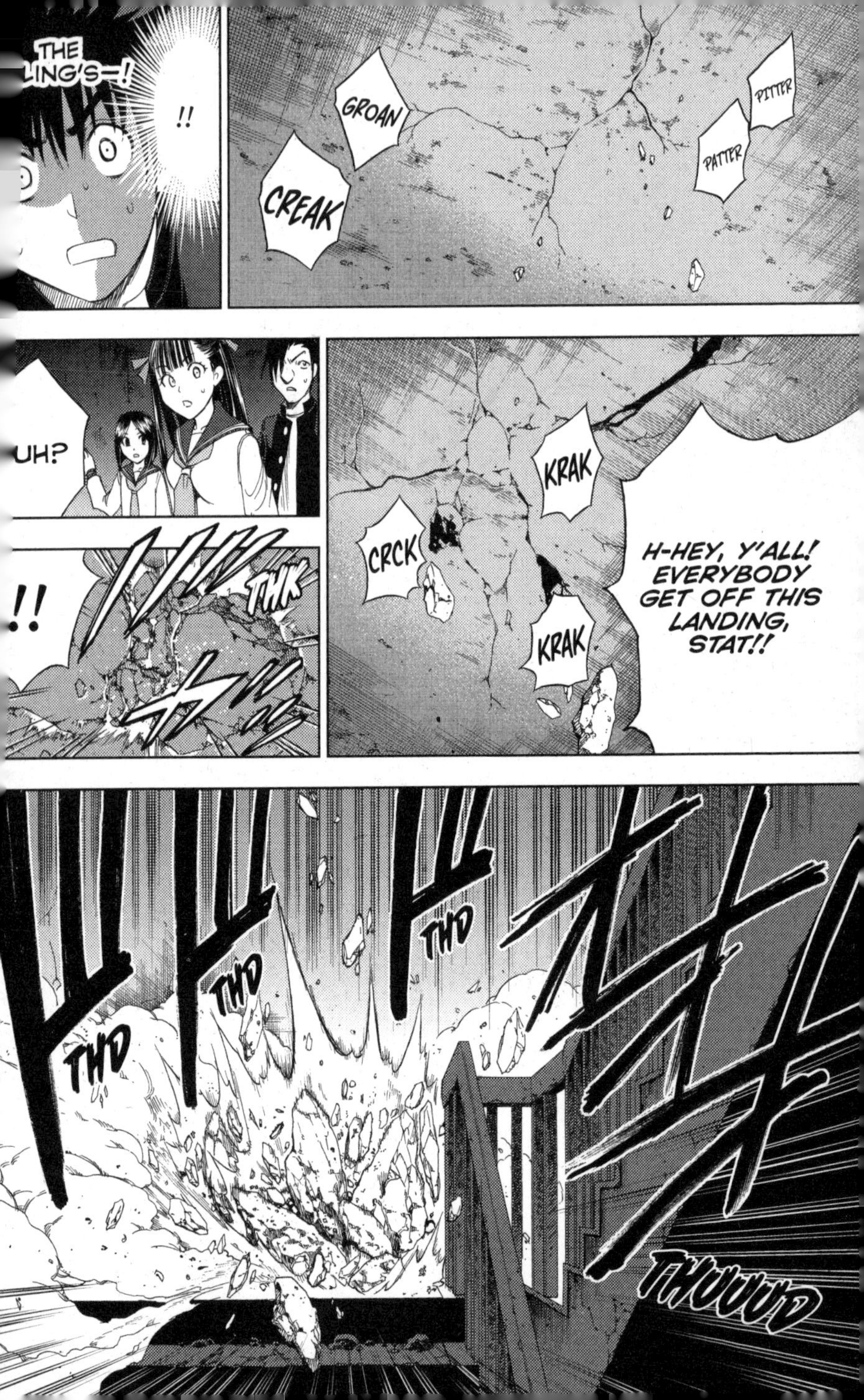
PITTER
PATTER
GROAN
CREAK
!!
THE
LING'S—!
H-HEY, Y'ALL! EVERYBODY GET OFF THIS LANDING, STAT!!
KRAK
CRCK
KRAK
UH?
THK
!!
THUUUUD
THD
THD
THD

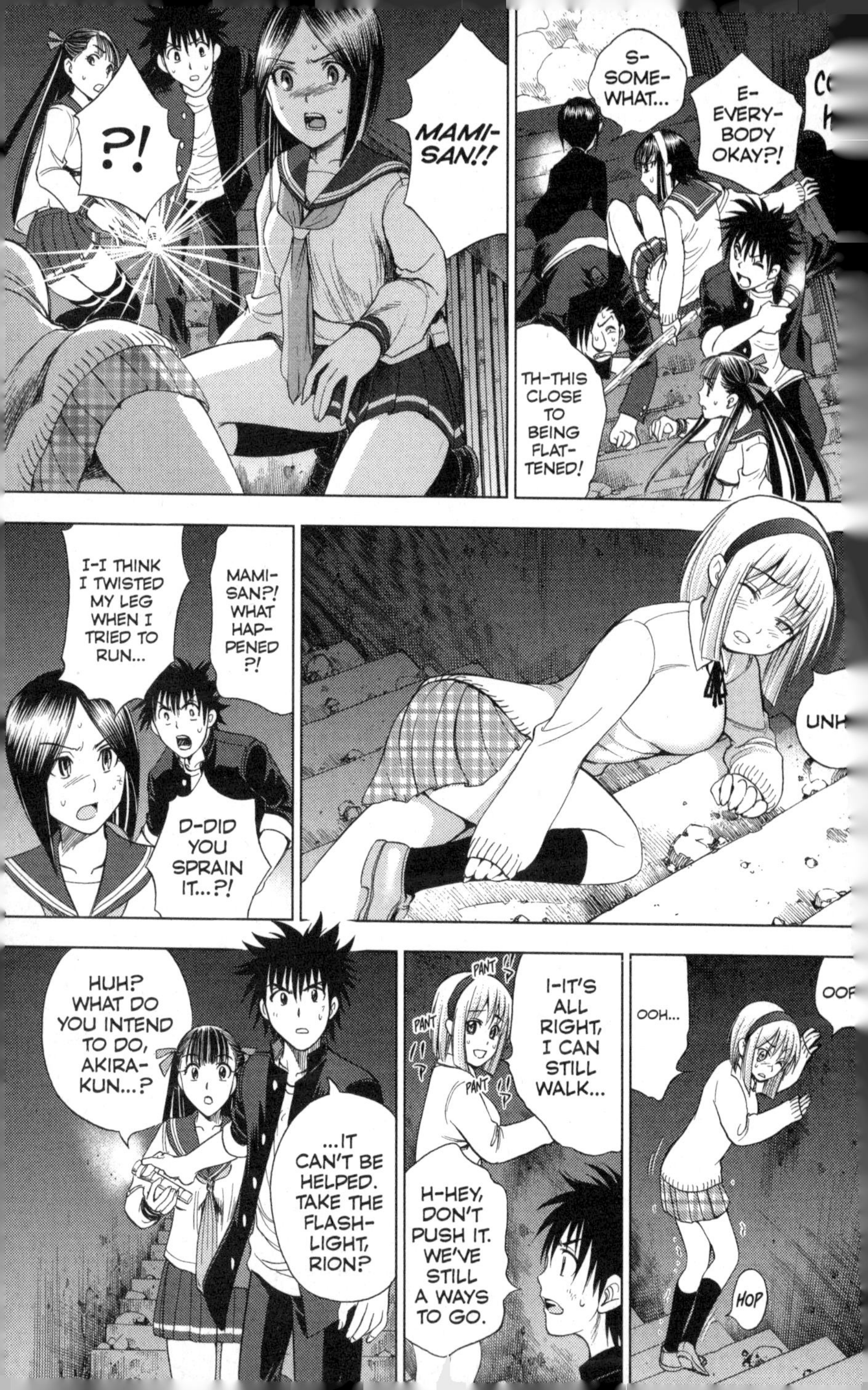
E-EVERYBODY OKAY?!
S-SOMEWHAT...
TH-THIS CLOSE TO BEING FLATTENED!
MAMI-SAN!!
?!
MAMI-SAN?! WHAT HAPPENED?!
I-I THINK I TWISTED MY LEG WHEN I TRIED TO RUN...
D-DID YOU SPRAIN IT...?!
OOH...
HOP
I-IT'S ALL RIGHT, I CAN STILL WALK...
PANT
PANT
PANT
H-HEY, DON'T PUSH IT. WE'VE STILL A WAYS TO GO.
HUH? WHAT DO YOU INTEND TO DO, AKIRA-KUN...?
...IT CAN'T BE HELPED. TAKE THE FLASHLIGHT, RION?

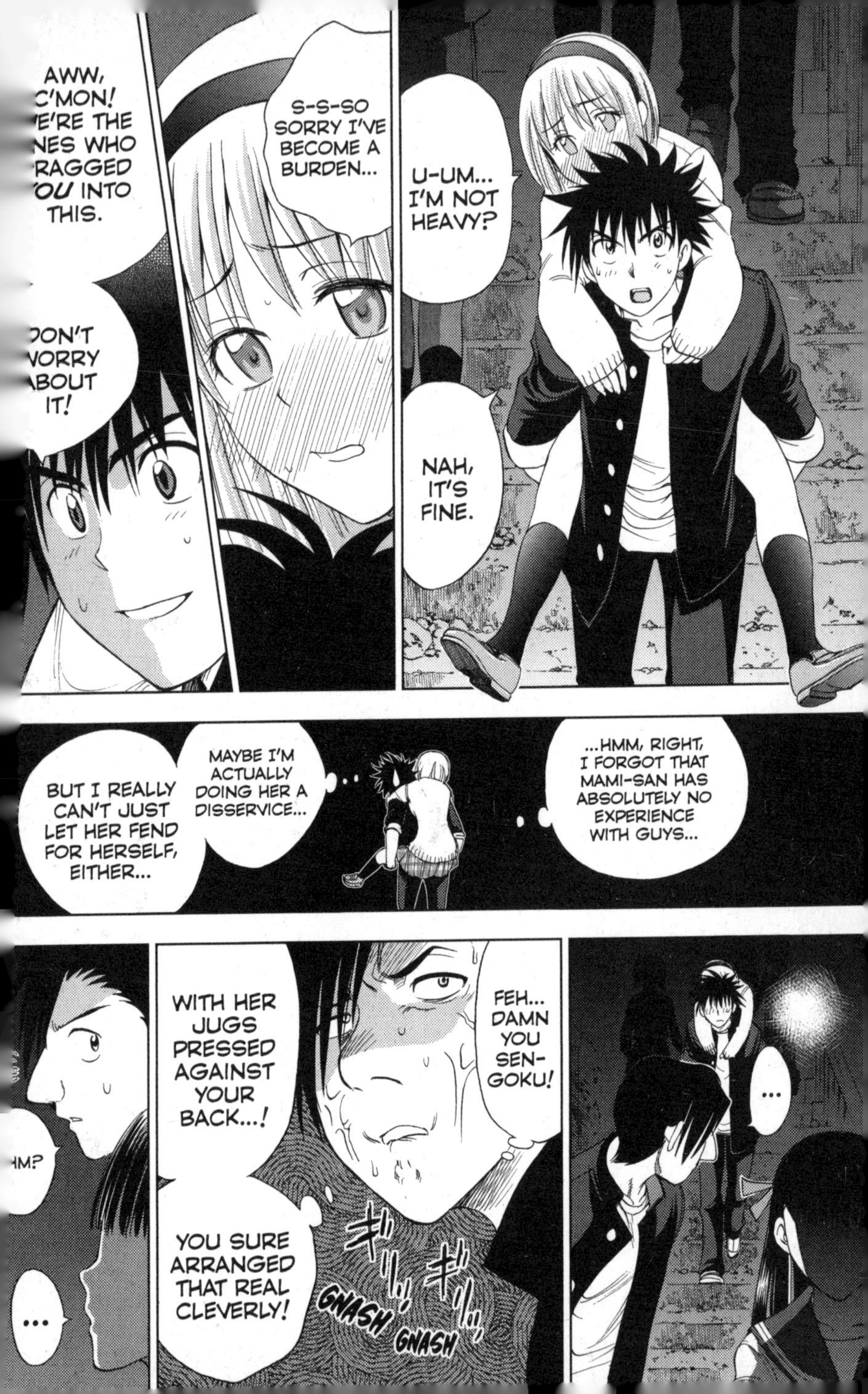
U-UM... I'M NOT HEAVY?
NAH, IT'S FINE.
S-S-SO SORRY I'VE BECOME A BURDEN...
AWW, C'MON! WE'RE THE ONES WHO DRAGGED YOU INTO THIS.
DON'T WORRY ABOUT IT!
...HMM, RIGHT, I FORGOT THAT MAMI-SAN HAS ABSOLUTELY NO EXPERIENCE WITH GUYS...
MAYBE I'M ACTUALLY DOING HER A DISSERVICE...
BUT I REALLY CAN'T JUST LET HER FEND FOR HERSELF, EITHER...
...
FEH... DAMN YOU SEN-GOKU!
WITH HER JUGS PRESSED AGAINST YOUR BACK...!
YOU SURE ARRANGED THAT REAL CLEVERLY!
GNASH
GNASH
HMM?
...

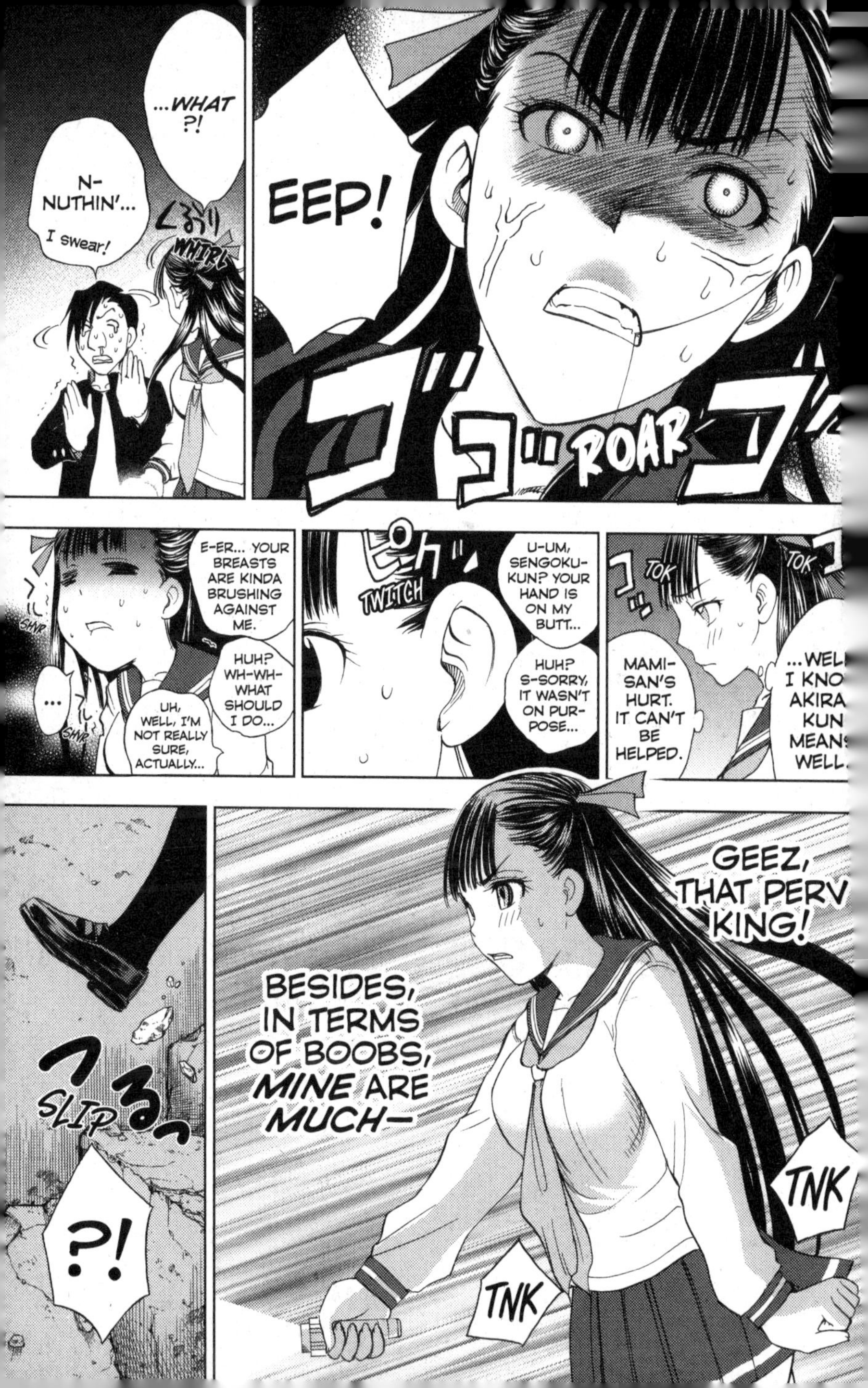
EEP!
ROAR
...WHAT ?!
くるり
WHIRL
N-NUTHIN'...
I swear!
TOK
TOK
...WEL
I KNO
AKIRA
KUN
MEAN
WELL.
MAMI-SAN'S HURT. IT CAN'T BE HELPED.
TWITCH
U-UM, SENGOKU-KUN? YOUR HAND IS ON MY BUTT...
HUH? S-SORRY, IT WASN'T ON PURPOSE...
E-ER... YOUR BREASTS ARE KINDA BRUSHING AGAINST ME.
SHVP
HUH? WH-WH-WHAT SHOULD I DO...
...
UH, WELL, I'M NOT REALLY SURE, ACTUALLY...
SHVP
GEEZ, THAT PERV KING!
BESIDES, IN TERMS OF BOOBS, MINE ARE MUCH—
TNK
TNK
SLIP
?!

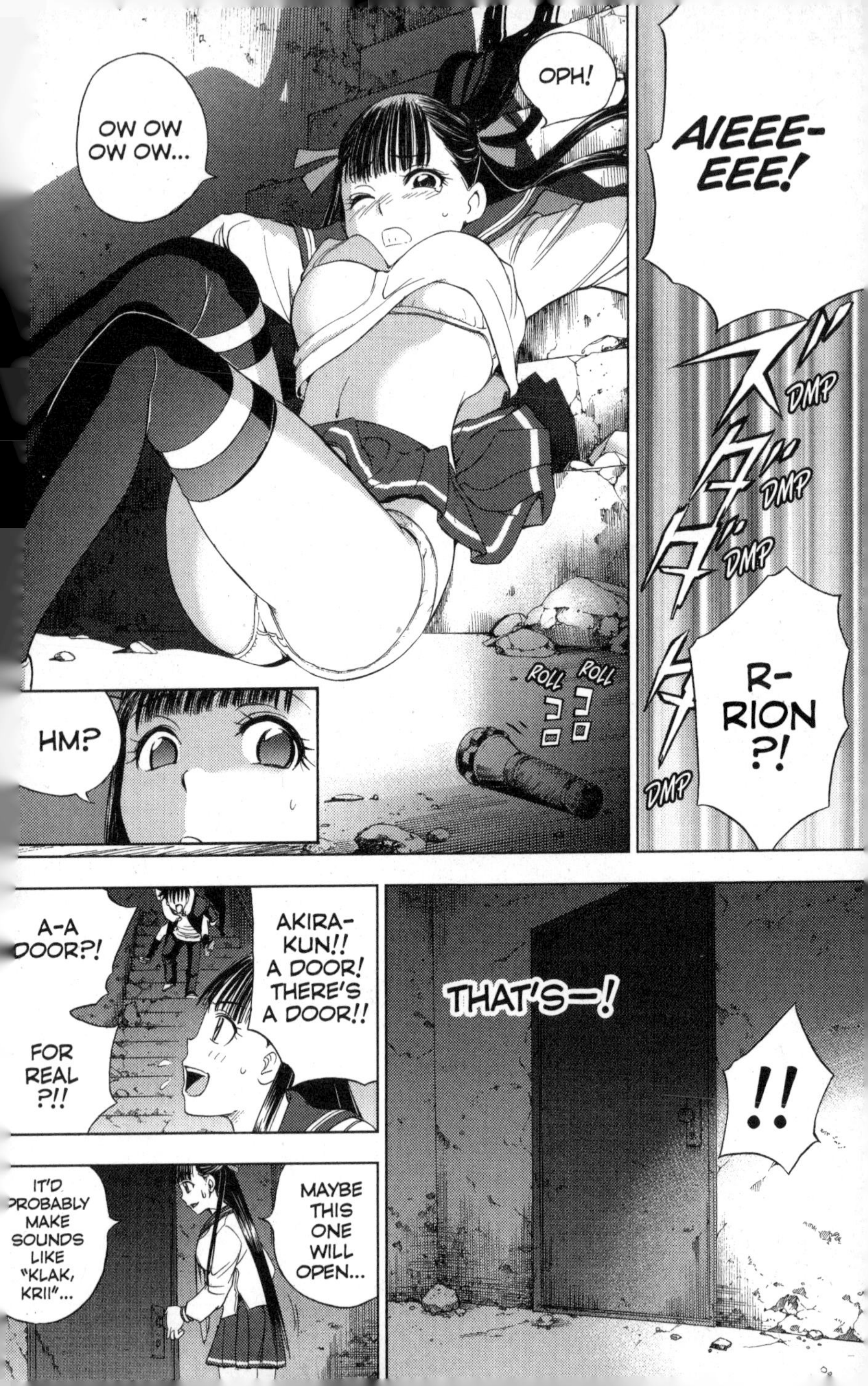
AIEEE-EEE!
DMP
DMP
DMP
DMP
R-RION?!
OPH!
OW OW OW OW...
ROLL
ROLL
HM?
THAT'S—!
!!
AKIRA-KUN!! A DOOR! THERE'S A DOOR!!
A-A DOOR?!
FOR REAL?!!
MAYBE THIS ONE WILL OPEN...
IT'D PROBABLY MAKE SOUNDS LIKE "KLAK, KRII"...

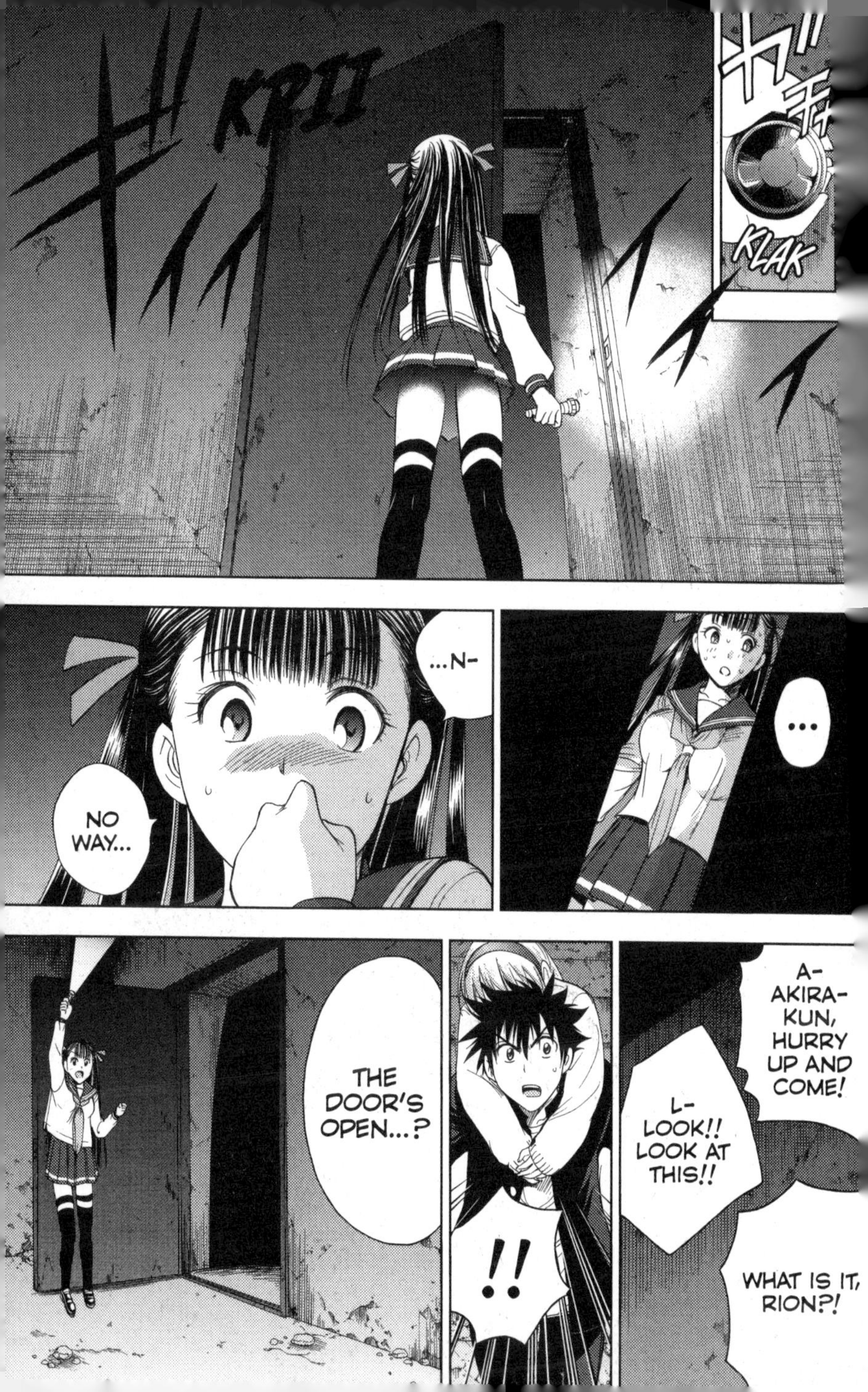
KLAK
KRII
...
...N-
NO WAY...
A-AKIRA-KUN, HURRY UP AND COME!
L-LOOK!! LOOK AT THIS!!
WHAT IS IT, RION?!
!!
THE DOOR'S OPEN...?

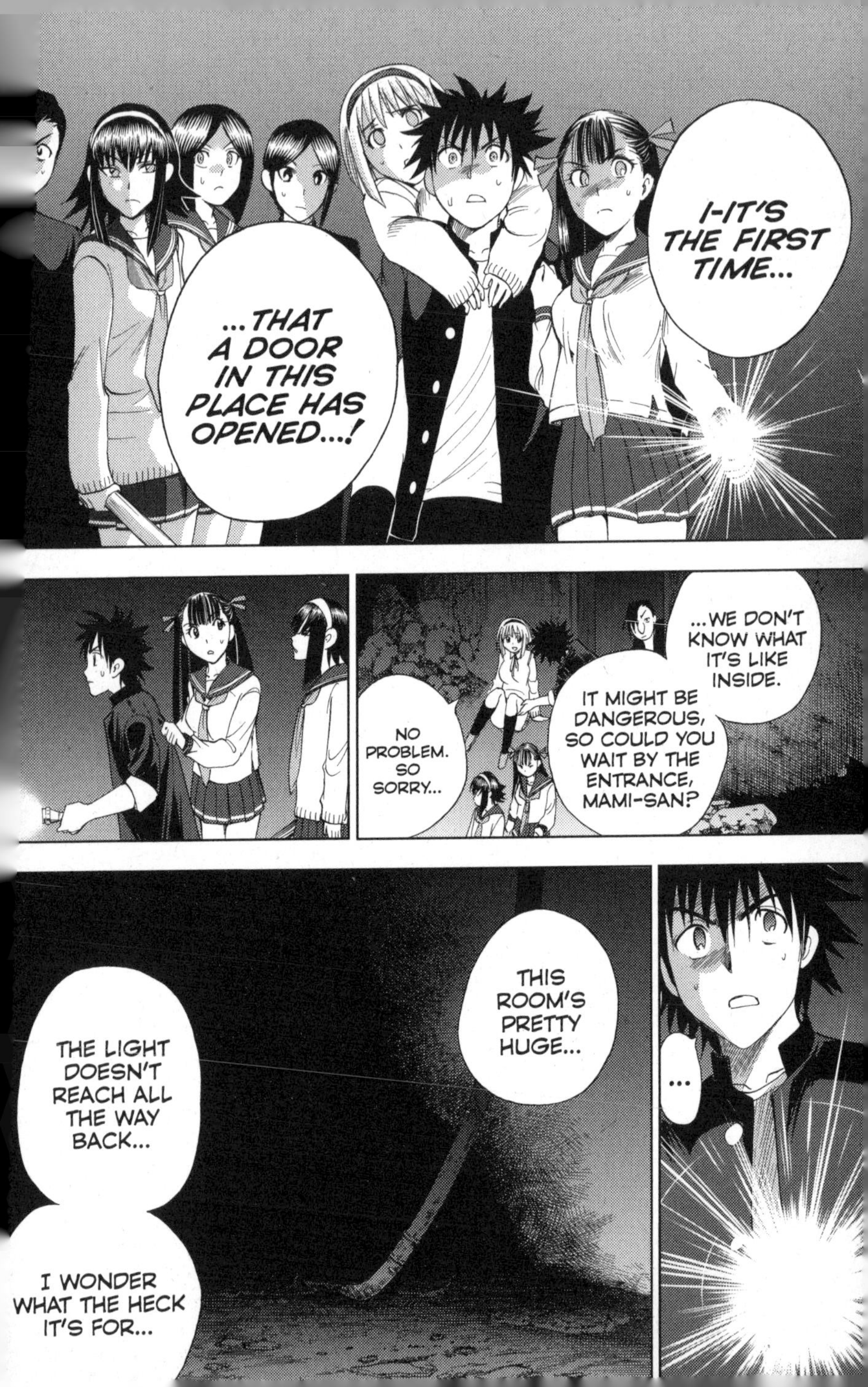
I-IT'S THE FIRST TIME...
...THAT A DOOR IN THIS PLACE HAS OPENED...!
...WE DON'T KNOW WHAT IT'S LIKE INSIDE.
IT MIGHT BE DANGEROUS, SO COULD YOU WAIT BY THE ENTRANCE, MAMI-SAN?
NO PROBLEM. SO SORRY...
...
THIS ROOM'S PRETTY HUGE...
THE LIGHT DOESN'T REACH ALL THE WAY BACK...
I WONDER WHAT THE HECK IT'S FOR...

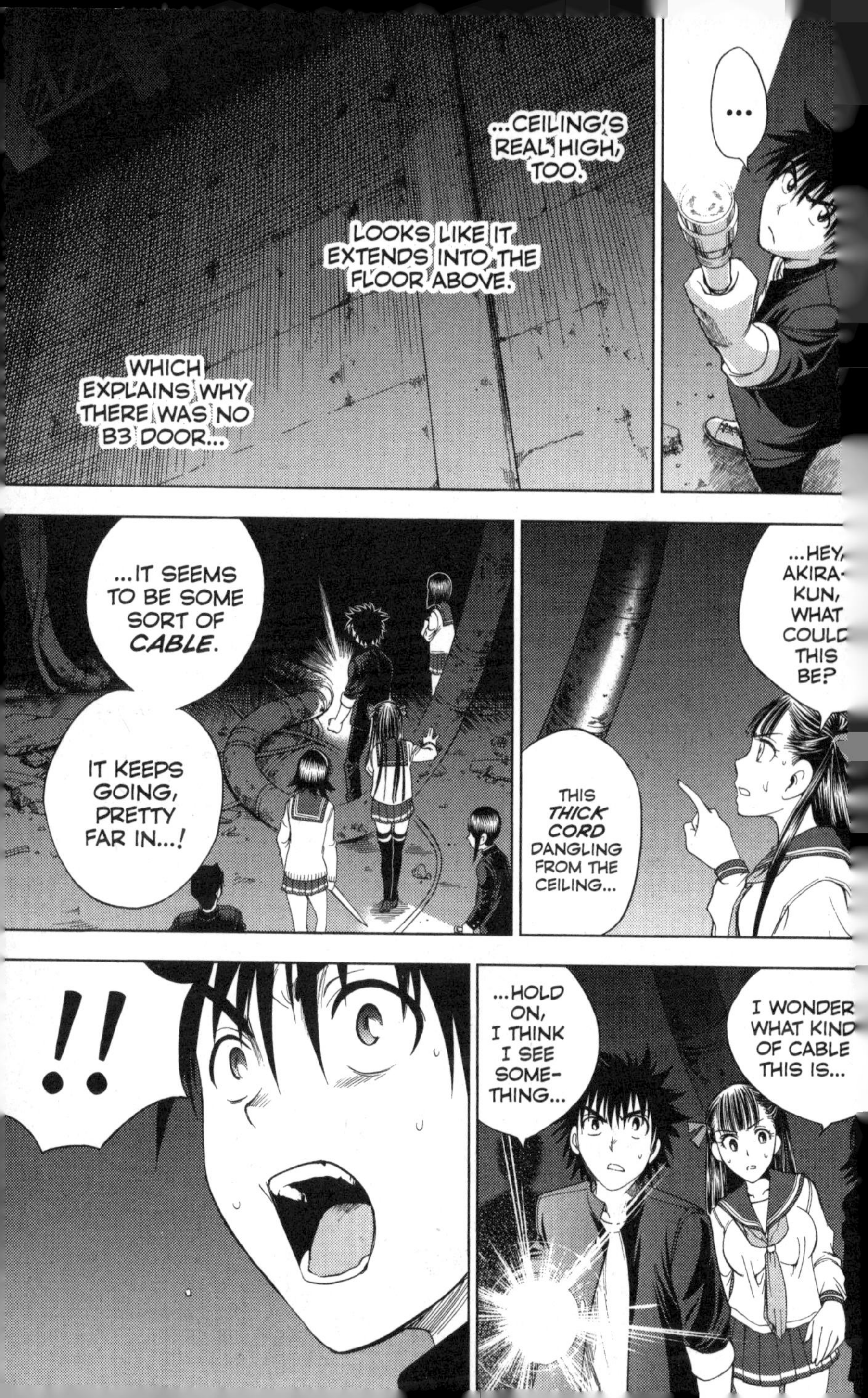
...
...CEILING'S REAL HIGH, TOO.
LOOKS LIKE IT EXTENDS INTO THE FLOOR ABOVE.
WHICH EXPLAINS WHY THERE WAS NO B3 DOOR...
...HEY, AKIRA-KUN, WHAT COULD THIS BE?
THIS *THICK CORD* DANGLING FROM THE CEILING...
...IT SEEMS TO BE SOME SORT OF *CABLE*.
IT KEEPS GOING, PRETTY FAR IN...!
I WONDER WHAT KIND OF CABLE THIS IS...
...HOLD ON, I THINK I SEE SOME-THING...
!!

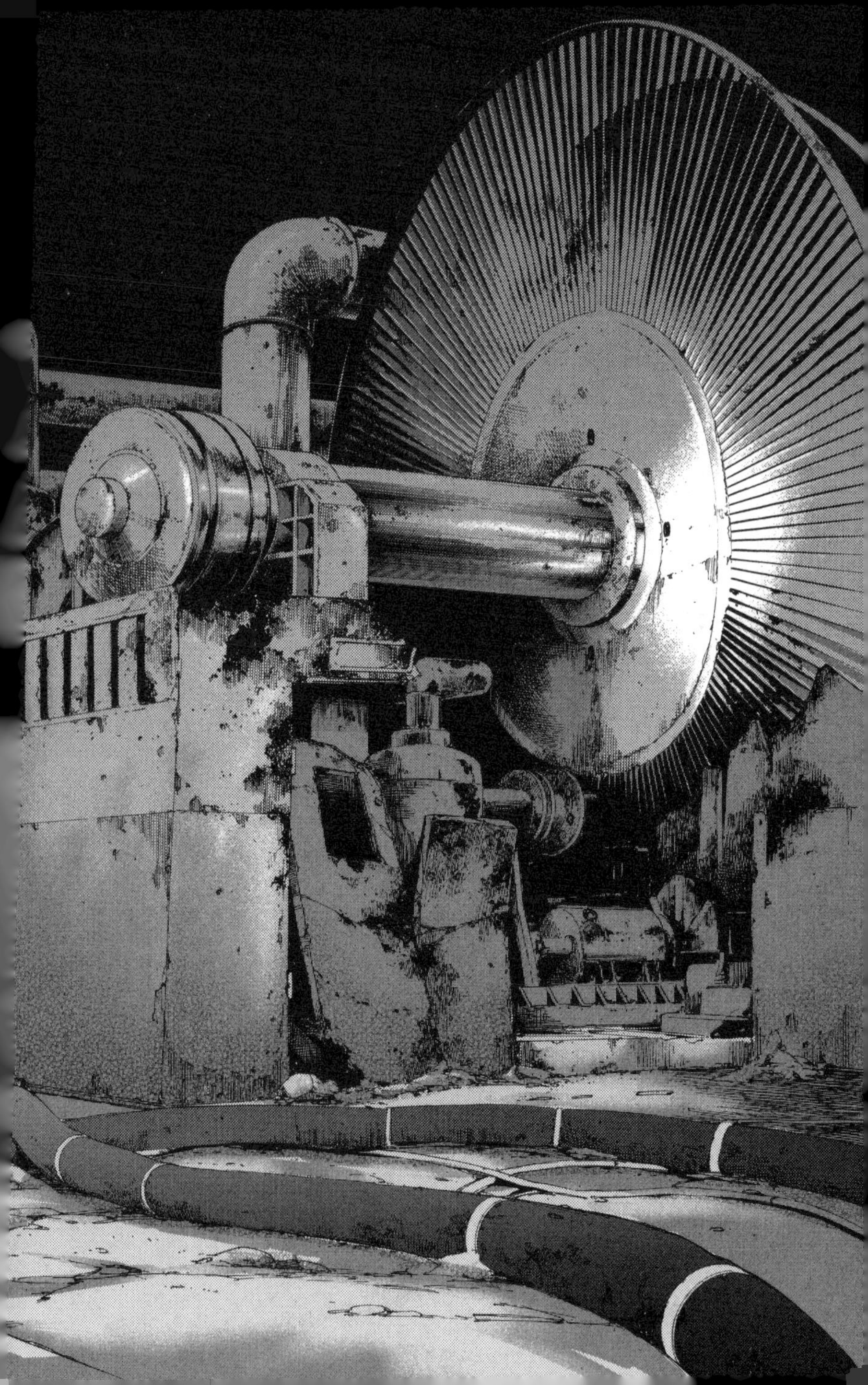

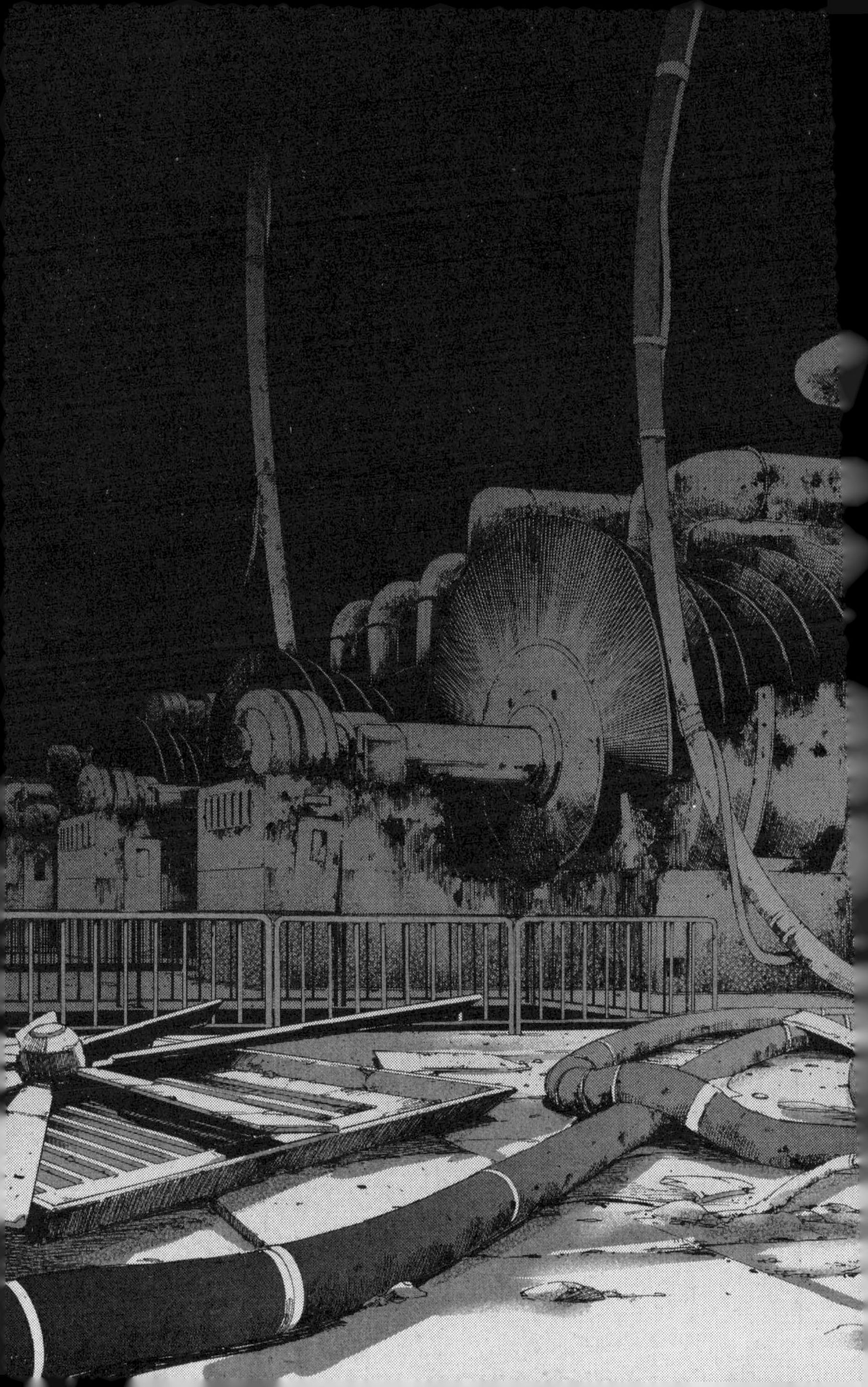

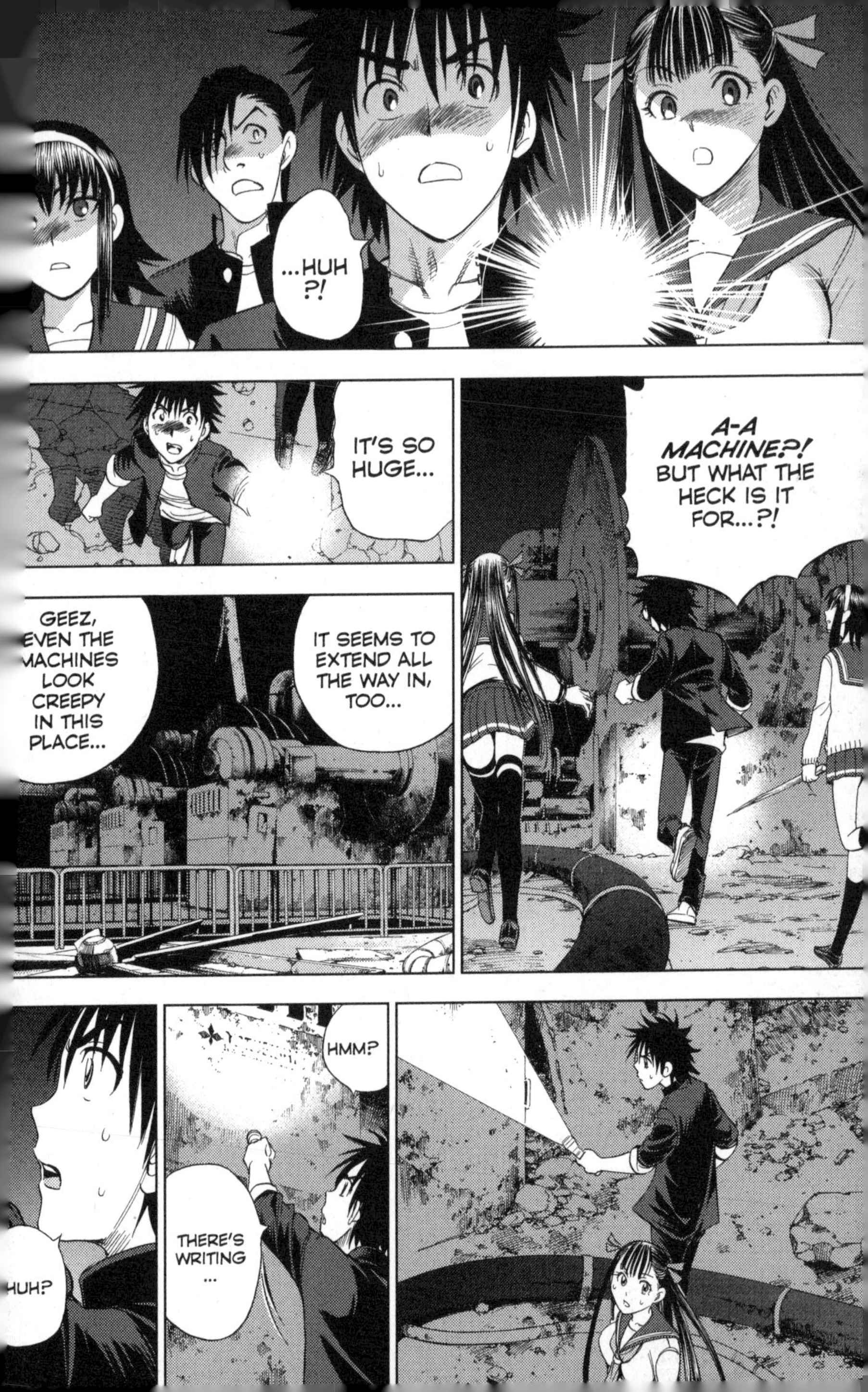
...HUH ?!
A-A MACHINE?! BUT WHAT THE HECK IS IT FOR...?!
IT'S SO HUGE...
IT SEEMS TO EXTEND ALL THE WAY IN, TOO...
GEEZ, EVEN THE MACHINES LOOK CREEPY IN THIS PLACE...
HMM?
THERE'S WRITING ...
HUH?

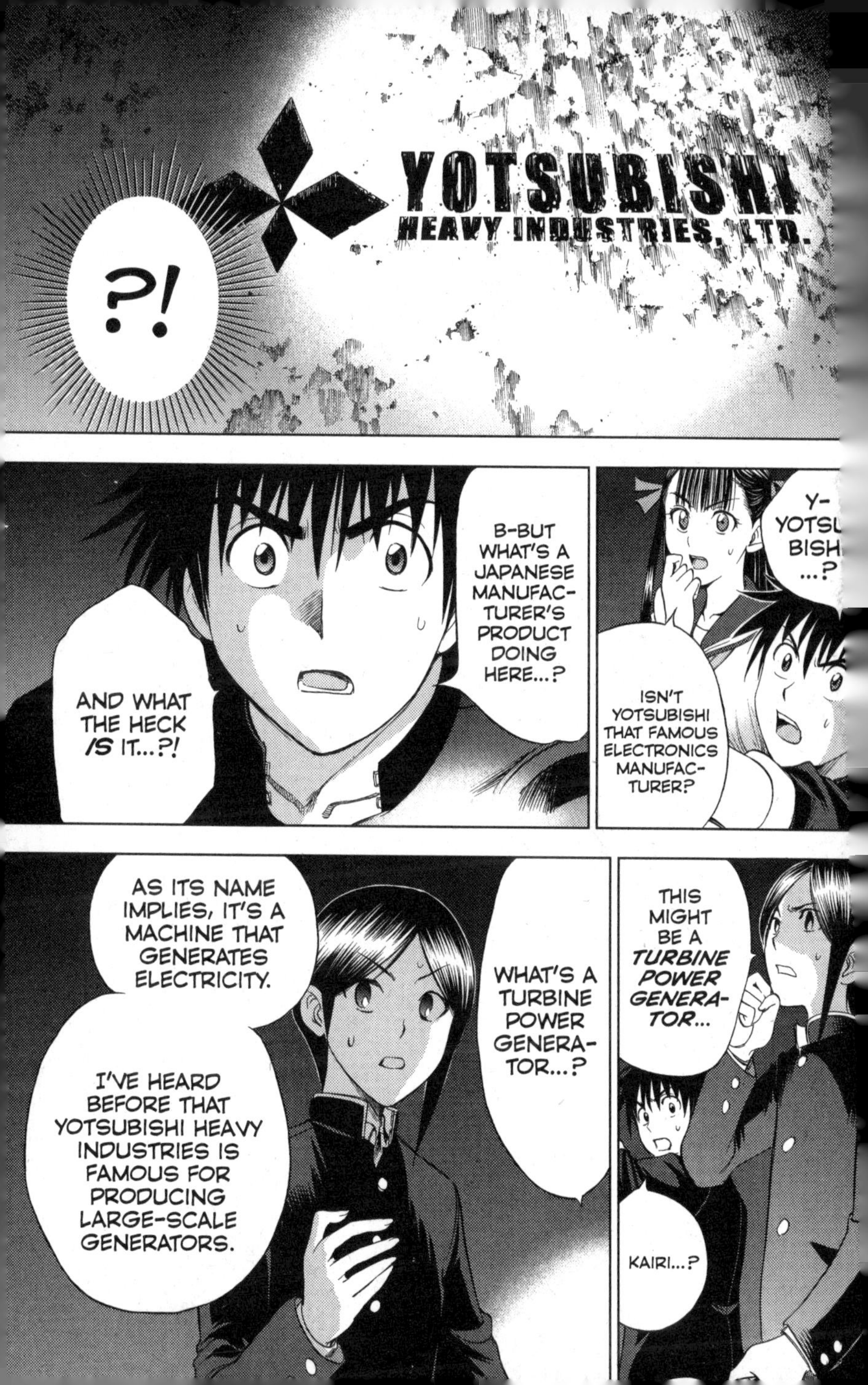
YOTSUBISHI
HEAVY INDUSTRIES, LTD.
?!
Y-YOTSUBISH...?
ISN'T YOTSUBISHI THAT FAMOUS ELECTRONICS MANUFACTURER?
B-BUT WHAT'S A JAPANESE MANUFACTURER'S PRODUCT DOING HERE...?
AND WHAT THE HECK *IS* IT...?!
THIS MIGHT BE A *TURBINE POWER GENERATOR*...
KAIRI...?
WHAT'S A TURBINE POWER GENERATOR...?
AS ITS NAME IMPLIES, IT'S A MACHINE THAT GENERATES ELECTRICITY.
I'VE HEARD BEFORE THAT YOTSUBISHI HEAVY INDUSTRIES IS FAMOUS FOR PRODUCING LARGE-SCALE GENERATORS.

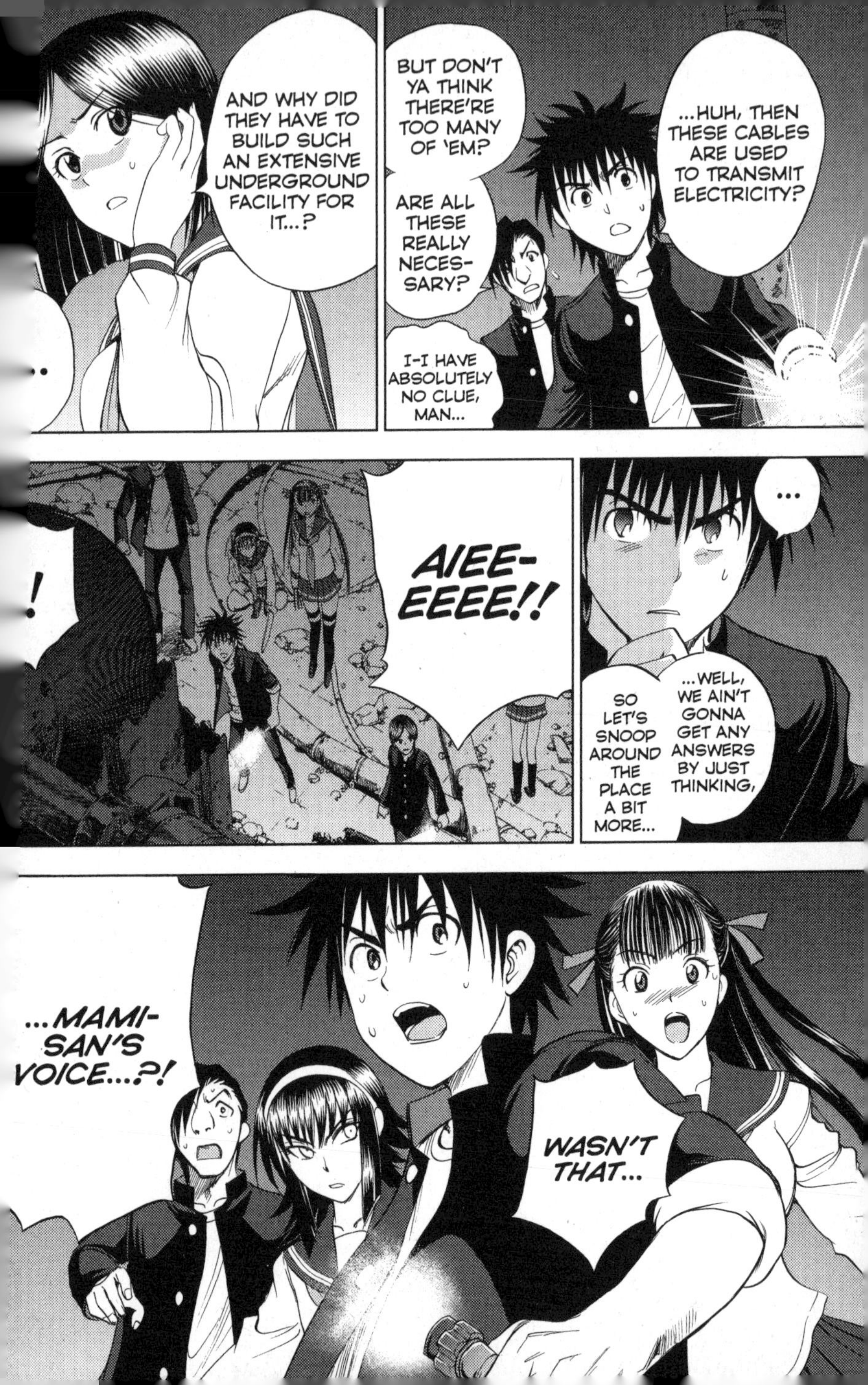
...HUH, THEN THESE CABLES ARE USED TO TRANSMIT ELECTRICITY?
BUT DON'T YA THINK THERE'RE TOO MANY OF 'EM?
ARE ALL THESE REALLY NECES-SARY?
I-I HAVE ABSOLUTELY NO CLUE, MAN...
AND WHY DID THEY HAVE TO BUILD SUCH AN EXTENSIVE UNDERGROUND FACILITY FOR IT...?
...
...
...WELL, WE AIN'T GONNA GET ANY ANSWERS BY JUST THINKING,
SO LET'S SNOOP AROUND THE PLACE A BIT MORE...
AIEE-EEEE!!
!
WASN'T THAT...
...MAMI-SAN'S VOICE...?!

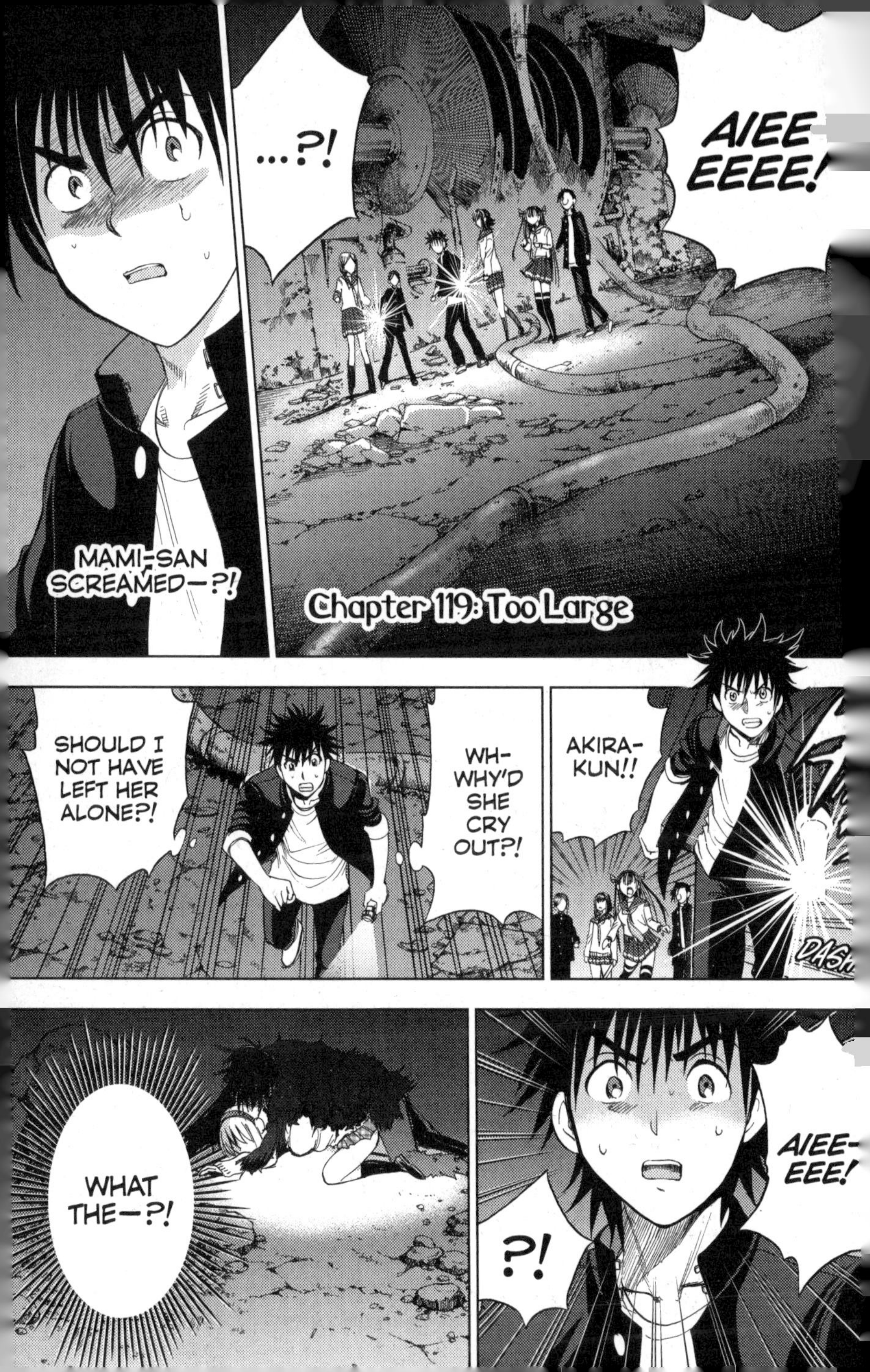
AIEE EEEE!
...?!
Chapter 119: Too Large
MAMI-SAN SCREAMED—?!
AKIRA-KUN!!
WH-WHY'D SHE CRY OUT?!
SHOULD I NOT HAVE LEFT HER ALONE?!
AIEE-EEE!
?!
WHAT THE—?!

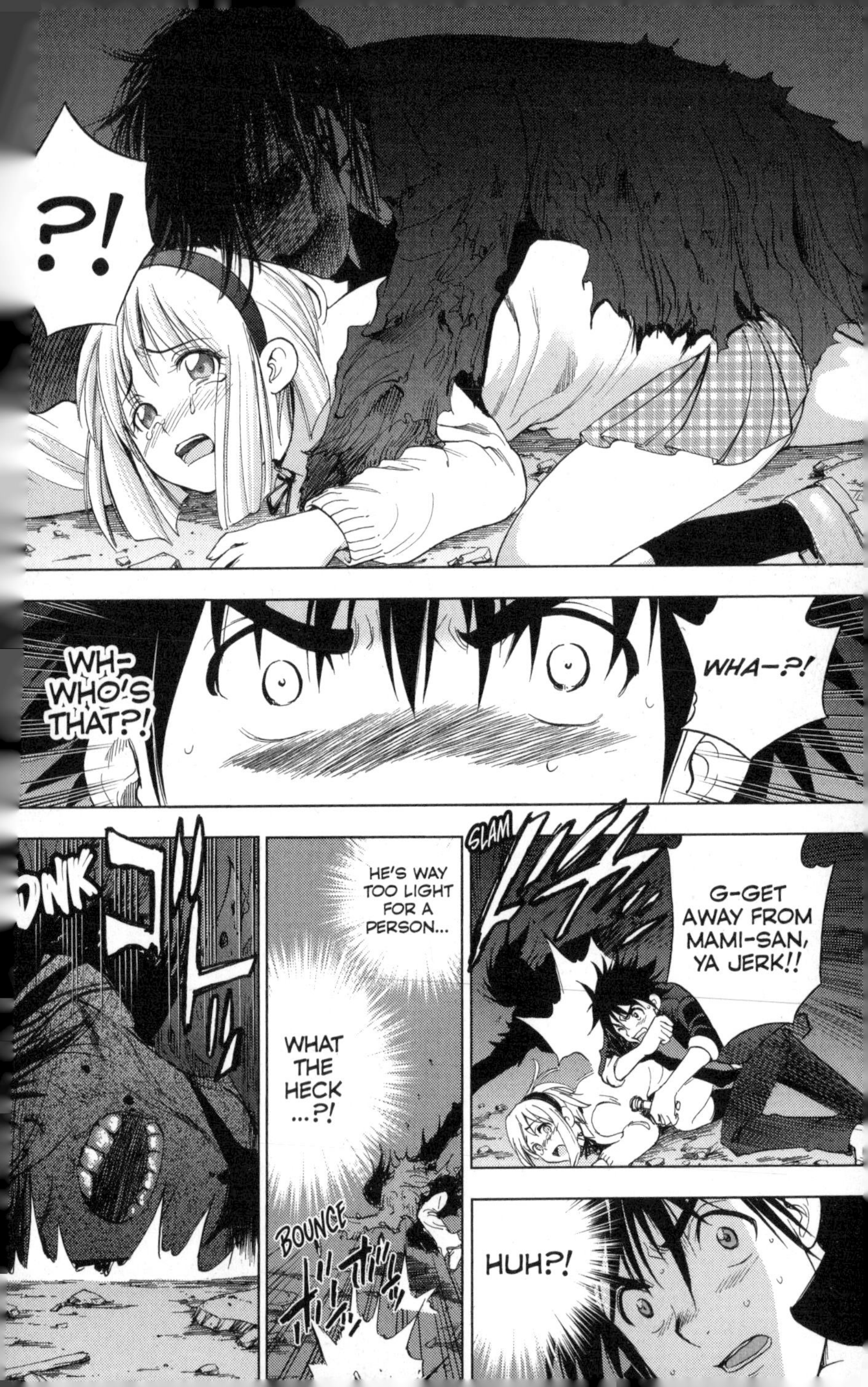

?!
WHA-?!
WH- WHO'S THAT?!
SLAM
G-GET AWAY FROM MAMI-SAN, YA JERK!!
HUH?!
HE'S WAY TOO LIGHT FOR A PERSON...
WHAT THE HECK ...?!
BOUNCE
DNK

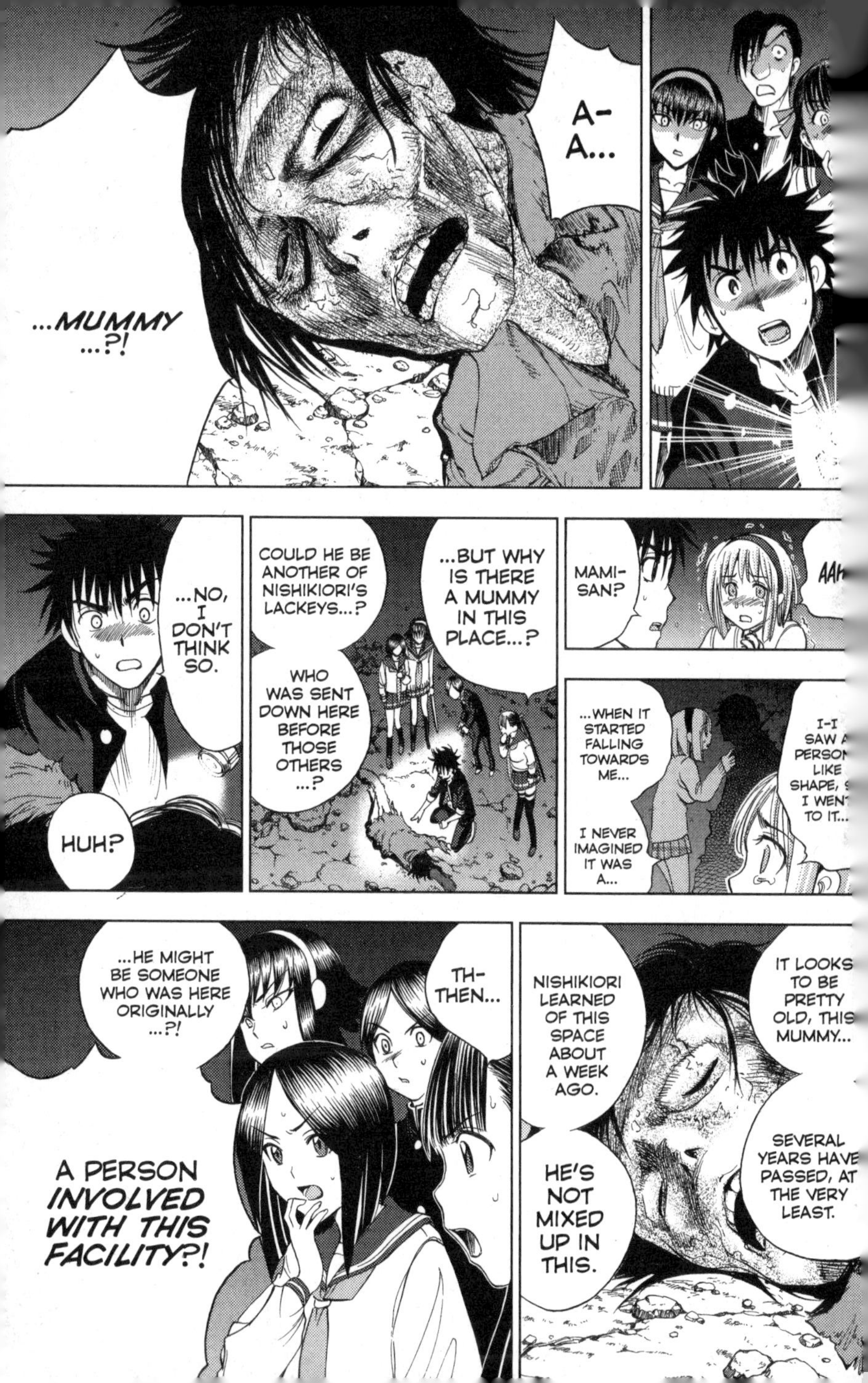
A-
A...
...MUMMY ...?!
AAH
MAMI-SAN?
I-I SAW A PERSON LIKE SHAPE, S I WENT TO IT...
...WHEN IT STARTED FALLING TOWARDS ME...
I NEVER IMAGINED IT WAS A...
...BUT WHY IS THERE A MUMMY IN THIS PLACE...?
COULD HE BE ANOTHER OF NISHIKIORI'S LACKEYS...?
WHO WAS SENT DOWN HERE BEFORE THOSE OTHERS ...?
...NO, I DON'T THINK SO.
HUH?
IT LOOKS TO BE PRETTY OLD, THIS MUMMY...
NISHIKIORI LEARNED OF THIS SPACE ABOUT A WEEK AGO.
SEVERAL YEARS HAVE PASSED, AT THE VERY LEAST.
HE'S NOT MIXED UP IN THIS.
TH- THEN...
...HE MIGHT BE SOMEONE WHO WAS HERE ORIGINALLY ...?!
A PERSON INVOLVED WITH THIS FACILITY?!

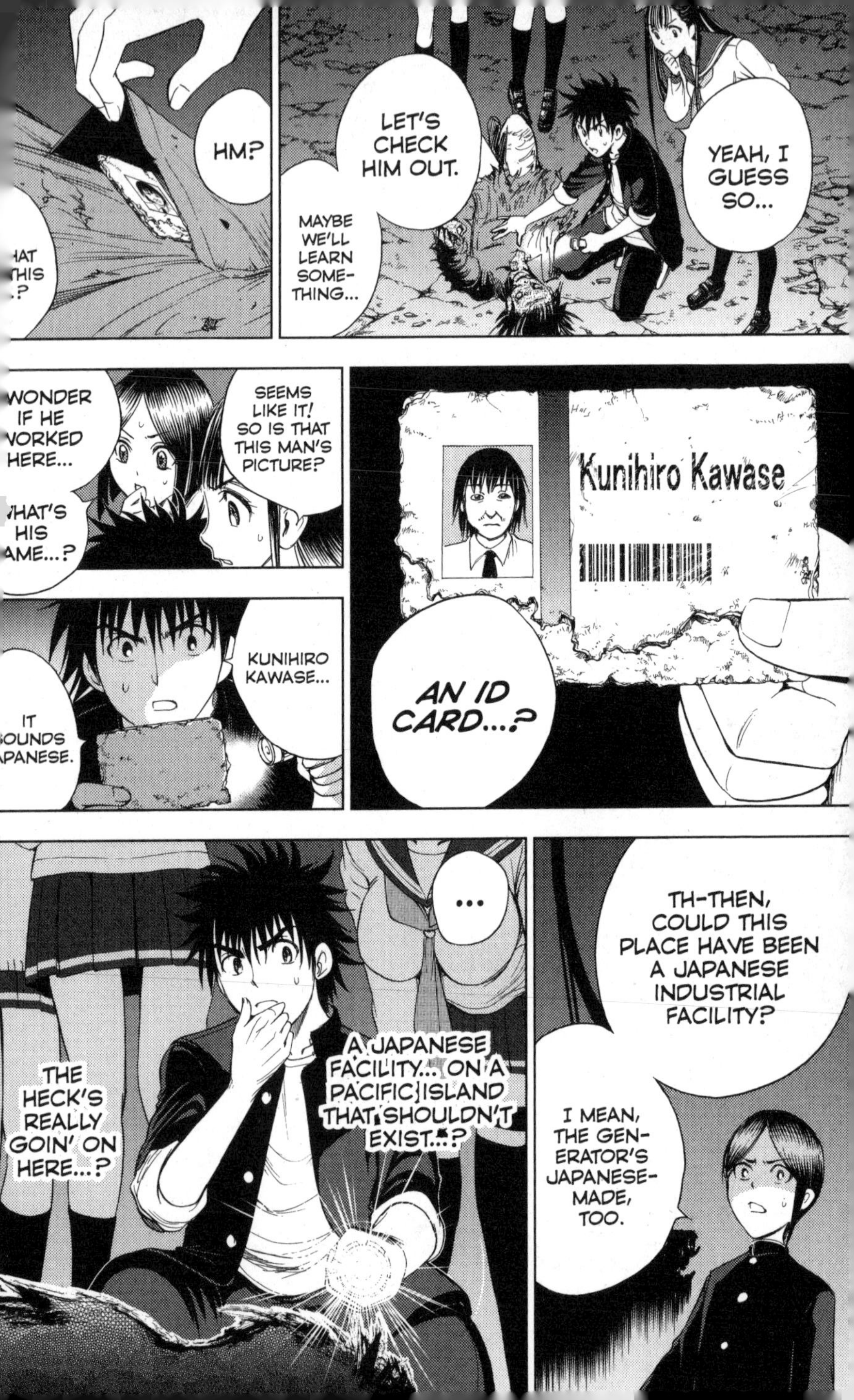
YEAH, I GUESS SO...
LET'S CHECK HIM OUT.
MAYBE WE'LL LEARN SOME-THING...
HM?
Kunihiro Kawase
AN ID CARD...?
SEEMS LIKE IT! SO IS THAT THIS MAN'S PICTURE?
WONDER IF HE WORKED HERE...
WHAT'S HIS NAME...?
KUNIHIRO KAWASE...
IT SOUNDS JAPANESE.
TH-THEN, COULD THIS PLACE HAVE BEEN A JAPANESE INDUSTRIAL FACILITY?
I MEAN, THE GEN-ERATOR'S JAPANESE-MADE, TOO.
...
A JAPANESE FACILITY... ON A PACIFIC ISLAND THAT SHOULDN'T EXIST...?
THE HECK'S REALLY GOIN' ON HERE...?

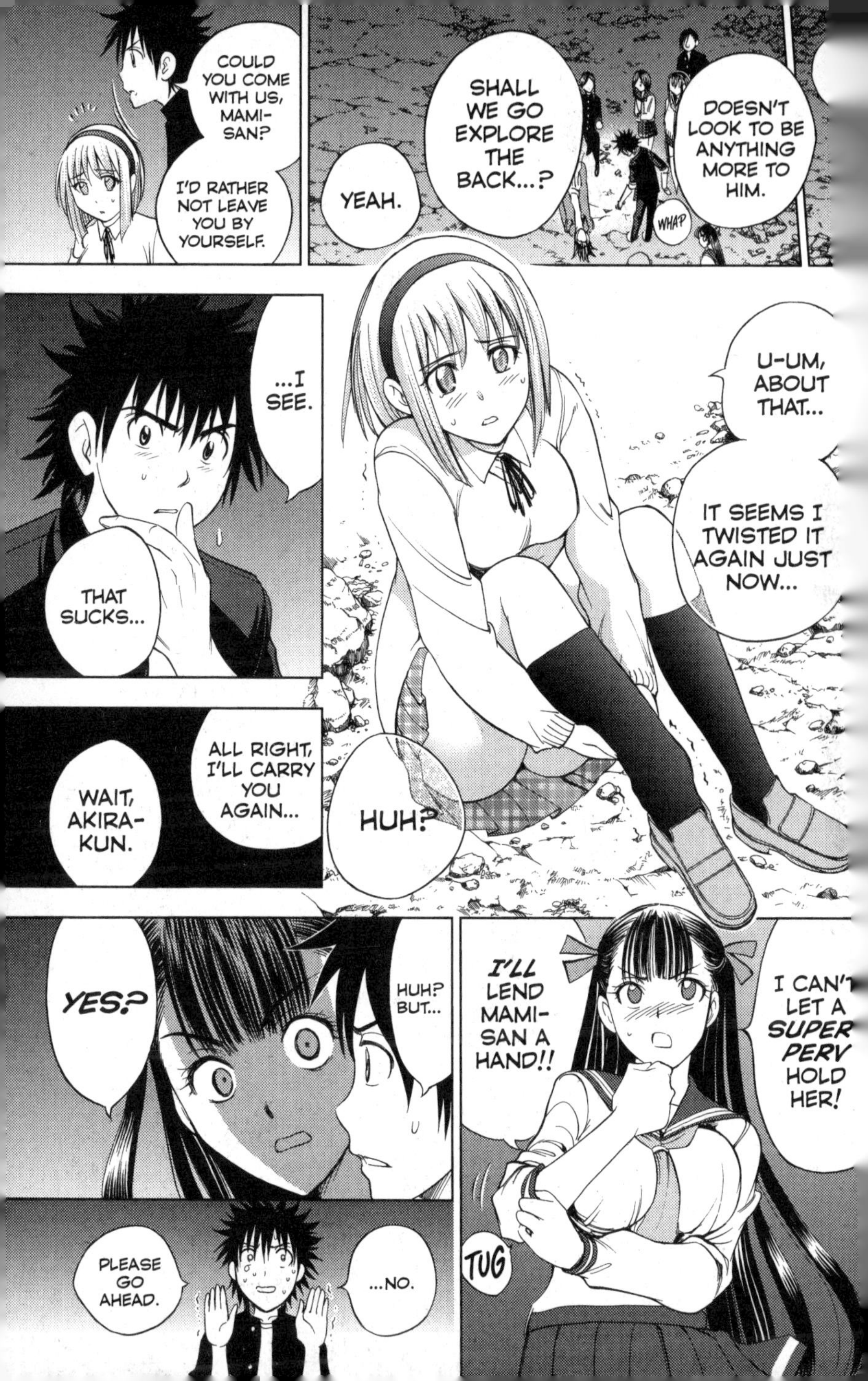
DOESN'T LOOK TO BE ANYTHING MORE TO HIM.
WHAP
SHALL WE GO EXPLORE THE BACK...?
YEAH.
COULD YOU COME WITH US, MAMI-SAN?
I'D RATHER NOT LEAVE YOU BY YOURSELF.
U-UM, ABOUT THAT...
IT SEEMS I TWISTED IT AGAIN JUST NOW...
HUH?
...I SEE.
THAT SUCKS...
ALL RIGHT, I'LL CARRY YOU AGAIN...
WAIT, AKIRA-KUN.
I CAN'T LET A SUPER PERV HOLD HER!
I'LL LEND MAMI-SAN A HAND!!
TUG
HUH? BUT...
YES?
...NO.
PLEASE GO AHEAD.

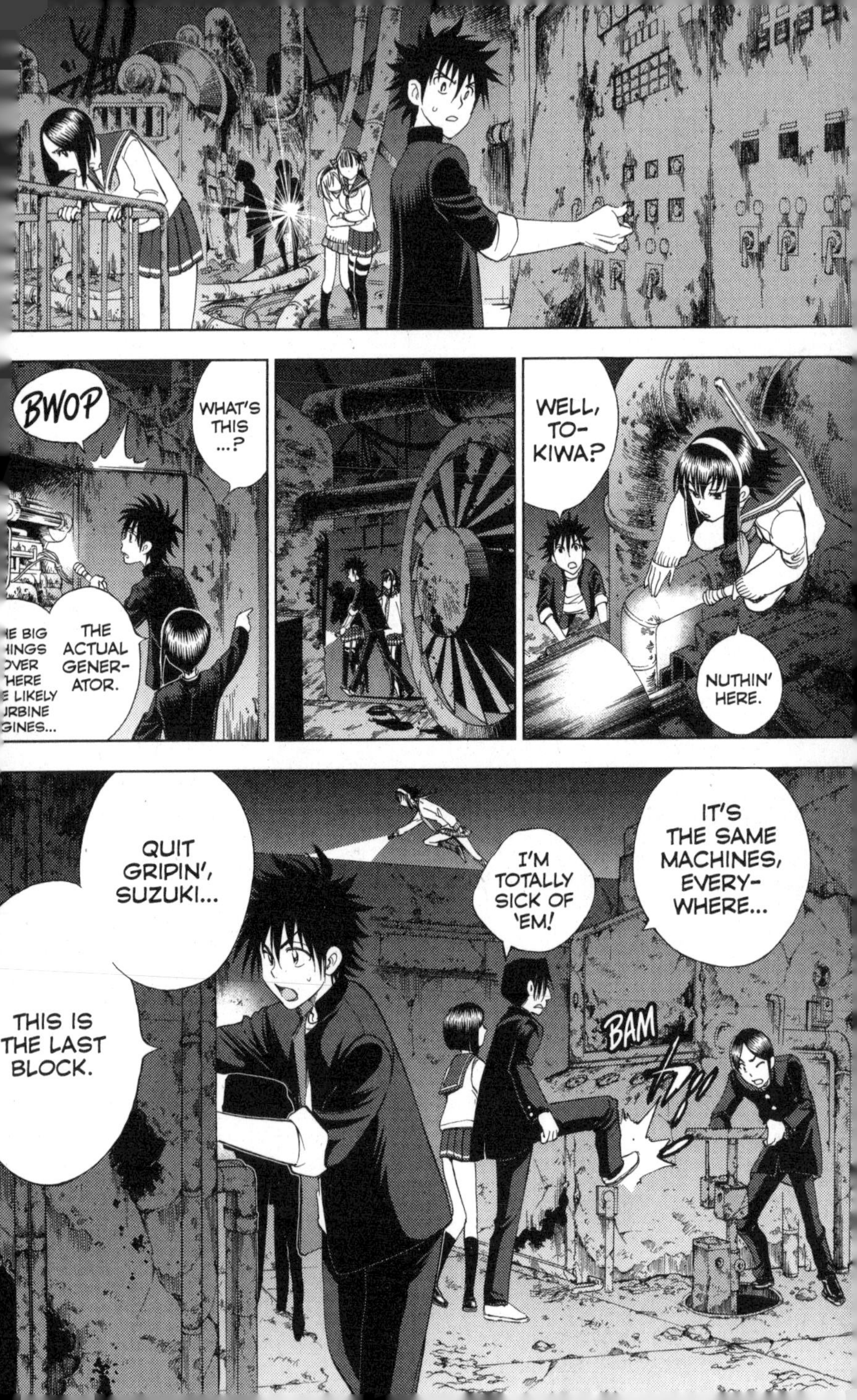
WELL, TO-KIWA?
NUTHIN' HERE.
WHAT'S THIS ...?
BWOP
THE ACTUAL GENER-ATOR.
HE BIG HINGS OVER HERE E LIKELY URBINE GINES...
IT'S THE SAME MACHINES, EVERY-WHERE...
I'M TOTALLY SICK OF 'EM!
QUIT GRIPIN', SUZUKI...
THIS IS THE LAST BLOCK.
BAM

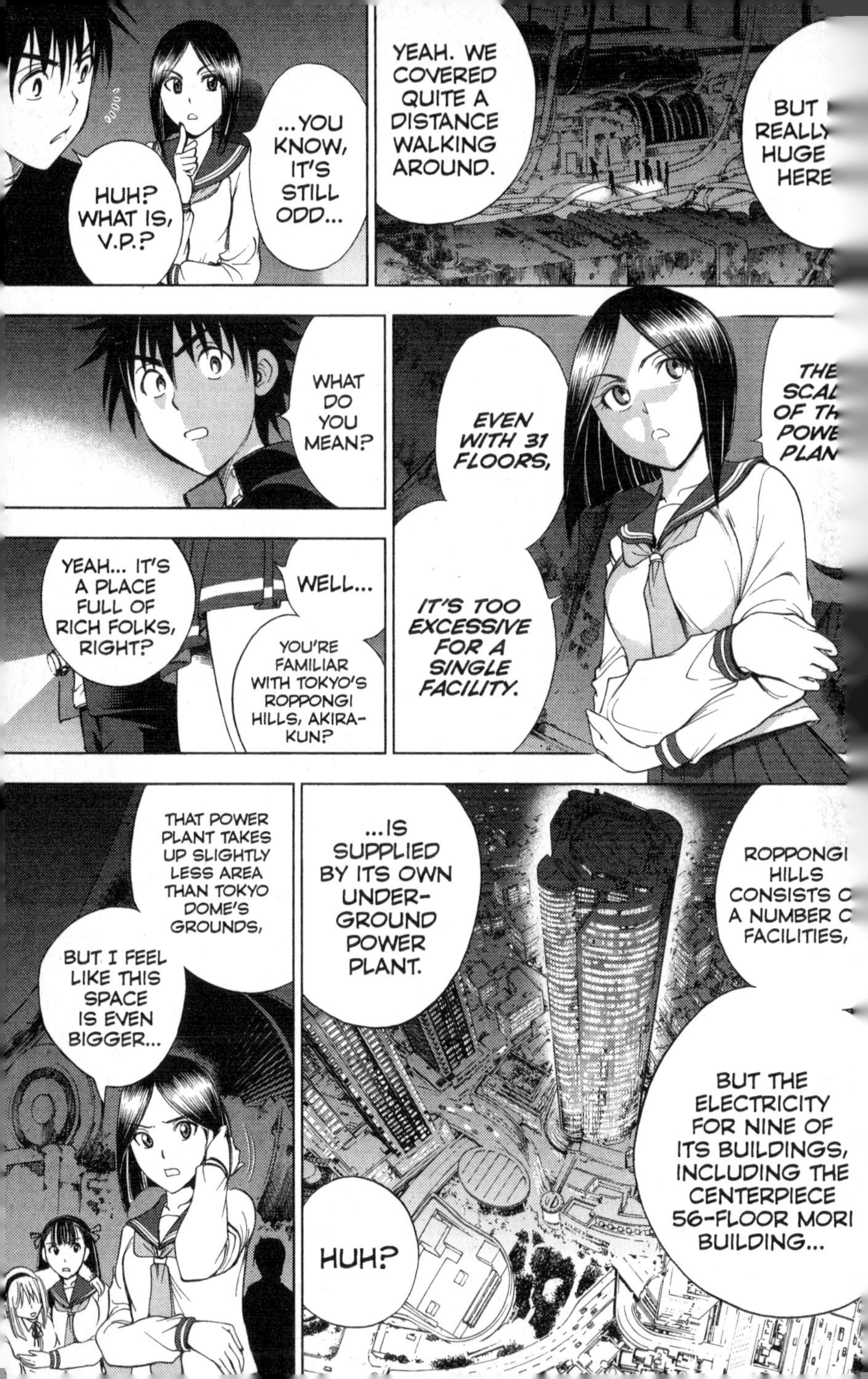
BUT I
REALLY
HUGE
HERE
YEAH. WE COVERED QUITE A DISTANCE WALKING AROUND.
...YOU KNOW, IT'S STILL ODD...
HUH? WHAT IS, V.P.?
THE
SCAL
OF TH
POWE
PLAN
EVEN WITH 31 FLOORS,
IT'S TOO EXCESSIVE FOR A SINGLE FACILITY.
WHAT DO YOU MEAN?
WELL...
YOU'RE FAMILIAR WITH TOKYO'S ROPPONGI HILLS, AKIRA-KUN?
YEAH... IT'S A PLACE FULL OF RICH FOLKS, RIGHT?
ROPPONGI HILLS CONSISTS O
A NUMBER O
FACILITIES,
BUT THE ELECTRICITY FOR NINE OF ITS BUILDINGS, INCLUDING THE CENTERPIECE 56-FLOOR MORI BUILDING...
...IS SUPPLIED BY ITS OWN UNDER-GROUND POWER PLANT.
HUH?
THAT POWER PLANT TAKES UP SLIGHTLY LESS AREA THAN TOKYO DOME'S GROUNDS,
BUT I FEEL LIKE THIS SPACE IS EVEN BIGGER...

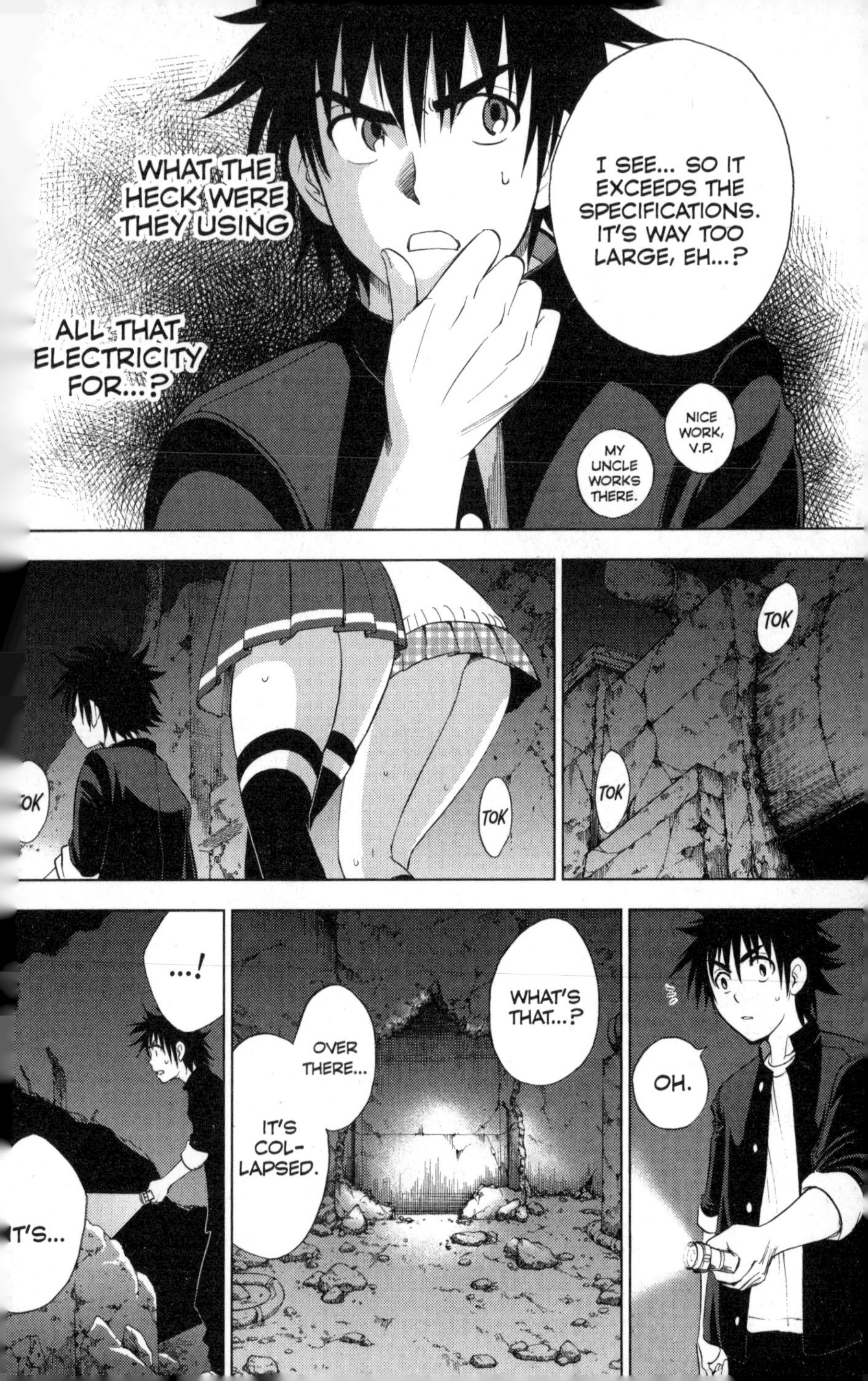
I SEE... SO IT EXCEEDS THE SPECIFICATIONS. IT'S WAY TOO LARGE, EH...?
WHAT THE HECK WERE THEY USING
ALL THAT ELECTRICITY FOR...?
NICE WORK, V.P.
MY UNCLE WORKS THERE.
TOK
TOK
TOK
OH.
WHAT'S THAT...?
OVER THERE...
IT'S COL-LAPSED.
...!
IT'S...

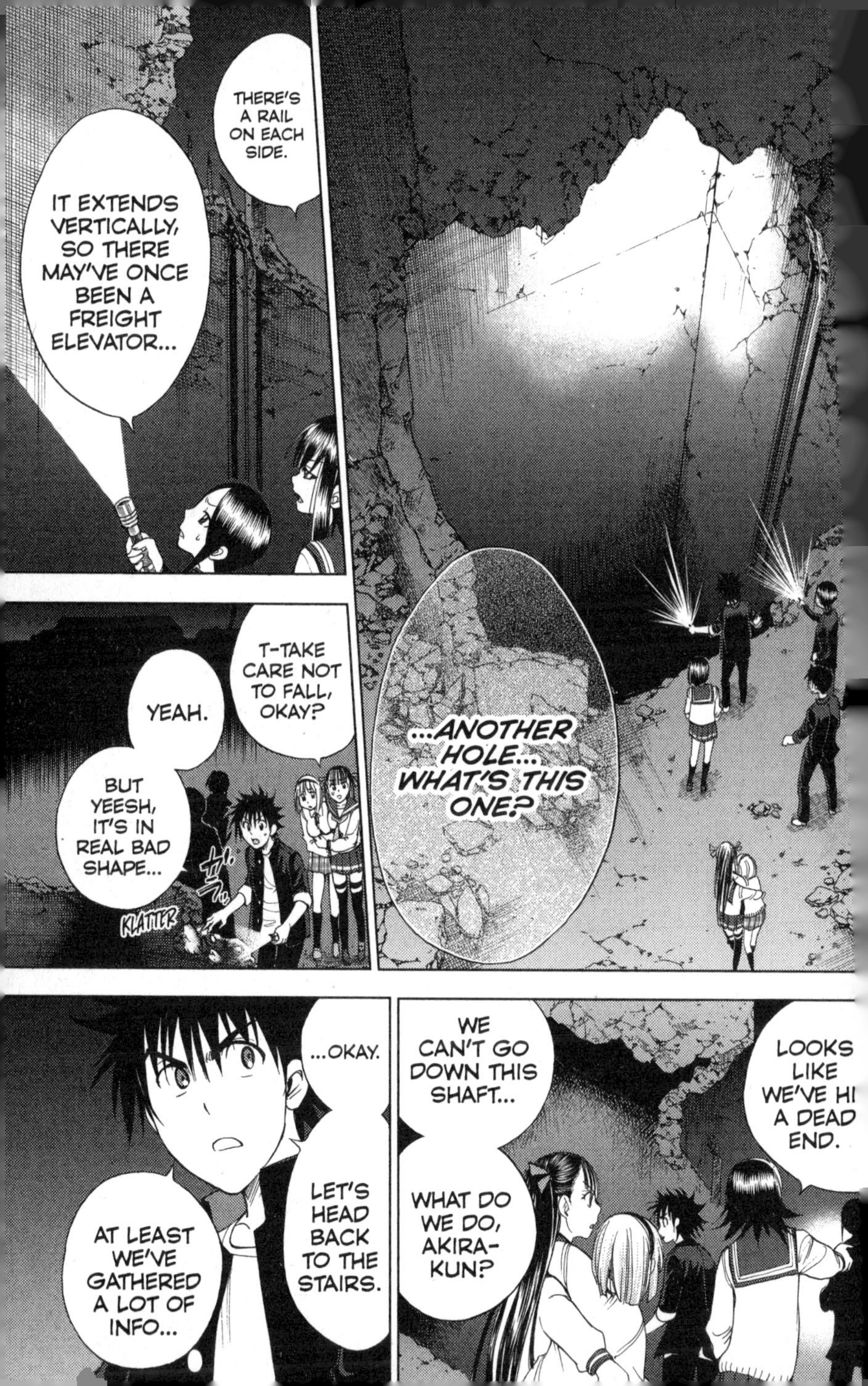
...ANOTHER HOLE... WHAT'S THIS ONE?
THERE'S A RAIL ON EACH SIDE.
IT EXTENDS VERTICALLY, SO THERE MAY'VE ONCE BEEN A FREIGHT ELEVATOR...
T-TAKE CARE NOT TO FALL, OKAY?
YEAH.
BUT YEESH, IT'S IN REAL BAD SHAPE...
KLATTER
LOOKS LIKE WE'VE HI A DEAD END.
WE CAN'T GO DOWN THIS SHAFT...
WHAT DO WE DO, AKIRA-KUN?
...OKAY.
LET'S HEAD BACK TO THE STAIRS.
AT LEAST WE'VE GATHERED A LOT OF INFO...

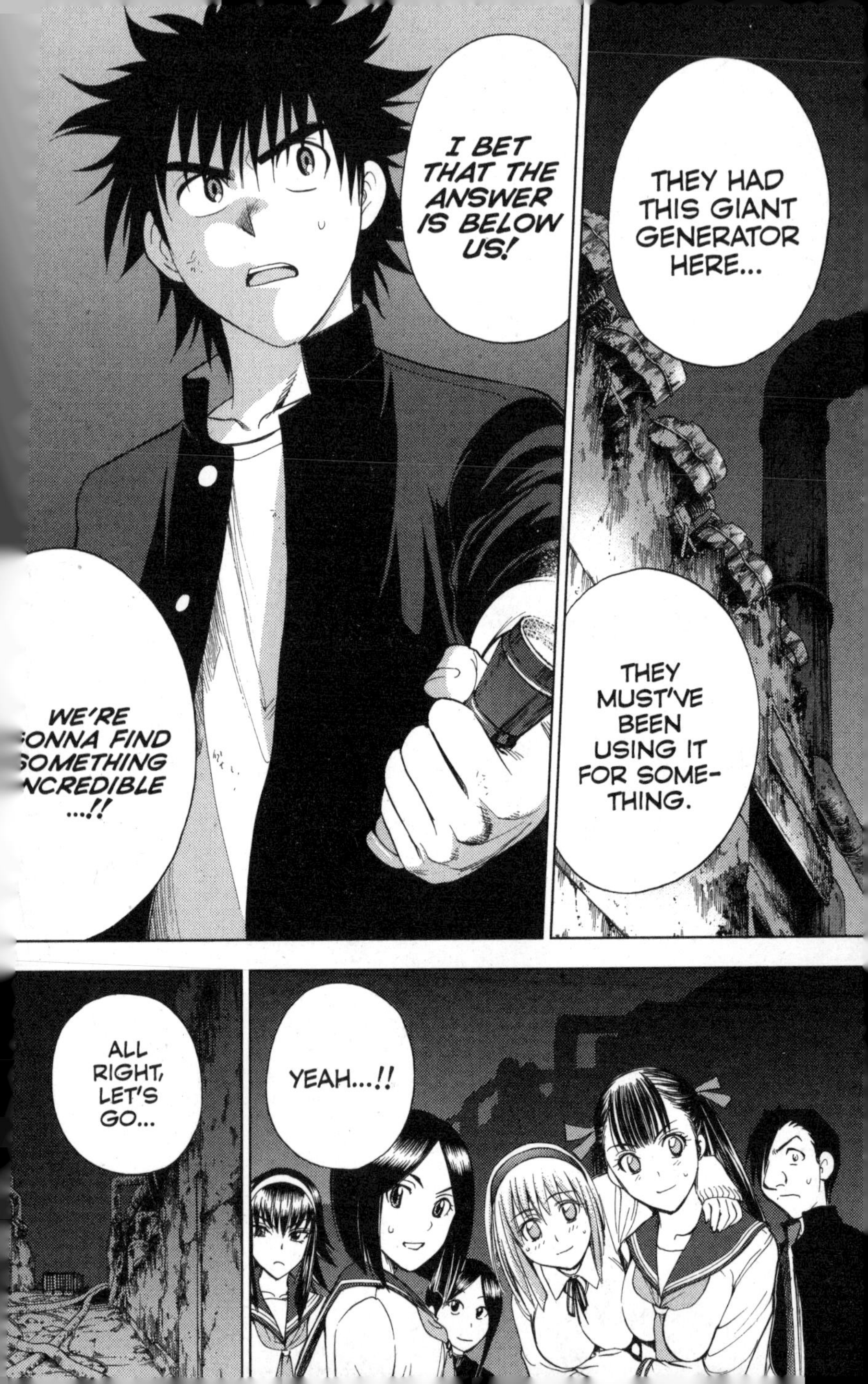
THEY HAD THIS GIANT GENERATOR HERE...
THEY MUST'VE BEEN USING IT FOR SOME-THING.
I BET THAT THE ANSWER IS BELOW US!
WE'RE GONNA FIND SOMETHING INCREDIBLE ...!!
YEAH...!!
ALL RIGHT, LET'S GO...

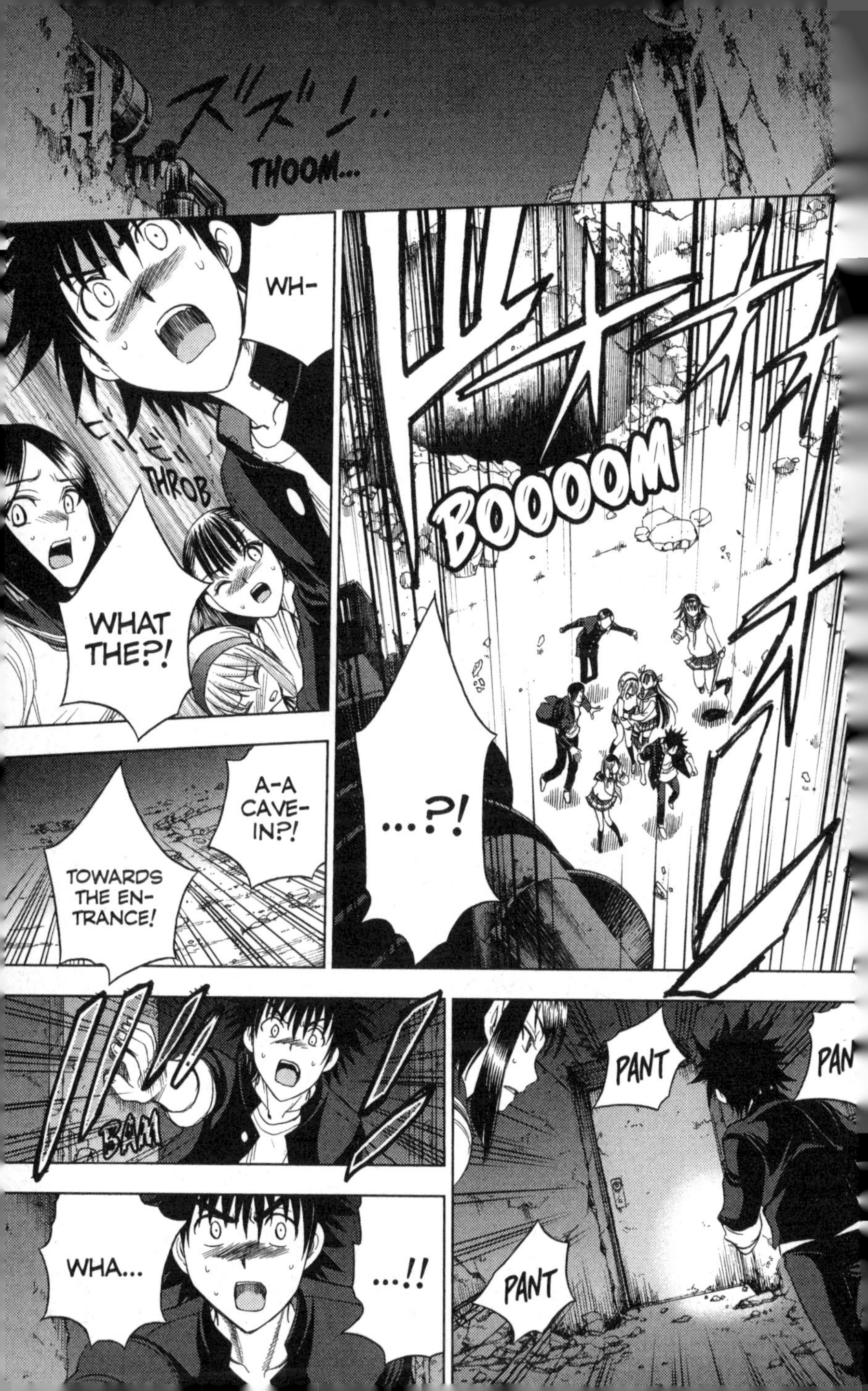
ズズン..
THOOM...
BOOOOM
...?!
WH-
THROB
WHAT THE?!
A-A CAVE-IN?!
TOWARDS THE EN-TRANCE!
PAN
PANT
PANT
BAM
...!!
WHA...

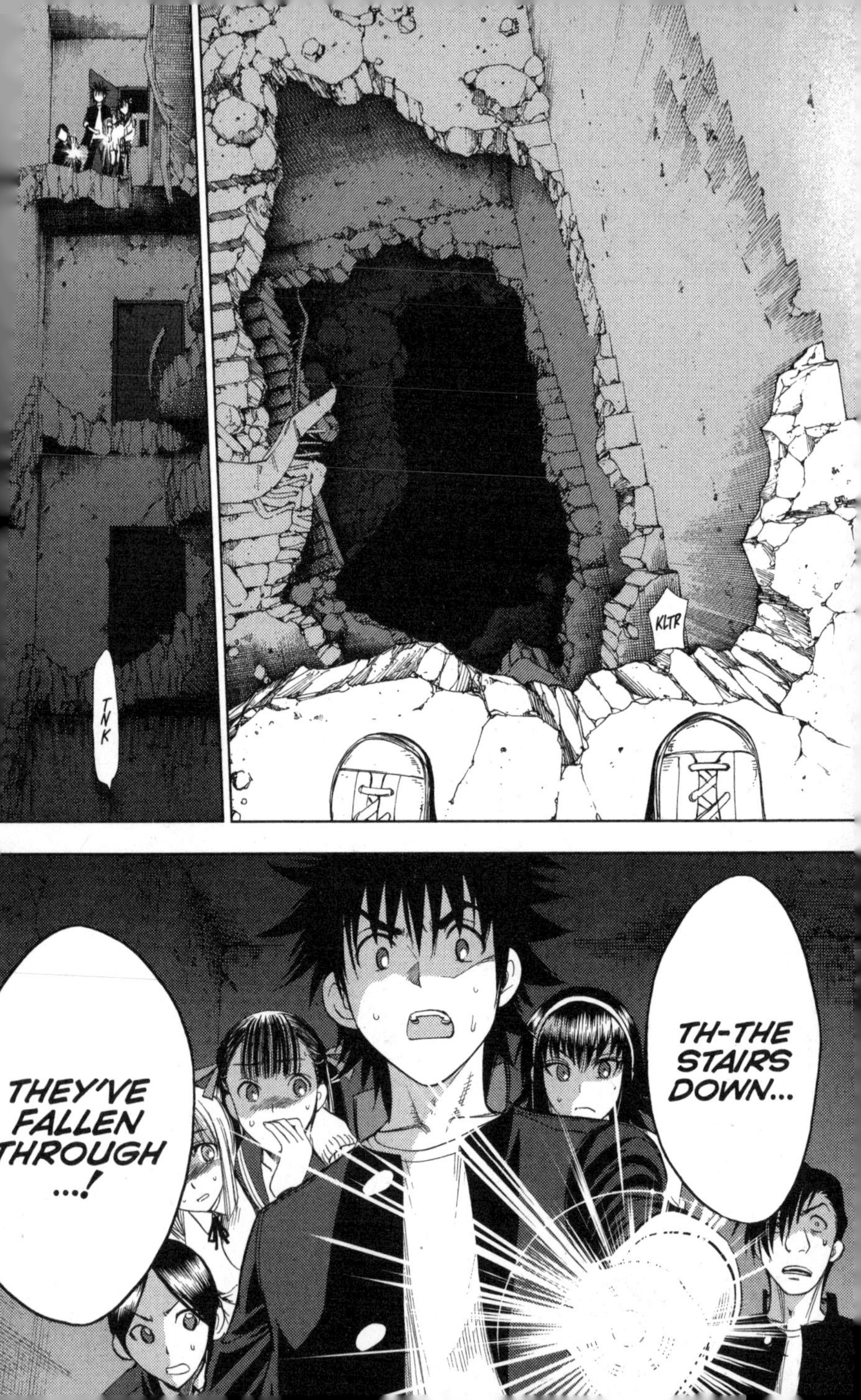
KLTR
TNK
TH-THE STAIRS DOWN...
THEY'VE FALLEN THROUGH ...!

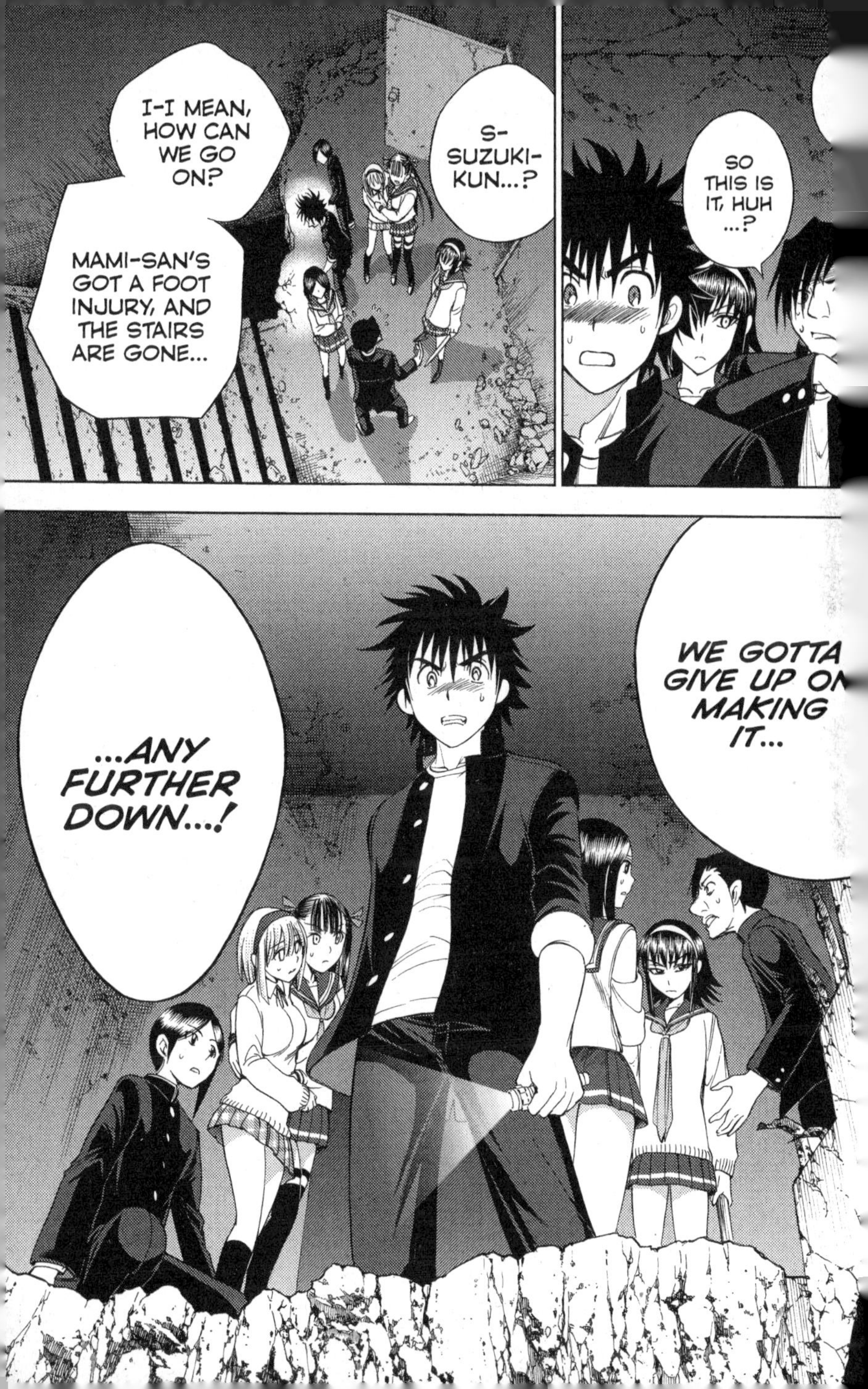
SO THIS IS IT, HUH ...?
S-SUZUKI-KUN...?
I-I MEAN, HOW CAN WE GO ON?
MAMI-SAN'S GOT A FOOT INJURY, AND THE STAIRS ARE GONE...
WE GOTTA GIVE UP ON MAKING IT...
...ANY FURTHER DOWN...!

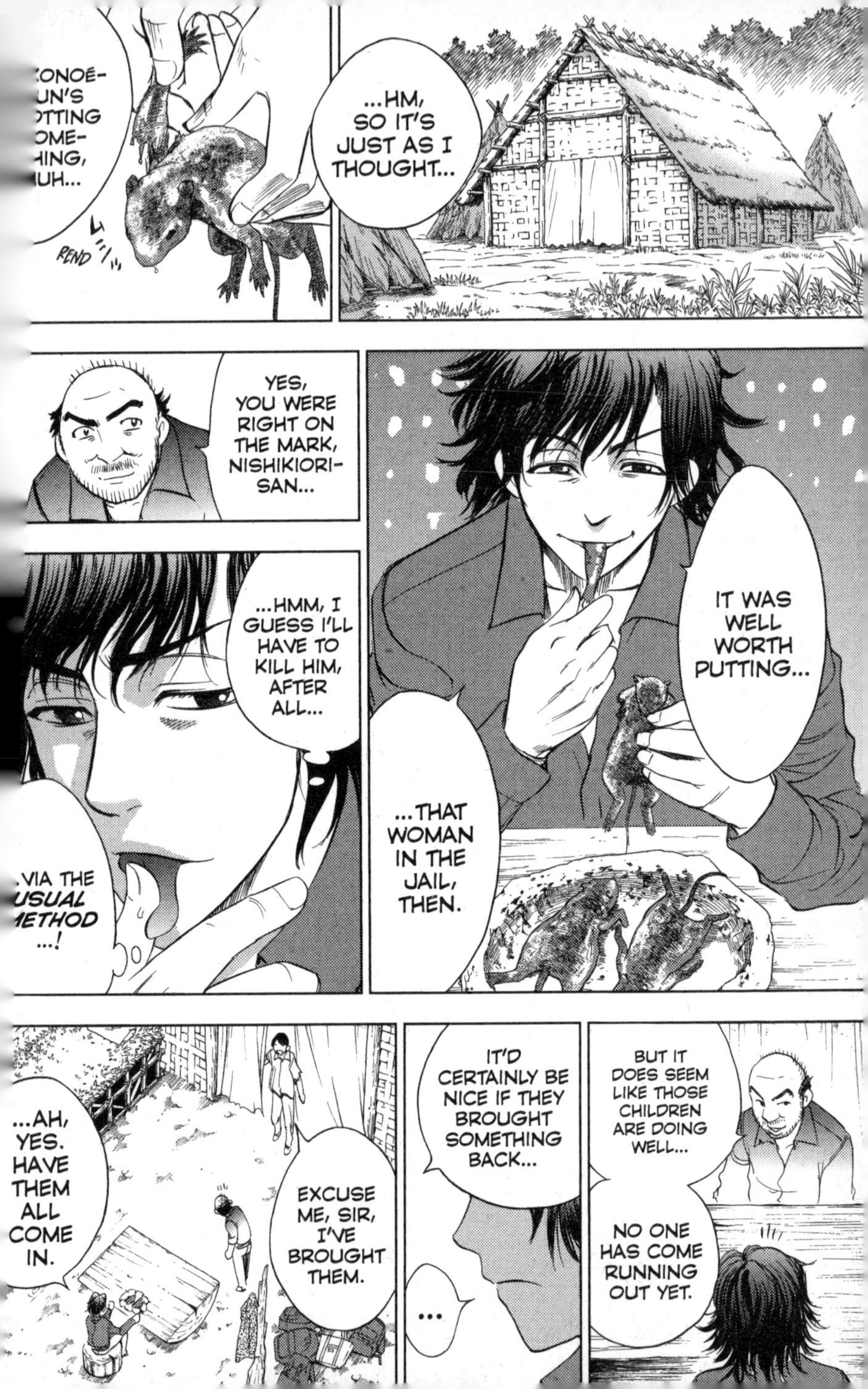
...HM, SO IT'S JUST AS I THOUGHT...
ONOE-
UN'S
OTTING
OME-
HING,
UH...
REND
IT WAS WELL WORTH PUTTING...
...THAT WOMAN IN THE JAIL, THEN.
YES, YOU WERE RIGHT ON THE MARK, NISHIKIORI-SAN...
...HMM, I GUESS I'LL HAVE TO KILL HIM, AFTER ALL...
.VIA THE
USUAL
ETHOD
...!
BUT IT DOES SEEM LIKE THOSE CHILDREN ARE DOING WELL...
NO ONE HAS COME RUNNING OUT YET.
IT'D CERTAINLY BE NICE IF THEY BROUGHT SOMETHING BACK...
...
EXCUSE ME, SIR, I'VE BROUGHT THEM.
...AH, YES. HAVE THEM ALL COME IN.

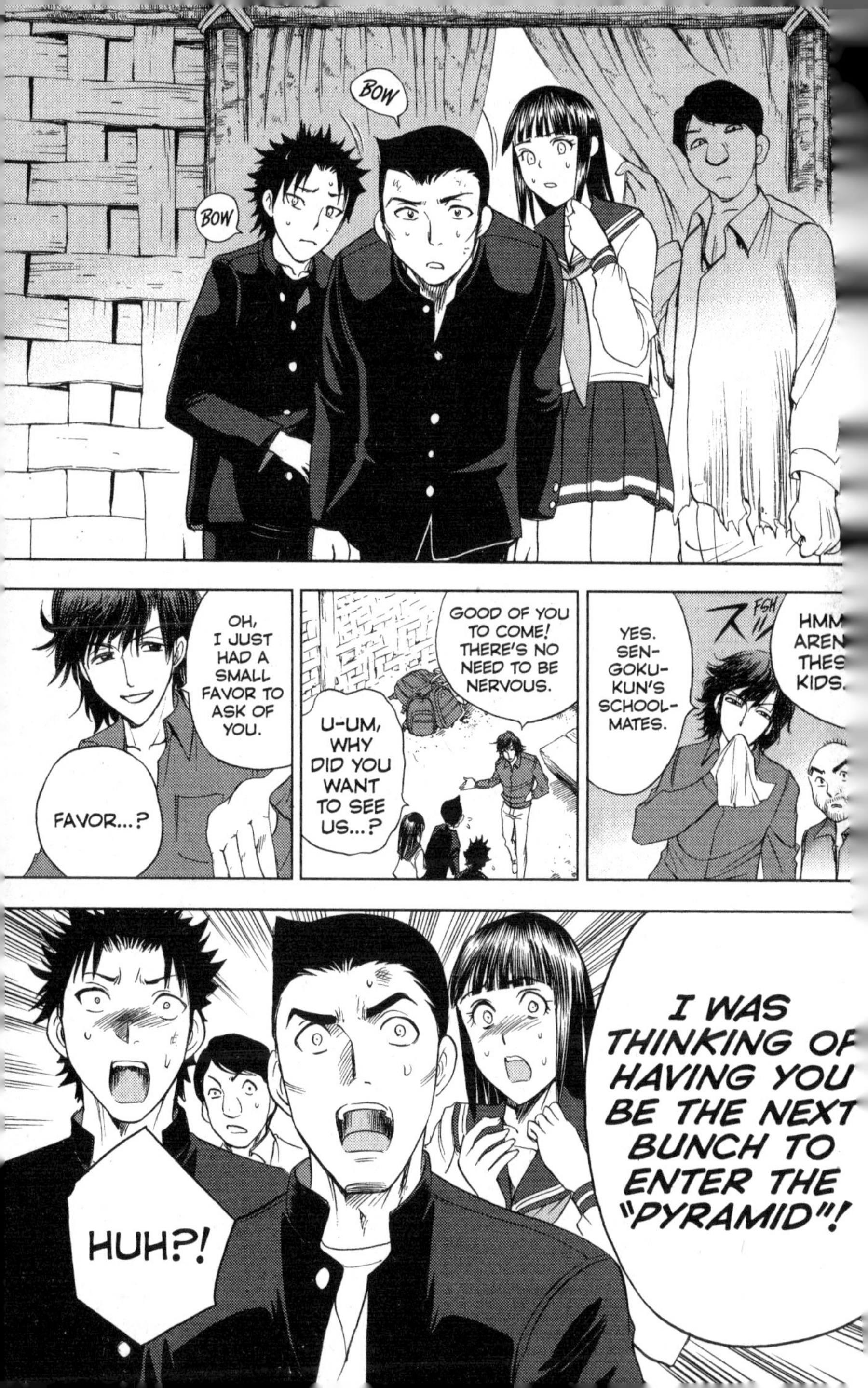

BOW
BOW
HMM
AREN
THES
KIDS.
スッ FSH
YES. SEN-GOKU-KUN'S SCHOOL-MATES.
GOOD OF YOU TO COME! THERE'S NO NEED TO BE NERVOUS.
U-UM, WHY DID YOU WANT TO SEE US...?
OH, I JUST HAD A SMALL FAVOR TO ASK OF YOU.
FAVOR...?
I WAS THINKING OF HAVING YOU BE THE NEXT BUNCH TO ENTER THE "PYRAMID"!
HUH?!

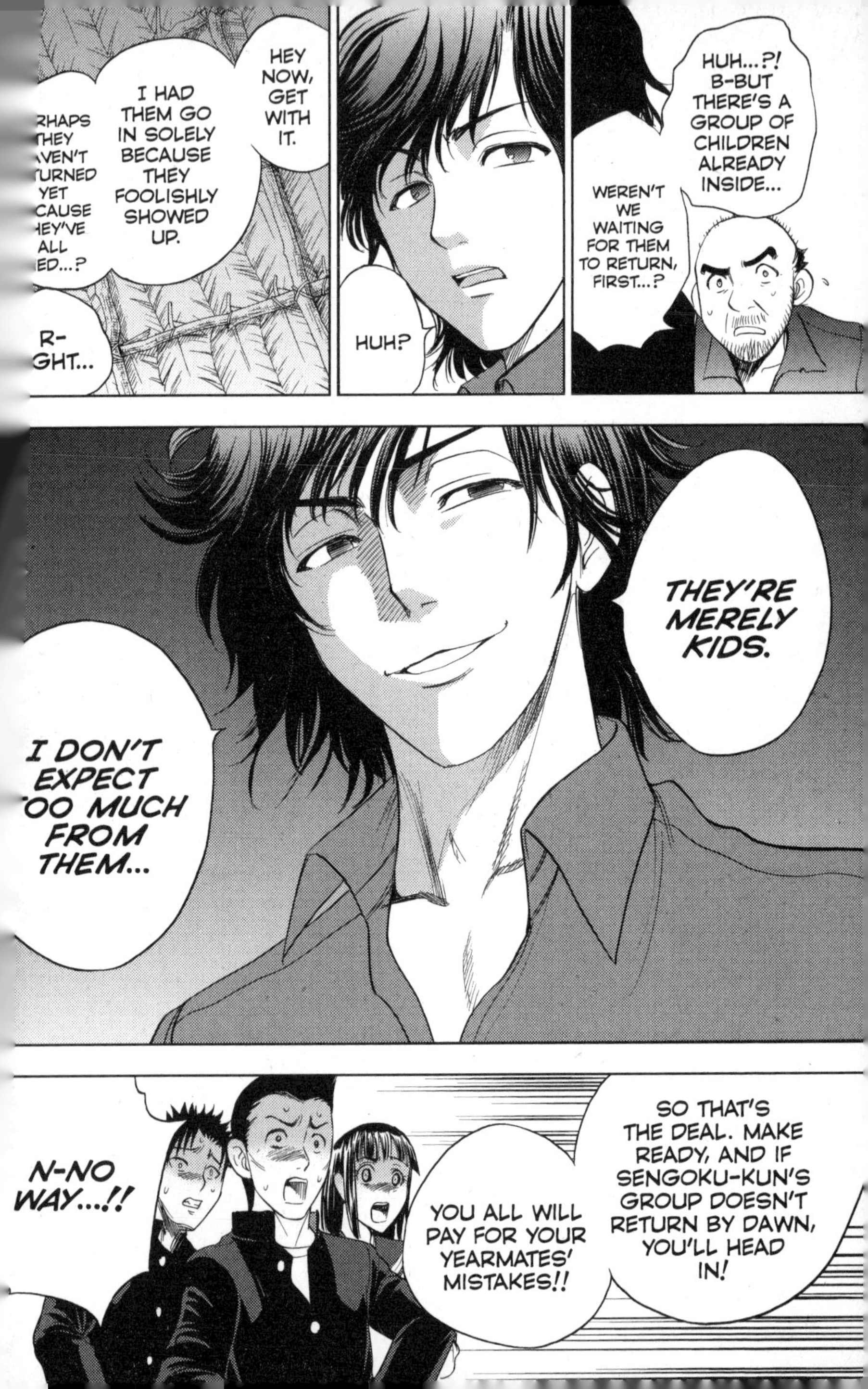

HUH...?! B-BUT THERE'S A GROUP OF CHILDREN ALREADY INSIDE...
WEREN'T WE WAITING FOR THEM TO RETURN, FIRST...?
HEY NOW, GET WITH IT.
HUH?
I HAD THEM GO IN SOLELY BECAUSE THEY FOOLISHLY SHOWED UP.
RHAPS THEY VEN'T TURNED YET CAUSE HEY'VE ALL ED...?
R-GHT...
THEY'RE MERELY KIDS.
I DON'T EXPECT OO MUCH FROM THEM...
SO THAT'S THE DEAL. MAKE READY, AND IF SENGOKU-KUN'S GROUP DOESN'T RETURN BY DAWN, YOU'LL HEAD IN!
YOU ALL WILL PAY FOR YOUR YEARMATES' MISTAKES!!
N-NO WAY...!!

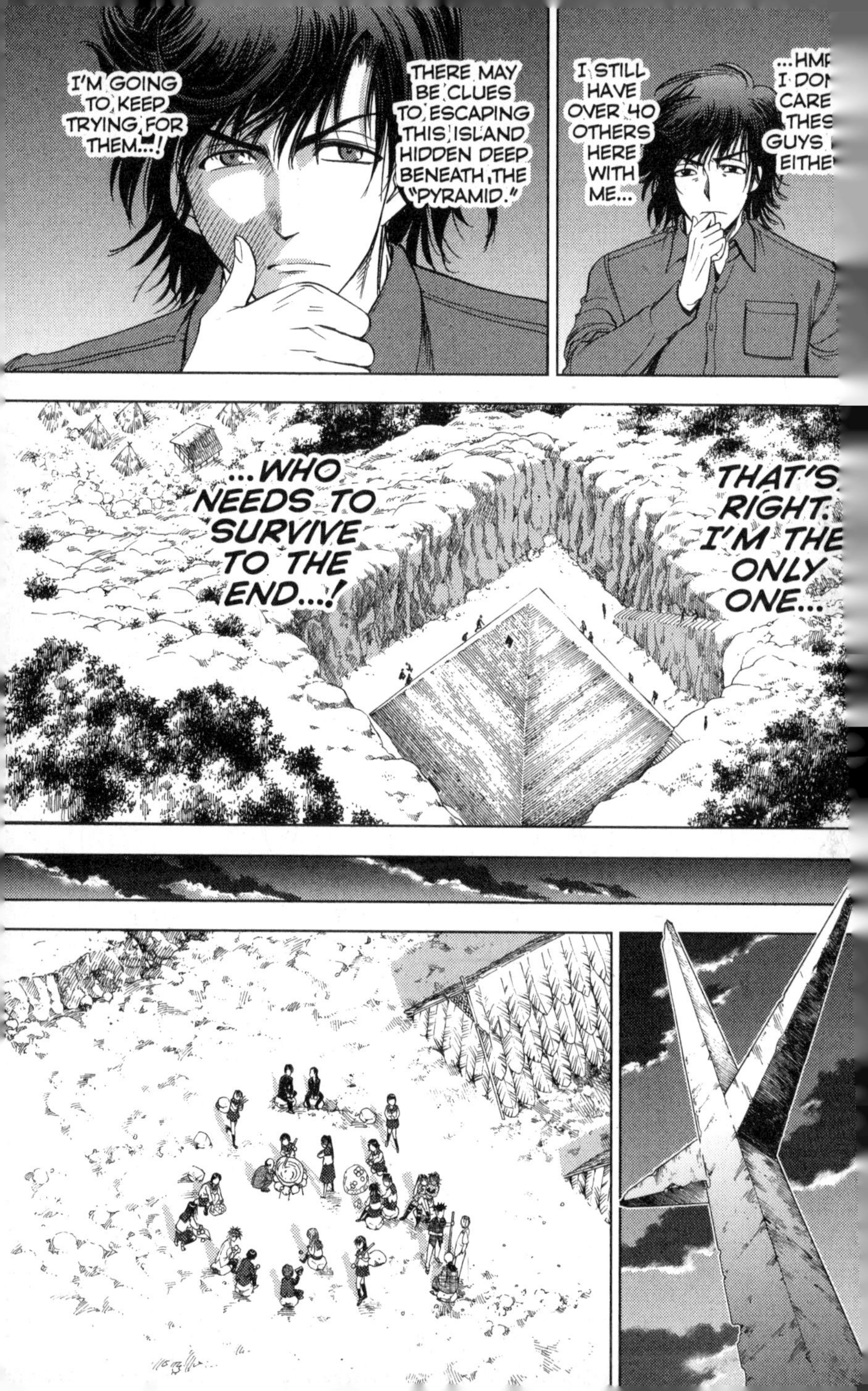
...HMP I DON CARE THES GUYS EITHE
I STILL HAVE OVER 40 OTHERS HERE WITH ME...
THERE MAY BE CLUES TO ESCAPING THIS ISLAND HIDDEN DEEP BENEATH THE "PYRAMID."
I'M GOING TO KEEP TRYING FOR THEM...!
THAT'S RIGHT. I'M THE ONLY ONE...
...WHO NEEDS TO SURVIVE TO THE END...!

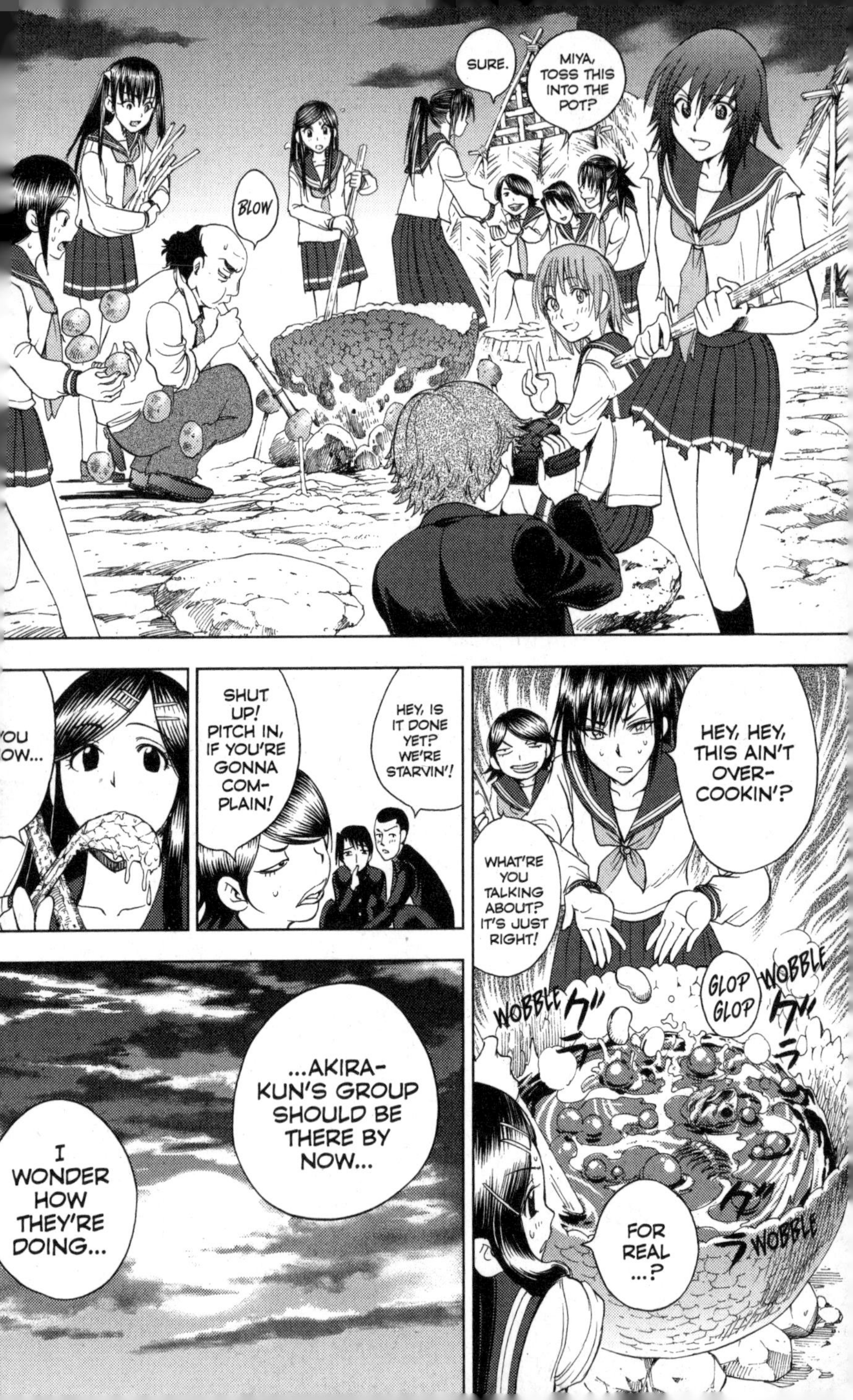
MIYA, TOSS THIS INTO THE POT?
SURE.
BLOW
HEY, HEY, THIS AIN'T OVER-COOKIN'?
WHAT'RE YOU TALKING ABOUT? IT'S JUST RIGHT!
GLOP GLOP
WOBBLE グラ
WOBBLE グラ
WOBBLE グラ
FOR REAL ...?
HEY, IS IT DONE YET? WE'RE STARVIN'!
SHUT UP! PITCH IN, IF YOU'RE GONNA COM-PLAIN!
YOU OW...
...AKIRA-KUN'S GROUP SHOULD BE THERE BY NOW...
I WONDER HOW THEY'RE DOING...

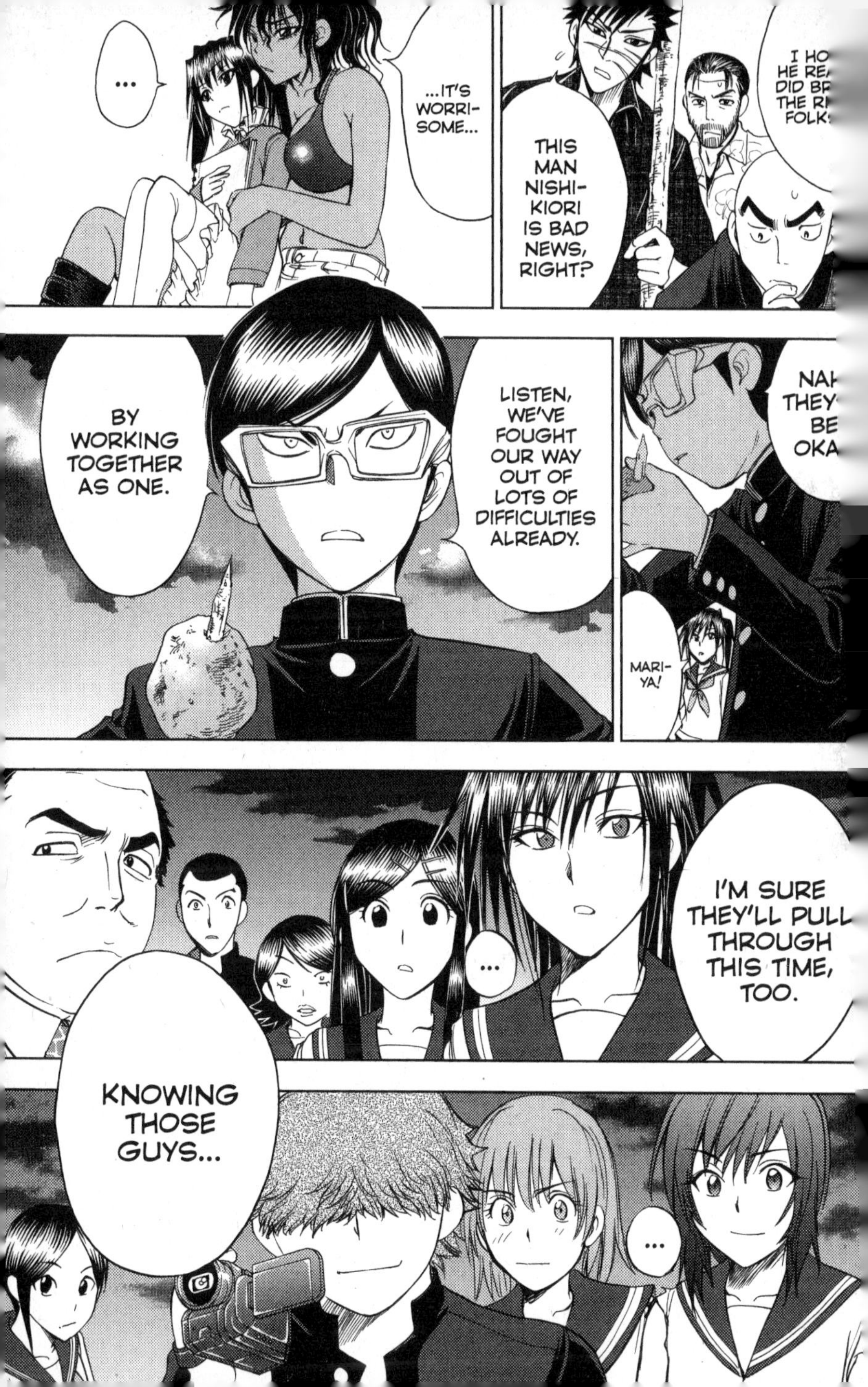
I HO HE REA DID BR THE RI FOLKS
THIS MAN NISHIKIORI IS BAD NEWS, RIGHT?
...IT'S WORRISOME...
...
NAH THEY' BE OKA
MARIYA!
LISTEN, WE'VE FOUGHT OUR WAY OUT OF LOTS OF DIFFICULTIES ALREADY.
BY WORKING TOGETHER AS ONE.
I'M SURE THEY'LL PULL THROUGH THIS TIME, TOO.
...
...
KNOWING THOSE GUYS...

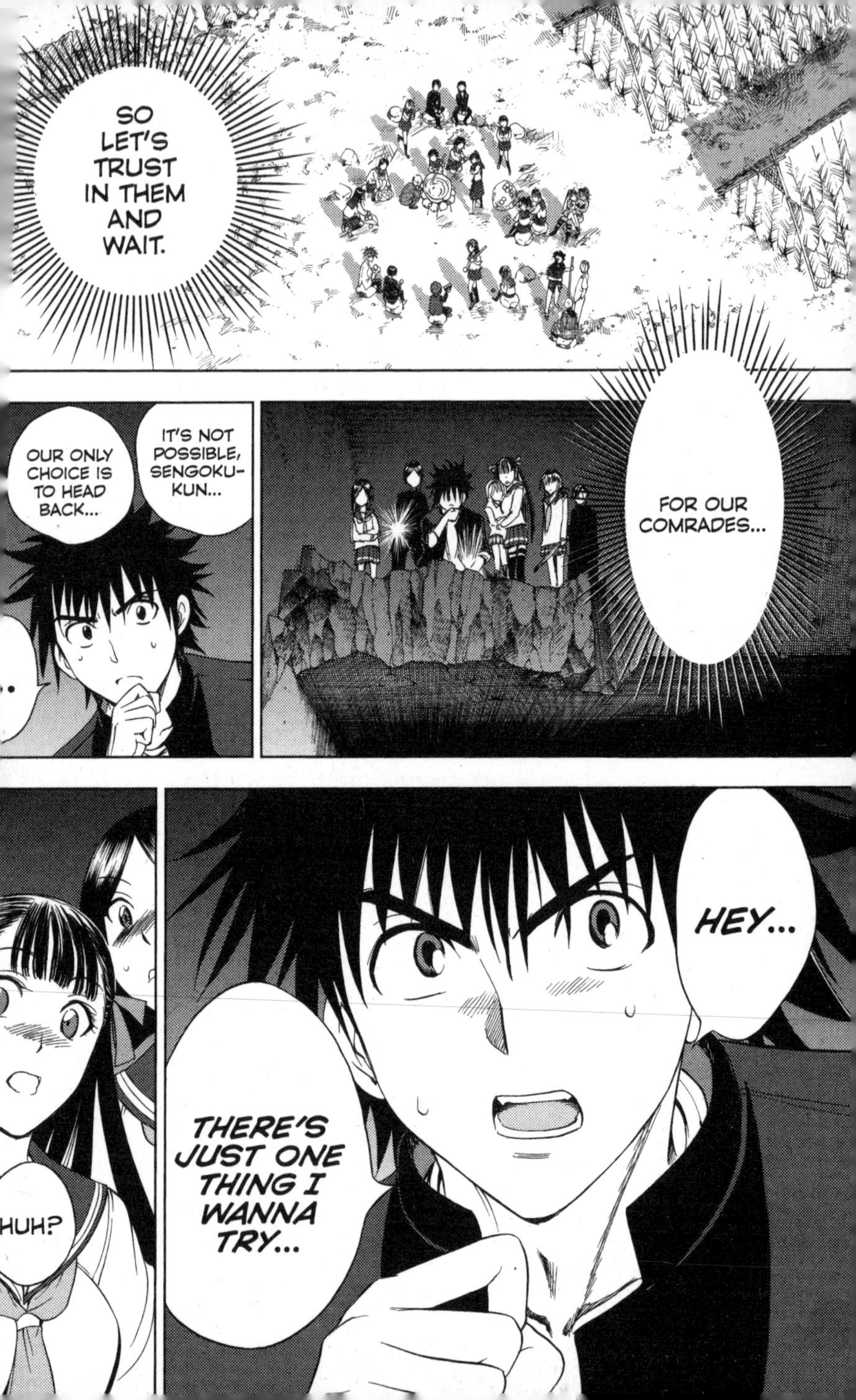
SO LET'S TRUST IN THEM AND WAIT.
FOR OUR COMRADES...
IT'S NOT POSSIBLE, SENGOKU-KUN...
OUR ONLY CHOICE IS TO HEAD BACK...
HEY...
THERE'S JUST ONE THING I WANNA TRY...
HUH?

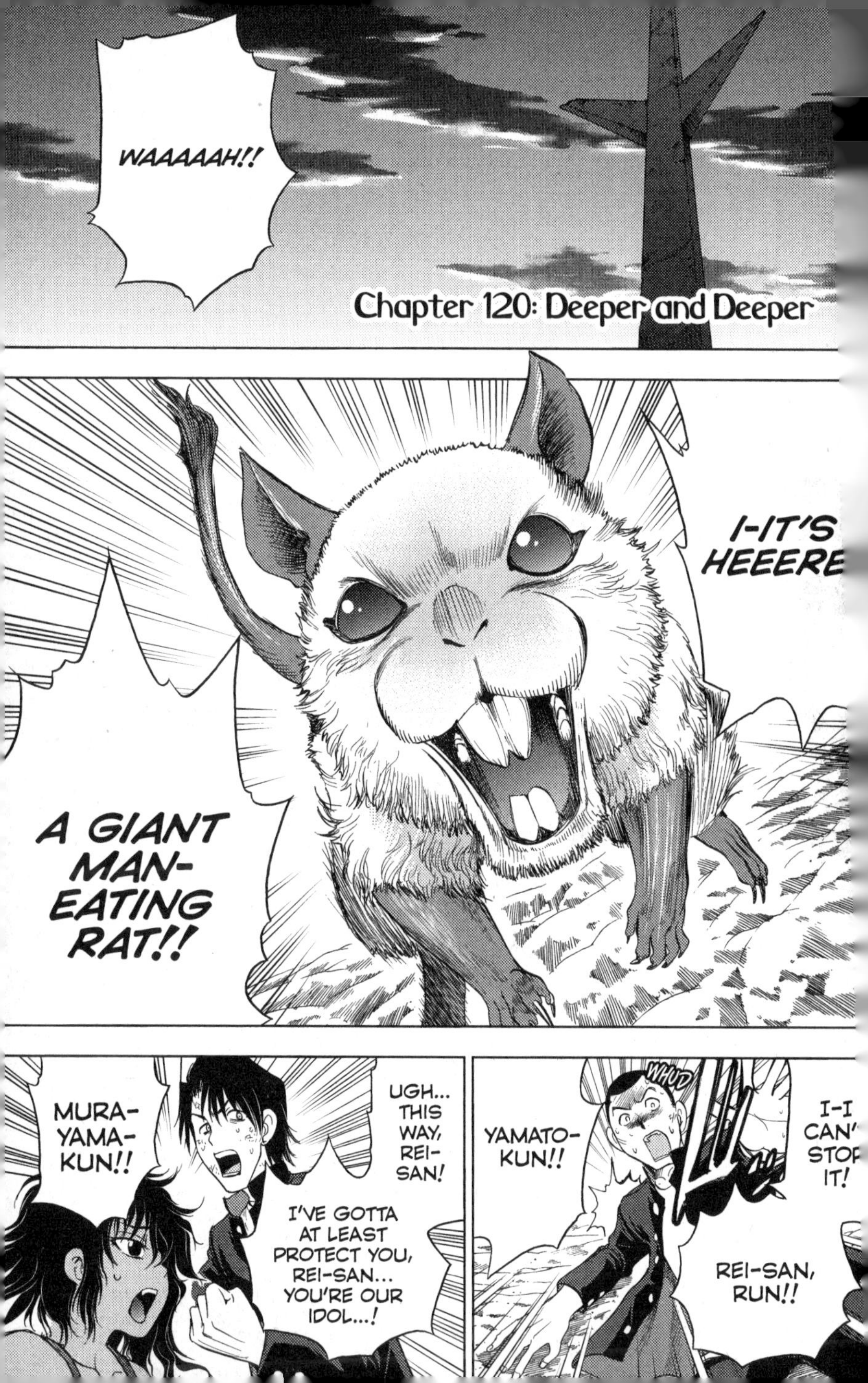
WAAAAAH!!
Chapter 120: Deeper and Deeper
I-IT'S HEEERE
A GIANT MAN-EATING RAT!!
WHUD
I-I CAN'T STOP IT!
YAMATO-KUN!!
REI-SAN, RUN!!
UGH... THIS WAY, REI-SAN!
MURA-YAMA-KUN!!
I'VE GOTTA AT LEAST PROTECT YOU, REI-SAN... YOU'RE OUR IDOL...!

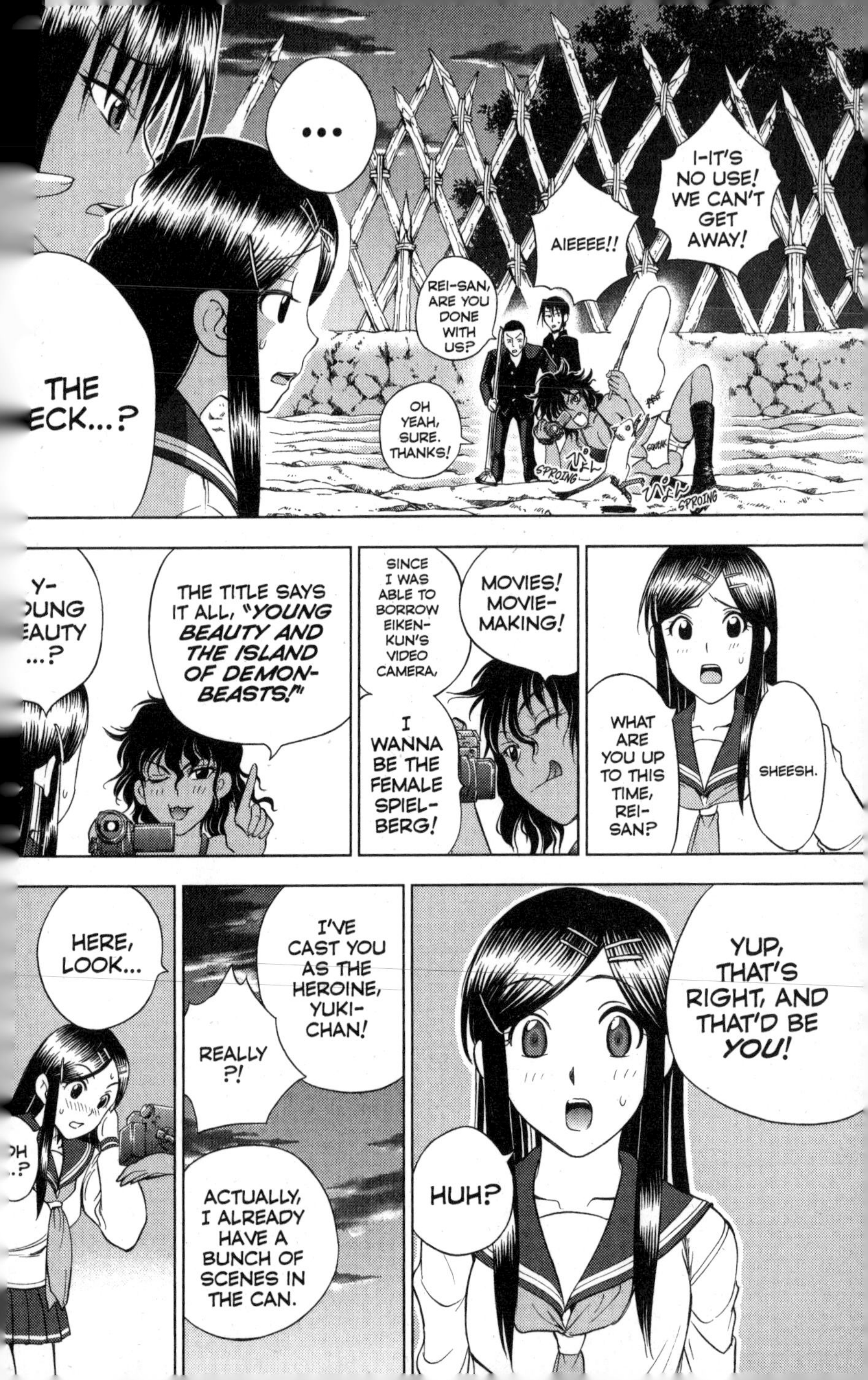
I-IT'S NO USE! WE CAN'T GET AWAY!
AIEEEE!!
REI-SAN, ARE YOU DONE WITH US?
OH YEAH, SURE. THANKS!
SPROING
SPROING
...
THE
ECK...?
SHEESH.
WHAT ARE YOU UP TO THIS TIME, REI-SAN?
MOVIES! MOVIE-MAKING!
SINCE I WAS ABLE TO BORROW EIKEN-KUN'S VIDEO CAMERA,
I WANNA BE THE FEMALE SPIEL-BERG!
THE TITLE SAYS IT ALL, *"YOUNG BEAUTY AND THE ISLAND OF DEMON-BEASTS!"*
Y-
OUNG
EAUTY
...?
YUP, THAT'S RIGHT, AND THAT'D BE *YOU*!
HUH?
I'VE CAST YOU AS THE HEROINE, YUKI-CHAN!
REALLY?!
ACTUALLY, I ALREADY HAVE A BUNCH OF SCENES IN THE CAN.
HERE, LOOK...

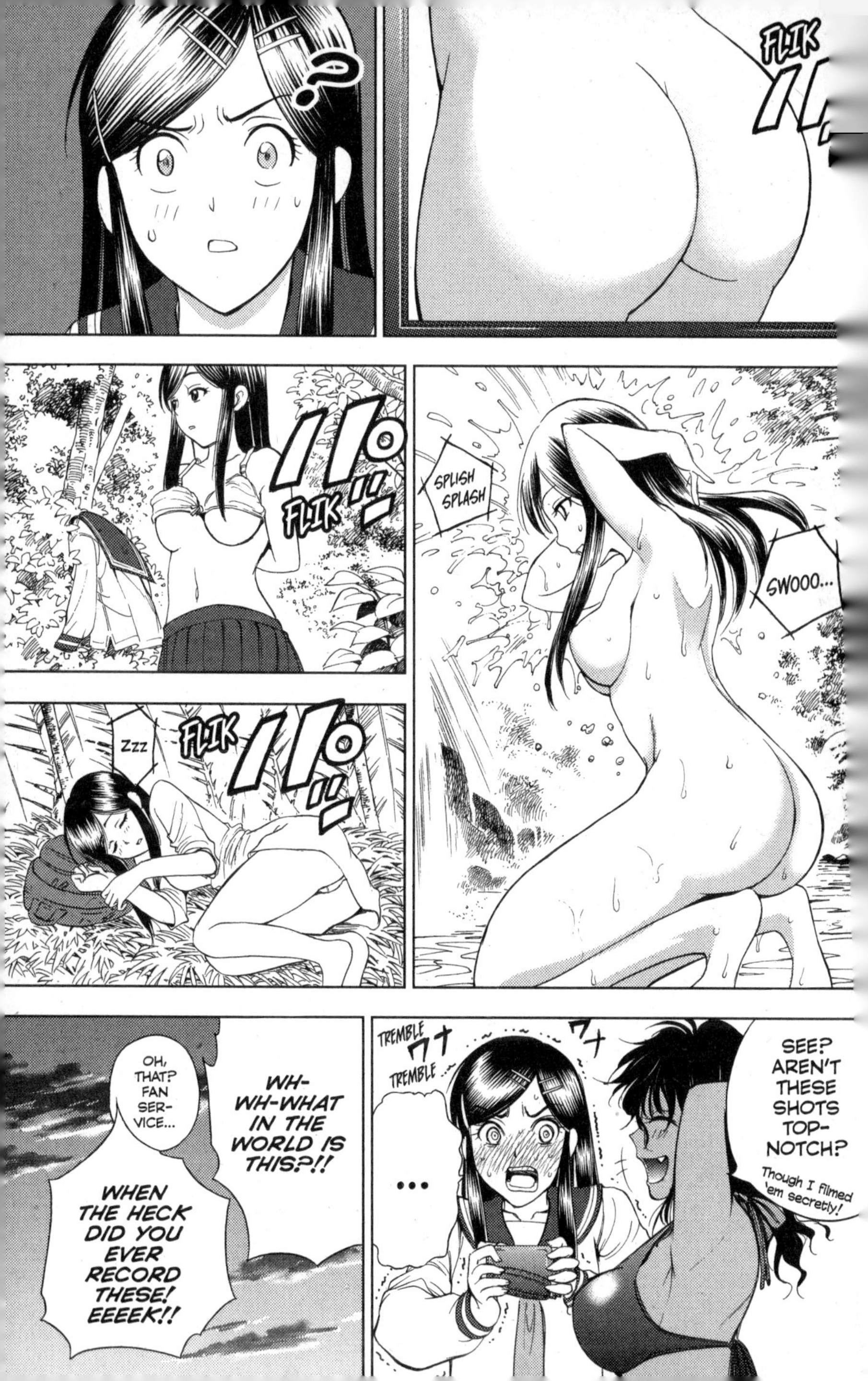
FLIK
SPLISH SPLASH
SWOOO...
FLIK
Zzz
FLIK
SEE? AREN'T THESE SHOTS TOP-NOTCH?
Though I filmed 'em secretly!
TREMBLE TREMBLE
...
WH-WH-WHAT IN THE WORLD IS THIS?!!
OH, THAT? FAN SER-VICE...
WHEN THE HECK DID YOU EVER RECORD THESE! EEEEK!!

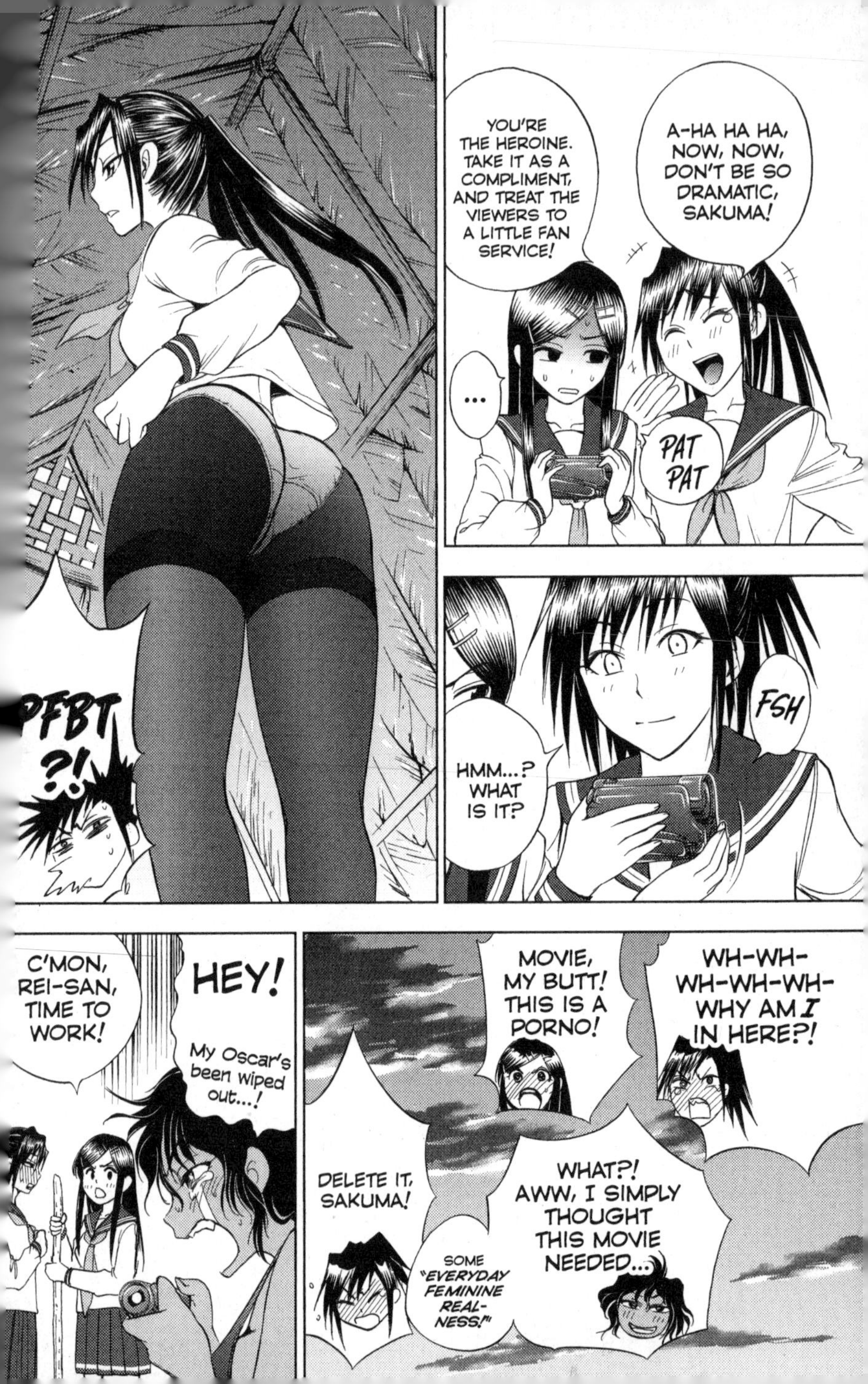
A-HA HA HA, NOW, NOW, DON'T BE SO DRAMATIC, SAKUMA!
YOU'RE THE HEROINE. TAKE IT AS A COMPLIMENT, AND TREAT THE VIEWERS TO A LITTLE FAN SERVICE!
PAT PAT
...
FSH
HMM...? WHAT IS IT?
PFBT ?!
WH-WH-WH-WH-WH-WHY AM *I* IN HERE?!
MOVIE, MY BUTT! THIS IS A PORNO!
WHAT?! AWW, I SIMPLY THOUGHT THIS MOVIE NEEDED...
SOME *"EVERYDAY FEMININE REAL-NESS!"*
DELETE IT, SAKUMA!
HEY!
C'MON, REI-SAN, TIME TO WORK!
My Oscar's been wiped out...!

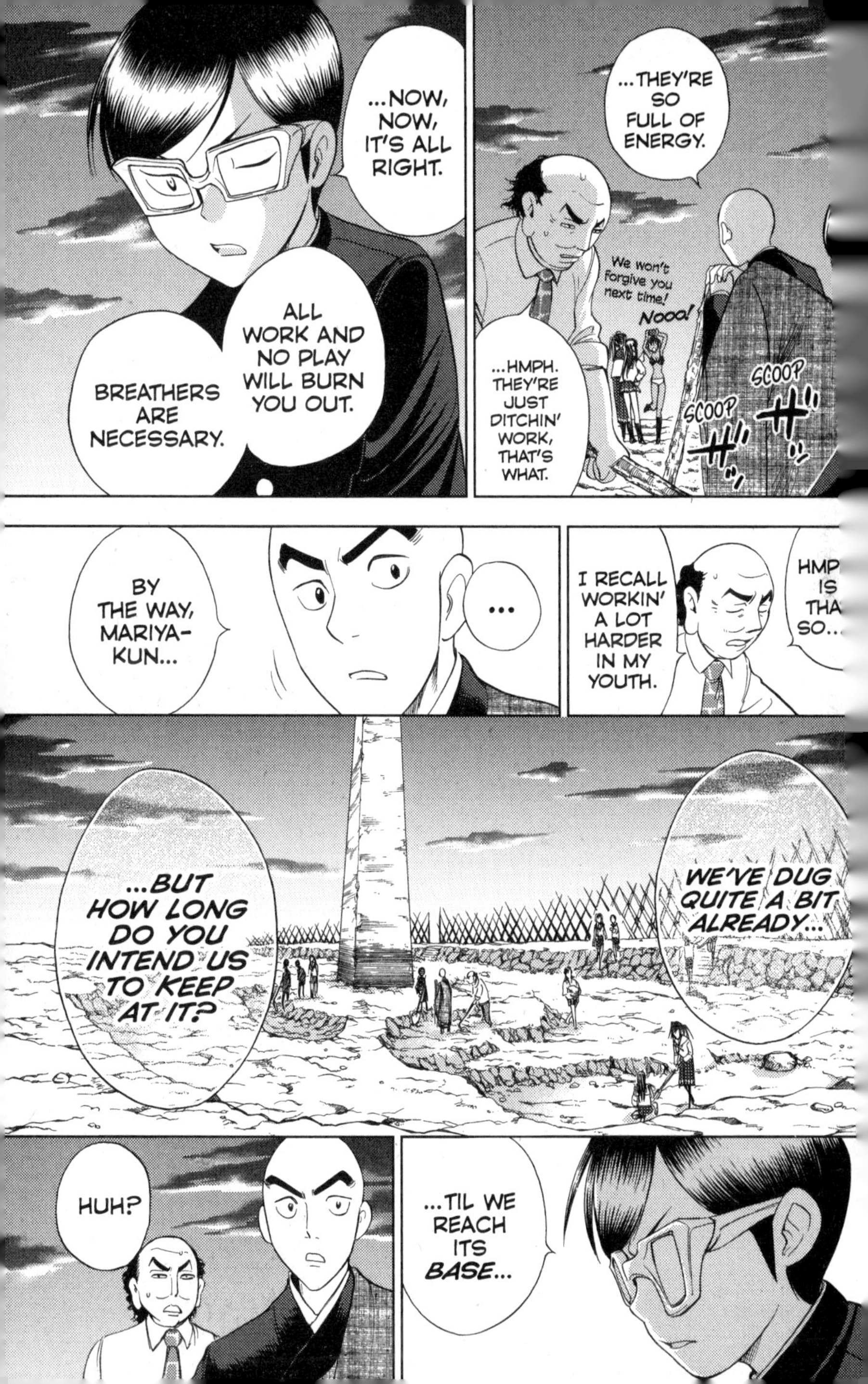
...THEY'RE SO FULL OF ENERGY.
We won't forgive you next time!
Nooo!
SCOOP
SCOOP
...HMPH. THEY'RE JUST DITCHIN' WORK, THAT'S WHAT.
...NOW, NOW, IT'S ALL RIGHT.
ALL WORK AND NO PLAY WILL BURN YOU OUT.
BREATHERS ARE NECESSARY.
HMP IS THA SO...
I RECALL WORKIN' A LOT HARDER IN MY YOUTH.
...
BY THE WAY, MARIYA-KUN...
WE'VE DUG QUITE A BIT ALREADY...
...BUT HOW LONG DO YOU INTEND US TO KEEP AT IT?
...TIL WE REACH ITS BASE...
HUH?

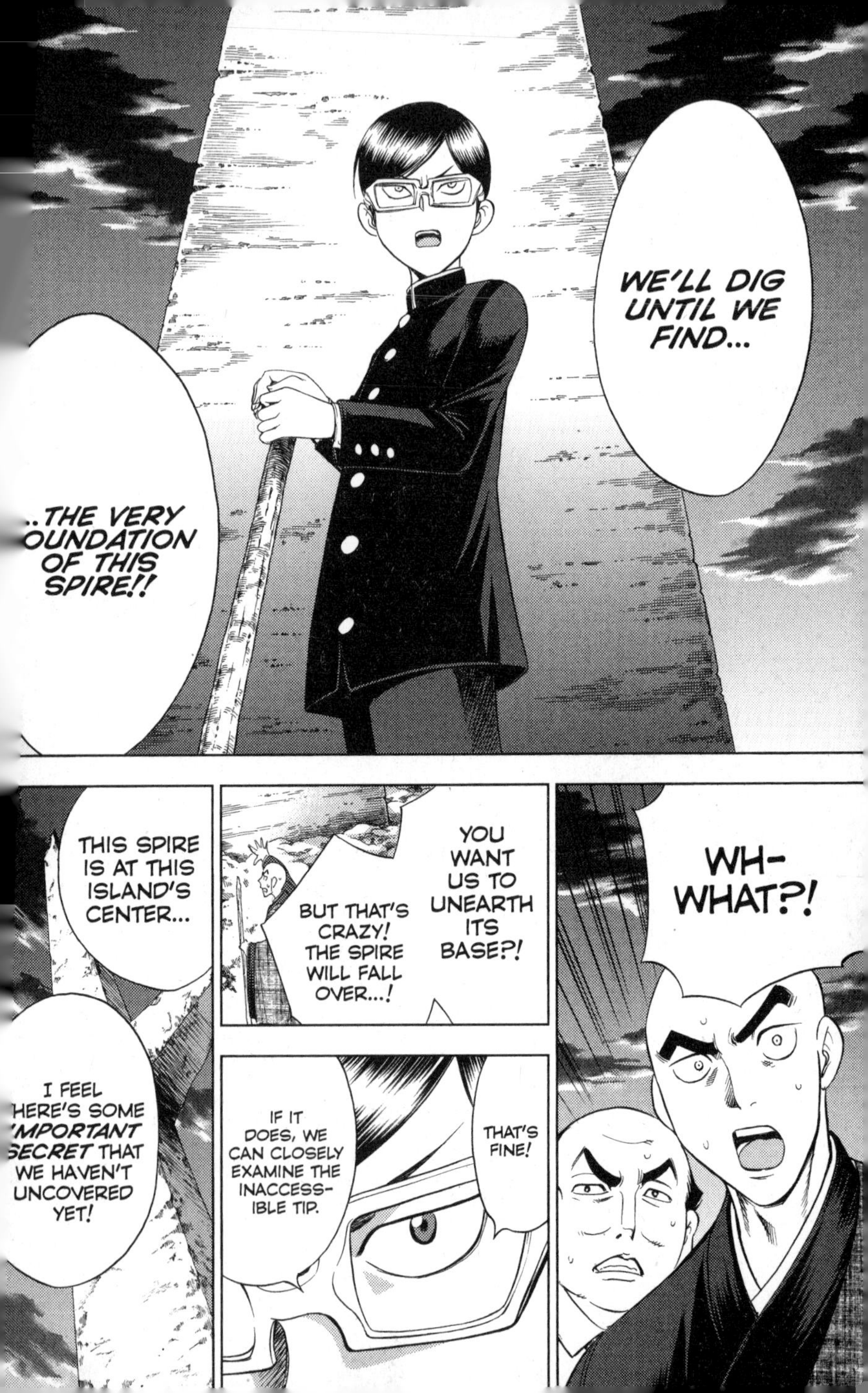
WE'LL DIG UNTIL WE FIND...
..THE VERY OUNDATION OF THIS SPIRE!!
WH-WHAT?!
YOU WANT US TO UNEARTH ITS BASE?!
BUT THAT'S CRAZY! THE SPIRE WILL FALL OVER...!
THAT'S FINE!
IF IT DOES, WE CAN CLOSELY EXAMINE THE INACCESS-IBLE TIP.
THIS SPIRE IS AT THIS ISLAND'S CENTER...
I FEEL HERE'S SOME MPORTANT SECRET THAT WE HAVEN'T UNCOVERED YET!

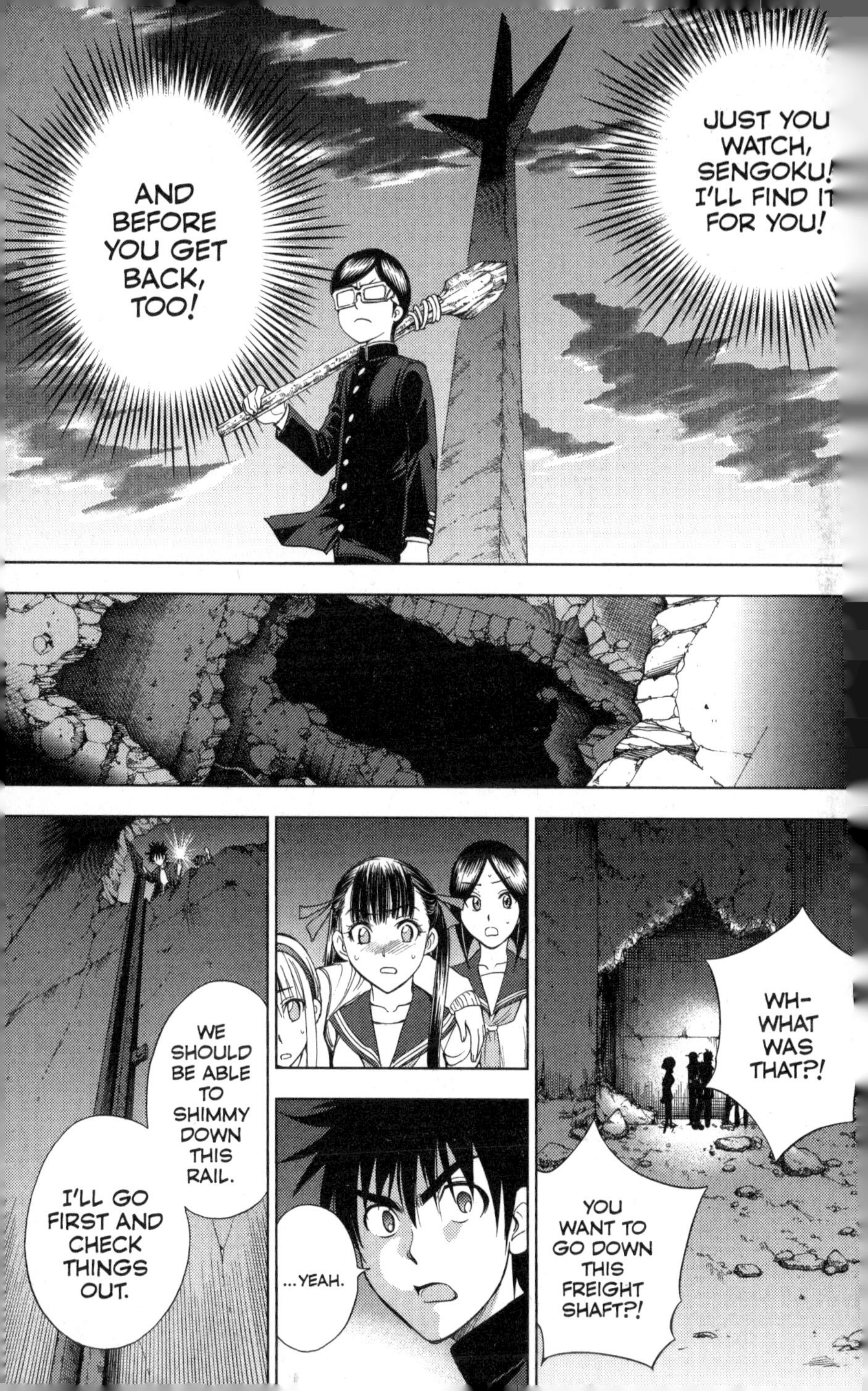
JUST YOU WATCH, SENGOKU! I'LL FIND IT FOR YOU!
AND BEFORE YOU GET BACK, TOO!
WH-WHAT WAS THAT?!
YOU WANT TO GO DOWN THIS FREIGHT SHAFT?!
...YEAH.
WE SHOULD BE ABLE TO SHIMMY DOWN THIS RAIL.
I'LL GO FIRST AND CHECK THINGS OUT.

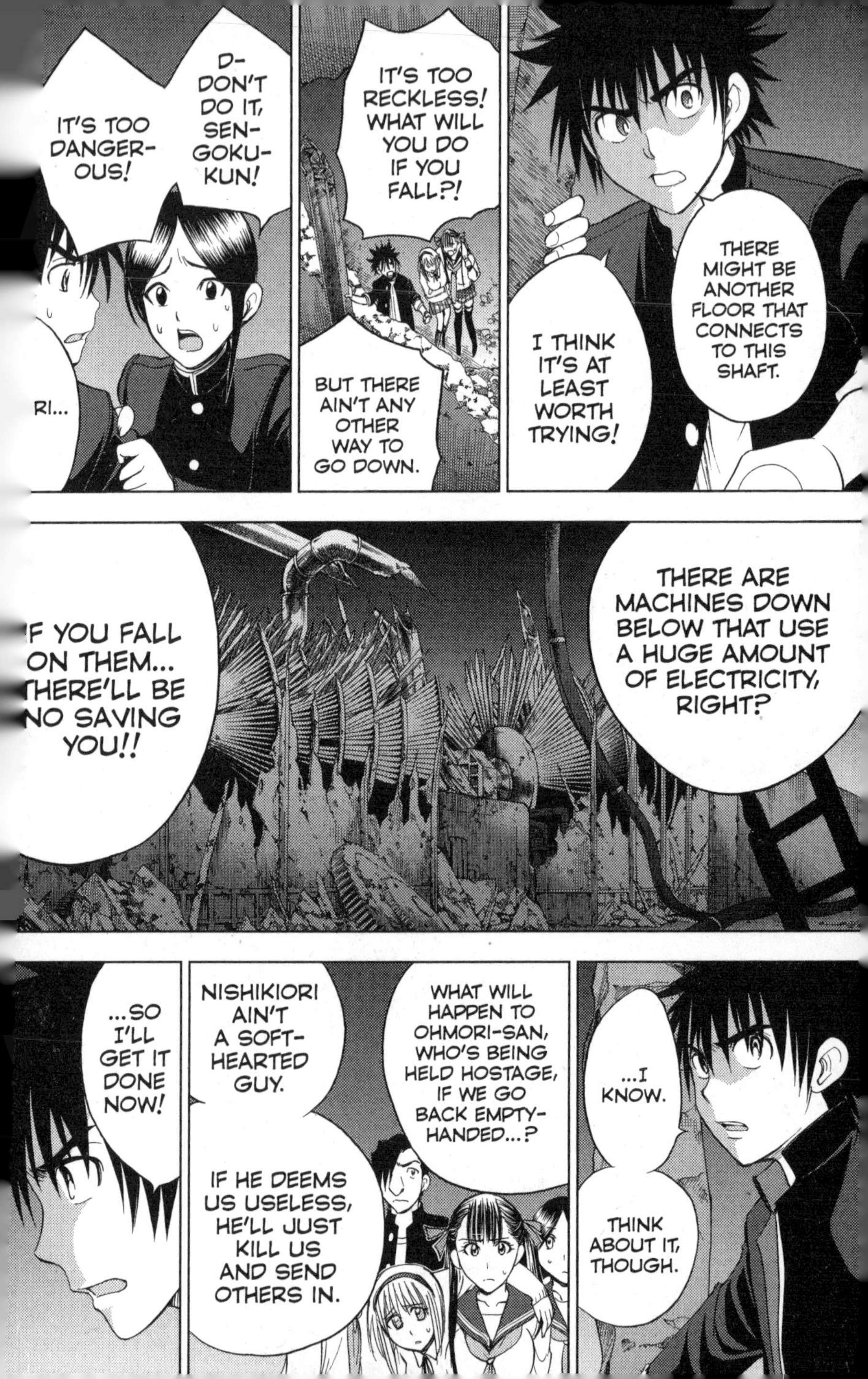
THERE MIGHT BE ANOTHER FLOOR THAT CONNECTS TO THIS SHAFT.
I THINK IT'S AT LEAST WORTH TRYING!
IT'S TOO RECKLESS! WHAT WILL YOU DO IF YOU FALL?!
BUT THERE AIN'T ANY OTHER WAY TO GO DOWN.
D-DON'T DO IT, SEN-GOKU-KUN!
IT'S TOO DANGER-OUS!
RI...
THERE ARE MACHINES DOWN BELOW THAT USE A HUGE AMOUNT OF ELECTRICITY, RIGHT?
IF YOU FALL ON THEM... THERE'LL BE NO SAVING YOU!!
...I KNOW.
THINK ABOUT IT, THOUGH.
WHAT WILL HAPPEN TO OHMORI-SAN, WHO'S BEING HELD HOSTAGE, IF WE GO BACK EMPTY-HANDED...?
NISHIKIORI AIN'T A SOFT-HEARTED GUY.
IF HE DEEMS US USELESS, HE'LL JUST KILL US AND SEND OTHERS IN.
...SO I'LL GET IT DONE NOW!

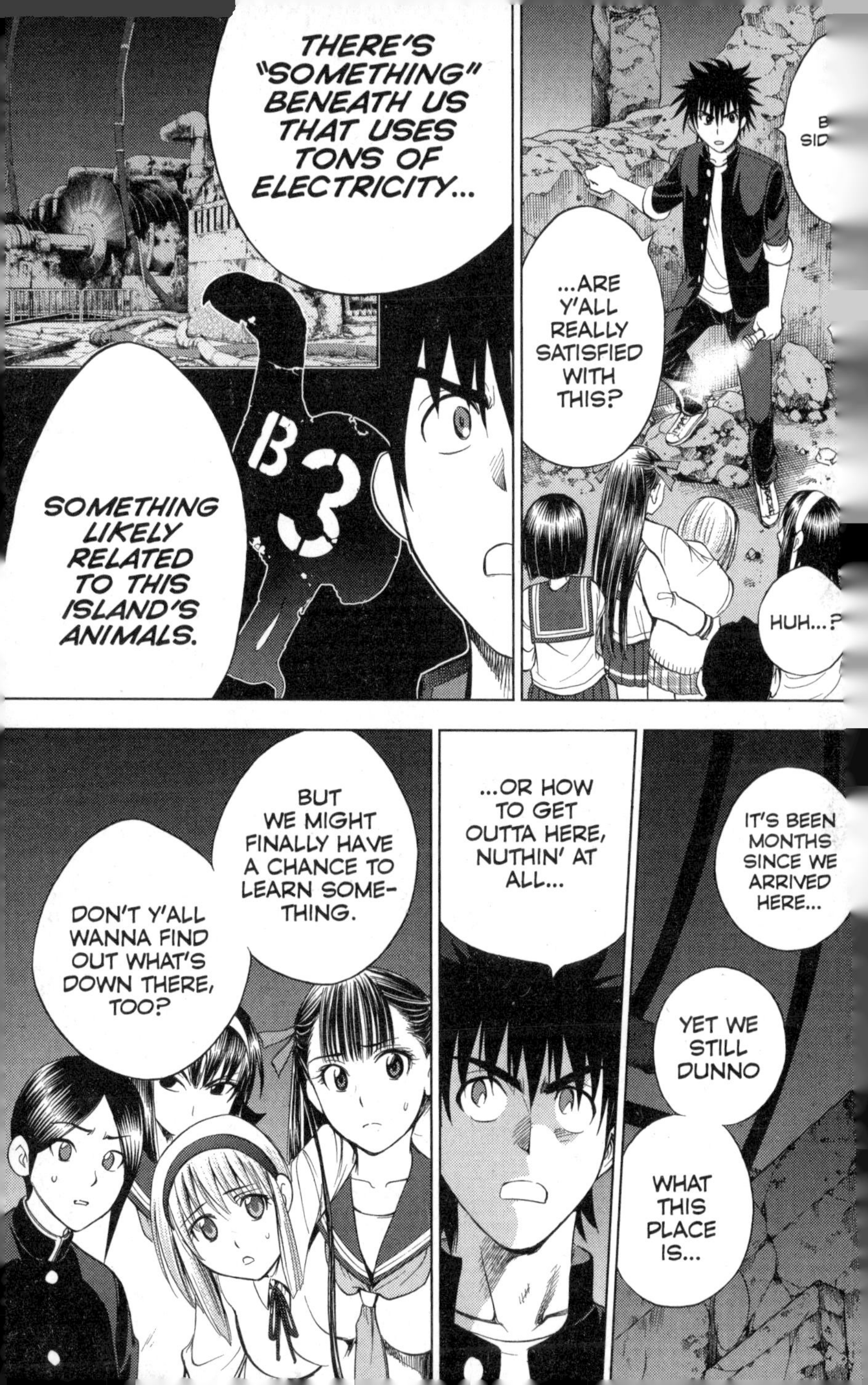
...ARE Y'ALL REALLY SATISFIED WITH THIS?
HUH...?
THERE'S "SOMETHING" BENEATH US THAT USES TONS OF ELECTRICITY...
B3
SOMETHING LIKELY RELATED TO THIS ISLAND'S ANIMALS.
IT'S BEEN MONTHS SINCE WE ARRIVED HERE...
YET WE STILL DUNNO
WHAT THIS PLACE IS...
...OR HOW TO GET OUTTA HERE, NUTHIN' AT ALL...
BUT WE MIGHT FINALLY HAVE A CHANCE TO LEARN SOME-THING.
DON'T Y'ALL WANNA FIND OUT WHAT'S DOWN THERE, TOO?

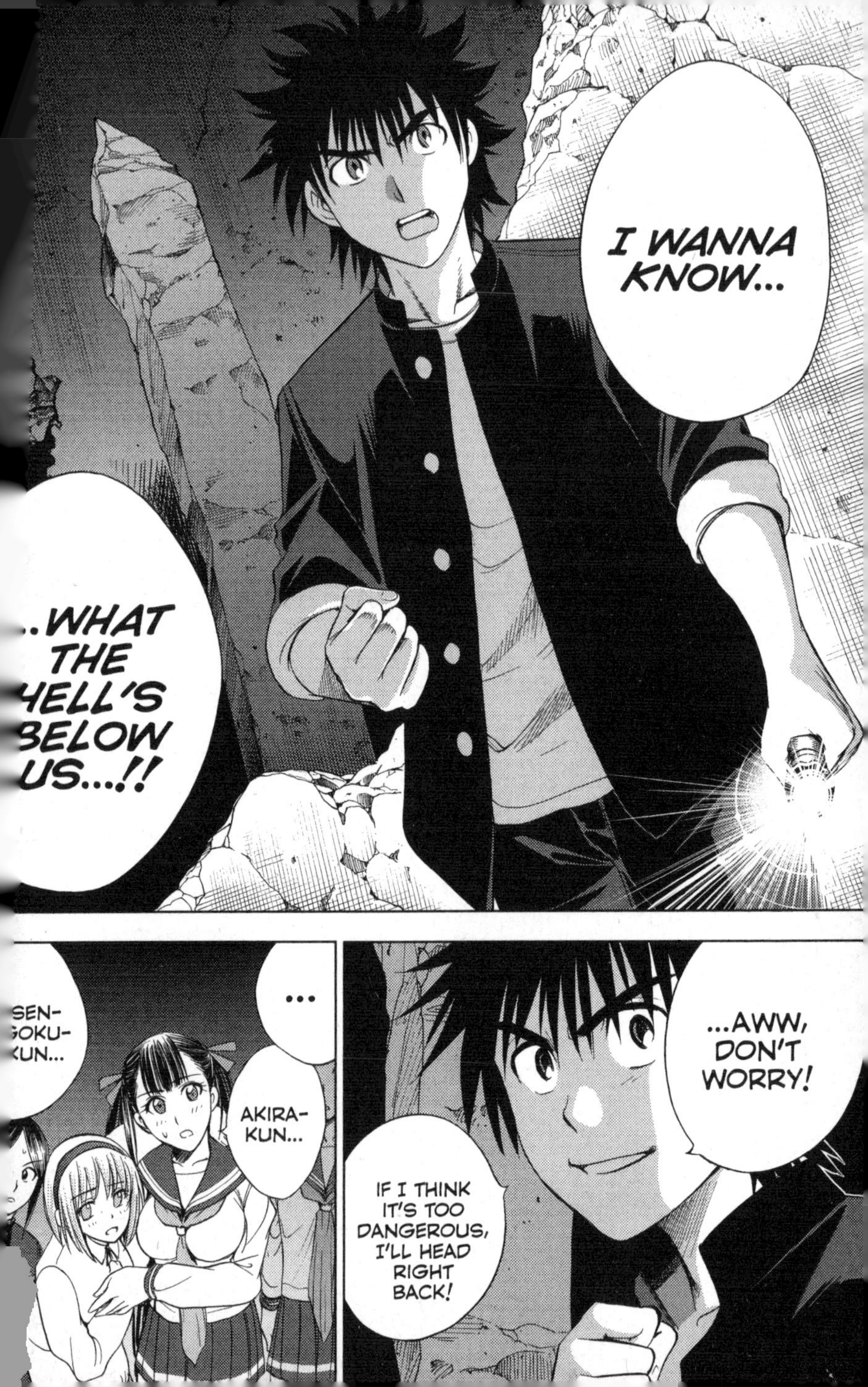
I WANNA KNOW...
...WHAT THE HELL'S BELOW US...!!
...AWW, DON'T WORRY!
IF I THINK IT'S TOO DANGEROUS, I'LL HEAD RIGHT BACK!
...
SEN-GOKU-KUN...
AKIRA-KUN...

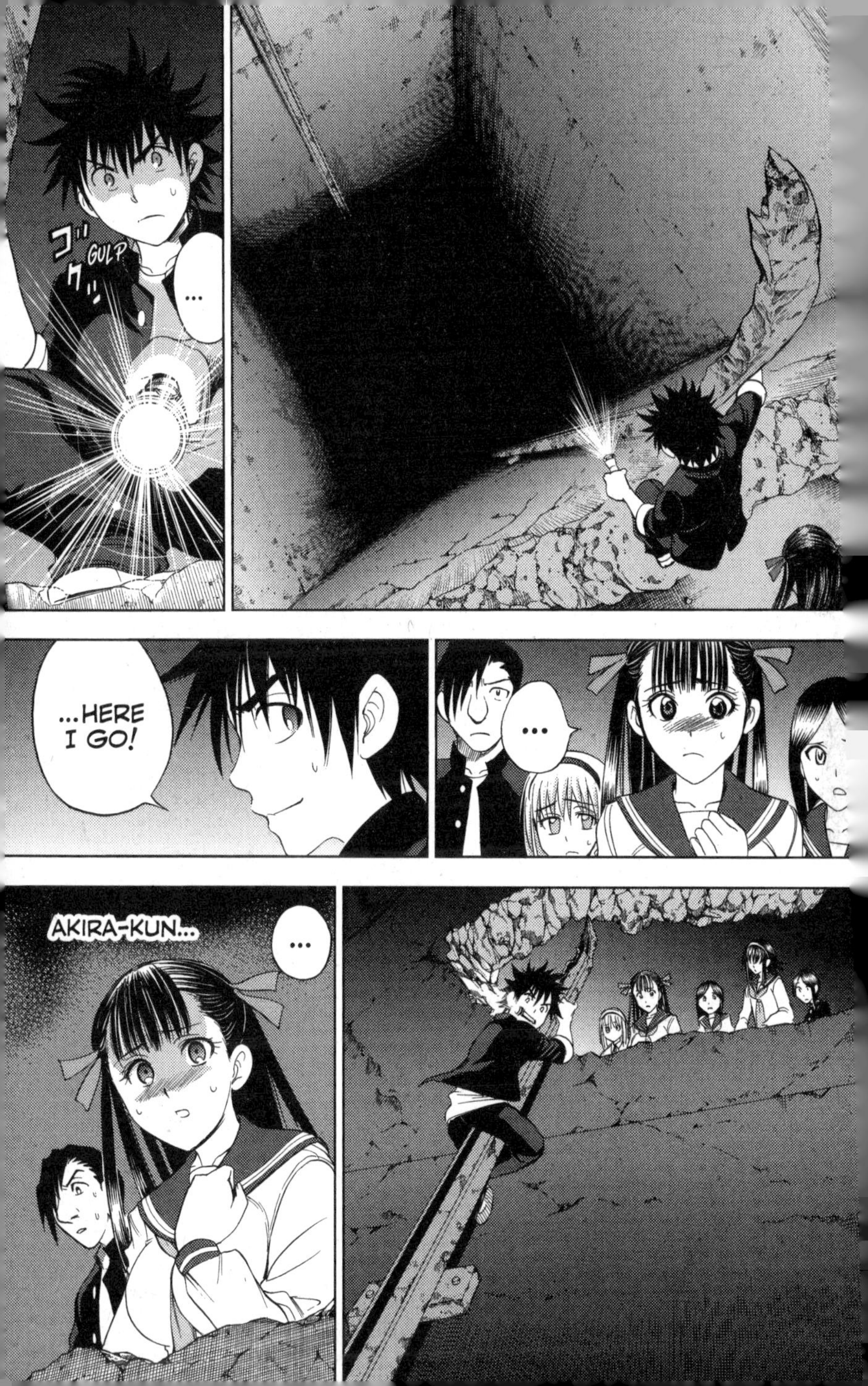
...
ゴクッ
GULP
...
...HERE I GO!
...
AKIRA-KUN...

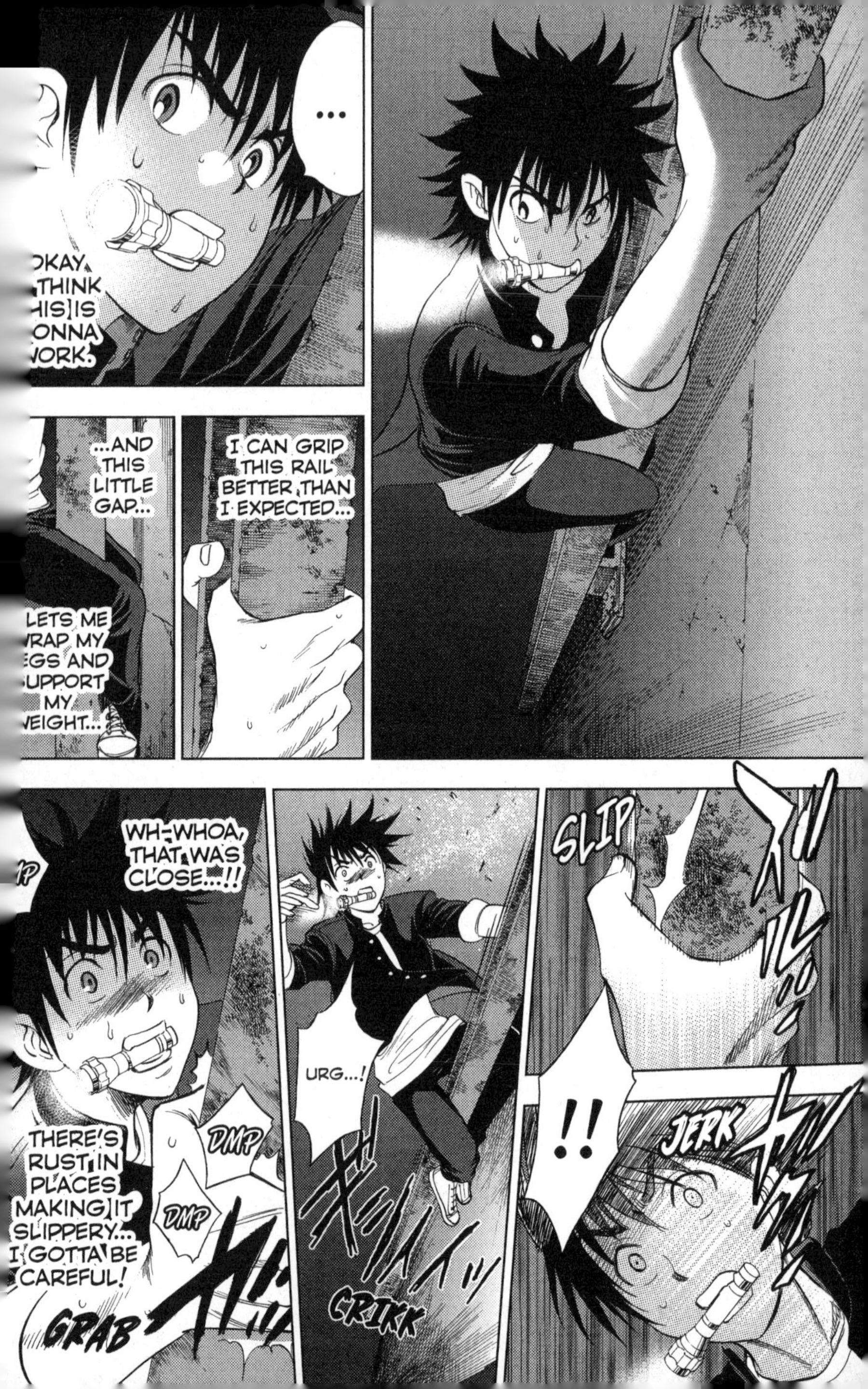
...
OKAY. THINK HIS IS ONNA WORK.
I CAN GRIP THIS RAIL BETTER THAN I EXPECTED...
...AND THIS LITTLE GAP...
LETS ME WRAP MY EGS AND UPPORT MY EIGHT...
SLIP
!!
JERK
URG...!
CRIKK
WH-WHOA, THAT WAS CLOSE...!!
THERE'S RUST IN PLACES MAKING IT SLIPPERY... I GOTTA BE CAREFUL!
DMP
DMP
GRAB

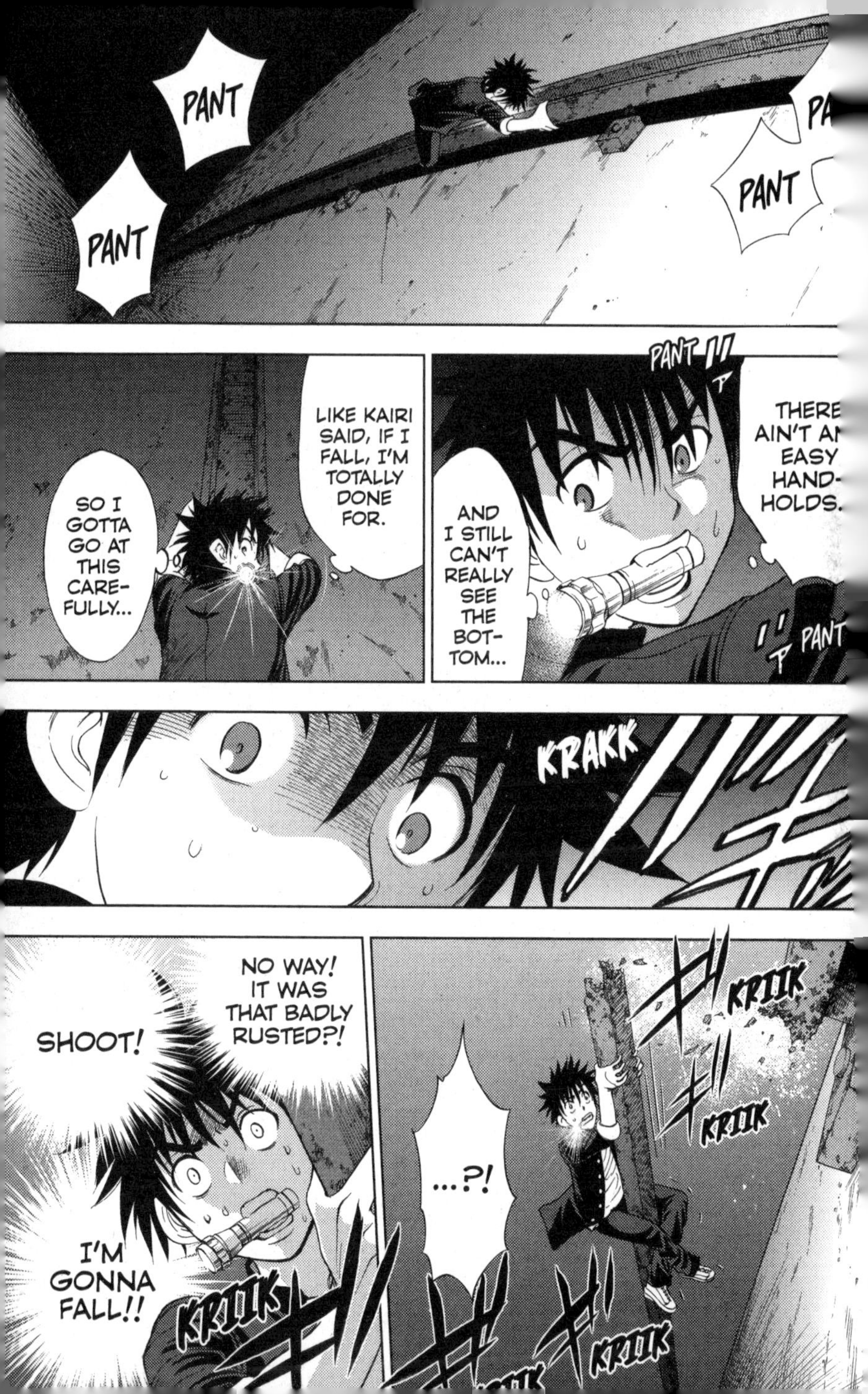
PANT
PANT
PANT
PANT!!
THERE AIN'T A EASY HAND-HOLDS.
AND I STILL CAN'T REALLY SEE THE BOT-TOM...
PANT
LIKE KAIRI SAID, IF I FALL, I'M TOTALLY DONE FOR.
SO I GOTTA GO AT THIS CARE-FULLY...
KRAKK
KRIIK
KRIIK
...?!
KRIIK
NO WAY! IT WAS THAT BADLY RUSTED?!
SHOOT!
I'M GONNA FALL!!
KRIIK

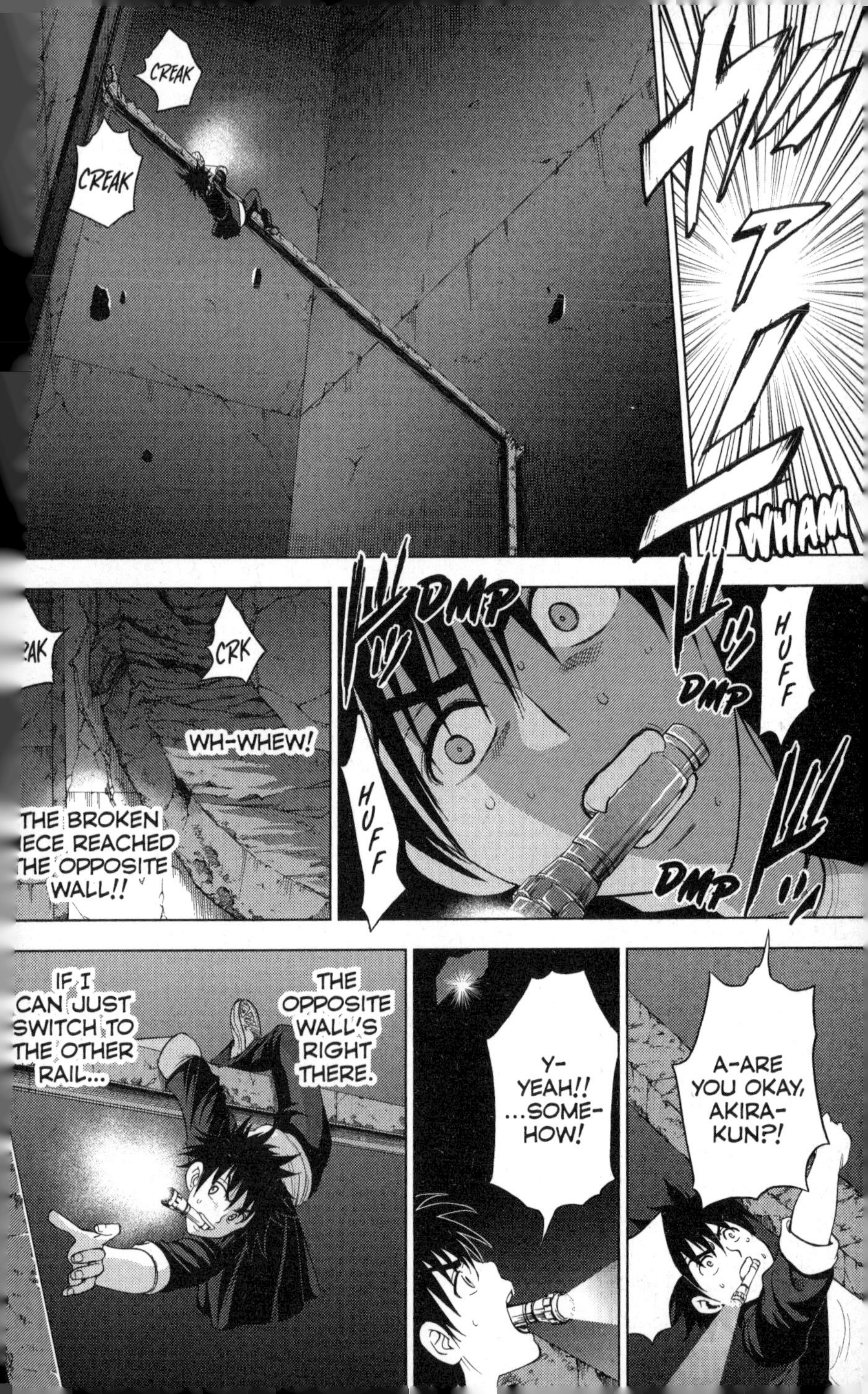
CREAK
CREAK
WHAM
HUFF
DMP
DMP
DMP
HUFF
CRK
WH-WHEW!
THE BROKEN
ECE REACHED
THE OPPOSITE
WALL!!
A-ARE YOU OKAY, AKIRA-KUN?!
Y-YEAH!! ...SOME-HOW!
THE OPPOSITE WALL'S RIGHT THERE.
IF I CAN JUST SWITCH TO THE OTHER RAIL...

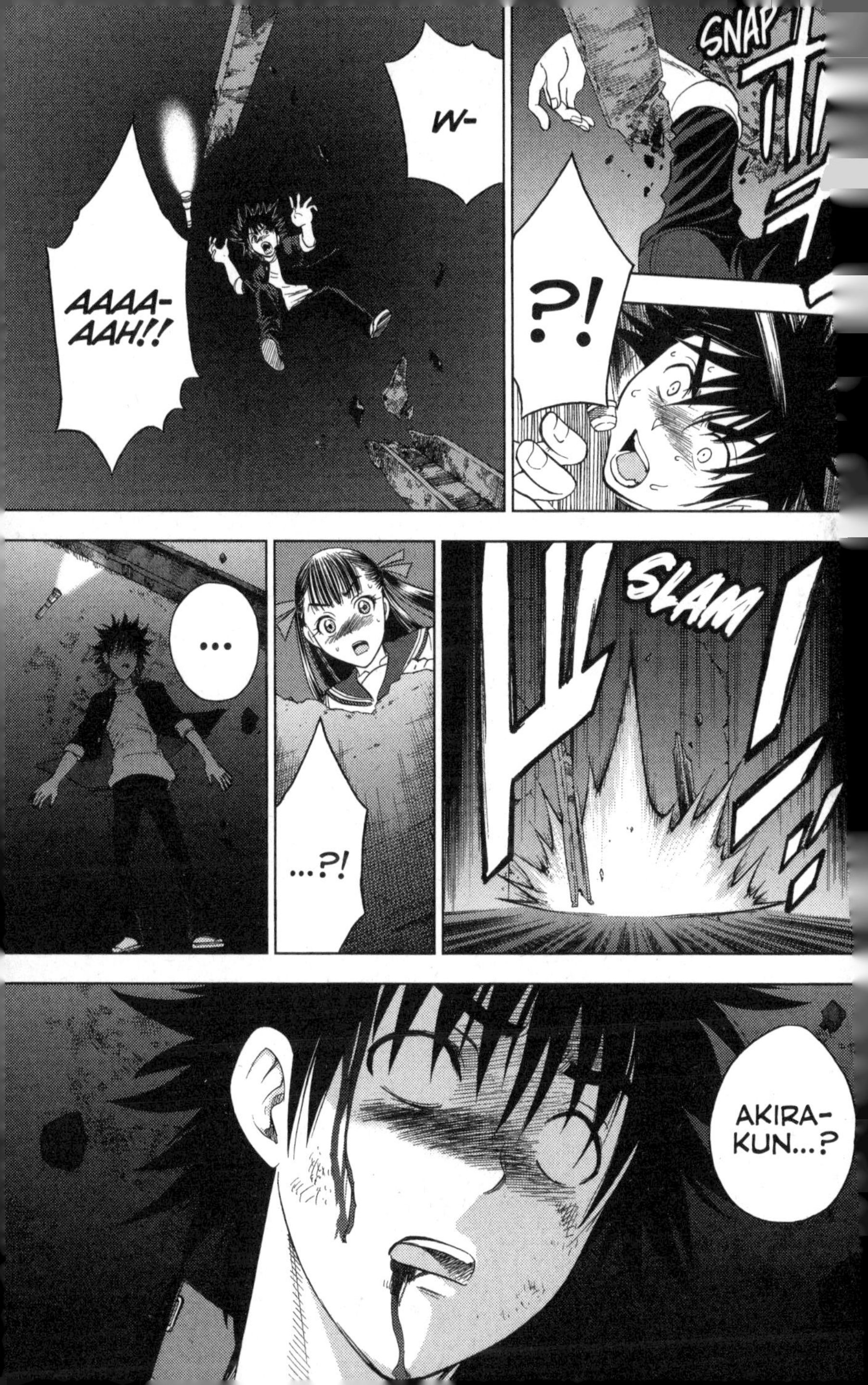
SNAP
?!
W-
AAAA-AAH!!
SLAM
...?!
...
AKIRA-KUN...?

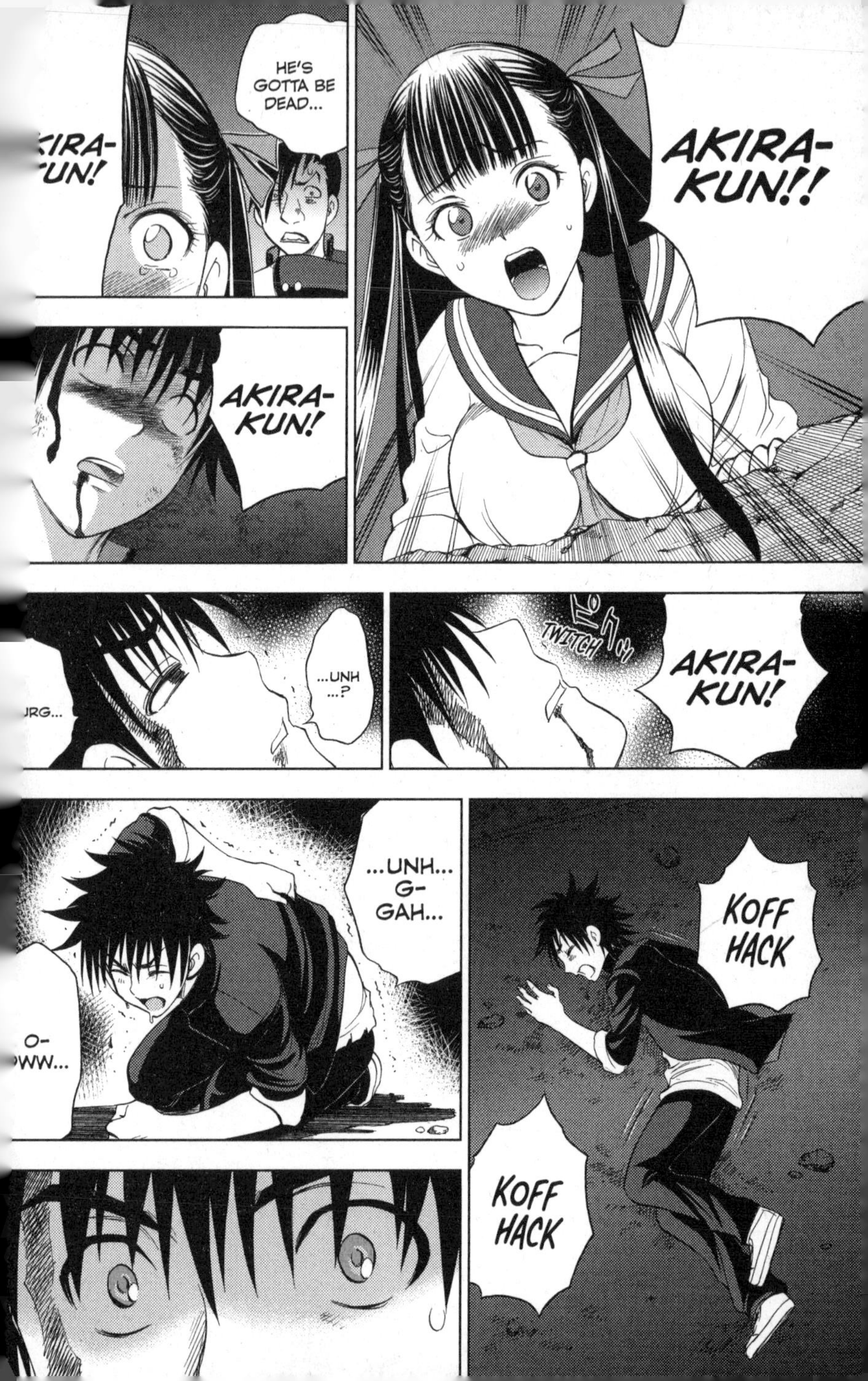
AKIRA-KUN!!
HE'S GOTTA BE DEAD...
KIRA-UN!
AKIRA-KUN!
TWITCH
AKIRA-KUN!
...UNH ...?
URG...
KOFF HACK
KOFF HACK
...UNH... G-GAH...
O-OWW...

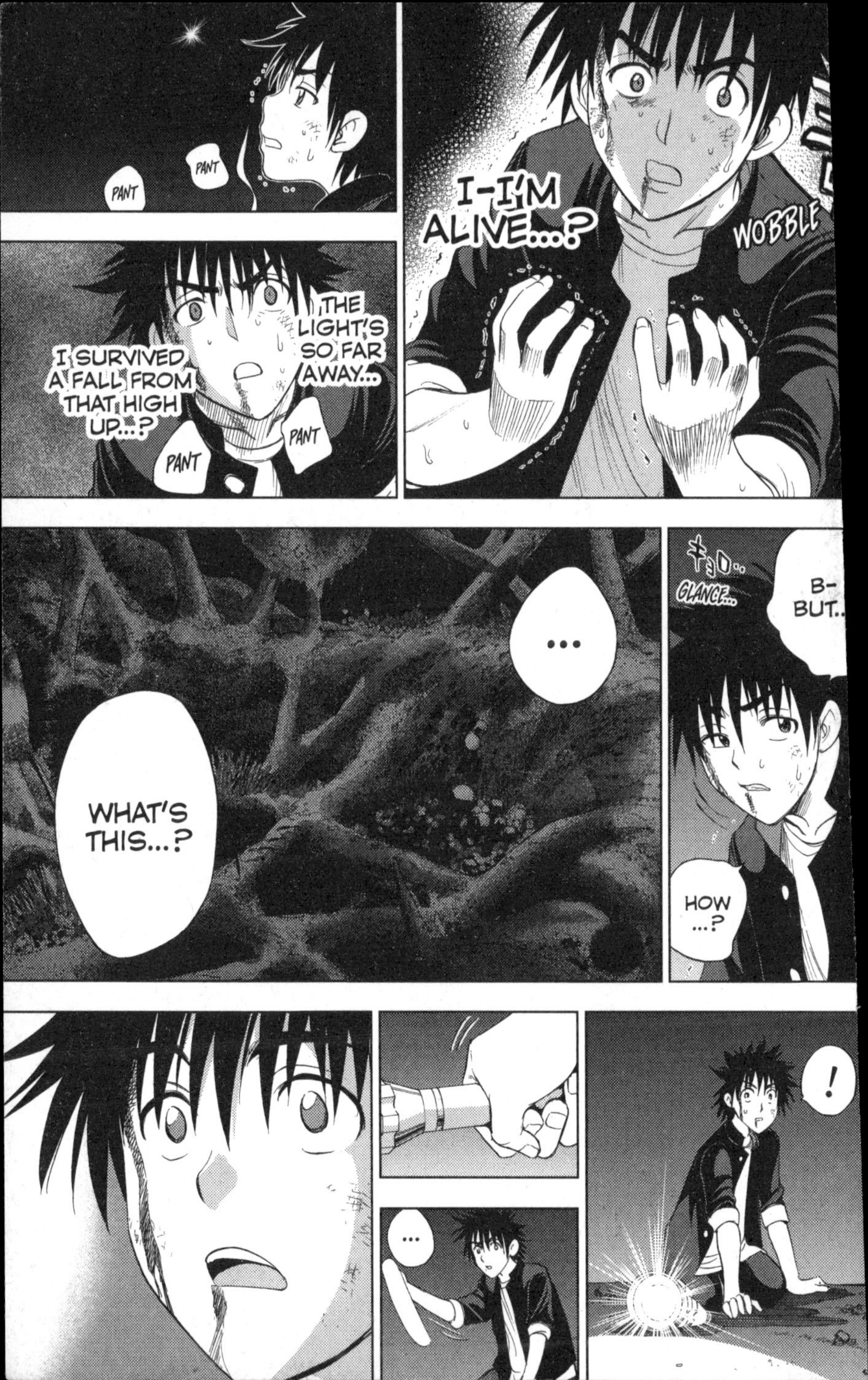
I-I'M ALIVE...?
WOBBLE
PANT
PANT
THE LIGHT'S SO FAR AWAY...
I SURVIVED A FALL FROM THAT HIGH UP...?
PANT
PANT
キョロ..
GLANCE...
B-BUT..
HOW ...?
...
WHAT'S THIS...?
!
...

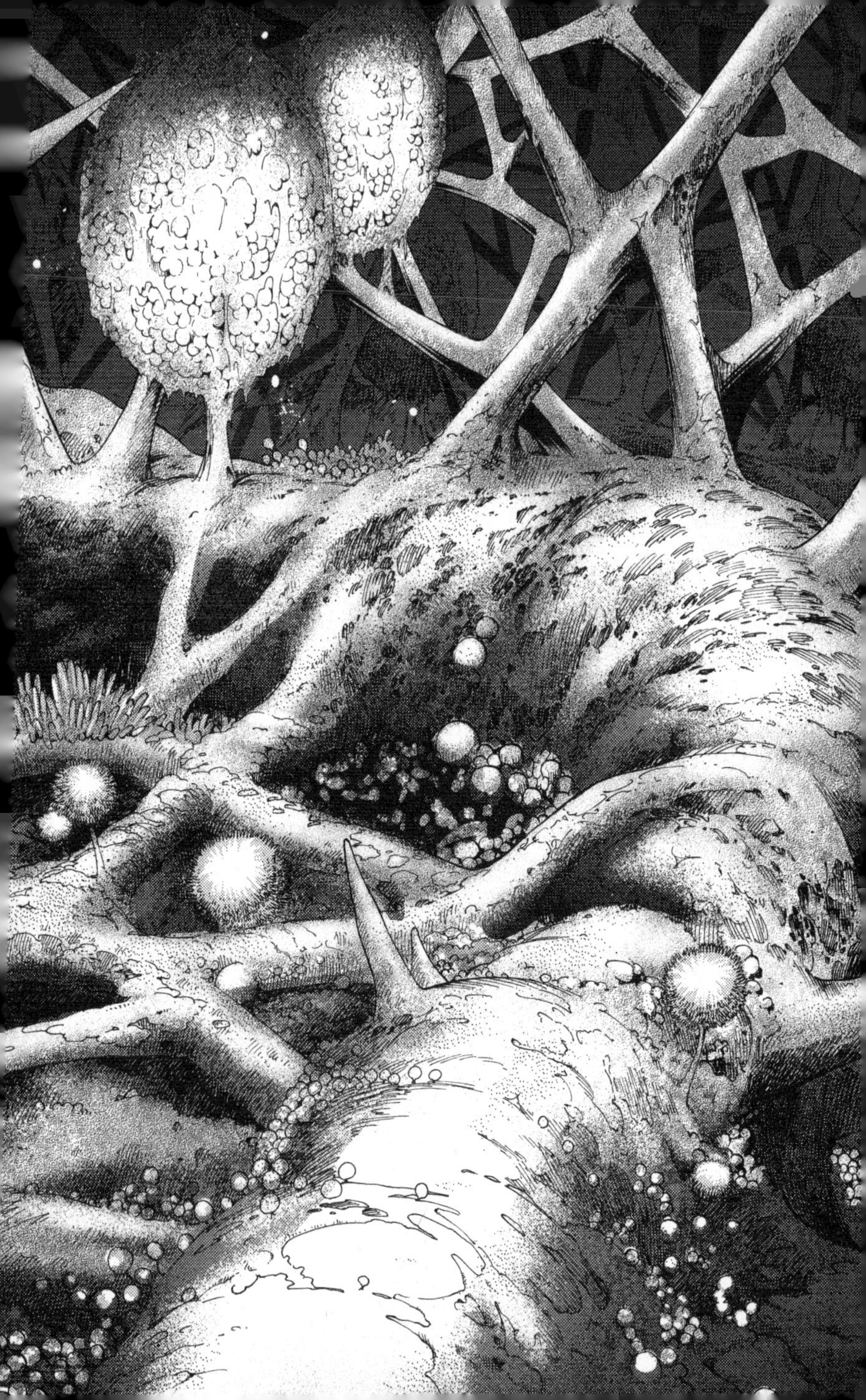

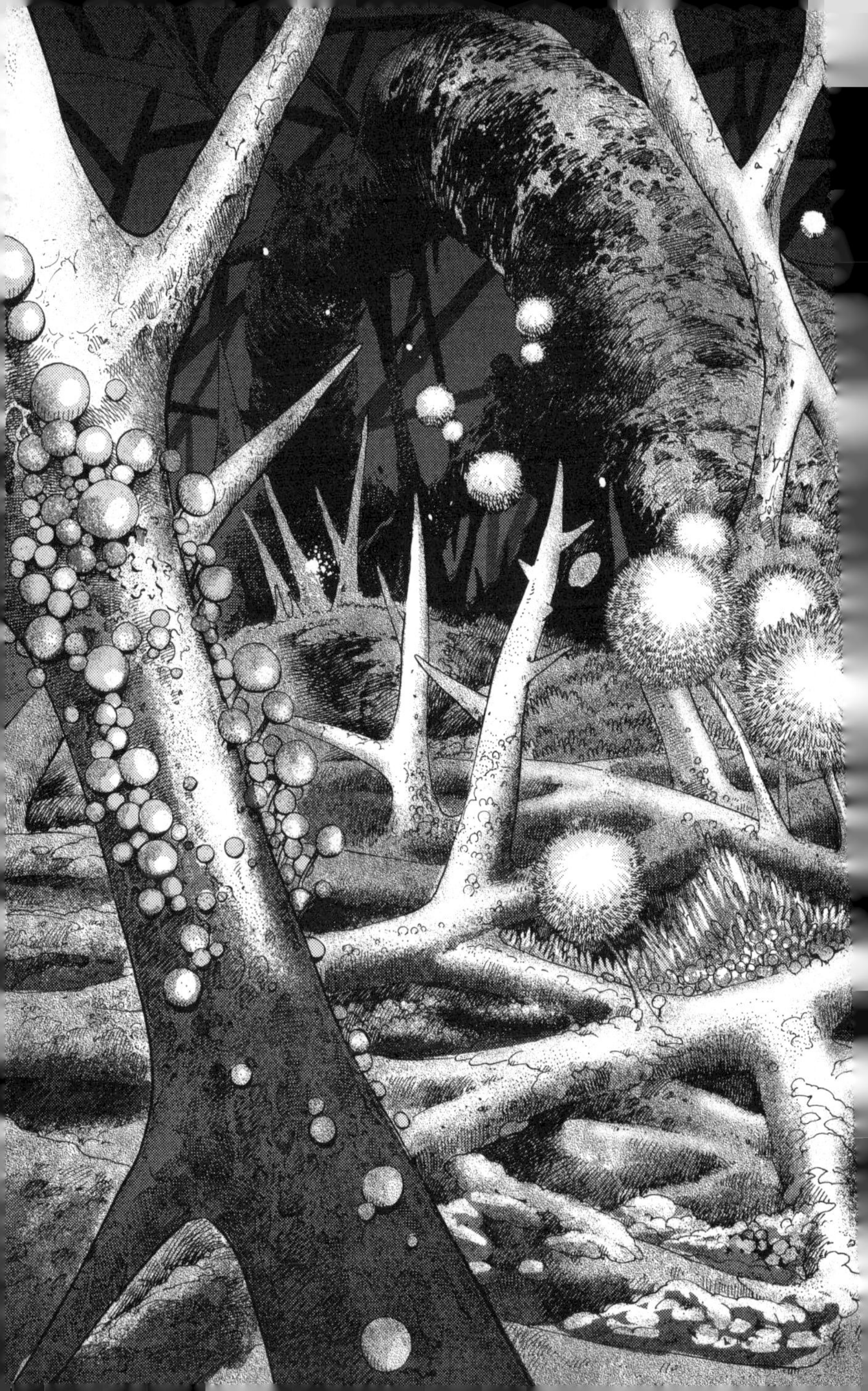

BUT STILL...

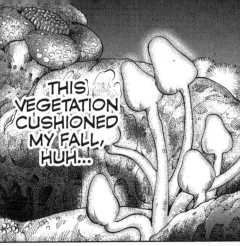

THIS VEGETATION CUSHIONED MY FALL, HUH...

...WHAT THE HECK *IS THIS* ...?!

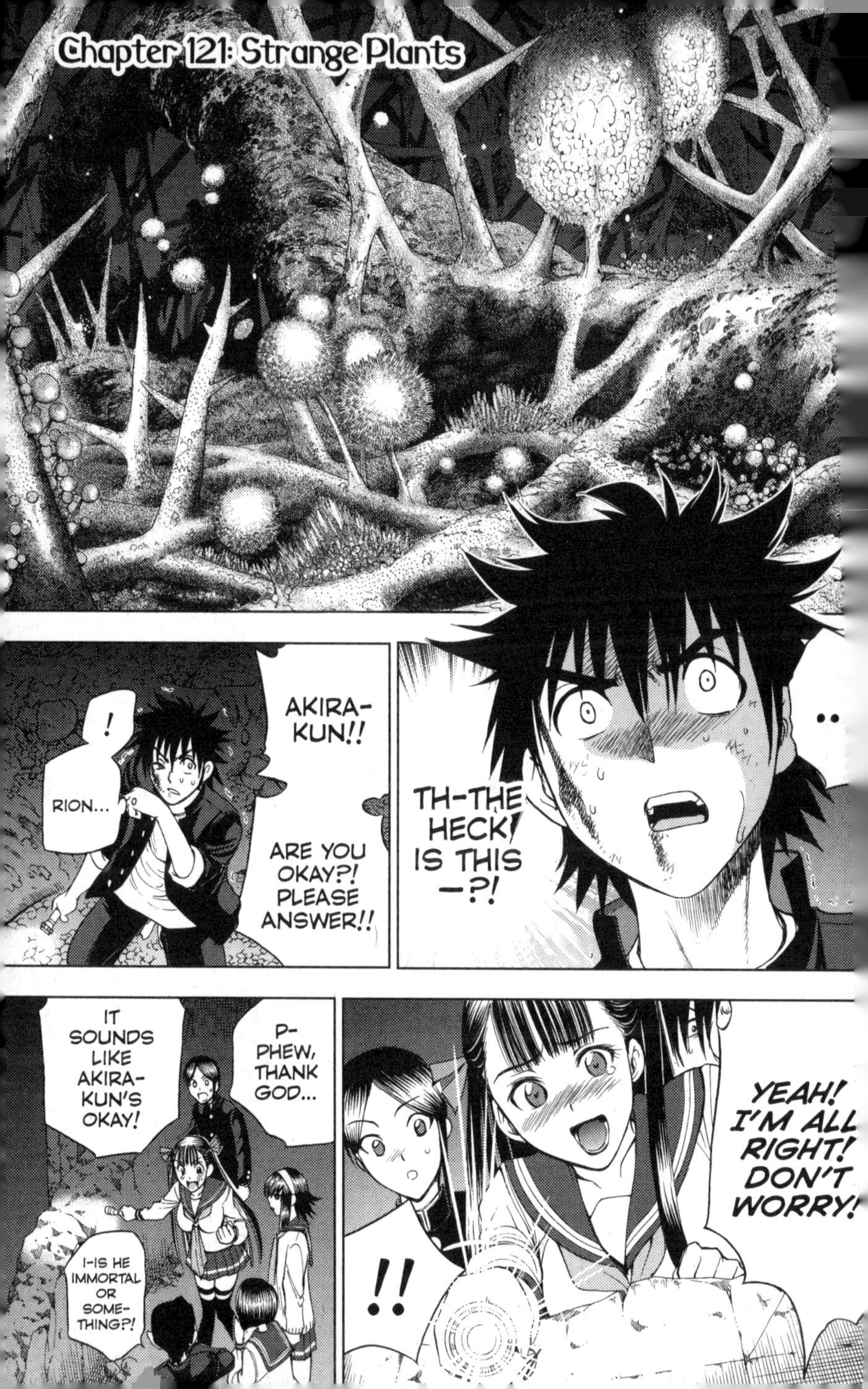

Chapter 121: Strange Plants
..
TH-THE HECK IS THIS—?!
AKIRA-KUN!!
ARE YOU OKAY?! PLEASE ANSWER!!
!
RION...
YEAH! I'M ALL RIGHT! DON'T WORRY!
!!
P-PHEW, THANK GOD...
IT SOUNDS LIKE AKIRA-KUN'S OKAY!
I-IS HE IMMORTAL OR SOMETHING?!

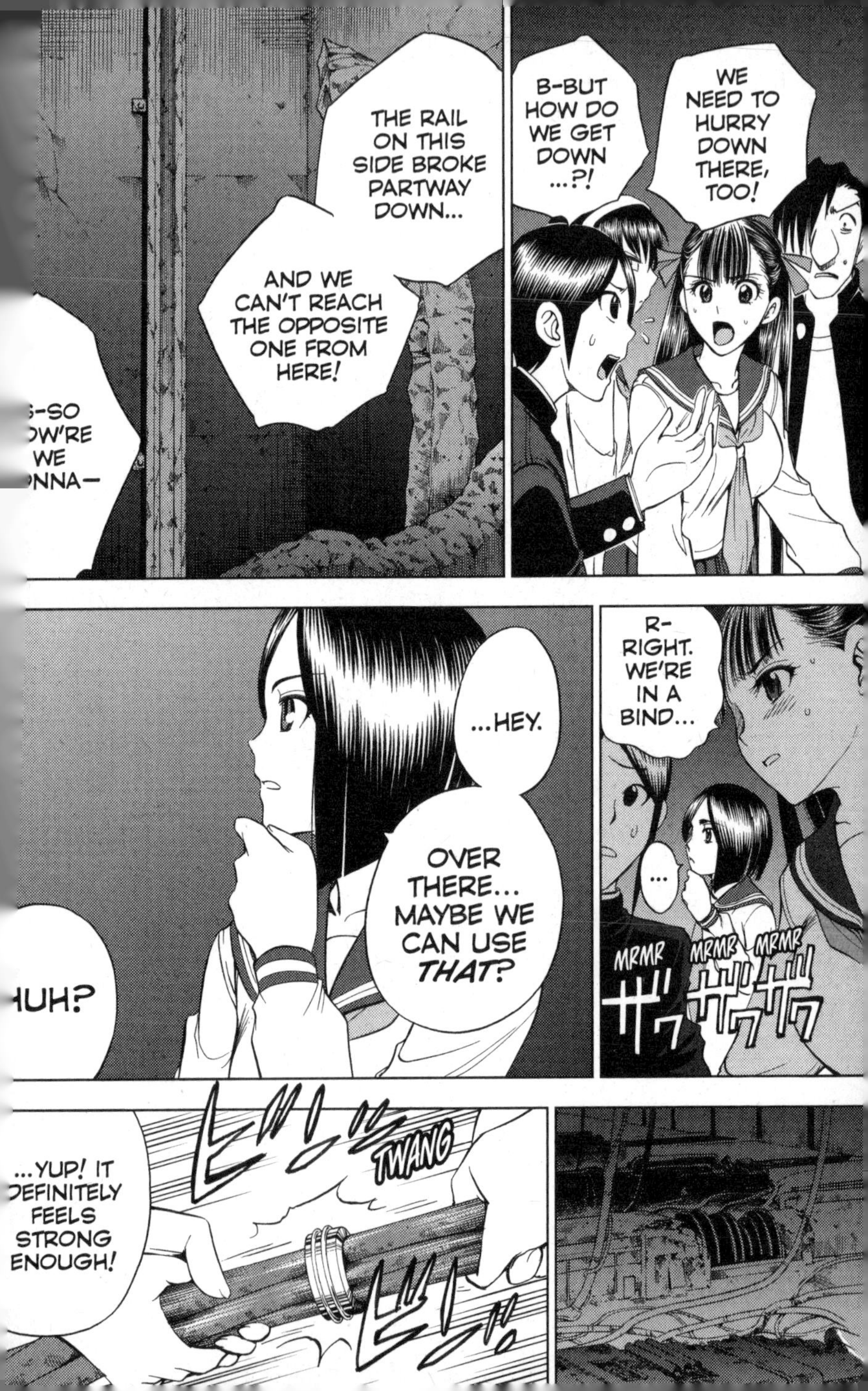
WE NEED TO HURRY DOWN THERE, TOO!
B-BUT HOW DO WE GET DOWN ...?!
THE RAIL ON THIS SIDE BROKE PARTWAY DOWN...
AND WE CAN'T REACH THE OPPOSITE ONE FROM HERE!
-SO OW'RE WE ONNA—
R-RIGHT. WE'RE IN A BIND...
...
MRMR MRMR MRMR
ザワザワザワ
...HEY.
OVER THERE... MAYBE WE CAN USE *THAT*?
HUH?
ビンッ
TWANG
...YUP! IT DEFINITELY FEELS STRONG ENOUGH!

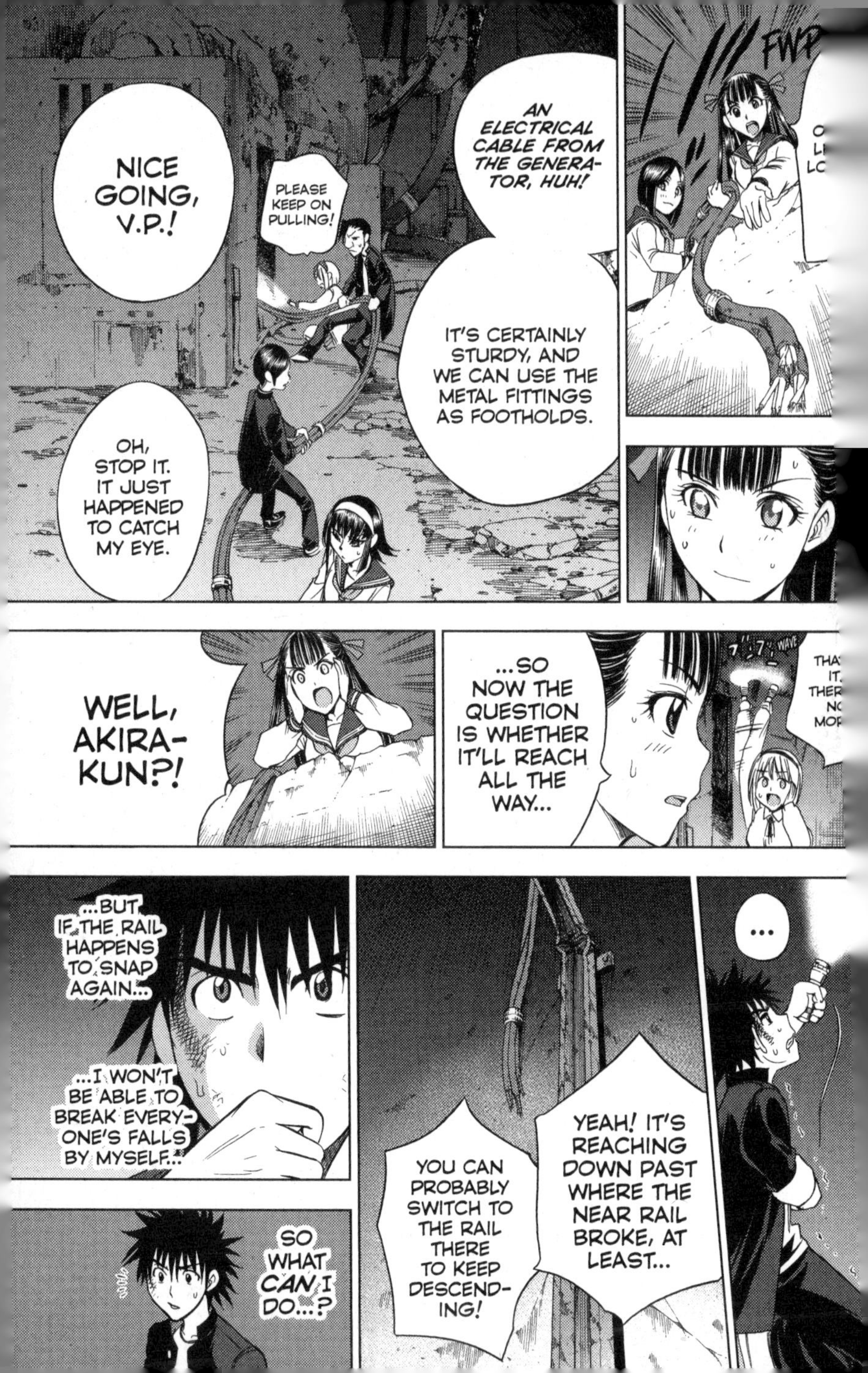
AN ELECTRICAL CABLE FROM THE GENERATOR, HUH!
IT'S CERTAINLY STURDY, AND WE CAN USE THE METAL FITTINGS AS FOOTHOLDS.
PLEASE KEEP ON PULLING!
NICE GOING, V.P.!
OH, STOP IT. IT JUST HAPPENED TO CATCH MY EYE.
WAVE
...SO NOW THE QUESTION IS WHETHER IT'LL REACH ALL THE WAY...
WELL, AKIRA-KUN?!
...
YEAH! IT'S REACHING DOWN PAST WHERE THE NEAR RAIL BROKE, AT LEAST...
YOU CAN PROBABLY SWITCH TO THE RAIL THERE TO KEEP DESCENDING!
...BUT IF THE RAIL HAPPENS TO SNAP AGAIN...
...I WON'T BE ABLE TO BREAK EVERYONE'S FALLS BY MYSELF...
SO WHAT CAN I DO...?

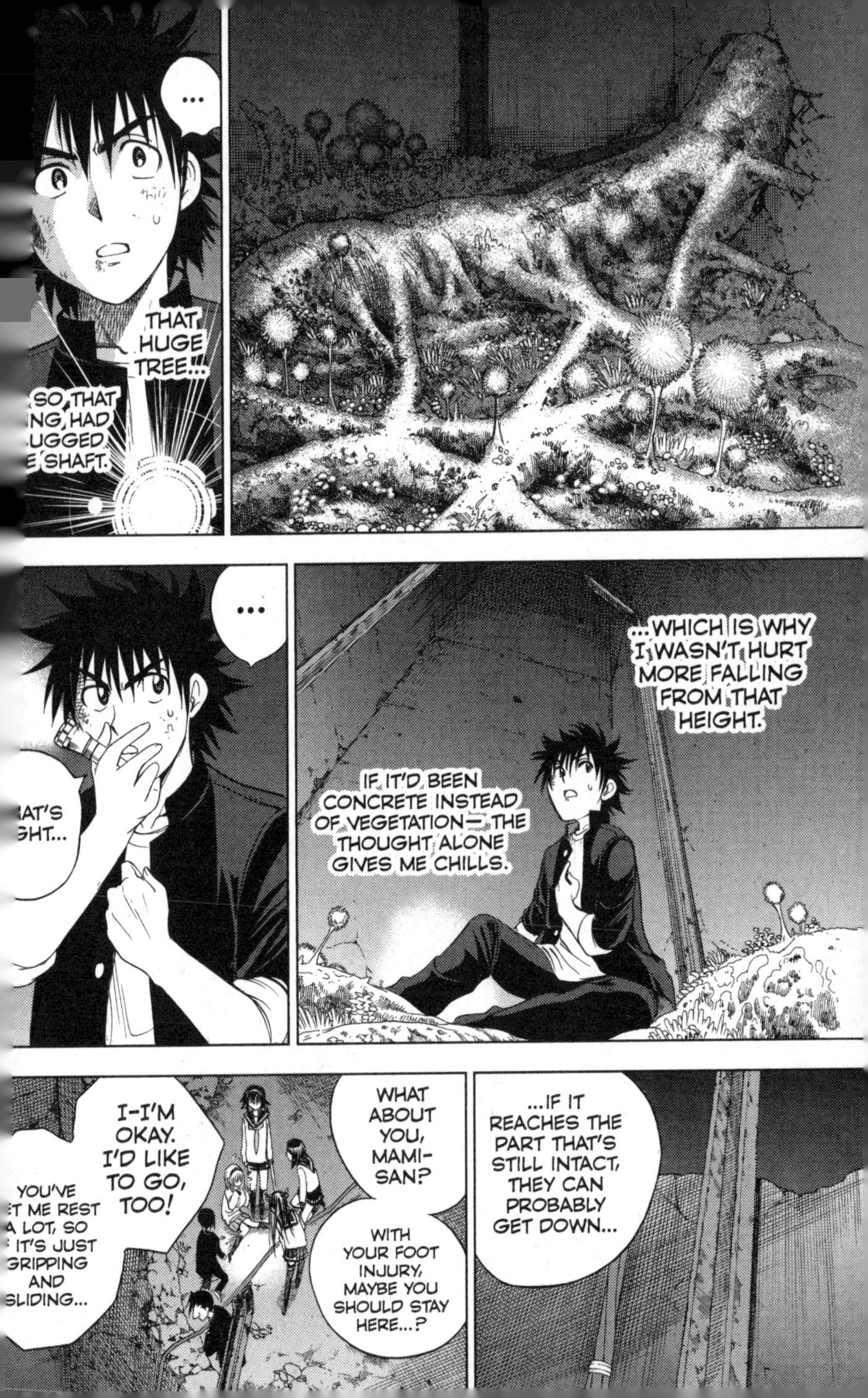
...
THAT HUGE TREE...
SO THAT NG HAD UGGED E SHAFT.
...WHICH IS WHY I WASN'T HURT MORE FALLING FROM THAT HEIGHT.
IF IT'D BEEN CONCRETE INSTEAD OF VEGETATION— THE THOUGHT ALONE GIVES ME CHILLS.
...
AT'S GHT...
...IF IT REACHES THE PART THAT'S STILL INTACT, THEY CAN PROBABLY GET DOWN...
WHAT ABOUT YOU, MAMI-SAN?
WITH YOUR FOOT INJURY, MAYBE YOU SHOULD STAY HERE...?
I-I'M OKAY. I'D LIKE TO GO, TOO!
YOU'VE ET ME REST A LOT, SO IT'S JUST GRIPPING AND SLIDING...

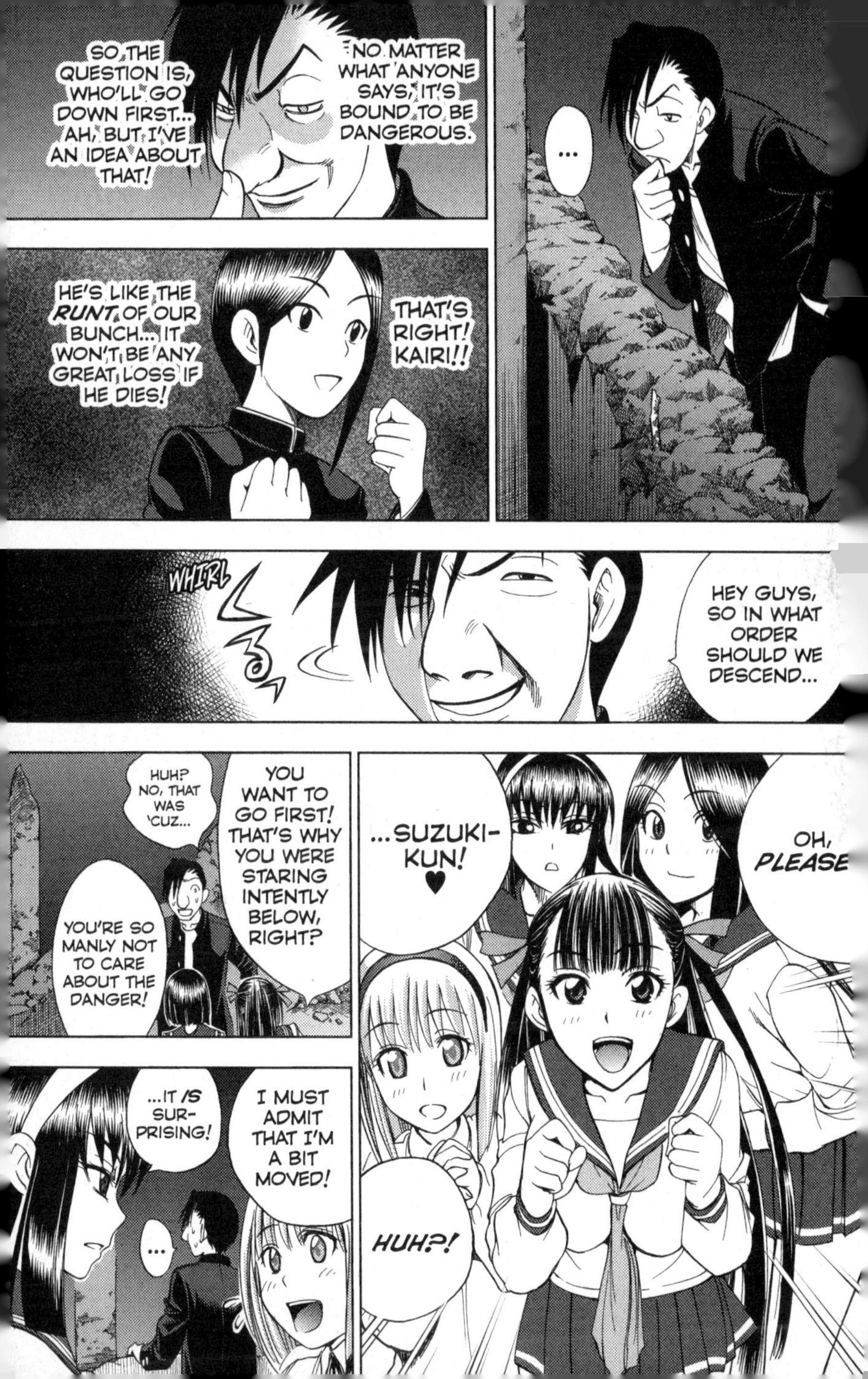
...
NO MATTER WHAT ANYONE SAYS, IT'S BOUND TO BE DANGEROUS.
SO THE QUESTION IS, WHO'LL GO DOWN FIRST... AH, BUT I'VE AN IDEA ABOUT THAT!
THAT'S RIGHT! KAIRI!!
HE'S LIKE THE *RUNT* OF OUR BUNCH... IT WON'T BE ANY GREAT LOSS IF HE DIES!
HEY GUYS, SO IN WHAT ORDER SHOULD WE DESCEND...
WHIRL
OH, *PLEASE*
...SUZUKI-KUN! ♥
HUH?!
YOU WANT TO GO FIRST! THAT'S WHY YOU WERE STARING INTENTLY BELOW, RIGHT?
HUH? NO, THAT WAS 'CUZ...
YOU'RE SO MANLY NOT TO CARE ABOUT THE DANGER!
I MUST ADMIT THAT I'M A BIT MOVED!
...IT *IS* SUR-PRISING!
...

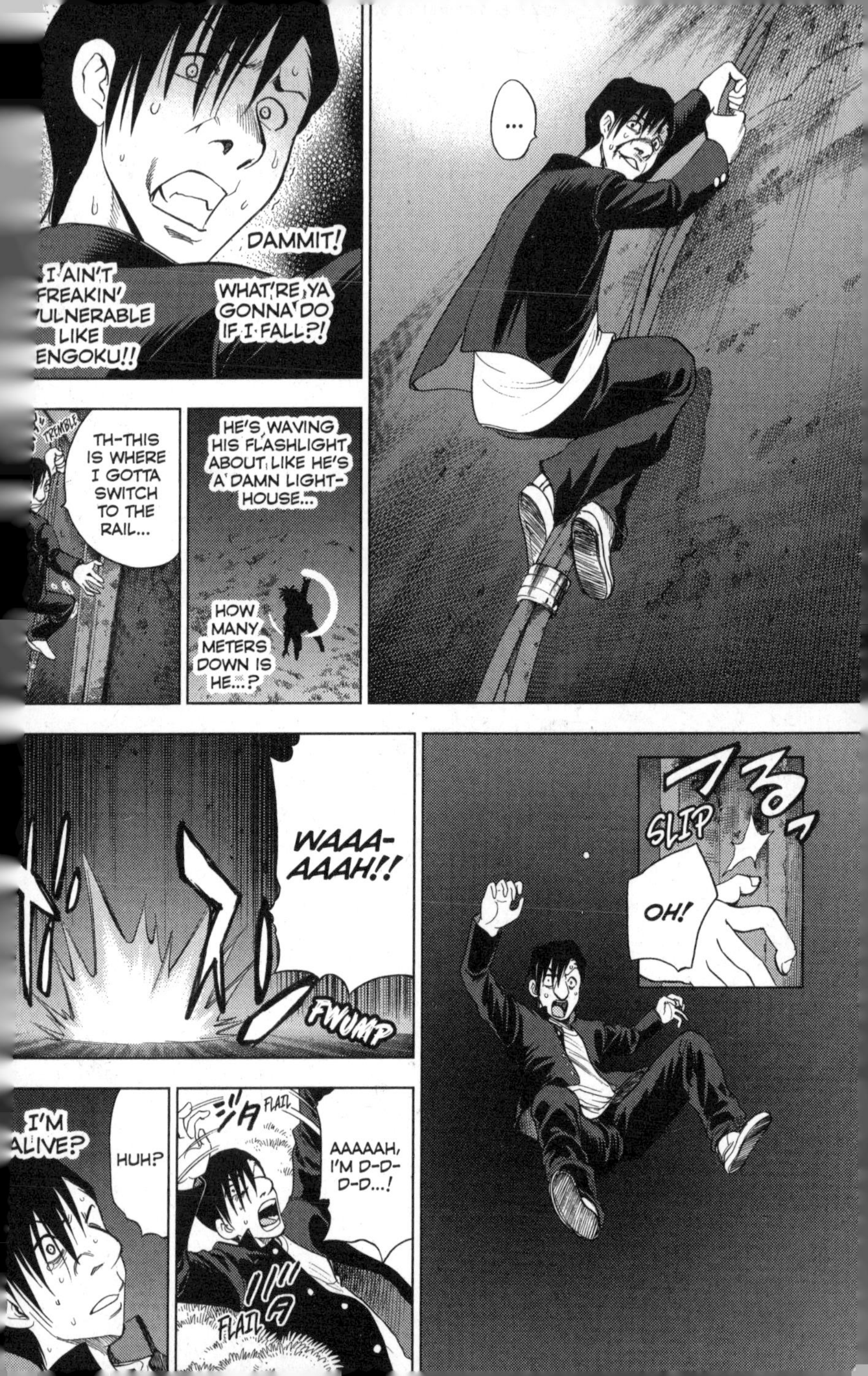
...
DAMMIT!
WHAT'RE YA GONNA DO IF I FALL?!
I AIN'T FREAKIN' VULNERABLE LIKE ENGOKU!!
HE'S WAVING HIS FLASHLIGHT ABOUT LIKE HE'S A DAMN LIGHT-HOUSE...
HOW MANY METERS DOWN IS HE...?
TREMBLE
TH-THIS IS WHERE I GOTTA SWITCH TO THE RAIL...
SLIP
OH!
WAAAAAAH!!
FWUMP
FLAIL
AAAAAH, I'M D-D-D-D...!
FLAIL
HUH?
I'M ALIVE?

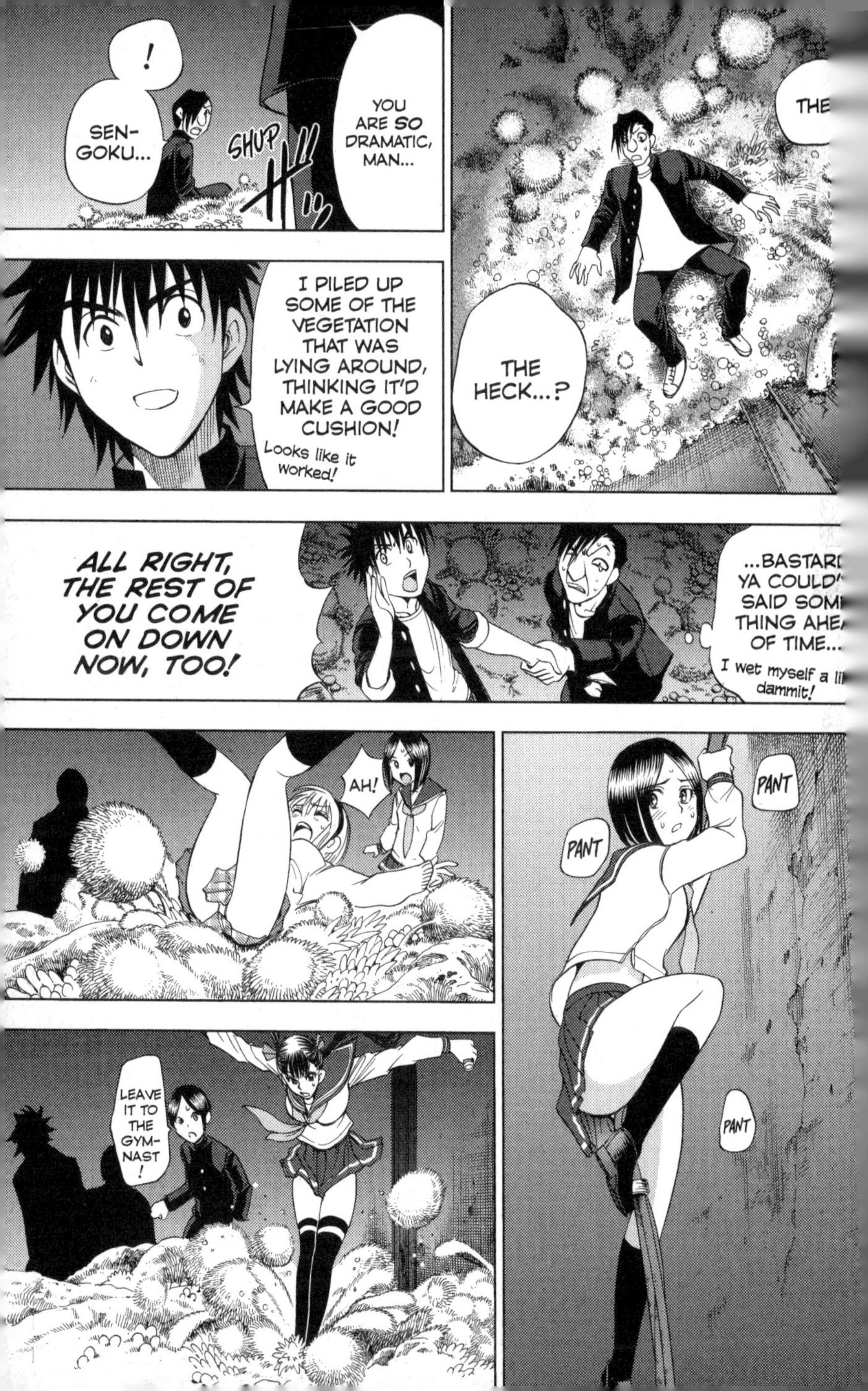
THE
THE HECK...?
YOU ARE SO DRAMATIC, MAN...
SHUP
!
SEN-GOKU...
I PILED UP SOME OF THE VEGETATION THAT WAS LYING AROUND, THINKING IT'D MAKE A GOOD CUSHION!
Looks like it worked!
...BASTARD YA COULD'
SAID SOME THING AHEA OF TIME...
I wet myself a li dammit!
ALL RIGHT, THE REST OF YOU COME ON DOWN NOW, TOO!
PANT
PANT
PANT
AH!
LEAVE IT TO THE GYM-NAST!

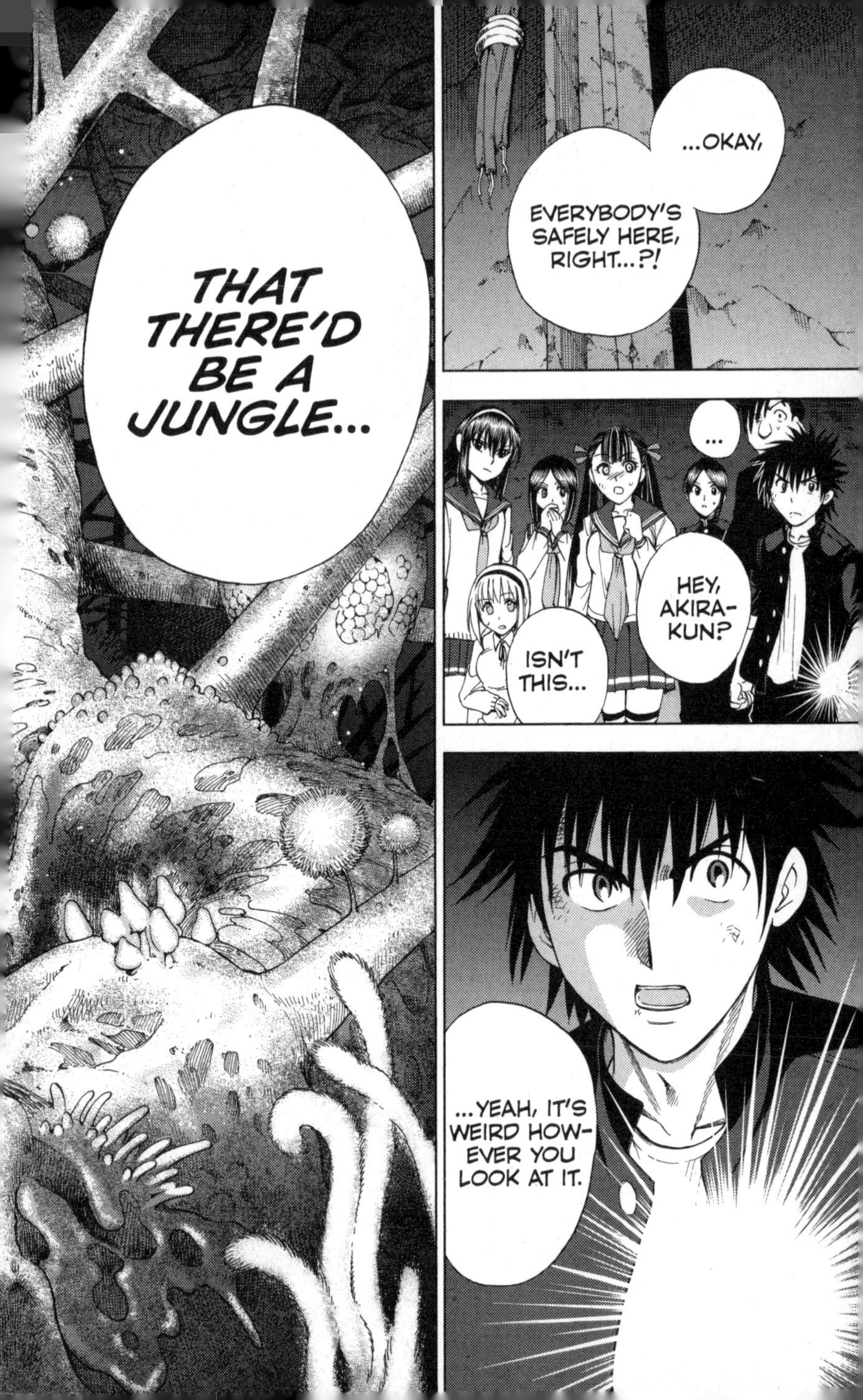
...OKAY,
EVERYBODY'S SAFELY HERE, RIGHT...?!
...
HEY, AKIRA-KUN?
ISN'T THIS...
...YEAH, IT'S WEIRD HOW-EVER YOU LOOK AT IT.
THAT THERE'D BE A JUNGLE...

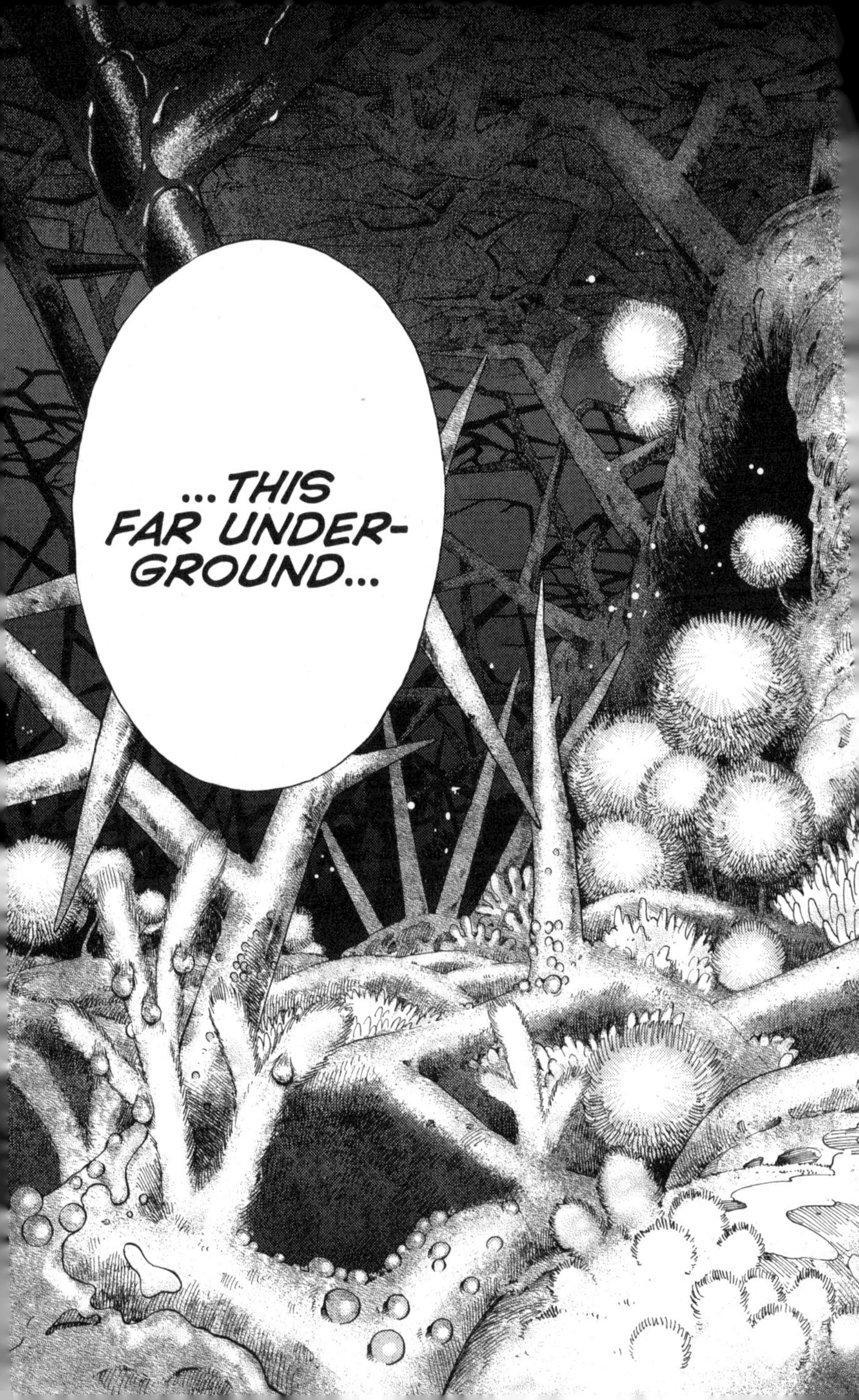
...THIS FAR UNDER-GROUND...

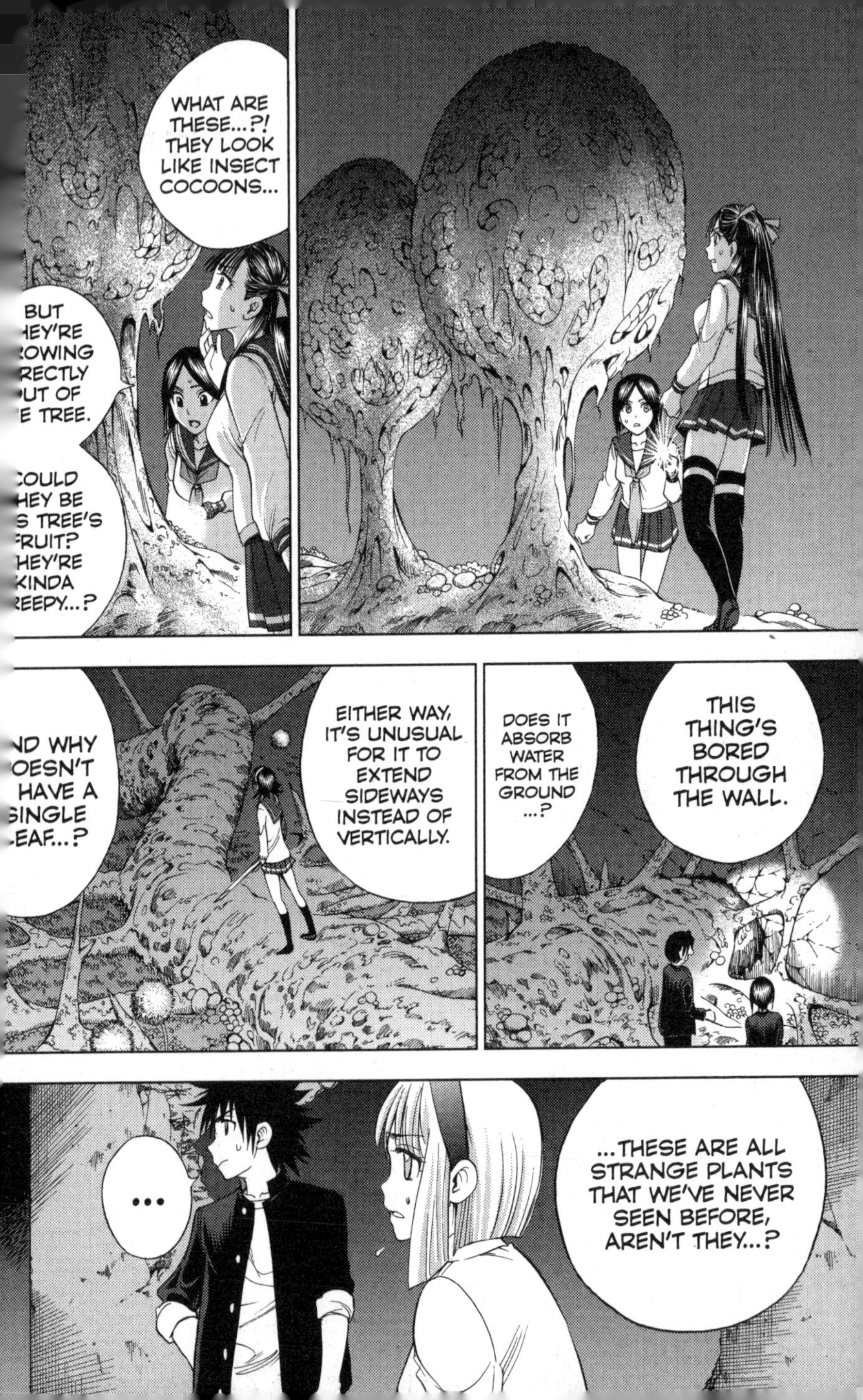
WHAT ARE THESE...?! THEY LOOK LIKE INSECT COCOONS...
BUT HEY'RE ROWING RECTLY UT OF E TREE.
COULD HEY BE S TREE'S FRUIT? HEY'RE KINDA REEPY...?
THIS THING'S BORED THROUGH THE WALL.
DOES IT ABSORB WATER FROM THE GROUND ...?
EITHER WAY, IT'S UNUSUAL FOR IT TO EXTEND SIDEWAYS INSTEAD OF VERTICALLY.
ND WHY OESN'T HAVE A SINGLE EAF...?
...THESE ARE ALL STRANGE PLANTS THAT WE'VE NEVER SEEN BEFORE, AREN'T THEY...?
...

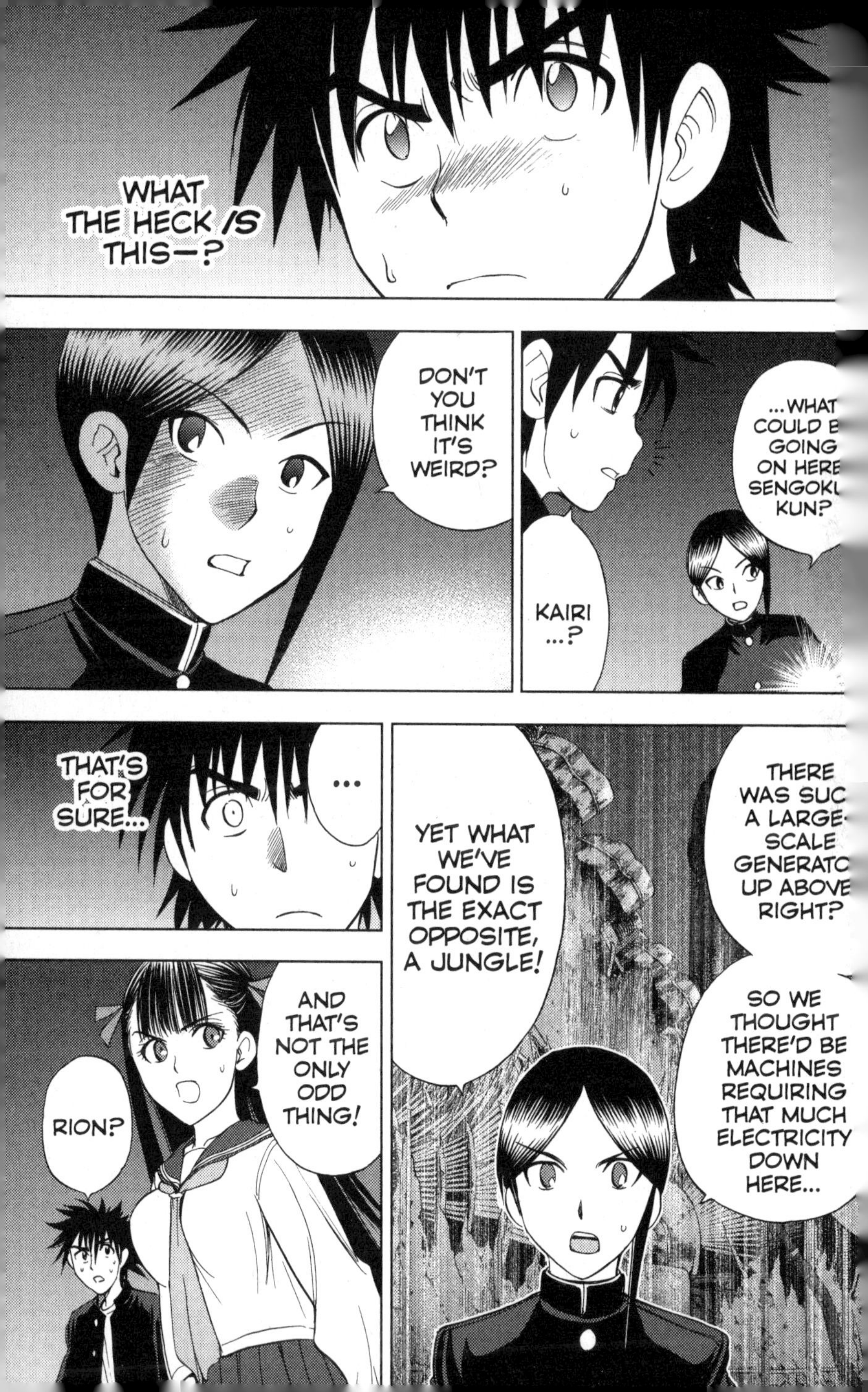
WHAT THE HECK IS THIS—?
...WHAT COULD B GOING ON HERE SENGOKU KUN?
KAIRI ...?
DON'T YOU THINK IT'S WEIRD?
THERE WAS SUC A LARGE-SCALE GENERATO UP ABOVE RIGHT?
SO WE THOUGHT THERE'D BE MACHINES REQUIRING THAT MUCH ELECTRICITY DOWN HERE...
YET WHAT WE'VE FOUND IS THE EXACT OPPOSITE, A JUNGLE!
...
THAT'S FOR SURE...
AND THAT'S NOT THE ONLY ODD THING!
RION?

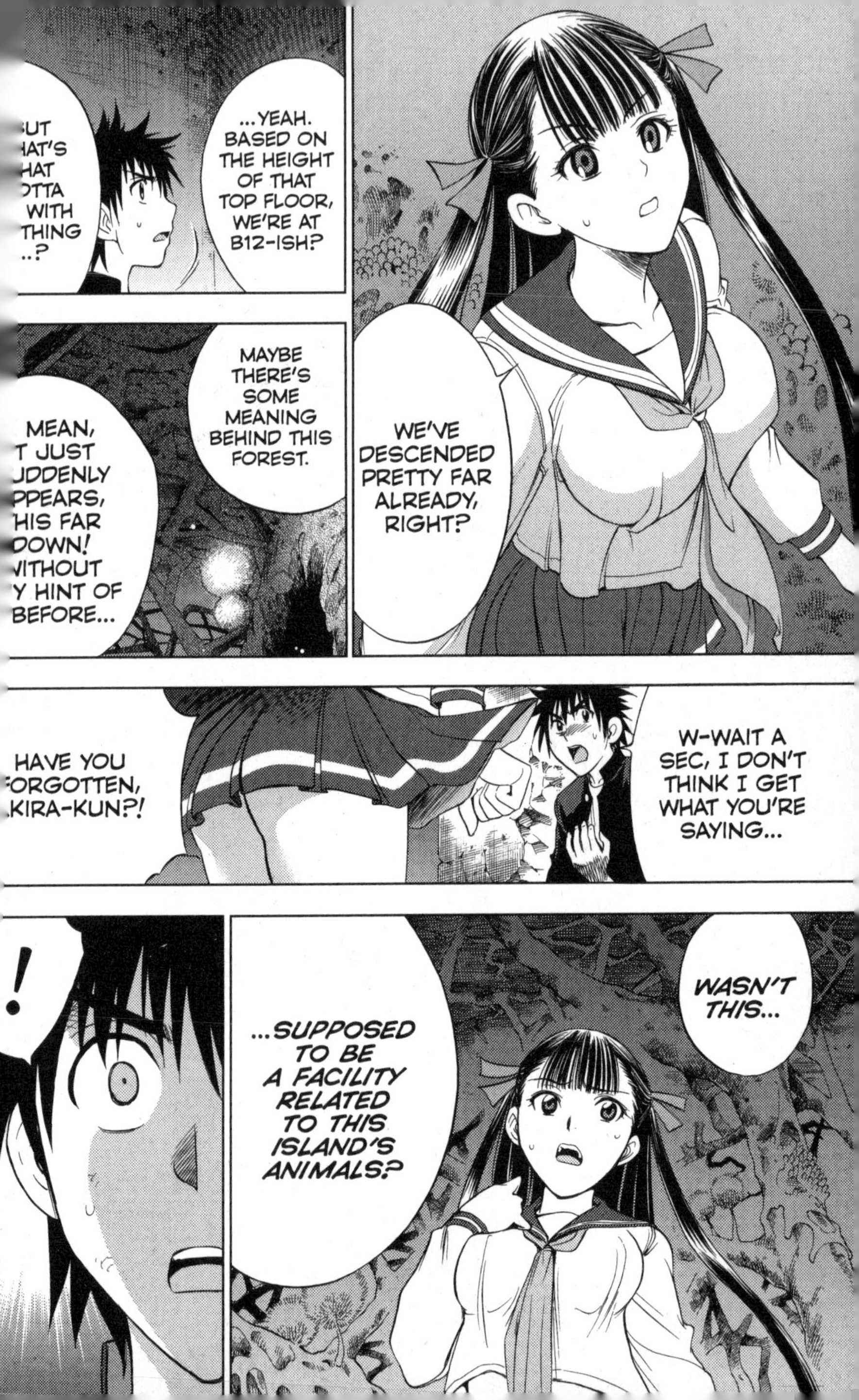
WE'VE DESCENDED PRETTY FAR ALREADY, RIGHT?
...YEAH. BASED ON THE HEIGHT OF THAT TOP FLOOR, WE'RE AT B12-ISH?
UT AT'S HAT OTTA WITH THING ..?
MAYBE THERE'S SOME MEANING BEHIND THIS FOREST.
MEAN, T JUST UDDENLY PPEARS, HIS FAR DOWN! VITHOUT Y HINT OF BEFORE...
W-WAIT A SEC, I DON'T THINK I GET WHAT YOU'RE SAYING...
HAVE YOU FORGOTTEN, KIRA-KUN?!
WASN'T THIS...
...SUPPOSED TO BE A FACILITY RELATED TO THIS ISLAND'S ANIMALS?
!

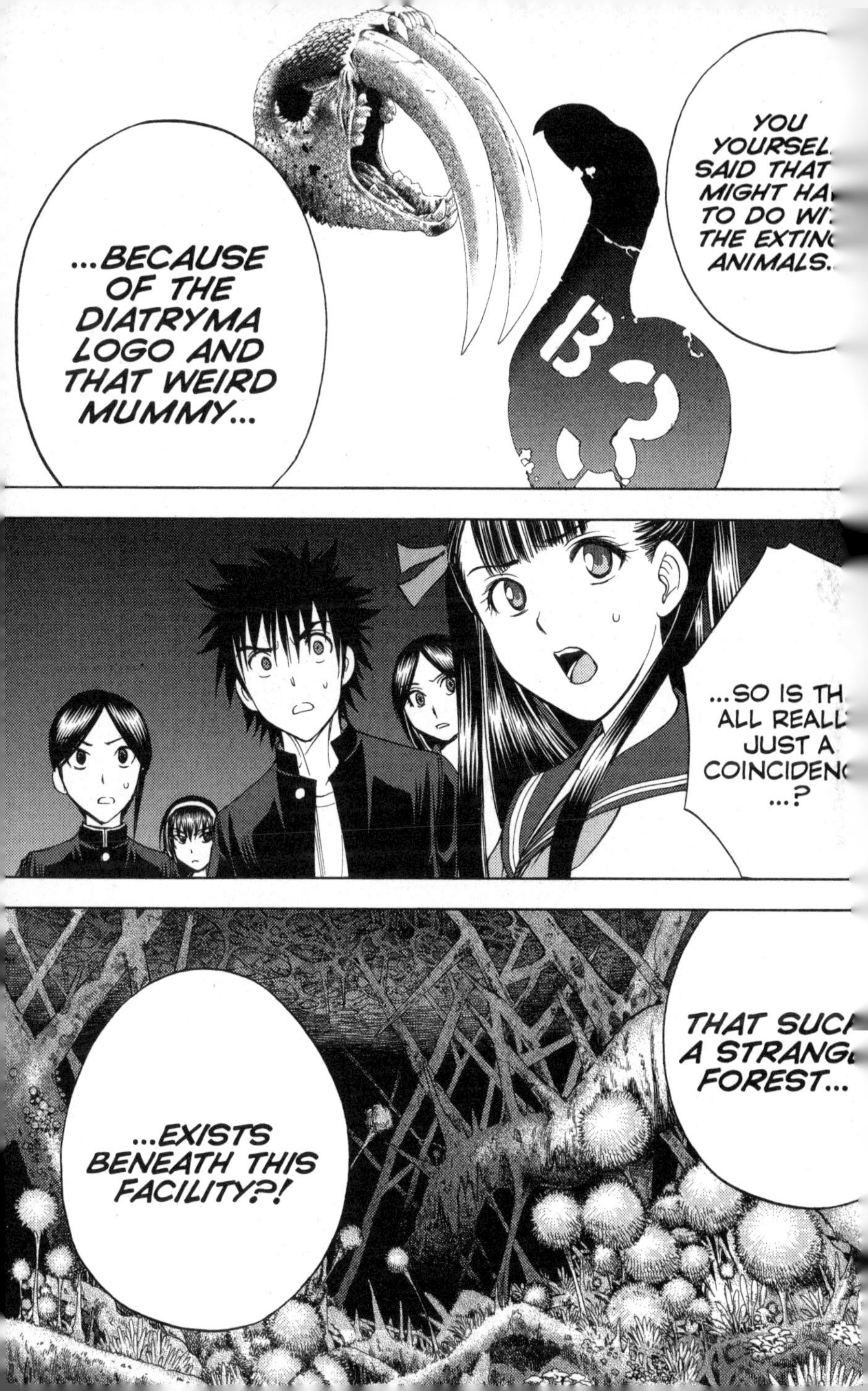
YOU YOURSEL SAID THAT MIGHT HA TO DO WI THE EXTIN ANIMALS.
...BECAUSE OF THE DIATRYMA LOGO AND THAT WEIRD MUMMY...
...SO IS TH ALL REALL JUST A COINCIDEN ...?
THAT SUC A STRANG FOREST...
...EXISTS BENEATH THIS FACILITY?!

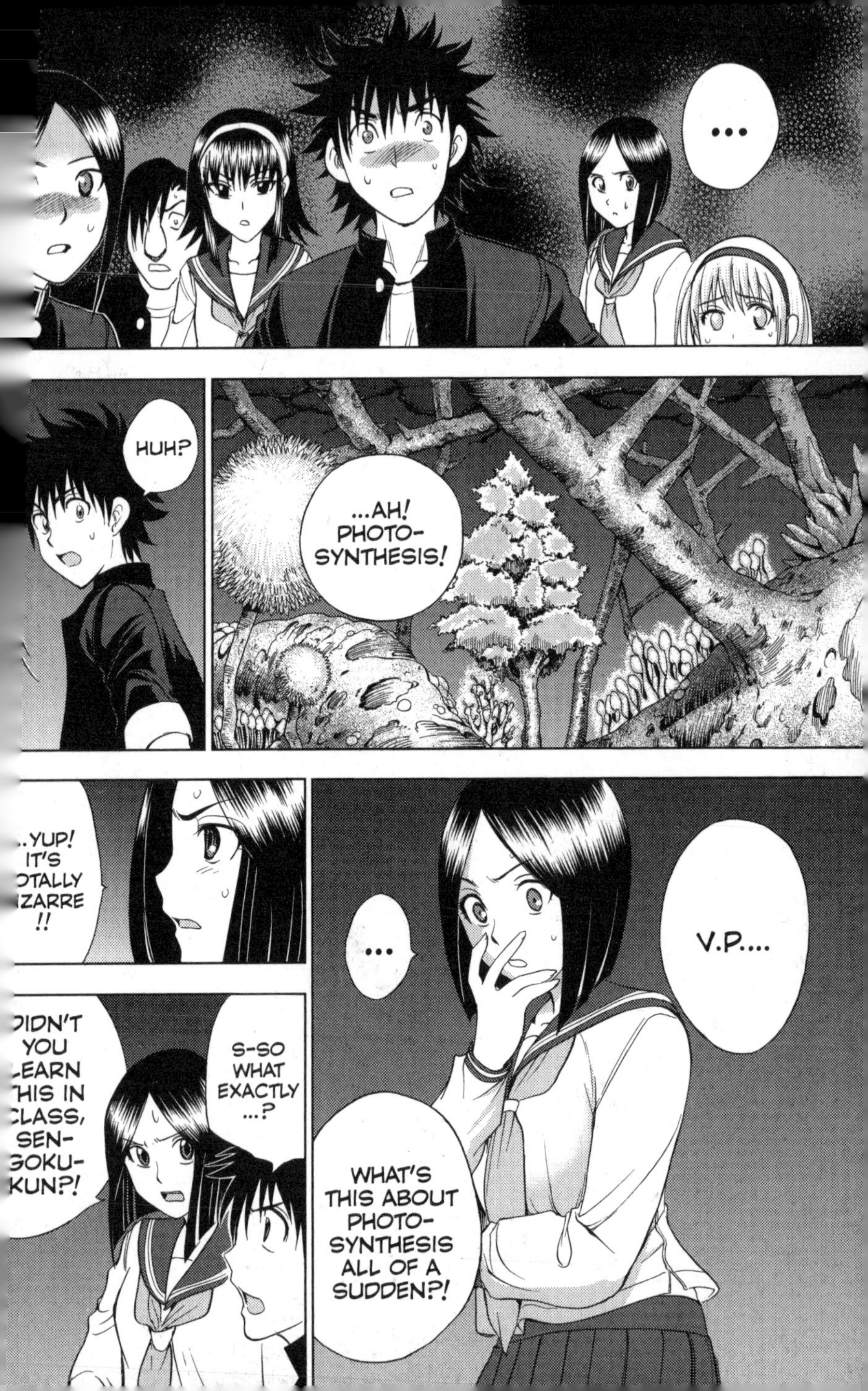
...
...AH! PHOTO-SYNTHESIS!
HUH?
V.P....
...
WHAT'S THIS ABOUT PHOTO-SYNTHESIS ALL OF A SUDDEN?!
..YUP! IT'S OTALLY ZARRE !!
S-SO WHAT EXACTLY ...?
IDN'T YOU EARN HIS IN LASS, SEN-GOKU-KUN?!

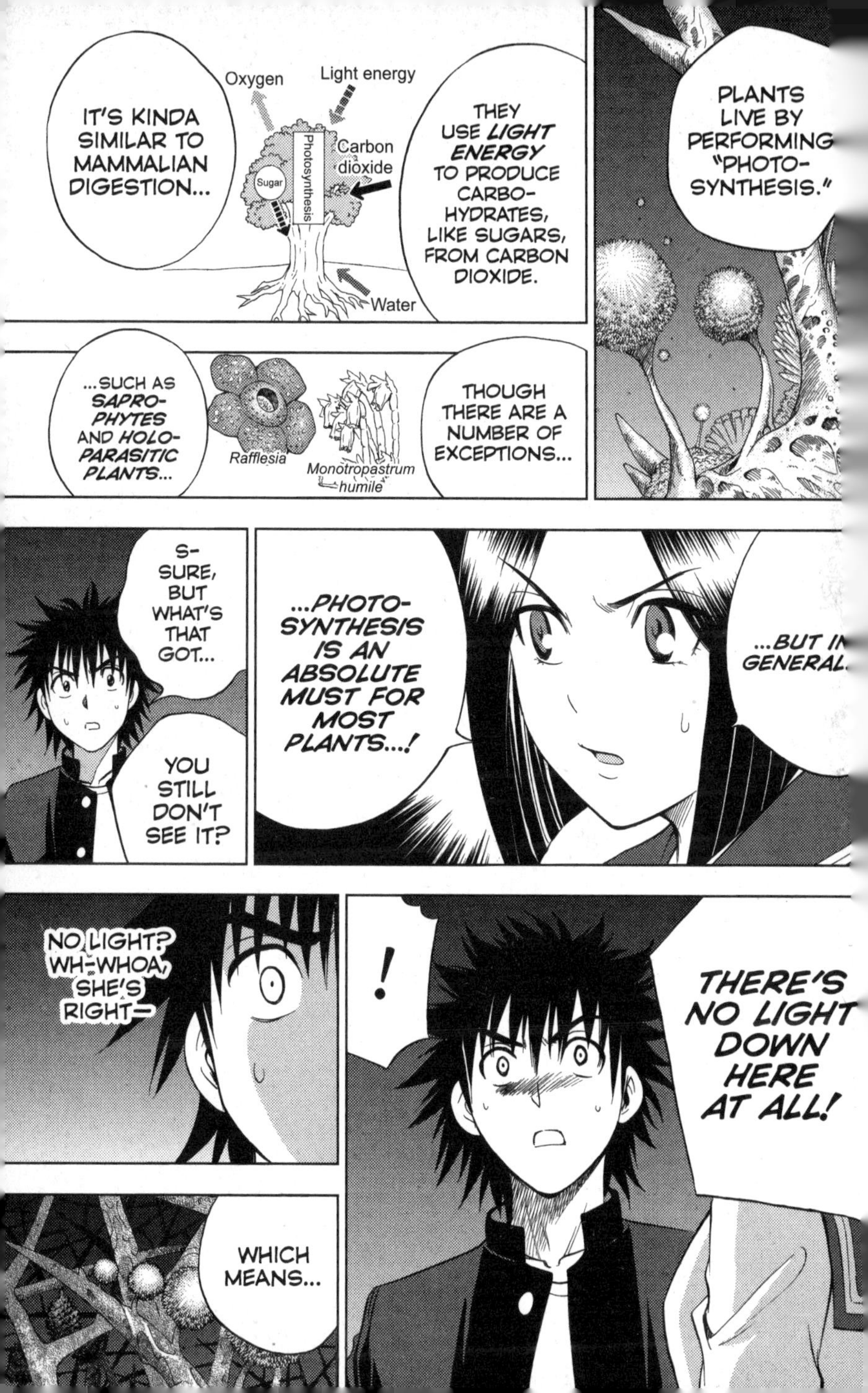
PLANTS LIVE BY PERFORMING "PHOTO-SYNTHESIS."
THEY USE LIGHT ENERGY TO PRODUCE CARBO-HYDRATES, LIKE SUGARS, FROM CARBON DIOXIDE.
Light energy
Oxygen
Carbon dioxide
Photosynthesis
Sugar
Water
IT'S KINDA SIMILAR TO MAMMALIAN DIGESTION...
THOUGH THERE ARE A NUMBER OF EXCEPTIONS...
Monotropastrum humile
Rafflesia
...SUCH AS SAPRO-PHYTES AND HOLO-PARASITIC PLANTS...
...BUT IN GENERAL
...PHOTO-SYNTHESIS IS AN ABSOLUTE MUST FOR MOST PLANTS...!
S-SURE, BUT WHAT'S THAT GOT...
YOU STILL DON'T SEE IT?
THERE'S NO LIGHT DOWN HERE AT ALL!
!
NO LIGHT? WH-WHOA, SHE'S RIGHT—
WHICH MEANS...

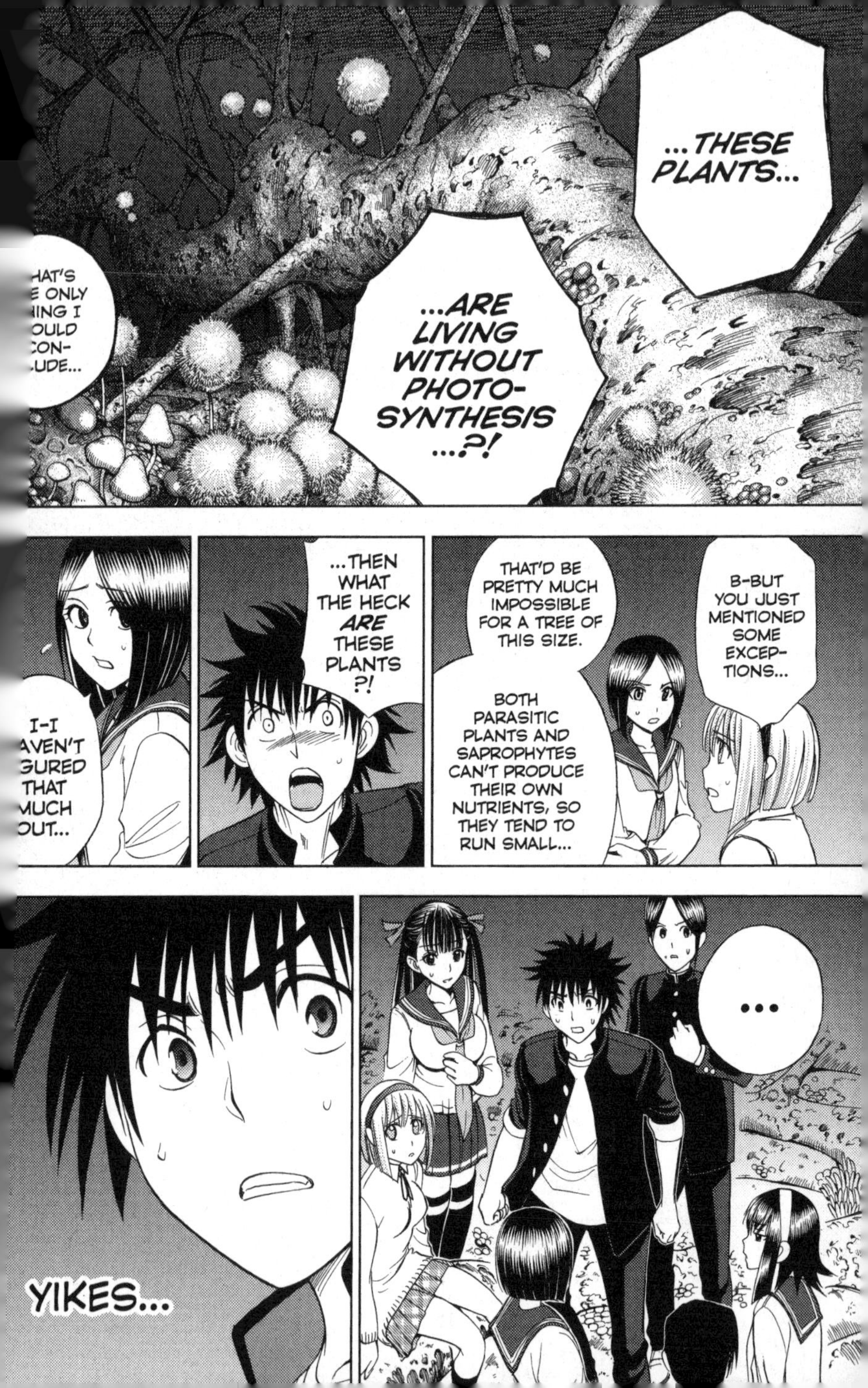
...THESE PLANTS...
...ARE LIVING WITHOUT PHOTO-SYNTHESIS ...?!
HAT'S E ONLY HING I OULD CON- LUDE...
B-BUT YOU JUST MENTIONED SOME EXCEP-TIONS...
THAT'D BE PRETTY MUCH IMPOSSIBLE FOR A TREE OF THIS SIZE.
BOTH PARASITIC PLANTS AND SAPROPHYTES CAN'T PRODUCE THEIR OWN NUTRIENTS, SO THEY TEND TO RUN SMALL...
...THEN WHAT THE HECK *ARE* THESE PLANTS ?!
I-I AVEN'T IGURED THAT MUCH OUT...
...
YIKES...

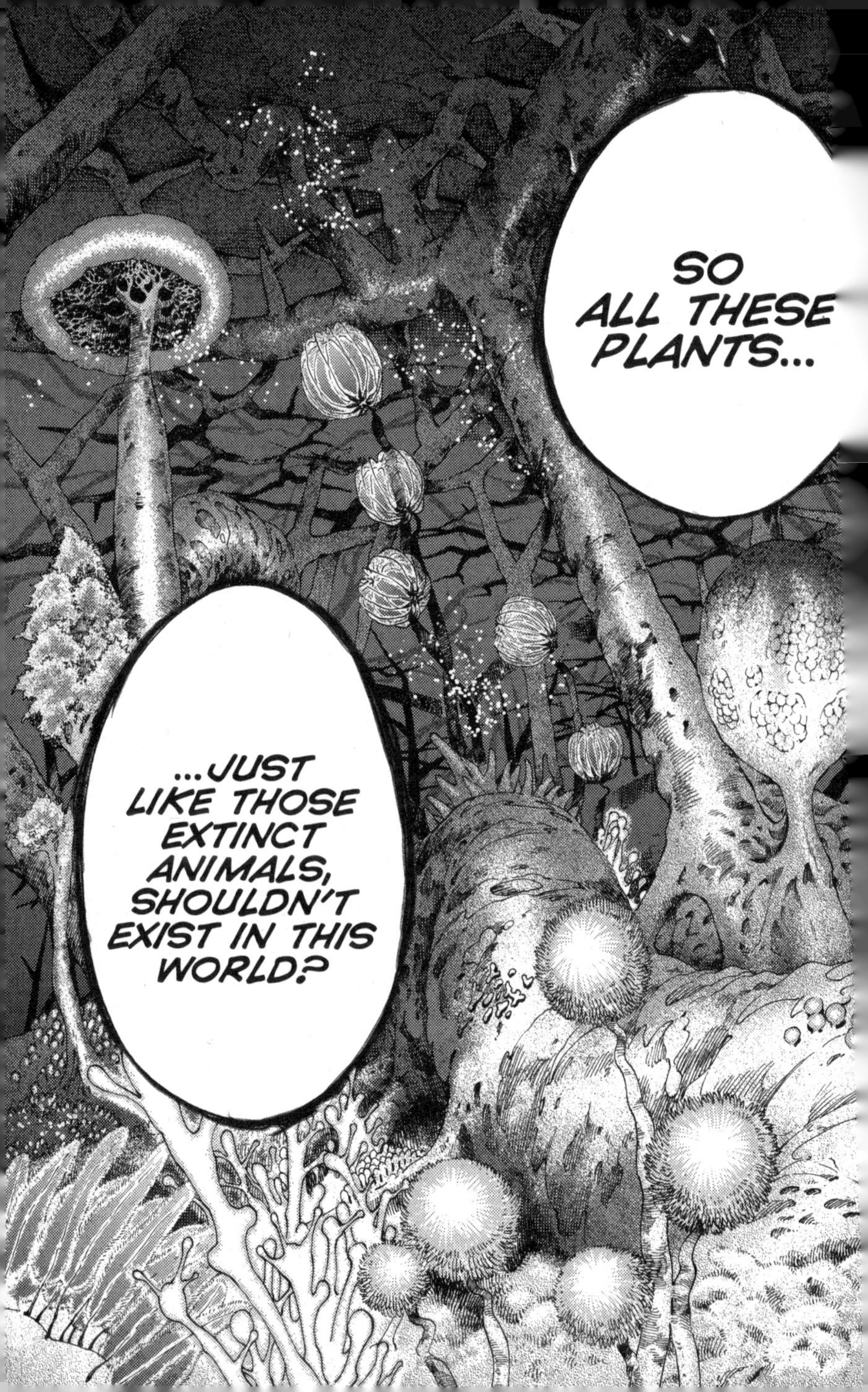
SO ALL THESE PLANTS...
...JUST LIKE THOSE EXTINCT ANIMALS, SHOULDN'T EXIST IN THIS WORLD?

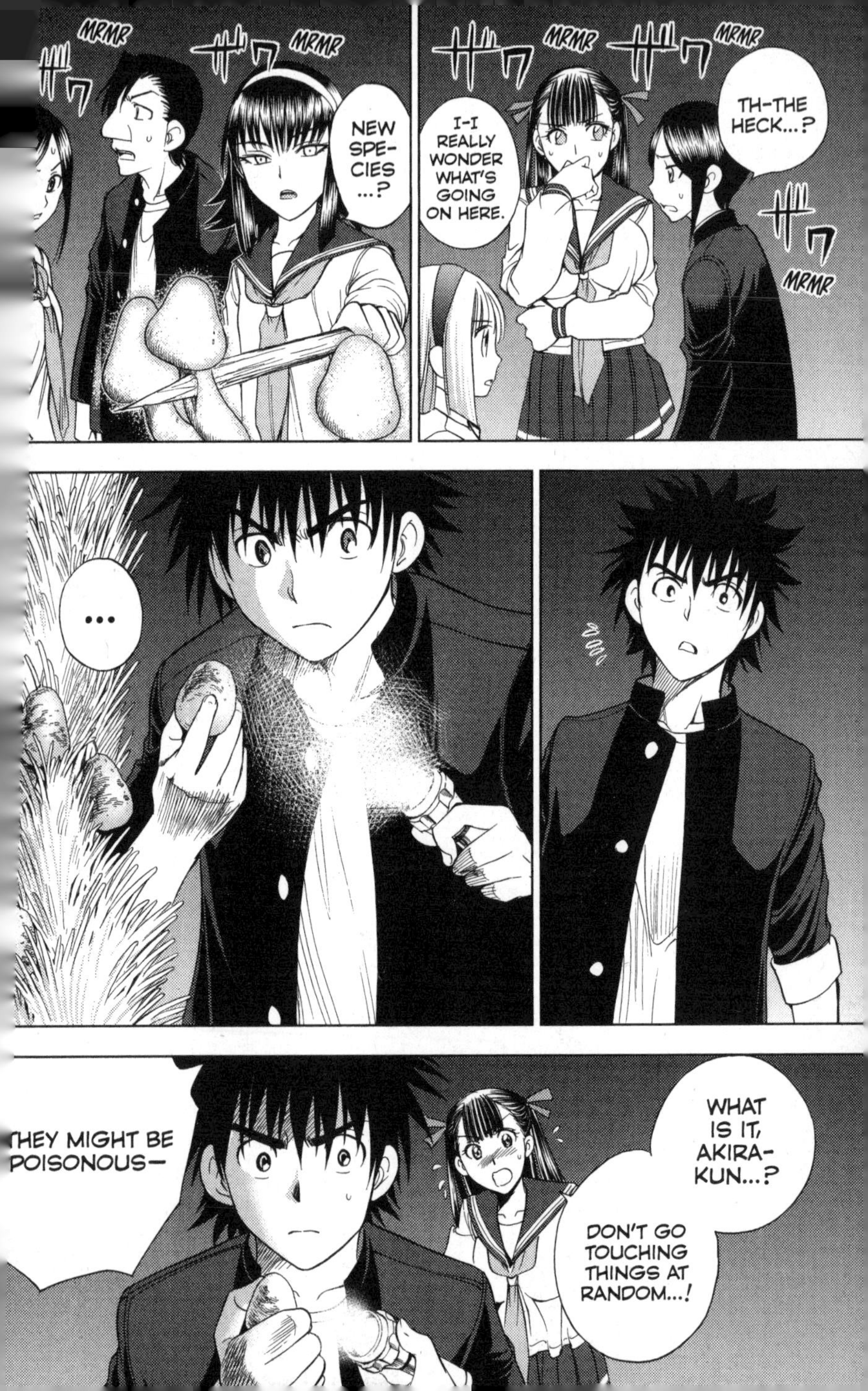
ザワ
MRMR
TH-THE HECK...?
ザワ
MRMR
I-I REALLY WONDER WHAT'S GOING ON HERE.
ザワ
MRMR
NEW SPE-CIES ...?
ザワ
MRMR
ザワ
MRMR
...
WHAT IS IT, AKIRA-KUN...?
DON'T GO TOUCHING THINGS AT RANDOM...!
THEY MIGHT BE POISONOUS—

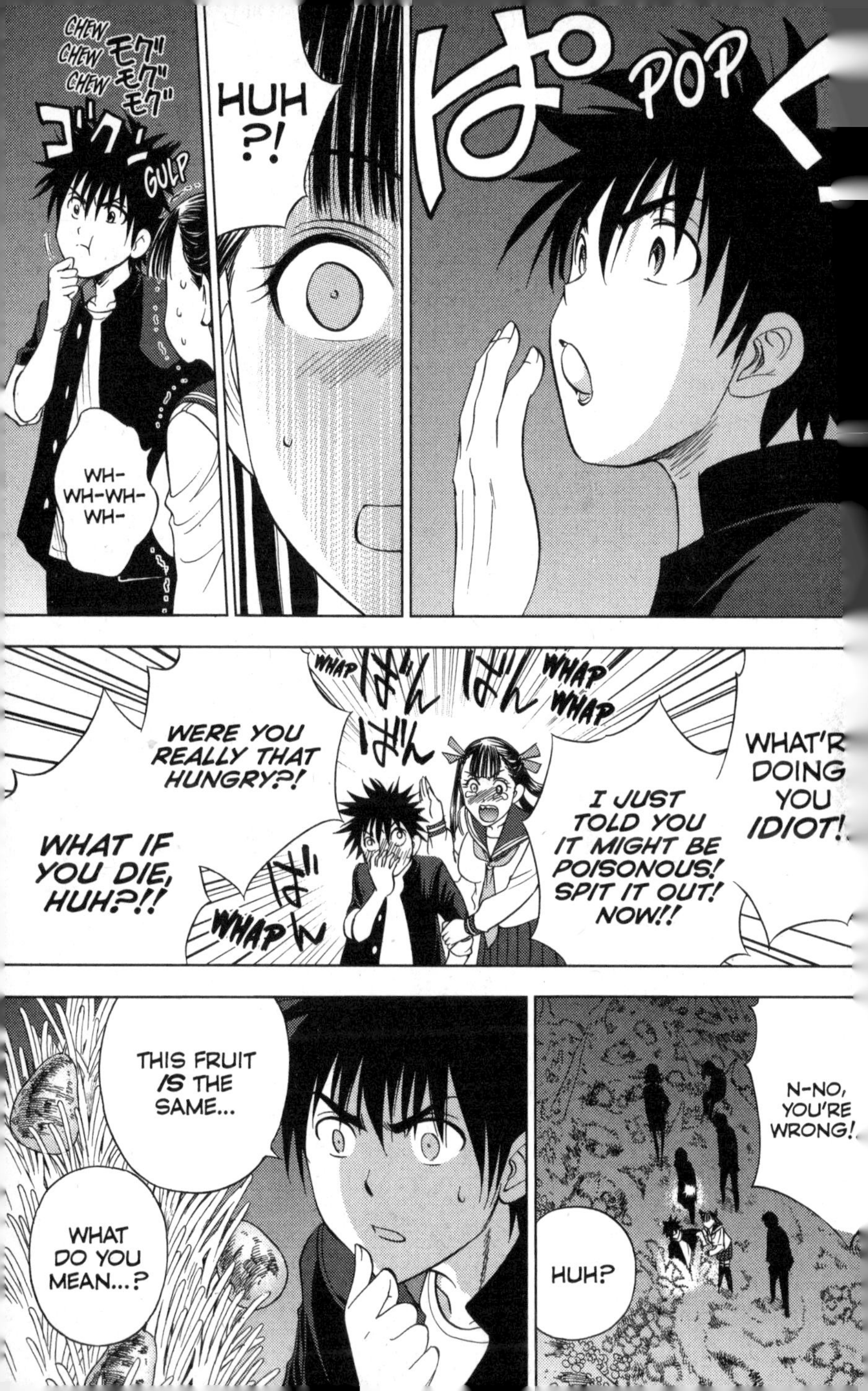
ぱ
POP
HUH ?!
CHEW CHEW CHEW
モグモグモグ
ゴクン
GULP
WH- WH-WH-WH- WH-
WHAT'R DOING YOU IDIOT!
I JUST TOLD YOU IT MIGHT BE POISONOUS! SPIT IT OUT! NOW!!
WHAP ばん ばん WHAP WHAP ばん
WERE YOU REALLY THAT HUNGRY?!
WHAT IF YOU DIE, HUH?!!
ばん WHAP
N-NO, YOU'RE WRONG!
HUH?
THIS FRUIT IS THE SAME...
WHAT DO YOU MEAN...?

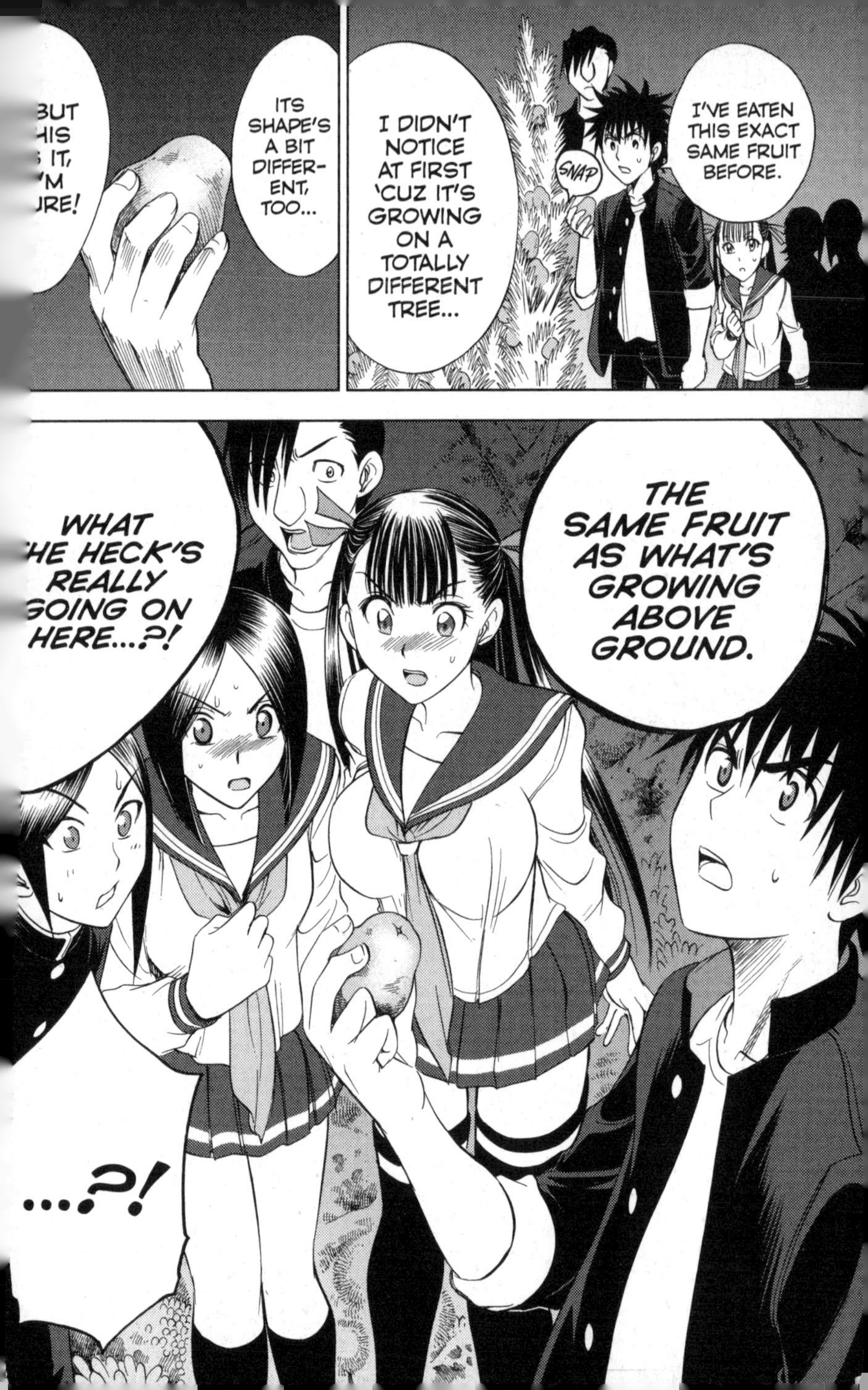
I'VE EATEN THIS EXACT SAME FRUIT BEFORE.
SNAP
I DIDN'T NOTICE AT FIRST 'CUZ IT'S GROWING ON A TOTALLY DIFFERENT TREE...
ITS SHAPE'S A BIT DIFFER-ENT, TOO...
BUT HIS S IT, 'M URE!
THE SAME FRUIT AS WHAT'S GROWING ABOVE GROUND.
WHAT HE HECK'S REALLY GOING ON HERE...?!
...?!

To be continued...

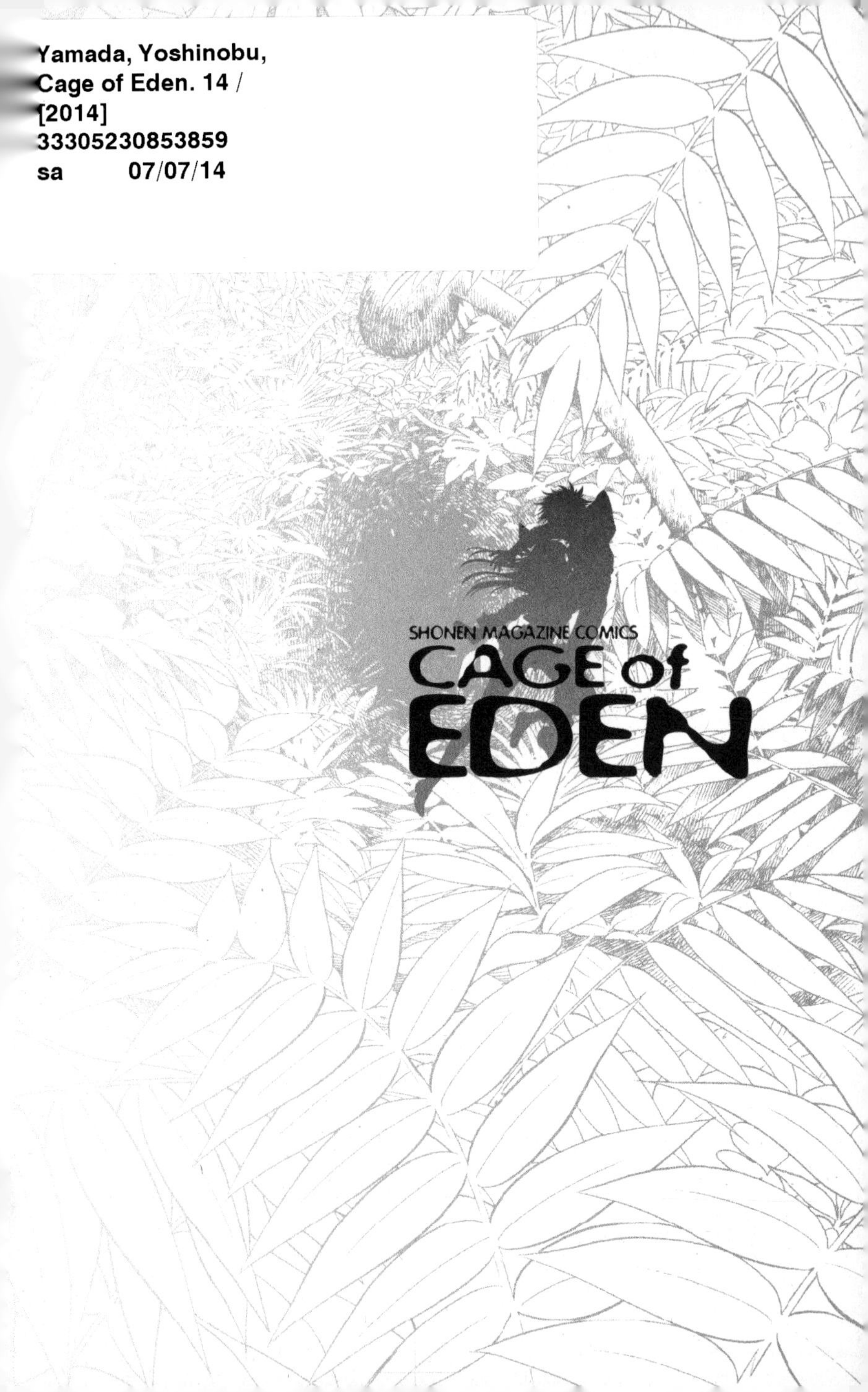
SHONEN MAGAZINE COMICS
CAGE of EDEN

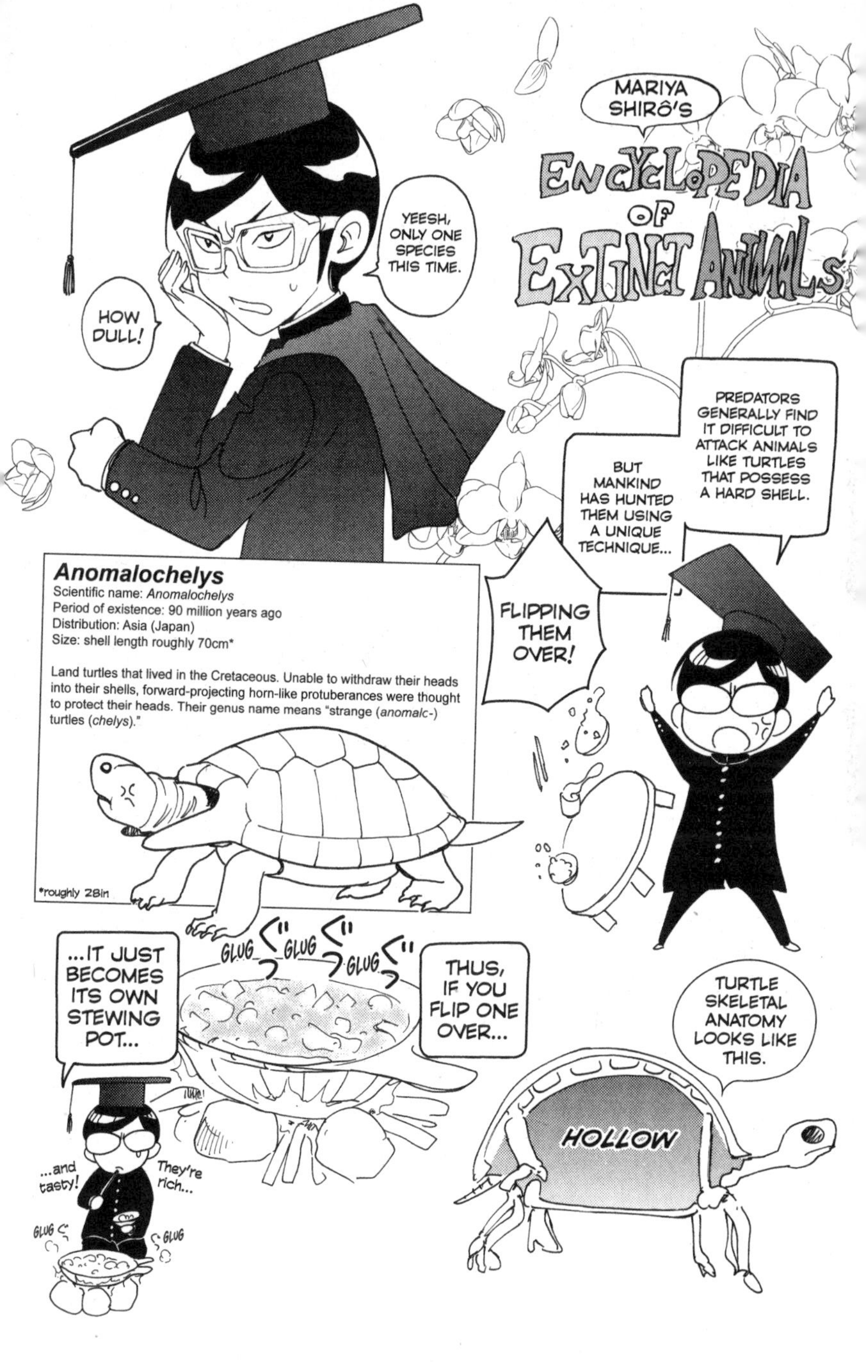
MARIYA SHIRÔ'S
ENCYCLOPEDIA OF EXTINCT ANIMALS
YEESH, ONLY ONE SPECIES THIS TIME.
HOW DULL!
PREDATORS GENERALLY FIND IT DIFFICULT TO ATTACK ANIMALS LIKE TURTLES THAT POSSESS A HARD SHELL.
BUT MANKIND HAS HUNTED THEM USING A UNIQUE TECHNIQUE...
FLIPPING THEM OVER!
Anomalochelys
Scientific name: Anomalochelys
Period of existence: 90 million years ago
Distribution: Asia (Japan)
Size: shell length roughly 70cm*
Land turtles that lived in the Cretaceous. Unable to withdraw their heads into their shells, forward-projecting horn-like protuberances were thought to protect their heads. Their genus name means "strange (anomalc-) turtles (chelys)."
*roughly 28in
TURTLE SKELETAL ANATOMY LOOKS LIKE THIS.
HOLLOW
THUS, IF YOU FLIP ONE OVER...
GLUG GLUG GLUG
...IT JUST BECOMES ITS OWN STEWING POT...
They're rich...
...and tasty!
GLUG GLUG

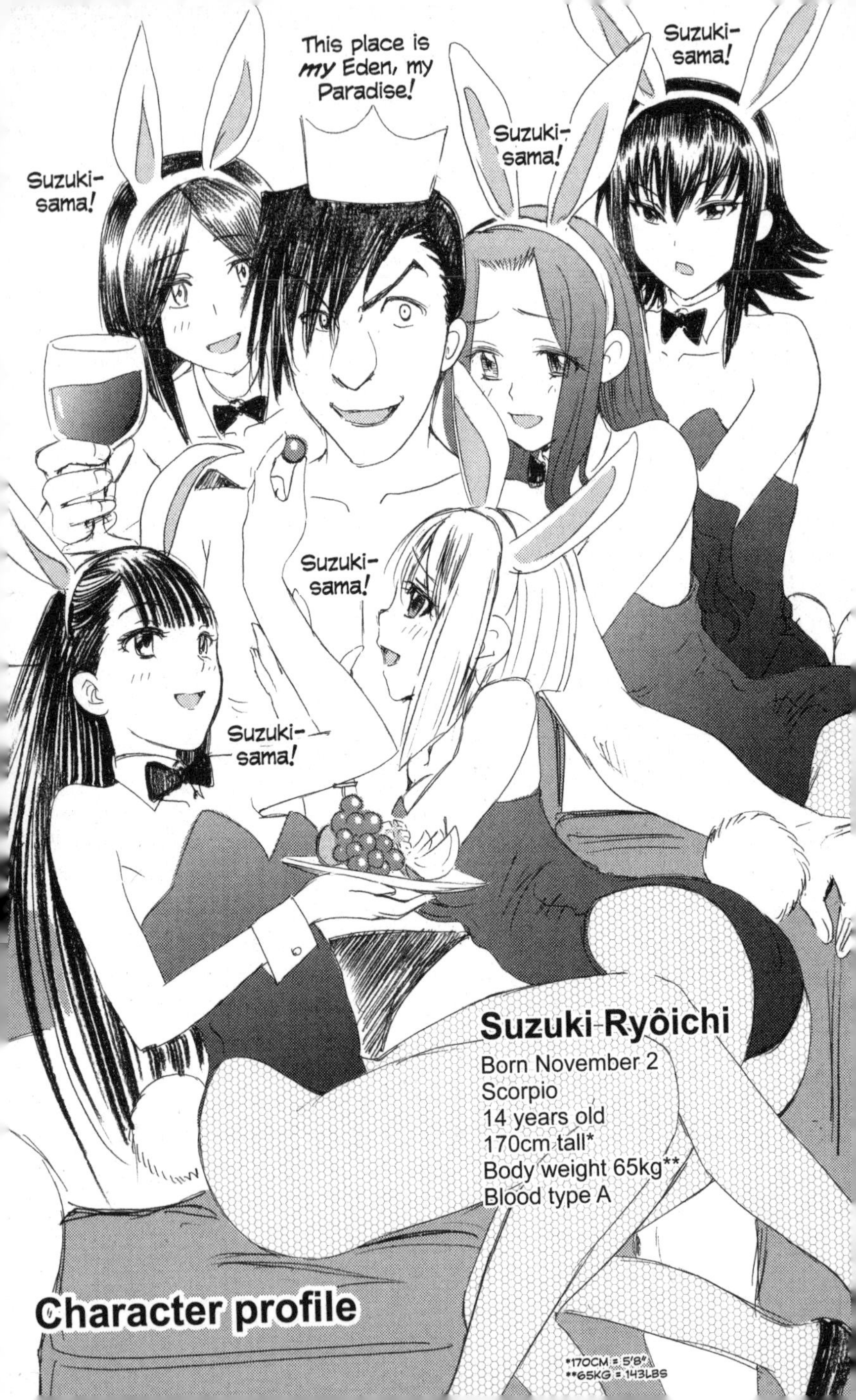
Suzuki-sama!
This place is *my* Eden, my Paradise!
Suzuki-sama!
Suzuki-sama!
Suzuki-sama!
Suzuki-sama!
Suzuki Ryôichi
Born November 2
Scorpio
14 years old
170cm tall*
Body weight 65kg**
Blood type A
Character profile
*170CM = 5'8"
**65KG = 143LBS

Hatsusé Shizuka

Born September 24
Libra
15 years old
157cm tall*
Blood type B
BWH: 83•56•84**

*157cm = 5'3"
**83•56•84 = 33•22•34

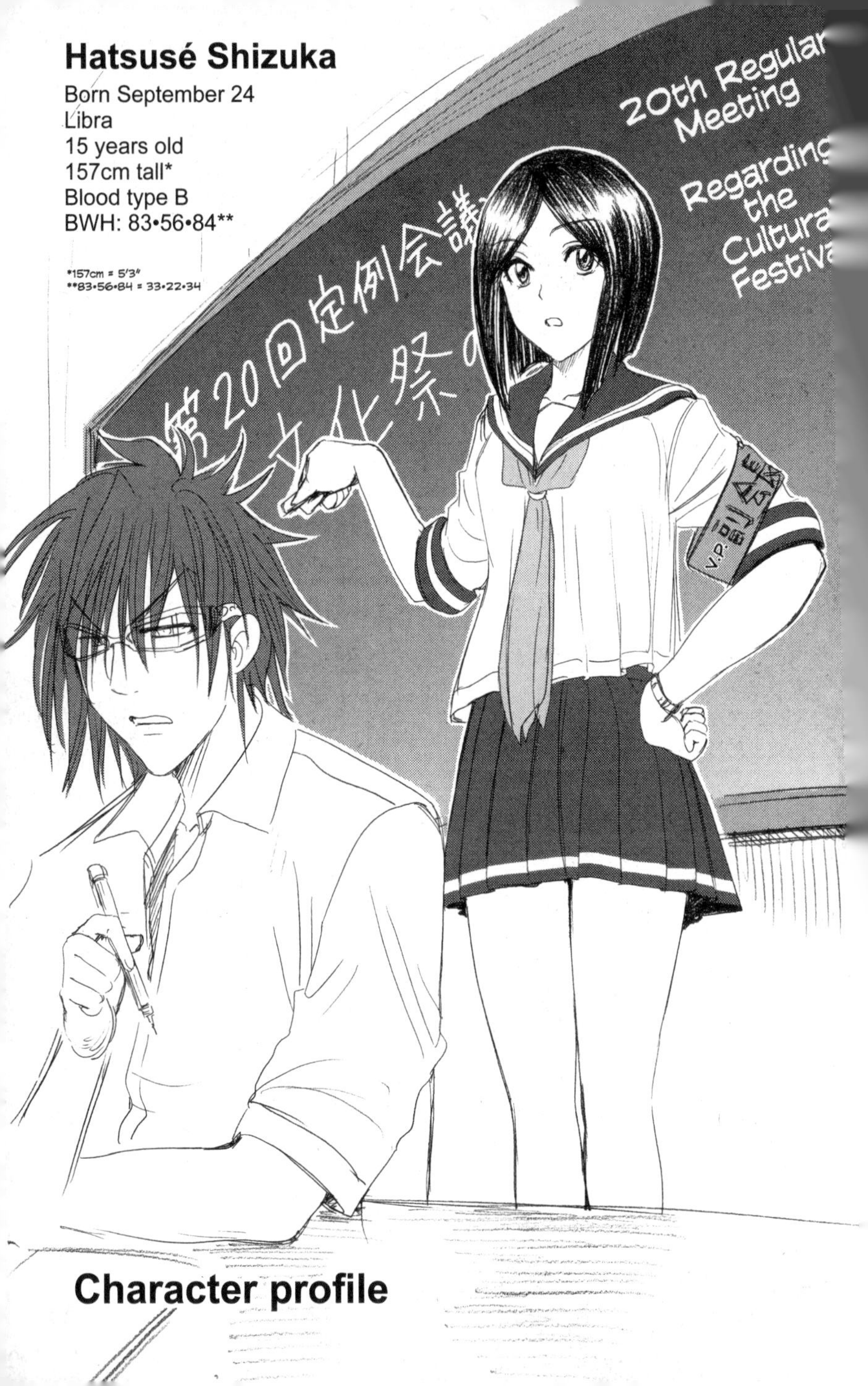
第20回定例会議
文化祭の
20th Regular
Meeting
Regarding
the
Cultura
Festiva

Character profile

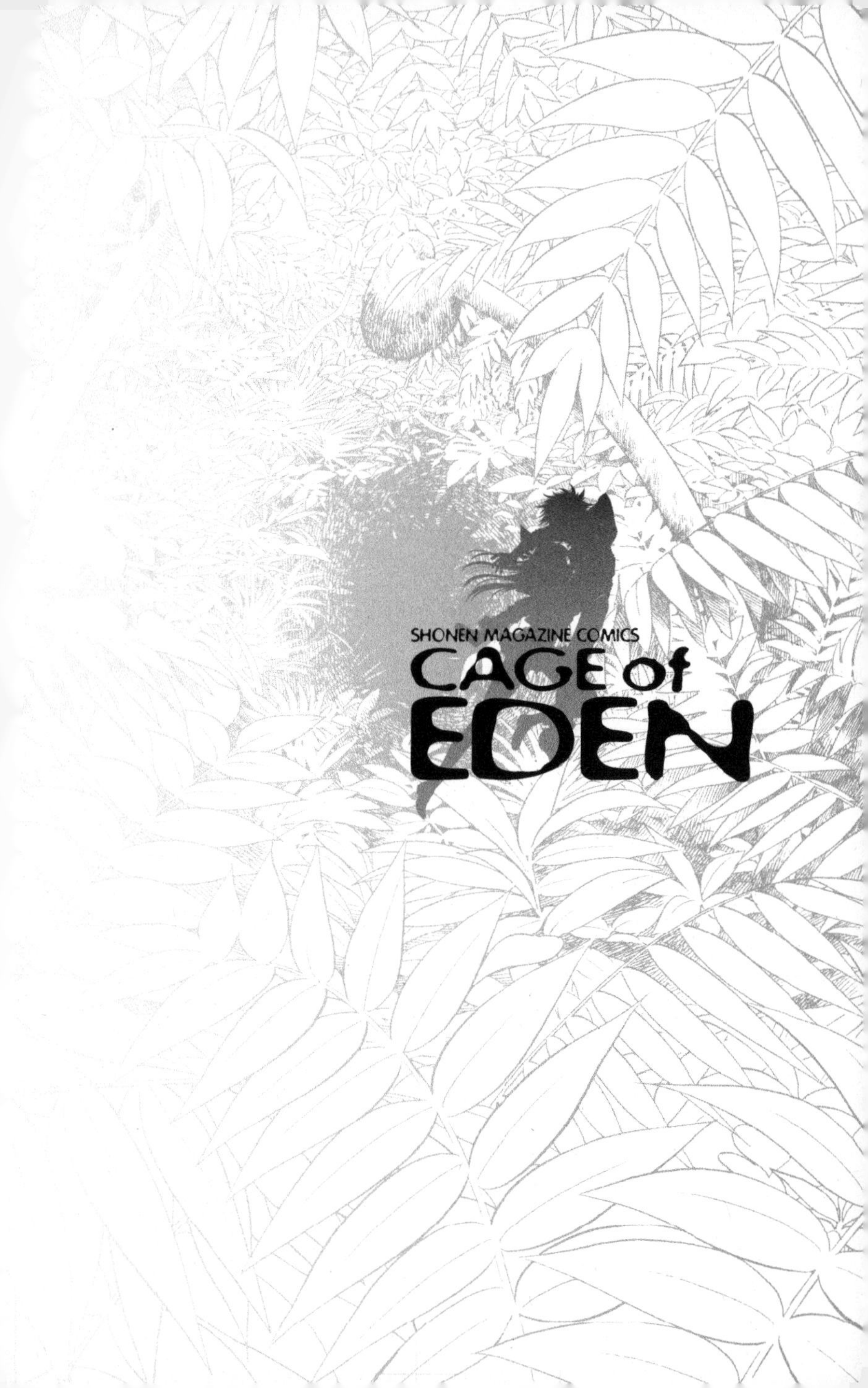
SHONEN MAGAZINE COMICS
CAGE of EDEN

Translation Notes

Suigetsu, page 029
Translated as "Moon in the Water," it refers to an uppercut to the celiac or solar plexus.

Yotsubishi Heavy Industries, page 121
Likely an homage to Mitsubishi Heavy Industries, which is part of the Mitsubishi Group conglomerate. "Mitsubishi" means "three diamonds (diamond-shapes)" and "yotsubishi" means "four diamonds." This is also reflected in the brand logo, which resembles Mitsubishi's except with the lower two diamonds moved upward to allow for an extra diamond at the bottom.

Roppongi Hills and Tokyo Dome, page 129
The centerpiece of the Roppongi Hills complex is actually Mori Tower, not Mori Building, and only has 54 floors as opposed to 56, though it does indeed have its own onsite power plant located underneath it. Also, Tokyo Dome's field has an area of 140,000 square feet.

Monotropastrum humile, page 177
A type of plant species that almost completely lacks chlorophyll, and thus cannot perform sufficient photosynthesis to survive on its own. It is known as a myco-heterotroph because it parasitizes and obtains its nutrients from fungal species instead, in this case mycorrhizal fungi, which in turn are in symbiotic relationships with vascular plants (specifically their roots) themselves.

Rafflesia, page 177
A genus of parasitic plants native to southeastern Asia, its distinctive foul odor likened to rotting flesh has earned it the nickname "corpse flower" and "meat flower," though the titan arum also boasts this moniker. Rafflesia do not have any chlorophyll, and are completely dependent on its host, Tetrastigma vines.

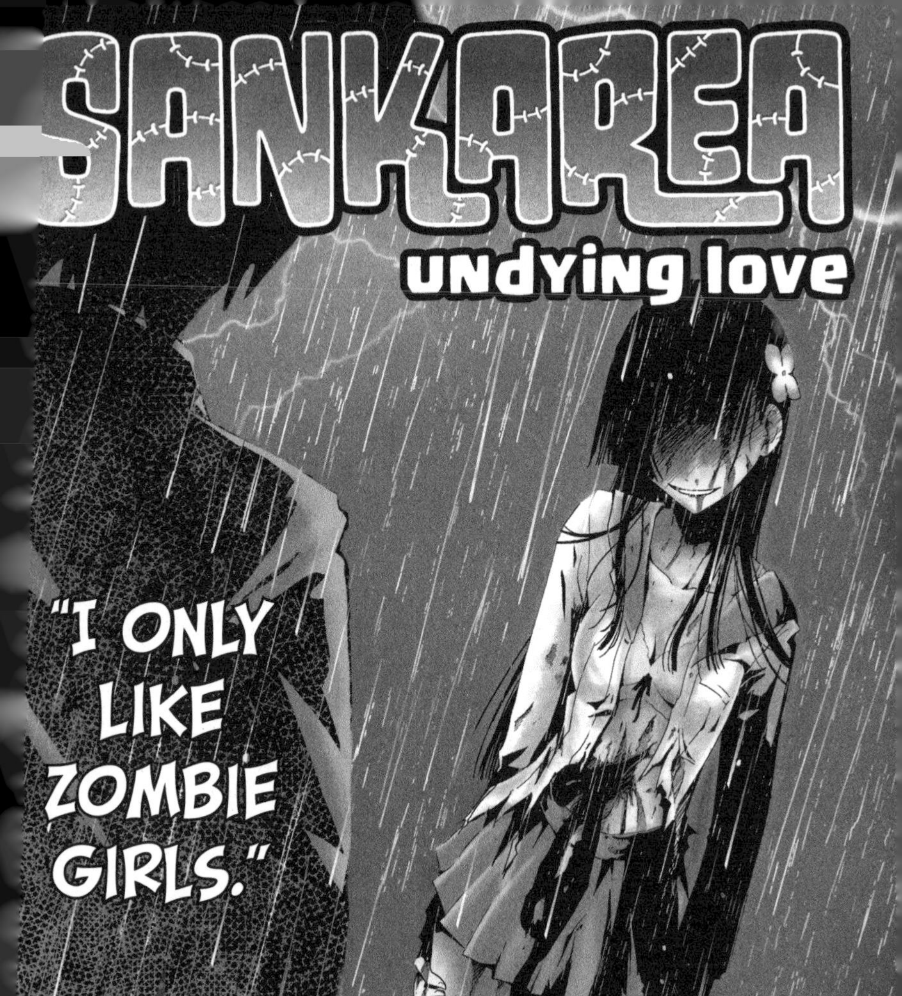

SANKAREA

undying love

"I ONLY LIKE ZOMBIE GIRLS."

...hihiro has an unusual connection to zombie movies. He doesn't feel bad for ...he survivors – he wants to comfort the undead girls they slaughter! When ...s pet passes away, he brews a resurrection potion. He's discovered by ...ocal heiress Sanka Rea, and she serves as his first test subject!

A Kodansha Comics Trade Paperback Original.

Cage of Eden volume 14 copyright © 2011 Yoshinobu Yamada
English translation copyright © 2014 Yoshinobu Yamada

All rights reserved.

Published in the United States by Kodansha Comics, an imprint of Kodansha USA Publishing, LLC, New York.

Publication rights for this English edition arranged through Kodansha Ltd., Tokyo.

First published in Japan in 2011 by Kodansha Ltd., Tokyo, as *Eden no Ori* 14

ISBN 978-1-61262-263-7

Printed in the United States of America.

www.kodanshacomics.com

9 8 7 6 5 4 3 2 1

Translator: Mari Morimoto
Lettering: Morgan Hart

TOMARE!

[STOP!]

You are going the wrong way!

Manga is a completely different type of reading experience.

To start at the *beginning*, go to the *end*!

That's right! Authentic manga is read the traditional Japanese way—from right to left, exactly the *opposite* of how American books are read. It's easy to follow: Just go to the other end of the book, and read each page—and each panel—from the right side to the left side, starting at the top right. Now you're experiencing manga as it was meant to be.